Dominion of Capital
The Politics of Big Business and
the Crisis of the Canadian Bourgeoisie,
1914–1947

In the critical decades following the First World War, the Canadian political landscape was shifting in ways that significantly recast the relationship between big business and government. As public pressures changed the priorities of Canada's political parties, many of Canada's most powerful businessmen struggled to come to terms with a changing world that was less sympathetic to their ideas and interests than before. *Dominion of Capital* offers a new account of relations between government and business in Canada during a period of transition between the established expectations of the National Policy and the uncertain future of the twentieth century.

Don Nerbas tells this fascinating story through close portraits of influential business and political figures of this period – including Howard P. Robinson, Charles Dunning, Sir Edward Beatty, R.S. McLaughlin, and C.D. Howe – that provide insight into how events in different sectors of the economy and regions of the country shaped the political outlook and strategies of the country's business elite. Drawing on business, political, social, and cultural history, Nerbas revises standard accounts of government-business relations in this period and sheds new light on the challenges facing big business in early twentieth-century Canada.

(Canadian Social History Series)

DON NERBAS is an assistant professor in the Department of History and Culture at Cape Breton University.

Dominion of Capital

The Politics of Big Business and the Crisis of the Canadian Bourgeoisie, 1914–1947

Don Nerbas

UNIVERSITY OF TORONTO PRESS
Toronto Buffalo London

ISBN 978-1-4426-4545-5 (cloth)
ISBN 978-1-4426-1352-2 (paper)

Printed on acid-free, 100% post-consumer recycled paper with
vegetable-based inks

Library and Archives Canada Cataloguing in Publication

Nerbas, Don, 1980–
Dominion of capital : the politics of big business and the crisis
of the Canadian bourgeoisie, 1914–1947 / Don Nerbas.

(Canadian social history series)

Includes bibliographical references and index.
ISBN 978-1-4426-4545-5 (bound). – ISBN 978-1-4426-1352-2 (pbk.)

1. Industrial policy – Canada – History – 20th century.
2. Canada – Economic conditions – 1918–1945. 3. Canada –
Politics and government – 1914–1945. I. Title. II. Series:
Canadian social history series

HD3616.C32N47 2013   338.971009'041   C2013-903486-2

University of Toronto Press acknowledges the financial assistance to its publishing
program of the Canada Council for the Arts and the Ontario Arts Council.

Canada Council   Conseil des Arts
for the Arts   du Canada

University of Toronto Press acknowledges the financial support of the Government of
Canada through the Canada Book Fund for its publishing activities.

Contents

Acknowledgments   vii

Introduction: Canadian Capital in the Age of Empire   3

Part One: Big Business from Triumph to Crisis

1 Provincial Man of Mystery: Howard P. Robinson and the Politics of Capital in New Brunswick   29
2 Charles A. Dunning: A Progressive in Business and Politics   69
3 The Dilemma of Democracy: Sir Edward Beatty, the Railway Question, and National Government   114

Part Two: Continentalism and the Managerial Ethic

4 Stewardship and Dependency: Sam McLaughlin, General Motors, and the Labour Question   157
5 Engineering Canada: C.D. Howe and Canadian Big Business   201

Conclusion: Après le déluge   242

Notes   251
Index   357

Illustrations follow page 192

Acknowledgments

This work has benefited from support in various forms and from various sources. David Frank read numerous drafts, provided valuable feedback, and has been a mentor to me; I hold an enormous amount of gratitude for him, which will be easily understandable to anyone who knows him. I also received insightful feedback from Jeff Brown, Alvin Finkel, Greg Kealey, Margaret McCallum, and Suzanne Morton, who all read earlier versions of the manuscript in its entirety. During the course of my research, colleagues and friends offered places to stay, intellectual stimulation, and kindness, making this journey much more enjoyable. In particular, I would like to thank Matt Baglole, Marty Clark, Val Deacon, Steve Grainger, Mark McLaughlin, David Meren, Kirk Niergarth, and William Vinh-Doyle. Christine McLaughlin not only arranged for me to stay with her family while I was in Oshawa, she also provided excellent feedback. I presented some of the research in this book at various conferences, including the annual meeting of the Canadian Historical Association, the Atlantic Canada Studies Conference, the Business History Conference, the annual meeting of the Social Science History Association, and the Montreal History Group's Les Jeudis d'histoire seminar series; I thank everyone for their thoughtful comments. The anonymous reviewers also provided very helpful input.

Archivists and librarians at many institutions offered crucial assistance during my research. I would like to thank the staffs at Library and Archives Canada, Queen's University Archives, the Harriett Irving

Library, the Archives of Ontario, the Canadian Pacific Railway Archives, the Provincial Archives of New Brunswick, the New Brunswick Museum, the McLaughlin branch of the Oshawa Public Libraries, and the Oshawa Community Museum and Archives.

This project received financial support from the Social Sciences and Humanities Research Council of Canada and the University of New Brunswick. Professor Joe Martin, director of Canadian business history at the Rotman School of Management, played an instrumental role in guiding this work through the later stages of the publishing process. Crucial support towards the publication of this book was also received from Dr Richard Currie. I offer them my sincere thanks. I also offer sincere thanks to Len Husband, editor, University of Toronto Press, whose commitment to this project was untiring.

My family has been a constant source of support, and Courtney MacIsaac has lived with this project more than anyone else. They keep me going.

Dominion of Capital
The Politics of Big Business and the Crisis of the Canadian Bourgeoisie, 1914–1947

Introduction
Canadian Capital in the Age of Empire

The tall buildings lining St James Street can be seen from miles away, a cluster of grey structures hovering above Montreal's bustling cityscape. From the street itself the neoclassical architecture is even more imposing, creating an almost cavernous effect and projecting the impression of timeless wisdom. Well-dressed men march about purposefully in heavy coats; perhaps a few carry the Montreal *Gazette* or the *Financial Post* under their arm. On this frosty January day in 1929, the septuagenarian president of the Royal Bank of Canada, Sir Herbert Holt, is scheduled to address the bank's directors for its annual meeting at eleven o'clock in the morning. From his mansion on Stanley Street in Montreal's Square Mile, an old enclave of the city's bourgeoisie extending from the southern section of Mount Royal, Holt's journey to the office is short. The tallest building in Montreal, the new headquarters of the Royal Bank at 360 St James Street serves as a testament to the bank's rising stature in business and finance, and with assets totaling more than $900 million, the directors are at ease while Holt addresses them. The year 1928 had been good, and Holt anticipates more of the same in 1929. He propounds an expansive, global vision of capital accumulation that hitherto had served the bank well. The postwar political turmoil in Europe having calmed, Holt declares, "the world stands upon the verge of a period of prosperity similar to that which is now being experienced in North America, and ... the volume of our international trade will soon rise to new and unprecedented levels." The potential problems ahead, to Holt's mind, are simply the problems of meeting the conditions for further expansion, and thus he warns that a substantial increase in immigration is necessary. "I believe, however," he concludes, "that at the moment it is no exaggeration to summarize the general situation by saying that there is no other part of the world more prosperous than Canada."[1]

This was the setting of the Royal Bank's annual meeting on 10 January 1929. Holt's optimism was not unusual; it evinced the élan of a conquering national bourgeoisie. With an involvement in utilities, textiles, coal and steel, as well as pulp and paper, the tentacles of Holt's economic activity extended well beyond banking; indeed, his non-bank business interests represented hundreds of millions of dollars in capital investment. But Holt's optimism, and his business interests, would be thrown into question by the onset of economic crisis later in the year. Having actively participated in the economic growth of the National Policy period preceding the First World War, when western expansion, European immigration and settlement, railway building, and protective tariffs established and consolidated Canada's position in North America, a project of both nation building and imperial expansion under the Union Jack, Holt and many other capital-rich Canadians anticipated a future that would follow the experience of the recent past. However, the contradictions of that expansion would soon disrupt these expectations and create a new array of challenges and opportunities for a changing national elite.

This study examines Canada's economic elite as they confronted new circumstances and as they tried to build and maintain the politico-economic order – as they understood it – during the thirty years following the First World War. As with Holt, the expectations and assumptions of the country's elite during this period continued to be shaped by the experience of the National Policy period. The 1920s, as Holt's language revealed, was a successful decade for Canadian big business, especially as emerging industries such as pulp and paper and automobiles provided new opportunities for capital accumulation. It was also a decade of marked political success. Following the retreat of the postwar farmer-labour revolt during the early 1920s, Canadian big business regained its swagger.[2] Drawing upon the influence of progressivism and meritocratic ideals, big business advanced its political influence and shored up its legitimacy as the wealthiest Canadians made renewed claims to their stewardship of the Dominion.

Yet evidence of change could be seen at the very heart of the nation's economy within one of its most heavily capitalized sectors: the railways. As Richard White has recently shown, transcontinental railways had become central to the political life of nation-states in North America by the late nineteenth century, a development that had been spurred along by railway entrepreneurs who had achieved a startling ability to cultivate relationships with politicians to serve their own aims. White concluded that the railways had "thoroughly insinuated themselves into the modern state."[3] But during the First World War the capacity of private enterprise to control Canada's transcontinental railway system was significantly undermined, as the crucial flow of capital from Britain was cut off after the onset of war. The Canadian Northern, the Grand Trunk, and the Grand Trunk Pacific fell into deep financial trouble. They were eventually taken over by the federal government and consolidated into one state-run system, the Canadian National Railways (CNR), during the period from 1917 to 1923. Prime Minister Robert Borden's Union administration acted to rescue the railway companies from bankruptcy and receivership, and to avoid the massive economic fallout that would have resulted from their failure. The ordeal reduced Canadian Northern Railway president Sir William Mackenzie to tears, while the powerful group of capitalists centred around the Canadian Pacific Railway (CPR), including Sir Herbert Holt and Edward Beatty (who was appointed president of the CPR in 1918), became infuriated with the creation of a government-owned competitor. This structural transition, which gave the state a more active and autonomous role in the nation's economic life, set the framework for the political crisis that would confront big business during the 1930s. As both railway companies fell into financial difficulties during the Great Depression of the 1930s, businessmen argued that CNR deficits, combined with other government spending, threatened the solvency of the Canadian state. The "railway question" gained a central role in the politics of big business as the debate achieved wider ideological resonance as part of a larger debate about political economy and the role of the state in society. Beatty played a lead role in the unfolding political conflict, as he and his St James Street allies faced a significant historical failure.

This study tells the story of that political failure. It does so by examining the *mentalité* as well as the political and accumulation strategies of

Canadian big business through a series of comparative biographical case studies. Holt, Beatty, and many others embraced an outlook based upon an earlier phase of capitalist expansionism that had unfolded within the framework of the British Empire and was deeply interconnected with Canadian nation building. Railway building, protective tariffs, and immigration and settlement had played key roles in this earlier period of capitalist expansionism, animated by a liberal vision of limited government involvement in the domestic economy and a sense of Canada as a British nation, which before the First World War had been strongly reinforced by Canadian business's widespread connection to the British financial market.[4] The basis of this old political economy was already being undermined in the 1920s, not only through increased government intervention in sectors such as the railways but also through the expansion of a new type of U.S. influence in Canada's economy, especially apparent in the rise of the automobile industry. With this, the traditional outlook of Canada's business elite encountered difficulties. A profound contradiction became apparent in Canadian businessmen such as General Motors of Canada president Colonel Sam McLaughlin, whose business success represented a new junior partnership with U.S. capital, but whose cultural sensibilities remained decidedly British.

While the structural reorientation of the Canadian economy during the 1920s gradually began to undermine the residual culture and worldview of Canadian big business, the Great Depression of the 1930s and the experience of the wartime economy of the 1940s would generate a broader and deeper crisis that would challenge the political power of the nation's economic elite. The genesis of a new logic – one that allowed greater freedom for state intervention, was more managerial, and was more oriented towards the United States – was apparent in the activities and beliefs of engineering contractor-turned-politician C.D. Howe, and provided the basis for Howe's opposition to that traditional bastion of Canadian big business, the CPR. As minister of transport in the second half of the 1930s, Howe would embolden the CNR's management and offer stronger opposition to the CPR, not only in the field of railways but also in the airline business. As minister of munitions and supply, Howe functioned as Canada's industrial czar during the Second World War, a position he would maintain as minister of reconstruction during the transition to a peacetime economy. Howe played an important role in the 1930s and 1940s in promoting new forms of state intervention, often against the wishes of powerful capitalists. In so doing, he participated in recasting the state's relationship to the business elite. But the scope of his power was also quite limited after the Second World War; politicians and bureaucrats, embracing an enlarged sense of the state's capacity to play an active role in society, shaped the "mixed economy" and administered the so-called postwar settlement between capital and labour in ways that defied Howe's own relatively narrow, pro-business outlook. Canada's business elite emerged from this period with their power significantly diminished and their place within the Canadian political economy more tenuous than it had been a generation earlier.

Adaptation did come, but not in the manner generally perceived by scholars.[5] This account is less a story about prescient invention and adaptation than it is a story about the failure of extreme alternatives within a conservative elite and about a fundamental shift in power away from the historic locus of business power in Canada on St James Street. When he pronounced with such confidence about the future of Canadian capitalism in 1929, Sir Herbert Holt, the grizzled veteran of Canadian big business who had worked as a contractor and an engineer with the CPR during the railway's initial construction, failed to recognize that he was already near the height of his power. The political economy of the National Policy period gave rise to Holt and the CPR, but it was a political economy that would be undermined and challenged in unanticipated ways as the fiery embers of political struggle reshaped Canadian capitalism.

The National Policy, Capital, and the Exercise of Power

Unlike feudal or other noncapitalist elites, whose social position is determined by inheritance, legal title, or other markers of social distinction, the social power of business elites or bourgeoisies is based upon the ownership and/or control over capital. Since capital is always in movement, bourgeoisies have also been fluid and dynamic, their compositions moving in flux with changing commodity prices, business innovations, political regimes, and a range of other factors.[6] In Canada a national business elite grew in step with the expansion and consolidation of the nation-state during the late nineteenth and early twentieth centuries, reflecting a general process that was occurring throughout the advanced capitalist world. Characterized by the consolidation of national economies, the coalescence of banking and industry, protectionism, and the imperialism of territorial expansion, this new spate of capitalist growth – analysed by Rudolf Hilferding in terms of the rise of "finance capital" – was most developed in the emergent economies of the United States and Germany.[7]

Canada participated in these transformations associated with this "age of empire."[8] In 1879 the Canadian government introduced a protective tariff on manufactured goods and sought to encourage settlement and export-oriented agricultural production in the Prairie West. Known as the National Policy, this economic program demonstrated the growing political strength of manufacturing interests and created a spurt of industrialization in Central Canada and the Maritimes during the 1880s. Local merchants pooled their capital in industrial enterprises; artisans became industrialists; U.S. businesses set up factories in order to jump the protective tariff; and capital flowed into Canada from outside sources, especially Britain. The outcome was a rather diffuse, locally directed pattern of industrialization.[9] The construction of the Canadian Pacific Railway, completed in 1885, was the central project in the creation of a national economy, where the agricultural frontier of the West would serve as a captive market for the industrial centres of Ontario, Quebec, and the Maritimes.[10] This vision came to fruition after 1896 as the country entered a phase of stunning growth, benefiting from the general economic upturn throughout North America and Europe. Canada achieved rates of economic growth during the early twentieth century that surpassed even those of the United States.[11] During this period the capitalists associated with the CPR and other leading players in finance and industry based in Montreal and Toronto would extend and consolidate their control of Canadian economic life at the "commanding heights" of the business world; consolidation was intensified and linkages between a burgeoning industrial base and the nation's major banks became tighter, especially after the first Canadian merger wave of 1909–13.[12] As Robert Craig Brown and Ramsay Cook observed, "[t]he large corporation, the monopoly, and the trust became the characteristic form of business organization in these years. Business became national in scope."[13]

The significance of this general process has generated various conclusions. In the United States influential scholarly work has argued that the rise of the modern corporation ushered in a social revolution. Proponents of these views have claimed that salaried managers displaced the owners of capital, and diffuse stock holdings socialized ownership and undercut classical liberal concepts of individualism.[14] But, more recently, numerous U.S. historians have provided rich accounts of the political mobilizations of wealthy business elites and their impact upon national political life. Not only does this new scholarship insist upon the enduring importance of politics and social class in business history, much of it also demonstrates the various ways business elites sought to restore and revitalize their influence and legitimacy during the twentieth century.[15] In Canada, scholars had never been apt to emphasize the impact of the "managerial revolution," evidence of the fact that Canada never did produce an army of corporate administrators in proportion to those of its southern neighbour. And while Peter C. Newman has popularized the concept of "the Canadian Establishment" in his journalistic work on the ongoing exploits of Canadian business moguls, historians in Canada have tended to dismiss or avoid questions surrounding the manner in which economic elites exercise political power and behave as a social class, especially at the national level.[16] As a result, the Canadian business elite or bourgeoisie does not hold a clearly defined area of study within historiography – although a large body of literature emerged outside the discipline of history on the question of the Canadian bourgeoisie's contribution to economic dependency and "underdevelopment," especially as fears about the impact of U.S. ownership in the Canadian economy grew in the 1960s and 1970s.[17] Though they figure in almost every subfield of Canadian history, the bourgeoisie's social existence remains shrouded in many respects. In one study they preside over a royal commission, in another they sell war bonds, and in another they run for public office or finance a political campaign. The historical understanding of Canada's higher capitalist class remains surprisingly limited and fractured.[18] And while some historians in Canada have begun in recent years to examine the activities and ideas of elites within a broad societal context, class remains a highly problematic and contested concept.[19]

The Canadian Bourgeoisie

People who lived through the three decades following the First World War were not unfamiliar with the idea that a handful of bigwigs sat at the top of Canada's political and economic order. Louis Rosenberg identified "fifty big shots" in his popular pamphlet *Who Owns Canada?* – published in two editions, in 1935 and 1947.[20] Looking at many of the same people, Eugene Forsey identified the "economic cabinet of Canada" in a short article in 1934.[21] Certainly, Rosenberg and Forsey may have theorized their elites in a rather simplistic fashion, assuming a straightforward relationship between economic and political power. But it was hardly an invention to describe the existence of such an elite, just as the proverbial "1 per cent" of our day can hardly be dismissed as an imagined construction.

Though certain concepts of class have justly come to be considered old-fashioned, class itself, as Craig Heron has recently observed, continues to provide a relevant focus for historical investigation.[22] This study sets out to analyse Canadian big business and its politics within the wider social, cultural, and economic world from which business leaders emerged and operated. A picture of the Canadian bourgeoisie takes shape out of the broader context that is developed throughout this study: their environment, their ideas, and their activities – what E.P. Thompson described long ago as "experience."[23] In this way, to draw upon Heron's formulation, we shall see how "particular people" filled a category.[24] The term *bourgeoisie* is thus used in this study as a heuristic concept to describe a group of individuals who can be demonstrated to have acted collectively in class ways.[25]

Although the form of this social class was dramatically altered during the twentieth century with the fracturing of traditional bourgeois culture and the rise of the modern corporation, the bourgeoisie – defined fundamentally as a social class whose power is based upon the ownership and control of capital – can indeed be identified and studied into the twentieth century.[26] This book examines primarily the worlds of business and politics, and the focus in the pages that follow is upon a business bourgeoisie that embraced a particular *mentalité* and set of social practices. More particularly, this bourgeoisie formed the upper fraction of a national elite that was not only wealthy but occupied lead positions within the corporate structures of Canadian big business, controlling large pools of capital. Embracing a meritocratic ideology that usually erased the terminology of class, these individuals did not refer to themselves as a bourgeoisie, often preferring misleading euphemisms such as "representative citizens" to describe themselves. But, as we shall see, they nonetheless felt themselves to be a unique group, wielding power with an awareness of purpose. In the 1950s, American sociologist C. Wright Mills used a somewhat similar definition in describing the "power elite" in the United States, who represented, in his view, a "managerial reorganization of the propertied class" that helped sustain "the continuity of the higher capitalist class."[27] Although the group described in the pages to follow was far less coherent, organized, and politically effective than Mills's power elite, as proprietors, representatives, and administrators of corporate wealth, the Canadian bourgeoisie evinced characteristics that were of a similar nature: they moved easily from business to politics and back; they controlled a form of capital that socialized risk and lessened political division at the commanding heights of the economy; and their outlook and interests transcended their local environment.[28]

No attempt is made here to write the entire history of Canada's upper class, which would require a much broader analysis and much closer attention to the lives of elite women, their role in creating and preserving social and cultural capital, their important functions in philanthropy, and other activities worthy of scholarly attention. Thus, this study focuses upon a particularly concentrated and powerful part of the business elite, a gendered fraction of the bourgeoisie, since women were effectively barred from assuming lead roles in the world of Canadian business. And, indeed, as this book will show, gendered and racial understandings of the world were ubiquitous in structuring how elite men saw themselves and the world around them. This was an elite whose public face was very masculine indeed, as business and political leaders were cast within a meritocratic discourse that reified the supposed manly characteristics of aggressiveness and physical vitality, which U.S. cultural historian Jackson Lears has described as "the managerial revitalization of the rich."[29] And C.D. Howe carried gendered business ideals forward into the new environment of the 1940s, personally embodying aspects of what historian Christopher Dummitt has described as characteristics of the "manly modern," including anti-intellectualism, decisiveness, and a willingness to engage in calculated risk.[30] This elite was in practice, as well, almost always Anglo-Celtic, although a few French Canadians could also claim a place in this exclusive world from time to time. Ethnicity thus functioned as a cohesive force for an elite that racialized itself as British within a Canadian society that remained decidedly part of a larger "British world." This, of course, was in stark contrast to the experience of the country's ethnically diverse working class, which was often seriously divided by ethnic identities that were reproduced in residential patterns and at the workplace as well as in cultural and political life.[31] For stylistic reasons, the terms *business elite, economic elite, Canadian bourgeoisie, big bourgeoisie, bourgeoisie, business class, moneyed Canadians, capital-rich Canadians,* and even *upper class* are used in this study to refer to this small but powerful social group who presided over Canadian big business.

The Anatomy of an Elite

We may map out this economic elite's general sociological characteristics through quantitative analysis. Using principally the 1917 *Annual Financial Review*, supplemented with biographical data from the *Who's Who and Why,* a list of 102 leading businessmen has been compiled to provide a glimpse of the structure of Canada's business elite at the beginning of our period of study, a period when war offered new accumulation opportunities through a sudden boost in the export market while also creating new financial strains that seriously disrupted the structure of the bourgeoisie's economic activity.[32] In compiling the list, priority was given to the number of directorships and to the economic prominence of the companies with which individuals were connected. On average, individuals held six directorships listed in the 1917 *Annual Financial Review.* The goal here was to isolate key figures of national import who operated above local elites. Some consideration was also given to individuals whose political influence was well known. Though impressionistic, this method allows us to draw a fairly reliable general portrait of the national business elite.

Several spheres coalesced to bring these men into contact with one another. First, the data reveal an unmistakable geographic concentration. Of the group, 75 per cent were residents of either Montreal or Toronto. Montreal was by far the most important centre, home to forty-seven individuals, compared to only twenty-nine from Toronto. The collective dominance of these two urban centres in Canadian big business is revealed by the fact that the third largest urban contingent was from Hamilton, with a total of only six, followed closely by Halifax and Winnipeg, with five each. Elite social clubs also played an important role in fostering sociability among the upper strata of national economic life. The most important social club for the country's elite in 1917 was Montreal's Mount Royal Club, which had been founded by members of the CPR-Bank of Montreal group as a super-exclusive preserve for the wealthy and well connected. Fifty members of our group were members of the Mount Royal Club. As might be expected, slightly fewer – forty-five in all – were members of Montreal's more inclusive St James's Club. Reflecting the geographical location of the group, the Toronto social clubs were well represented in this elite circle too, with thirty-six and thirty-five individuals holding memberships in the York and Toronto clubs, respectively. While only three individuals in the group were residents of Ottawa, Ottawa's Rideau Club commanded a membership of thirty-five individuals. The reasons for this appear obvious: the policies of the federal government mattered dearly to these capital-rich men, and the Rideau Club represented a key point of access to politicians in the nation's capital. These individuals operated above the local sphere. The scope of their activities was national and even transnational.

Though their business interests were wide, their social origins were narrow. Their average age in 1917 was fifty-nine, and more than 75 per cent were Canadian-born.[33] Of those not born in Canada, all but two were born in England, Scotland, Ireland, the United States, or Newfoundland – and, of the two, only one was not of Anglo-Celtic descent.[34] A number of these men inherited businesses, revealed in part by the substantial number of individuals born in Montreal (eighteen) and Toronto (nine). The relative homogeneity in religious denomination provides further evidence of the group's narrow social origins. Of the seventy-three individuals whose religious denomination was listed in *Who's Who*, thirty-five were Presbyterian, and twenty-three were

Anglican. Thus, of those whose religious denomination was listed, nearly 80 per cent were either Presbyterian or Anglican. And a small but important Methodist group was based in Toronto.[35] Only four Catholics were included in the 1917 group, an indication of the small number of French Canadians who operated within the upper-stratum of the nation's business elite – although one of this number, CPR president Lord Shaughnessy, was Irish Catholic. The three French Catholics, interestingly, were all politically active, suggestive of their unique role within an essentially Anglo-Celtic elite.[36]

The Case Studies

In the following pages, attention has been paid to incorporate figures from different regions and sectors of the economy, and each case reveals a different trajectory. Aside from this, selection was based upon sheer economic and political influence – which explains the somewhat ubiquitous role of railway politics in these pages – as well as the availability of sufficient relevant source material. And, whereas the average date of birth from our 1917 group was 1858, the average date of birth of the five individuals selected for the case studies was 1879: these men were of a different generation. They found their place in the nation's business elite *during* the three decades after the First World War, and thus this study offers a window into a process of class formation. Though these men may not have represented typical experiences, their trajectories were archetypal. The biographical approach also offers an opportunity to explore their *mentalité*. This study, after all, is just as much about what these men thought they were doing as it is about what they actually did; it is just as much about political failure as it is about political success. By looking at this subject anew through the biographical approach, we can appreciate the extent to which business magnates perceived their own failure to influence public policy. Thus, while Alvin Finkel has correctly emphasized the prominent role of business in the reform process during the 1930s, the individual reforms he examined were distinct from what Arthur Meighen described in 1939 as "the big towering issues facing Canada," such as the railway question, empire, national debt, and industrial unionism.[37] The business elite often refused to adapt on these issues. Furthermore, while businessmen could support government intervention in aid of the private sector, they in many instances remained hostile to government expansion in areas already inhabited by private business. Moreover, they often remained ideologically opposed to the idea of government intervention, no matter how often this conflicted with the actual practice of business in a national economy characterized by monopoly and oligopoly wherein the state already played an active role.

Part 1 of this study covers three individuals, each from a different region, who all became associated with St James Street and embraced residual outlooks associated with the experience of the National Policy period: the crisis of the old political economy was their crisis. Chapter 1 examines Howard P. Robinson (1874–1950), a Saint John, New Brunswick, newspaper owner who was also interested in utilities and an array of other business endeavours. Robinson rose from relatively modest circumstances to become one of the Maritime region's most influential capitalists of the interwar period and played an important political role in facilitating New Brunswick's transition to pulp and paper during the 1920s. Maintaining links to outside capital, both U.S. and Central Canadian, Robinson represented a more ambiguous version of the "community-oriented entrepreneur" than had existed in the past. Nonetheless, his experience points to the continued vitality of regional elites in the context of a highly centralized national economy. Robinson worked as a behind-the-scenes political operator who succeeded in championing the ascendance of big capital in New Brunswick. In his case we see, therefore, that the growing influence of large, corporate capital was not merely an economic process born of the greater economies of scale and capital reserves of large companies but that it was also part of a broader political campaign, which depended upon the support of regional elites such as Robinson.[38] Moreover, Robinson had taken control of Saint John's entire daily press by 1927, which signalled the more generalized shift towards a nonpartisan press sensitive to the general interests of business, as displayed by Canadian press barons of the period, including Lord Atholstan and later J.W. McConnell of the Montreal *Star*, Smeaton White of the Montreal *Gazette*, and, in the 1930s, C. George McCullagh of the Toronto *Globe and Mail*. As Canada descended into economic turmoil in the 1930s, Robinson reacted angrily against government interventionism and articulated the regionalist lament that Confederation had been a mistake.[39] A strong British imperialist and strident believer in private enterprise, Robinson was aghast at the social-democratic and continental direction in which Canada appeared to be heading during the 1930s and 1940s. However, even Robinson accepted that tactical adaptation must be within his repertoire, and he remained aware of the necessity to, as he put it, "compromise with the assassins."[40]

Chapter 2 follows a different regional trajectory associated with the experience of the National Policy period. It examines Charles Avery Dunning (1885–1958), a leader of Saskatchewan's cooperative grain marketing movement, a farmers' representative and western progressive who became a Liberal premier of Saskatchewan in the 1920s before moving into Mackenzie King's federal cabinet as minister of railways and canals and later as minister of finance. After the defeat of the King Liberals in the 1930 federal election, Dunning moved into the private sector in Montreal and became associated with numerous enterprises, but especially the CPR. When he resumed his place in King's cabinet as minister of finance in 1935, the erstwhile progressive was widely perceived as a representative of big business – and correctly so. The chapter examines the manner in which Dunning's brand of western progressivism coalesced with the outlook of big business and for a time seemed to create an effective political formula. As Dunning moved to St James Street and developed an outlook that was closer to the interests of the CPR, however, his political stock in the West tumbled quickly. His public image of vitality and high political probity suffered during the 1930s from the taint of big money, as Dunning came to be seen as a stodgy plutocrat representing the privileged interests of Montreal and Toronto. Ultimately, his term as minister of finance from 1935 to 1939 proved frustrating, as the pressures of government limited the range of his policies. While private enterprise and limited government intervention remained an ideal in Dunning's mind, he was forced to compromise these ideals, and he suffered the bitter irony of being the first minister of finance in Canada to oversee the government's initial experimentation with Keynesianism in 1938. He suffered a heart attack that year in the parliament building. With his health worn down and his ideology compromised, Dunning retired from politics in September 1939 and resumed his career in private business on St James Street.

Dunning's experience served as a lesson to businessmen frustrated by the party system. "Regardless of political stripe," claimed *Globe and Mail* president and publisher George McCullagh in January 1939, "I think most fair-minded people will agree that Charlie Dunning is a sincere public servant, trying to do a good job for the people. However, it is my firm conviction that he is suffering at the present time just as much from a broken heart as any physical ailment. In other words, he sees the hopelessness of doing a first-class job for the people, under our present political system. I could go on and name many other outstanding men in public life today whom the system effectively destroyed." To McCullagh's mind, Dunning's experience was a prime example of how talented individuals were effectively ruined by party politics.[41] McCullagh articulated a more generalized concern within the business elite concerning the pressures of popular opinion during a period of economic crisis. Indeed, some businessmen had hoped that Dunning could have led a nonpartisan "National Government" capable of implementing policies without interference from popular pressures or partisan calculations. And Dunning himself toyed with the idea. This was a recurring idea throughout the 1930s and into the 1940s.

It was an idea that was most strongly advanced by Sir Edward Beatty (1877–1943), the president of the CPR from 1918 to 1943 and the subject of chapter 3. The railway question was central to the politics of business during the 1930s, and Beatty was a lead player in the debate and commonly involved in the related political activism. Beatty and many other businessmen associated with St James Street believed that amalgamation of the CPR and CNR under private – that is, CPR – control was necessary in order to rescue the country from looming financial insolvency and general economic ruin. The major hurdle confronting this political drive was a public largely sceptical of the CPR's motivations as well as thousands of railway workers who were concerned about losing their jobs in the retrenchment that would follow railway unification. Beatty's support of the National Government campaign was prefigured by earlier efforts to publicize the railway question, particularly in the Royal Commission to Inquire into Railways and Transportation in Canada in 1931 and 1932. While Beatty had been encouraged by the commission's potential, he became frustrated by what he viewed as its ineffectual recommendation for increased cooperation between the two railway systems. And though the commission and the House of Commons hearings tarred his business rival, CNR president Sir Henry Thornton, Bennett's Conservative administration seemed more interested in revealing improprieties that occurred under Mackenzie King's watch than in following Beatty's suggestions regarding railway affairs. National Government offered a way out of this dilemma by insulating the government from the popular pressures inherent in party politics, which, to Beatty's mind, were stifling a constructive solution to the railway question. During the 1930s, Beatty also brought this somewhat embattled brand of elitist politics to the campus of McGill University, where as chancellor he waged a campaign against political radicalism. Beatty's ultimate failure to achieve railway unification revealed the waning political power of St James Street. However, St James Street's still formidable political clout ensured that nationalization of the CPR remained a decidedly remote prospect. The railway question also assumed a broader importance within the business community by the late 1930s, becoming tied to more general concerns about the state's expanding role in society.

The relative decline of the CPR was related to a more general shift in Canada's political economy. Part 2 examines two individuals associated with different aspects of this transition. Perhaps no company signalled Canada's changing economic structure after the First World War better than General Motors of Canada. Whereas the CPR was a largely British-owned company managed in Canada, General Motors of Canada was a subsidiary of a giant U.S. corporation firmly under the control of its U.S. head office, and thus it introduced a new form of dependency to the Canadian economy. Chapter 4 examines Colonel Sam McLaughlin (1871–1972), the president of General Motors of Canada. McLaughlin had well-established roots in Oshawa. His father operated a successful carriage company in Oshawa from the late 1870s to 1915, when Sam McLaughlin finally completed the transformation of the family business from the manufacture of carriages to the manufacture of automobiles. The carriage company had become the largest of its kind in Canada, a success story of National Policy industrialization. Given its size, the McLaughlin Carriage Company had a remarkably steady history of labour peace. After Sam McLaughlin and his brother, George, sold the business to General Motors in 1918, they succeeded in maintaining the earlier ethos of community stewardship, which the elder McLaughlin had cultivated around the carriage business. Indeed, during the 1920s, McLaughlin remained in many ways socially and economically detached from the national bourgeoisie, and the automobile industry had yet to acquire political recognition commensurate with its fast-expanding economic power. When the King Liberals lowered the tariff on automobiles in 1926, the community in Oshawa was quick to rally around GM of Canada in protest; and although a brief strike was staged two years later, Sam McLaughlin succeeded in encouraging a resolution of the dispute and sustained his claims to stewardship.

In the 1930s McLaughlin became more integrated into the social and economic life of the country's bourgeoisie as the automobile industry became even more important to the Canadian economy with the further expansion of the parts industry, and businessmen and politicians no longer seriously questioned the importance of the industry. These developments were paradoxical, since McLaughlin's path of dependent industrialization eventually undermined his claims to community stewardship in Oshawa as General Motors of Canada implemented massive cutbacks in response to the onset of economic crisis during the 1930s. The lessons that working-class Oshawa took from that experience were made apparent once the industry showed signs of recovery in the mid-1930s. The historic 1937 strike at General Motors in Oshawa not only signalled a breakthrough for industrial unionism in Canada, it was also plain evidence of McLaughlin's estrangement from the city's working class. He little understood the nature of the protest and reacted strongly against what he perceived as outside interference in the community; the Committee for Industrial Organization (CIO) was, after all, a U.S. organization. McLaughlin, as little as it squared up with his actual economic reality, remained a strident advocate of a right-wing version of the British tradition, articulating a profoundly conservative vision of the social order and advocating a hard-line stance against industrial unionism and the political left.

We may acquire a general sense of how these individuals fit into the business community after they had all come to occupy leading business positions during the 1930s. Table 1 utilizes the findings of Forsey and Rosenberg to provide an indication of the density of their business linkages through shared directorships. The banks, particularly the Royal Bank of Canada and the Bank of Montreal, were central institutions in the business life of the nation's bourgeoisie; but the most striking aspect of the group is the diversity of the men's interests, which is only partially revealed in the table. Transportation (Beatty, McLaughlin, and Robinson), mining (Beatty and McLaughlin), pulp and paper and hydroelectricity (Dunning and Robinson), and insurance and trust companies (Beatty, Dunning, and McLaughlin) are among the principal areas in which the group was represented in national and international business.

The meaning of the data shown in Table 1 can be enriched by considering the frequency with which key business figures identified by Rosenberg and Forsey appeared on the boards of the companies listed. Sir Herbert Holt and Ross H. McMaster, president of the Steel Company of Canada, lead the way, holding seven directorships each; they share at least one directorship with all four of our case-study subjects. Next is Sir Charles Gordon, president of the Bank of Montreal, who holds five. Following Gordon are five individuals, all holding four directorships, whose names are very familiar to Canadian business historians: W.A. Black, president of the Ogilvie Milling Company of Canada; Colonel Henry Cockshutt, chairman of Cockshutt Plow Company; J.W. McConnell, president and managing director of St Lawrence Sugar Corporation; James Richardson, Canada's most important grain dealer and president of James Richardson & Sons, Ltd; and C.F. Sise Jr, president of Bell Telephone of Canada. A slightly greater number held three directorships from the list above: Norman J. Dawes, president and managing director, National Breweries; S.C. Mewburn, solicitor and Bank of Montreal vice-president; Arthur Purvis, president and managing director of Canadian Industries Limited; Morris W. Wilson, managing director of the Royal Bank of Canada; Julian C. Smith, president of the Shawinigan Water and Power Company; and W.N. Tilley, whose law firm worked for the CPR.[42] Collectively, these men controlled capital that spread across many sectors, combining finance with productive industry. They operated within complex and deeply interconnected business networks that often allowed them to transcend their specific interests – in a certain business enterprise or sector – in pursuit of the broader objectives of their class, which could also be cultivated in elite social clubs.[43] Table 2 shows club memberships, and it reveals continuity from the pattern revealed in the 1917 group – evidence, too, of Montreal's persisting relative importance.

By the end of the 1930s, many of these individuals and others from their social class had rallied around conservative ideas that offered a set of right-wing alternatives to the perceived excesses and inadequacies of the political system. Defending the nation against the perils of radicalism, they subscribed to a residual worldview that combined a reverence for an imagined British tradition with a free-market ideology that had its roots in the old liberalism of the nineteenth century. An emergent capitalist ideology existed within Mackenzie King's cabinet, in the form of Clarence Decatur Howe (1886–1960), the subject of chapter 5. Trained as an engineer at the Massachusetts Institute of Technology, the U.S.-born Howe ran a successful business in Port Arthur, Ontario, designing and building grain elevators during the 1920s and into the 1930s. With the onset of economic hard times, Howe gravitated towards politics with the encouragement of Liberals whom he knew from the grain trade, namely Charles Dunning and Liberal organizer Norman Lambert. As minister of transport, Howe introduced businesslike methods to government, but not of the variety Beatty and others had been calling for. In the second half of the 1930s, he moved away from the cost cutting and retrenchment that had been forced upon the CNR under the Bennett administration and directed more attention towards setting up the company as a successfully functioning enterprise – not simply a political burden, as Bennett and his minister of railways and canals, R.J. Manion, had handled it. Moreover, with the formation of Trans-Canada Air Lines (TCA), Howe signalled his willingness to use the state to accomplish economic tasks of national importance. And, of course, these methods would become dramatically apparent when Howe served as minister of munitions and supply during the war. As an engineer, Howe privileged efficiency within a capitalist framework and was more willing to entertain ideas about economic management than was the case among those more wedded to the old political economy. And, during the 1940s, as classical liberal ideals lost traction with the experience of the wartime economy and as the influence of socialist and social-democratic alternatives became more widespread, especially as revealed by the growing popularity of the Co-operative

Table 0.1. Selected Directorships, circa 1935

	Robinson	Dunning	Beatty	McLaughlin	Number in the Rosenberg-Forsey Group
BANKING					
Bank of Montreal			X		18
Royal Bank of Canada	X				12
Dominion Bank				X	0
Barclays Bank (Canada)					NA
INSURANCE AND TRUST					
Sun Life Assurance Company of Canada			X		6
Mutual Life Insurance Company			X[a]		3
Ontario Equitable Life Insurance Company		X			0
Royal Trust			X	X	15
Maritime Trust	X				0
FORESTRY AND POWER					
Consolidated Paper		X			6
Howard Smith Paper Mills Ltd		X			2
Fraser Companies Limited	X[b]	X			0
International Hydro-Electric System and Subsidiary Companies	X				2

	Robinson	Dunning	Beatty	McLaughlin	Number in the Rosenberg-Forsey Group
MINING					
International Nickel Company of Canada (Inco)			X	X	4
Consolidated Mining and Smelting Company of Canada			X	X	4
TRANSPORTATION					
CPR			X	X	11
Canadian Airways	X		X		9
OTHER					
Canadian General Electric				X	6

[a]Trustee
[b]Voting trustee

Table 0.2. Club Memberships, circa 1935

	Robinson	Dunning	Beatty	McLaughlin	Number in the Rosenberg-Forsey Group
Mount Royal	X		X	X	39
St James's			X		26
Seigniory		X	X	X	N/A
Rideau		X	X		16
York			X	X	21
National				X	6

Commonwealth Federation (CCF), Howe's vision of state-managed business expansionism became part of a broader "passive revolution." Ironically, his ascent in national economic life during the 1930s and 1940s signalled the weakening political and economic position of St James Street, and the impact of Howe's ideas within the business elite remained limited immediately after the Second World War.

This study demonstrates the way in which social inequality functioned within the political system at the top of Canada's economic order, and it shows that the country's economic elite had a consciousness of their unique and privileged role in Canadian political life. But the exercise of political hegemony could prove elusive, especially in the context of the Great Depression of the 1930s, when the capitalist system was failing to deliver the results its champions promised. Capitalist crisis led to a political crisis within a national bourgeoisie too rigid and too classically liberal to respond effectively to the emerging political challenges created by the onset of the Depression. Underlying the political crisis lay broader economic changes that were undercutting the old political economy, exemplified by the relative decline of the CPR and St James Street; the government, encouraged by popular opinion, was compelled to play a more active role in economic and social life to meet the contingencies of the Depression and the Second

World War, and Canada's historic links with Britain – both economic and cultural – dissipated under the strain of continental integration. The more organized and managerial form of capitalism that emerged in this period, coupled with government concessions to popular social-democratic demands, often succeeded in the face of stiff resistance from the economic elite. *Dominion of Capital* thus offers an account of this historic change that integrates the Canadian bourgeoisie into the political history of modern Canada. In so doing, it suggests a new way of seeing that history. It suggests that the diminished political capacities of the country's economic elite was an important factor in creating the conditions for the state's more active role in economic and social life, which was managed by intellectuals and politicians operating with newfound authority.[44] Although the business elite enjoyed privileged access to positions of political power, they failed to truly carry the day as their political crisis deepened and as organizing from below reshaped Canada's political landscape. The expectations born of the National Policy period proved unrealistic. The conquering vision that Sir Herbert Holt articulated in 1929 never came to fruition, and the rule of big money was abortive during the tumultuous years that followed.[45]

PART ONE

Big Business From Triumph To Crisis

1

Provincial Man of Mystery: Howard P. Robinson and the Politics of Capital in New Brunswick

Aitken, Dunn, Killam, Pitfield: the best known Maritime-born financiers of the first half of the twentieth century all left their native region to make their mark.[1] Howard P. Robinson (1874–1950) was different. He stayed in New Brunswick to assemble a huge array of business connections that touched a wide range of sectors – all from a Saint John base. But his public profile was barely perceptible, and even regional specialists today have little more than vague knowledge of his activities. Robinson's influence in business, politics, and cultural life was, nonetheless, considerable, especially after the First World War, when he emerged as a leading provincial capitalist. His interest in the province's utilities sector, which began modestly in the telephone business in 1904, helped ensure that the defence of private property would remain a central tenet of his political philosophy until his death in 1950. Robinson's imposing role in the province's newspaper business, solidified by 1927, after he had acquired control of Saint John's entire daily press, also made certain that his interests and views were not to be taken lightly. By the 1920s, too, Robinson was beginning to forge more extensive links with the emerging pulp and paper industry. Though Robinson's business network was becoming more cosmopolitan in the decade after the First World War – and would become more so in the 1930s and 1940s as he entrenched his position within the ranks of the national business elite, accumulating directorships with the Royal Bank of Canada, the Canadian Pacific Railway (CPR) and numerous other firms – he was to remain committed to advancing what he believed were the economic and political interests of his home province. Unlike the Aitkens and Dunns, Robinson moved the tradition of the community-oriented entrepreneur into the twentieth century, remaining essentially a provincial capitalist, a forerunner of sorts to K.C. Irving.

That tradition, of course, was much more ambiguous in Robinson's time than in times past. In the nineteenth century, businessmen such as Alexander "Boss" Gibson – or even the financier John F. Stairs of Halifax – had attempted to consolidate control within the Maritime region and were guided by ideas of community stewardship and often paternalist convictions too.[2] Robinson was no paternalist and operated in a business world where proprietorship and control were increasingly complex. As a promoter early in his career he valued profit above control, but as he matured into a capitalist with more permanent associations with industry, he showed greater concern for the maintenance of provincial control; that said, he consistently collaborated with outside capital, and, indeed, such collaboration was essential to the economic stature he attained. He represented a new type of regional entrepreneur; a product of the integrated national economy of the early twentieth century, Robinson's brand of community-oriented entrepreneurship was fraught with contradictions and eventually collapsed under its own weight.[3]

Having ascended in business by forging relationships with outside capital, Robinson's autonomy and effectiveness as a provincial booster was limited, just as his political aims and ideological sensibilities were transgressed by the social and political ferment that emerged from the Great Depression of the 1930s and Canada's transition to state-managed capitalism in the 1940s. The social philosophy embraced by Robinson championed private enterprise but under monopolistic conditions.[4] The doctrine asserted the beneficence of private enterprise and argued against government intervention, even in sectors where "natural monopolies" prevailed. This worldview, rooted in the political economy of the National Policy period, posited that the state could play only a supporting role to private enterprise, and Robinson played an important political role, inviting big, outside capital into New Brunswick, demonstrative of the fundamentally political – and not merely economic – manner by which large corporations extended their influence within the Canadian economy.[5] His role as a provincial booster became harder to sustain ideologically as the public increasingly demanded more aggressive state intervention. The Maritime Rights progressivism he helped disseminate in the 1920s shed its popular appeal once the economic slump of the 1930s set in. In the 1920s Robinson was able to contribute to the political defeat of a provincial Liberal administration intent on developing publicly run hydroelectricity; but by the 1930s his political views lost popular appeal under the strains of the Great Depression; under these new conditions, Robinson's political priorities aligned more closely with the beliefs of capital-rich colleagues in Montreal and Toronto than with the priorities of many resident New Brunswickers.

While Robinson's business and political life remained firmly rooted in New Brunswick, his overall experience fit into the broader experience of the bourgeoisie's crisis of legitimacy. This experience was visible in the paradox of his career; while his structural power and business connections expanded, his political effectiveness diminished. Robinson's growing disillusionment during the 1930s and 1940s was shared by other capital-rich Canadians who lamented the eclipse of the old political economy and worried that society, as they knew it, was under grave threat by mounting government intervention and social-democratic concessions. Having grown suspicious about the efficacy of democracy in a time of economic crisis, Robinson and other members of Canada's economic elite retreated into conservative isolation.

Beginnings and Early Career

Born in the village of Elgin in Albert County in 1874, Robinson grew up in modest social circumstances. The relative paucity of source material on Robinson is particularly acute for his early years, but a general picture may be painted. Robinson's father, Robert D. Robinson, of some Loyalist ancestry, worked as a schoolteacher and later became superintendent for Albert County; this work was apparently supplemented by farming, as the 1871 and 1881 censuses list his occupation simply as "farmer." Robert Robinson also became a small manufacturer of birch spools for British thread mills. In the political fight over Confederation, he opposed the union.[6] Robinson's mother, Lavina J.

Robinson, came from a pre-Loyalist family (Stiles), which had originally migrated from New England to settle in Cornwallis, Nova Scotia. She embraced the Baptist faith, a particularly well-established denomination in the Maritimes, and seems to have exercised the matriarchal authority typical in religious matters during the nineteenth century.[7] Howard and his older sister Laura were both enumerated as Baptists in the census, even though Robert was Methodist. Howard's grandmother, Mary, also lived in the family household in Elgin; she, too, was Baptist.[8] Howard Robinson did not develop any particularly ardent sense of religiosity. He reminisced about reading Robert Louis Stevenson's *Treasure Island* and memorizing "Requiem" as a child. Conceding that he was "not orthodox" in religious belief, reading Stevenson's "prayers" had always been "an inspiration and a joy" to him.[9] Robinson later attended Mount Allison Academy in nearby Sackville, and one wonders whether fatherly influence was exercised to encourage this, Robinson's attendance at a Methodist institution.

In the early 1880s Robert Robinson moved the family to Sussex, centred within a relatively prosperous dairy region, where he established the printing business of R.D. Robinson & Company and later began to publish the *King's County Record*. He died in 1901, and Howard took over the business, which he reorganized into a limited liability company, R.D. Robinson Publishers Limited. Robinson's familial associations were not extensive, but he appears to have maintained an enduring emotional attachment to his mother, who passed away following an extended illness in 1932, at the age of eighty-seven, in Robinson's Saint John mansion; at the time, Robinson himself was recovering from a gastric ulcer and ignored a doctor-recommended European trip in order to remain with his ailing mother.[10] His older sister passed away the following year.[11] With his mother and sister gone, he appears to have had few relationships with blood relatives. Robinson willed his estate to his wife – Pearl Fox of Gagetown, whom he married in 1921 – but stipulated that, should his wife predecease him, nearly his entire estate would go to her relatives.[12]

Robinson had collaborated with his father to establish a farming newspaper, *The Maritime Farmer*, in 1895. Operating in Sussex, the paper made sense enough, but competition later arose from a Halifax-based paper, *The Maritime Homestead*, owned by William Dennis, proprietor of the *Halifax Herald*. *The Maritime Homestead*, the *Financial Post* reminisced in a 1937 biographical portrait of Robinson, "didn't anticipate much trouble in driving Mr. Robinson's Maritime Farmer to the boards." Robinson travelled to Halifax in an attempt to sell to his competitor, but Dennis was not interested. The *Financial Post* curtly reported the outcome: "the youthful proprietor of the Maritime Farmer went home to Sussex, borrowed money for his paper and won the fight."[13] Robinson's health declined soon after the victory. He sold *The Maritime Farmer* for $47,000 and left for Johns Hopkins Hospital in Baltimore.[14]

Robinson also became interested in the telephone business while he was still living in Sussex. His entry into the business was accidental. The 1937 *Financial Post* story claimed that he and a friend were planning a trip to the 1904 World's Fair in St Louis, but, in order for his unnamed friend to have cash for the trip, Robinson endorsed a note for him at the bank and took stock in the Central Telephone Company as security. Given that Senator Percy Burchill's later account of these events, based upon Robinson's testimony, makes no mention of the St Louis excursion and puts the value of the endorsed banknote at $50,000, it seems unlikely that Robinson was simply freeing up some spending money for a friend. In either case, the friend was unable to pay, and Robinson was left with stock in a company that owned a telephone system that, according to Robinson, "began nowhere and ended nowhere."[15]

His first instinct was, again, to sell his interest in Central Telephone to the more powerful competitor, the New Brunswick Telephone Company, which was affiliated with Bell Telephone of Montreal. As before, Robinson was turned away and "decided to fight." To save Central Telephone from bankruptcy, he convinced the prominent Saint John tea merchant T.H. Estabrooks to join the company's board of directors, along with a local Sussex lumberman, S.H. White; one of White's relations, C.T. White, had already developed an interest in the telephone business by establishing the first telephone system in Alma, Albert County.[16] Having fulfilled the demands of the company's creditors, aided by the leniency of Saint John industrialist J.L. McAvity in not demanding $4,000 owed him, Robinson embarked on a mission to create a functional telephone system by acquiring feeder lines across the province. It is evidence of his early Liberal party leanings that Robinson was able to obtain permission from H.R. Emmerson, Laurier's minister of railways and canals, to run telephone poles along the Intercolonial Railway's right-of-way.[17] This allowed Central Telephone to build a line reaching Bathurst, near the northern extremity of the province, ahead of New Brunswick Telephone, whose president, Senator F.B. Thompson, had a similar design as part of a larger plan towards the construction of a telephone system encircling the province. Intent on forcing a merger with New Brunswick Telephone from the beginning, Robinson's hand was strengthened when he received confidential information that Bell Telephone was dissatisfied with its New Brunswick service. He convinced Estabrooks to travel to Montreal with him to meet with C.F. Sise, president of the Bell Telephone Company of Canada, where the New Brunswick duo succeeded in obtaining a letter from Sise stating that Bell intended to abstain from voting in the upcoming New Brunswick Telephone shareholder meeting. Armed with this letter and control of the proxies belonging to the late Dr A.A. Stockton of Saint John, Robinson succeeded in 1906 in forcing a merger that gave Central Telephone directors representation equal to that of their New Brunswick Telephone counterparts, even though the arrangement was technically a takeover of Central Telephone.[18] That Robinson was appointed managing director of the reconstituted New Brunswick Telephone Company left little room to doubt the nature of the amalgamation. Robinson had won. He left Sussex for Saint John and was on his way to establishing himself as an important figure in the province's commercial capital.

In his early business career, Robinson valued capital accumulation above control of an individual enterprise, a mentality that was pervasive among early-twentieth-century promoters and financiers and apparent in Robinson's early attempts to force mergers. In search of new horizons of accumulation, Robinson left New Brunswick Telephone to work in the securities business, first as a manager of J.C. Mackintosh & Company, and later for his own company, Atlantic Bond Company Limited, which handled municipal and industrial bonds.[19] In 1912, however, "persistent demand for his services from the directors and shareholders" resulted in his return to New Brunswick Telephone as managing director.[20] As he resumed his position with

New Brunswick Telephone, Robinson was also beginning to consider a venture that would involve developing a power system in southern New Brunswick, which would also encompass Saint John's street railway system. The framework for Robinson's vision was largely achieved in 1916–17 with the formation of the New Brunswick Power Company and its acquisition of the St John Railway Company, owners of the city's street railway system. Robinson was able to finance the company through the Boston investment house of Harris, Forbes & Company, purchasers of the first issue of New Brunswick Power Company bonds. Support and advice were also forthcoming from Sir Herbert Holt, president of the Royal Bank of Canada. In November 1916, Robinson cited these facts in a letter to J.B.M. Baxter, attorney general of the province at the time, in an effort to increase the company's authorized capital. "In view of the fact that capital is at all times timid," Robinson explained,

> I trust that there will be no delay whatever in securing the authorization of the capitalization proposed. In the interest of the Province generally it must be borne in mind that we have succeeded in interesting outside capital to the extent of many millions of dollars, dependent upon the success of the application above referred to. We feel that in interesting such strong financial forces as these that we are doing something for the promotion of general prosperity in the district to be covered by our power lines and street railway extensions, and we sincerely trust your Government will give us all assistance possible.[21]

Attracting large amounts of outside capital and creating a general climate conducive to capital accumulation was viewed by Robinson as an unqualified benefit to the province. Harris, Forbes & Company advertised the first issue of $1,750,000 of New Brunswick Power bonds in the *New York Times* in March 1917, luring potential investors with the promise that "[t]he Company operates entirely without competition."[22] Unfortunately for Robinson and his associates interested in New Brunswick Power, the company's monopoly position was not lauded by a general public in Saint John, nor by local industrialists and merchants, desirous of cheap power rates.

Newspapers, Party Politics, and Public Power

The economic crisis that followed the First World War had especially
profound consequences for the Maritime region, which experienced a
crippling wave of deindustrialization in the early 1920s. The Liberal
New Brunswick government of W.E. Foster sought to shore up the
crumbling industrial economy of the province's most populous and
industrialized city, Saint John, by establishing the New Brunswick
Electric Power Commission in 1920 and soon after developing hydroelectricity on the Musquash River that would serve Saint John. The
government's public power leanings became even more pronounced
after Foster retired from active politics in 1923 and handed the reins of
government over to P.J. Veniot, New Brunswick's first Acadian premier. His government's administration of workmen's compensation,
its highway construction, and its pro-public power stance were indicative of a progressive vision for the province. Acquiring the nickname
"Good Roads" Veniot for his highway-building work as premier and
earlier as minister of public works, the progressive premier retained
solid support among Acadians, who were particularly concentrated in
the northeast arch of the province extending from Moncton to Edmundston, while also garnering support in the province's Anglophone south.
Veniot's vision for New Brunswick seemed, for a time, politically viable.[23] It was a vision that Robinson would vigorously oppose.

   Formerly a Liberal, Robinson had by this time left the party. The
evidence suggests the decisive break came during the First World War
with the formation of the Union government in 1917. The decision of
Conservative Prime Minister Robert Borden to forge a coalition government had been encouraged by the emerging view among significant
segments of the country's Anglophone population that the prosecution
of the war was too important for "party government"; conscription
was, of course, the main issue of contention. An ardent imperialist,
Robinson was an officer in the 3rd Artillery Regiment, a title undoubtedly conferred because of financial donations. Available biographical
accounts indicate that Robinson attempted to enlist for overseas service but was refused because of an unspecified "physical disability."
Remaining in Saint John, Robinson went on to play a leading role in

recruiting men for the New Brunswick Fighting 26th Battalion and served an active role in the Victory Loan campaigns.[24] If indeed Robinson still identified himself as a Liberal at the beginning of the war, by its end he certainly did not. As Sir Wilfrid Laurier, the Liberal leader, refused to acquiesce to conscription, pro-conscription Liberals jumped ship to become Unionist Liberals in a coalition government headed by Borden. Twenty years later, Prime Minister William Lyon Mackenzie King, who had remained loyal to Laurier in the moment of crisis, derisively referred to Robinson as "another Unionist."[25] The political fractures created within the Liberal Party in Saint John would be particularly severe.[26] Even though Premier W.E. Foster sympathized with the Union government, he did not offer the official support of his administration for fear of losing Acadian support, which his government relied upon heavily.[27] Thus, when the Liberal provincial administration sought to develop public power, Robinson was already opposed to the government on broader issues of imperial loyalty.

In 1922 Robinson gained control of Saint John's only remaining Conservative daily, the floundering Saint John *Standard*, later renamed the *Journal*, by injecting $90,000 into its operations; the Conservative Party had offered only $3,200 to keep the paper going.[28] Saint John's daily newspaper business, driven by political partisanship and overoptimism, had been saturated since before the First World War. Industrialist George McAvity, co-owner of the Liberal *Telegraph* and *Times*, reported in 1914 that the papers yielded no return on his investment. He called for the Liberal Party to take over the papers, but the party was apparently slow to act.[29] McAvity, along with Saint John lumberman John E. Moore, remained in control of the *Telegraph* in the early 1920s, when it continued to serve as an organ of the Liberals and had become a decidedly vocal advocate of public power development. In the wake of public hearings on New Brunswick Power in 1919, the provincial government's entry into power development in 1920, a bitter street railway strike in 1921, and growing support for public power development at the municipal level in Saint John, Robinson sold his interest in New Brunswick Power to Federal Light and Traction of New York in 1922.[30] The timing of Robinson's decision to enter the newspaper business, coinciding as it did with the growing debate over public power development, suggests that he may have been driven by political motivations from the beginning: namely, ensuring that the *Standard* remain an opponent of government intervention.[31] Whether he remained interested in New Brunswick Power at some level remains unclear; he was, however, without question an ideological and political ally.

The McAvity and Moore newspapers continued to oppose New Brunswick Power in 1923. The *Financial Post* reported: "The dispute between the New Brunswick Power Company and the owners of the Daily Telegraph and Evening Times, newspapers of St. John, is raging with intensity." The *Post* suggested that McAvity and Moore were following narrow self-interest, supporting the Saint John Power Commission because they owned land on the site of the Musquash dam – which was washed away by a freshet in the spring.[32] Though particular interests may have been at stake, the dispute also involved competing fractions of capital. Local industrial capital, which was also supported by small merchants, was desirous of cheap power rates, and the McAvity and Moore newspapers voiced its perspective. It was opposed by finance capital, embodied in New Brunswick Power but also including aligned local and regional capitalists.[33] Robinson represented the vanguard of the latter fraction and vigorously advanced its political mission.

Premier Veniot wished to achieve direct party control of the *Telegraph* and *Times-Star*, reporting to Mackenzie King in May 1923 that "[o]wing to the attitude of Moore the Telegraph and Times Star are becoming dangerous to the Liberal Party and we must obtain control or look to the organization of other means to carry on." Veniot suggested that only through the collective efforts of the prime minister, Minister of Public Works Dr James H. King, and Kings County Member of the Legislative Assembly J.D. McKenna could the Liberal Party hope to secure an option on the papers.[34] This was apparently done, but Veniot later reported to Mackenzie King that George McAvity "might not carry out the agreement entered into to transfer the papers to Mr. Andrew Haydon, who is acting in my behalf and other representative Liberals," because he believed "the option was secured by fraud." Emphasizing that the deal would serve to consolidate Liberal control of the papers, Veniot explained that J.D. McKenna "will more fully discuss matters with you."[35] McKenna acted as Veniot's representative; "he thoroughly understands the situation and you can depend on him,"

Veniot reassured King.[36] McKenna, however, also had personal associations with Howard Robinson: both men were connected to Sussex,
and McKenna had taken over the *Maritime Farmer*. The evidence is
patchy, though there is considerable reason to believe that McKenna –
who, in March, had "made complimentary references" to the incoming
premier in the New Brunswick legislature – was not the reliable Liberal
agent Veniot thought and helped Robinson gain control of the paper.[37]

The New Brunswick Publishing Company, whose authorized stock
was raised to $600,000 on 29 June, was used by Robinson as a holding
company to execute a merger of the Liberal *Telegraph* and Conservative
Journal and later "guide the destinies of the new publications."[38] The
Saint John *Globe* announced the incorporation of the company on 5
July, noting in its editorial section the following day that the company's
listed members, which consisted of a Fredericton lawyer and two young
women from York County, hardly squared up with the public assurance
that "the new company will have a representative board of directors,
including leading business men from widely scattered sections of this
province." This, the *Globe* suggested, was an indication that the individuals behind the merger wished "to remain unknown, not even letting
the left hand know what the right hand doeth."[39] When the first issue
of the *Telegraph-Journal* was published on 16 July, J.D. McKenna –
suggestive that an understanding between himself and Robinson had
been reached – headed the new operating company, and T.F. Drummie
served as business manager. Robinson would remain closely associated
with these individuals in the years to come. The paper made no specific
pronouncements regarding its policy "on either federal or provincial
politics," stating the universally inoffensive position that it would serve
"the interests of New Brunswick and the Maritime Provinces."[40] Robinson's true intentions were kept quiet, restricted to a small circle of investors, including lumbermen Angus McLean of Bathurst and Richard
O'Leary of Richibucto. The latter described Robinson's motivations in
private correspondence the following year: "to wipe out the St. John
Telegraph which had been injurious, every way, to the public utilities
of the province (in some of which we were interested) and as a political
sheet had been very obnoxious."[41]

Robinson had accomplished an impressive feat, since the merger depended upon nuanced financial dealings and on balancing the apparent

political scales so as not to alienate investors committed to either the Liberal or Conservative Parties – all necessarily done with consider-able deception. Robinson's ability to accommodate Liberals was not entirely insincere, but the result of a pro-business outlook that did not entail loyalty to any one party; from this perspective his willingness to mislead Foster and even King's deputy Andrew Haydon was simply a business strategy rather than a political betrayal. Angus McLean's move away from the Liberal Party in 1925 was to demonstrate this style of politics, where safeguarding the business climate was the overrid-ing political concern. Saint John Conservative MP J.B.M. Baxter un-derstood the transition, explaining in private correspondence to Arthur Meighen that much of the stock "is held by business interests which are not particularly interested in parties but are expected to respond to an approval based upon solid business." But Robinson also reassured Baxter that, though the merger eliminated Saint John's only Conser-vative paper, the Conservatives would still benefit.[42] This perhaps ex-plains Baxter's enthusiasm when reporting news of the merger on 12 July to R.B. Hanson, Conservative MP from Fredericton: "The deal is through and one of the most poisonous influences in N.B. politics [the *Telegraph*] is eliminated. The *most* poisonous [Veniot] remains and is in your city!"[43]

Though Robinson favoured the Conservative Party for his own po-litical and ideological reasons, he made it clear that representatives of the Conservative Party were in no position to dictate the news coverage of the *Telegraph-Journal*. This became evident in an exchange between Robinson and R.B. Hanson in December 1923. "I am, of course, sim-ply delighted at the manner in which the Telegraph-Journal has been handling the opposition side of the campaign in Kent," Hanson sar-castically wrote to Robinson in reference to a federal by-election cam-paign. Ending his letter on a more assertive note, Hanson proclaimed: "I am not complaining ... but if you live for the next ten years, believe me, your newspaper and all the rest will have to take notice of me."[44] The overzealous Hanson was quickly put in his place. Robinson wrote back: "There is one thing I don't think you nor our friend Baxter nor any of the Conservative party realize or appreciate, and that is the fact that, if it had not been for me, the Conservative party in this province would have had no paper prepared to publish anything but one side of a

political situation and that the side opposed to them." "On top of that,"
he continued, "I think I accomplished almost what was the impossible
when, after having fought the 'Telegraph,' I succeeded in securing an
option on it and eventually raised the money to buy it. There were a
thousand difficulties in the way, a thousand obstacles to be overcome,
not only of a financial but of a political character, and not one single
man of your party has come to me and expressed the slightest appreciation of what I have done." Robinson's letter then turned more personal:

> And not only that, but you personally sold your stock in my new company
> at fifty cents on the dollar. You offered it and it was bought by a man who
> had purchased a large quantity of bonds. The effect of your act upon my
> brokers can not be considered as either beneficial to my enterprise or as
> looking upon my changing the "Telegraph" from a violent Liberal paper
> to an independent paper as anything more than an unfriendly act so far as
> you can view it. Some of you Conservatives should at least appreciate the
> fact that if it had not been for me, you in this Province to-day would not
> have any paper except the Moncton "Times" which would even mention
> the fact that you were a factor in the Kent County campaign.
>
> Now, don't understand that I am finding fault, criticising or trying to
> be nasty. I just want more of you fellows to realize the way this whole sit-
> uation looks from the spot by the roadside where I am standing. Just think
> these facts over, and the next time you are prepared to criticise something
> which might appear in our news or editorial columns or through some
> slip in the publication of a news item ... please do not be so harsh or sus-
> picious or give away to your temper by doing an injury to your friend,
> the same way you did, when, in a moment of pique, you depreciated the
> value of the Preferred Stock I have been selling in this newspaper venture
> by talking and acting as you did.

Thus, not only was Hanson ungrateful, in Robinson's view, but de-
structively irresponsible in his sale of shares. Robinson closed by offering a warning, couched in the language of advice, that ultimately
extended an olive branch to his vociferous colleague:

> I think this sort of letter is coming to you, Dick, because it is written in
> an endeavor to keep you from a repetition of what has just taken place

in-so-far as my newspaper venture is concerned. There are some newspaper men in this country who, if you had done what you have done in this
situation, would give you just cause for complaint. I want to assure you
that, although I feel that you have acted in a most unfriendly manner towards me and that, whether intentionally or not, you have been the cause
of doing me a personal and business injury, it is not in any sense going
to affect the attitude of the paper toward the Conservative party nor my
personal attitude toward you.

If you are going to play the political game, you have got to play it in a
different way from that or you will make so many enemies that you will
be shot full of holes the first time you show your head above the tall grass.

Some day I can tell you just what the effect of this sale of your stock
has been and how very much you have endangered my plans, which
must ultimately work out to the advantage of your party as well as to you
personally.[45]

No response can be found in Hanson's papers. Robinson's point was
made. He would not accept such impudence from politicians, whose
sense of political strategy was, from Robinson's perspective, made
overly narrow and short-sighted by partisan considerations. Typical of
other business moguls, Robinson maintained a sense of superiority in
his dealings with political apparatchiks such as Hanson. As Mackenzie
King later observed, Robinson expected to be "courted."[46] Robinson's
political tactics were based upon an understanding of the power relationship between capitalists and politicians, in which the latter were
beholden to the former. And, indeed, Robinson's newfound role as a
press baron was part of a broader, nationwide transition in the newspaper business, as wealthy capitalists took over newspapers and diminished the influence of political parties over editorial policy.[47]

Politician and businessman were, of course, not mutually exclusive,
but rather each is best understood as a social role that could be acted out
by a single individual. Hanson, himself, was an example. He provided
legal counsel to Fraser Companies of Edmundston and sat on the board
of directors of the New Brunswick Telephone Company since 1922.[48]
Family association also integrated Hanson into the Canadian business
world; his brother-in-law, C.E. Neill, was vice-president of the Royal
Bank of Canada and had arranged Hanson's appointment as solicitor

for the bank's Fredericton branch. Interestingly, Neill had advised Hanson against becoming a politician; he told Hanson that politicians were generally not men of "a high type," and involvement in politics had "spoiled many good men and wrecked useful careers."[49] J.B.M. Baxter also straddled the business world; his law firm represented New Brunswick Telephone. Though they occupied different social roles, Robinson, Baxter, and Hanson were ideologically likeminded, coalescing around the defence of private property and the advancement of private enterprise, and they shared similar social experiences forged in places such as the Union Club in Saint John, social outings with the New Brunswick Telephone board, and a plethora of other activities that characterized the associational life of political and business elites.[50]

The 1925 Provincial Election

In 1924 and early 1925, as the Veniot government purchased the Grand Falls site from International Paper and proceeded to move ahead with its plans for public power development, opposing forces mobilized. Businessmen led the political mobilization at the upper levels of the New Brunswick Conservative Party in preparation for the 10 August 1925 provincial election. Prior attempts had been made by the Conservative Party to recruit a new provincial leader. In late 1923, Hanson expressed the opinion to J.B.M. Baxter that the provincial Conservatives should "get some outstanding business man, new to politics, to take up the burden" of party leader.[51] Baxter agreed, but the man they had in mind was reticent, Saint John resident W. Shives Fisher, owner of the Enterprise Foundry of Sackville.[52] The opposite transpired: the businessmen would recruit their politician of choice, J.B.M. Baxter. A party of about twenty-five businessmen, led by Angus McLean and likely Robinson too, approached Baxter in 1925 to request that he contest the election. A "financial madman," they argued, was running the province.[53] Baxter heeded their request, vacating his federal seat. Having served earlier in the decade in Arthur Meighen's government as minister of customs, Baxter was known as an opponent to public ownership and was on better terms with St James Street than Meighen, whose railway policy – inherited from Borden – had produced a nationalized railway system and had upset the federal Conservative Party's financial supporters in

Montreal centred around the CPR. Thus embracing "sound" economic views, Baxter left the uncertain world of federal politics for the more familiar, if not certain, political environ of New Brunswick.[54]

Grand Falls development was an issue upon which Robinson was willing to fight. In 1923 R.B. Hanson reported to George B. Jones, a fellow New Brunswick Conservative MP, that the *Telegraph-Journal* would pursue a strictly neutral, nonpartisan line should a provincial election arise, except if Veniot should attempt to develop Grand Falls. "I understand they will oppose development of Grand Falls by any Government," explained Hanson.[55] Veniot not only proceeded with plans to develop Grand Falls, but campaigned against the "Big Interests," promising that "[n]o private corporation will be permitted to lay a finger on our water power resources so long as I have the honour of remaining Premier of New Brunswick."[56] The fight was on.

The most visible group opposing Veniot were the province's forestry capitalists, concentrated largely in the northern section of the province. The emerging pulp and paper interests, with which Robinson was becoming associated, were provoked by Veniot's attempt to move the state into what they perceived as their rightful domain of economic activity, viewing it as a challenge to private enterprise. At the forefront of this group was Angus McLean, whose company, Bathurst Power and Paper, by the end of the decade would be included among New Brunswick's powerful pulp and paper triumvirate, which also consisted of International Paper of New York and Fraser Companies of Edmundston. McLean and Donald Fraser of Fraser Companies both left the Liberal Party to oppose Veniot. International Paper, the largest of the triumvirate, had reason to oppose Veniot as well, for the Liberal government had cancelled the company's contract to develop Grand Falls. A.R. Graustein, International Paper's president, admitted as much in private correspondence; and though the company's policy was to refrain from party politics, which included restricting its employees from running for public office, Graustein made an exception and allowed A.D. Taylor, manager of the Miramichi Lumber Company, an International Paper subsidiary, to run under the Conservative banner.[57] The smaller and economically troubled lumber barons, whose businesses were proving less and less viable, shared some of the concerns of the pulp and paper interests, such as stumpage rates, which they felt had become too high under Veniot's oversight. The forestry sector as a whole was unimpressed too by Veniot's administration of workmen's compensation, which, many lumbermen felt, placed too heavy a burden on operators. Indicative of the significant political realignments provoked by the 1925 election, the Conservatives ran three former Liberals in Northumberland County, prompting a Newcastle Conservative paper to withdraw its support of the Conservative candidates; even the Liberal and Conservative titles were largely discarded during the campaign in favour of the terms Government and Opposition to refer to the respective parties.[58] Robinson was an important, though quiet, ally of the province's forestry capitalists in 1925.

In this context, Robinson was willing to respond to specific demands from R.B. Hanson regarding the placement of news in the *Telegraph-Journal*, though in general the paper maintained a relatively neutral tone throughout the election.[59] Saint John Conservative candidate L.P.D. Tilley claimed, with considerable truth, that the *Telegraph-Journal* "leaned a little towards the Opposition" during the election campaign.[60] The appearance of neutrality was somewhat contrived, though, particularly when Angus McLean's five-part diatribe against Veniot and the Liberals was published as purchased advertising space.

The political strategy of the Conservatives was to tar Veniot personally, not to denounce popular initiatives such as public power development and workmen's compensation. Baxter, McLean, and others attacked Veniot as a proto-dictator, irresponsibly emptying the public purse more to satisfy personal vanity than the public good. They claimed he moved to develop Grand Falls without first obtaining "expert" advice as earlier promised, that he paid International Paper too much for the Grand Falls property in 1924, and that he was lining the pockets of favoured contractors. The thrust of the attack was, thus, not against public power development but against Veniot's handling of it.[61] Moreover, Angus McLean argued that Veniot's Grand Falls contract had ceded International Paper privileged access to Grand Falls power while endangering the access of native New Brunswick industries, thus suggesting that Veniot and International Paper were arrayed against local industry.[62]

Indeed, in Saint John the Conservatives attempted to appropriate public power and workmen's compensation for their own purposes. While

Baxter remained tight-lipped on the subject and McLean argued that public power was more expensive than private development, Saint John Conservative candidate and local businessman M.E. Agar was on record in favour of public development: "M.E. Agar Declares for Public Ownership," stated the *Telegraph-Journal* on 6 August.[63] Baxter, meanwhile, dubiously asserted the Workmen's Compensation Act had been passed by a Conservative government, claiming that Veniot was taking credit for something that he was merely overseeing; lumbermen supporting Baxter opposed workmen's compensation and probably interpreted such rhetoric for what it was – disingenuous politicking. The Conservatives gained political strength from their campaign's ambiguity and vaguely articulated intentions. This, no doubt, was a product of internal contradictions within the Opposition, but it was likely also born of a strategy designed to cultivate support beyond a narrow set of business interests, seen also in the *Telegraph-Journal*'s relatively subdued stance during the campaign.[64] The real trump card was the latent anti-Acadian and anti-Roman Catholic sentiment that the Opposition succeeded in arousing in southern New Brunswick and the St John River Valley. Indeed, a Klansman, J.S. Lord, was elected in Charlotte County, and correspondence in R.B. Hanson's papers demonstrates that Hanson maintained a rather friendly patronage relationship with a member of the Ku Klux Klan.[65]

It was a successful strategy. The Baxter Conservatives picked up thirty-seven of forty-eight seats in the election, winning in an unexpectedly lopsided fashion. The decisiveness of the Conservative victory suggested that bigotry played an important role in determining the outcome. And, indeed, the manner in which Veniot was defeated seemed to confirm as much. As one political scientist has observed, "[t]he seats won by the Veniot Government were almost entirely Acadian Catholic constituencies, while the English and Protestant constituencies went strongly for the Opposition."[66] Veniot was convinced that business interests had used their money to exploit the issues of race and religion during the campaign.[67] Announcement of Baxter's victory in the *Financial Post*, meanwhile, included the reassuring words that New Brunswick's new premier "is a lawyer of distinction and is financially interested in many important companies in his native province," as well as being knowledgeable "of the finer points of bridge."[68]

Robinson's contribution to the victory remains unclear; it seems to have been mostly of a passive, but calculated, nature. His control of the *Telegraph-Journal* ensured that the Conservative Party was able to get its message out to the voting public in Saint John, and private correspondence indicates his involvement in collecting campaign funds.[69] But Robinson remained aloof from active public involvement in the campaign, so much so that Mackenzie King seemed to believe that Angus McLean – and not Robinson – was controlling the press in Saint John.[70] Indeed, twenty years later Robinson would write that, even though he "owned and operated daily newspapers," he "never made a practice of writing editorials."[71] "I have an absolute horror of publicity," he would explain in 1937 when the *Financial Post* article highlighting his early business career appeared.[72] With Robinson remaining offstage, the party picked up all four seats in the City of Saint John, and the two seats in Saint John County. Robinson was likely most effective behind the scenes, particularly in Saint John, where direct opposition to public power would have been a highly unpopular stance, since low residential power rates in Saint John in 1925 were evidence to many residents of the benefits of public power development.[73] Moreover, capturing a significant portion of the working-class vote was necessary to win at the polls. The mysterious Robinson, once the main figure behind New Brunswick Power, would not have been an effective public figure for the Opposition.

An Ambiguous Ascent

With the 1925 Conservative victory, Robinson's central position within a new type of provincial bourgeoisie was strengthened. Robinson's role in the New Brunswick Telephone Company had long put him into contact with important businessmen across the province. But the rise of pulp and paper in the 1920s was, as Bill Parenteau has demonstrated, qualitatively changing the nature of entrepreneurship in the province's forestry sector, which had become even more central to the provincial economy in the wake of the deindustrialization of New Brunswick industrial centres, particularly Saint John. Less noncommittal about turning over Grand Falls to International Paper than his campaign rhetoric suggested, Baxter ceded huge tracts of land to the pulp and paper tri-umvirate and allowed the paternalistic lumber barons of the nineteenth century mould to be displaced by large joint-stock companies.[74] Rob-inson served as an intermediary between northern New Brunswick lumber barons such as J. Leonard O'Brien and G. Percy Burchill and outside financial and pulp and paper interests.[75] He also became as-sociated with all three major pulp and paper companies operating in New Brunswick. By the close of the decade, he had been appointed to the board of directors of Canadian International Paper, a subsidiary of International Paper, which, in turn, had acquired half of the Bathurst Power and Paper Company – and Robinson would gain a directorship with Bathurst Power in the 1930s. He was also appointed trustee of Fra-ser Companies bondholders during its reorganization in 1931.[76]

Robinson was involved in the Grand Falls project after the Conser-vative victory and appears to have been directly connected with the subsidiary company that International Paper formed to develop Grand Falls power, the Saint John River Power Company; Fraser Companies, too, was interested in the Grand Falls project. International Paper pres-ident A.R. Graustein wrote in June 1926 that he wished "to invite sev-eral representative citizens of New Brunswick to membership of the board." This included "not only Mr. Fraser himself, but also Mr. How-ard Robinson, and, although he is not directly interested, perhaps Mr. McLean also."[77] The pulp and paper triumvirate did not compete with one another; rather, each company marked out its spheres of influence on the provincial map while cultivating mutual interests. Grand Falls construction was delayed as International Paper and Fraser Companies demanded more concessions, which, Graustein suggested, were neces-sary to raise capital.[78] The New Brunswick pulp and paper industry by the second half of the 1920s was operating to consolidate monopoly and expand territorial control within a transnational business world. Robinson had, of course, been working in this milieu since his involve-ment with New Brunswick Power, which had brought him into con-tact with Boston and New York capital. Working as an intermediary to push along the commencement of construction at Grand Falls, Rob-inson advised Baxter that Graustein and Fraser intended to begin de-velopment as soon as the contract with the government was signed. "I would strongly urge you to bring this matter to conclusion just as soon as possible," wrote Robinson to Baxter in June 1926. "From all parts of the Province," he continued, "I get reports that the delay in proceeding with Grand Falls is being accepted as evidence that the whole situation has been trifled with. This provides an excellent excuse for many luke-warm supporters of yours to start talking against you and if the cause of their dissatisfaction is not removed soon, they will have gone 'over the fence' permanently."[79] Though construction did not proceed as quickly as Robinson hoped, he did eliminate Saint John's last dissenting voice to Baxter's handling of Grand Falls when the New Brunswick Publishing Company took over the Liberal Saint John *Globe* late in 1926.[80]

Three years later, on 14 March 1930, Robinson presided over the official ceremonies marking the opening of an enormous International Paper newsprint mill in Dalhousie, fed with power from the Grand Falls dam. He had been "instrumental, perhaps more than anyone else, in inducing the Canadian International Paper Company" to invest in the $14 million mill.[81] Robinson explained before the prominent audience at Dalhousie that the gathering marked the opening of one of the largest plants in New Brunswick's history. Such a development, he continued, "meant prosperity and money to the laboring people." Introducing J.B.M. Baxter, Robinson "said that he spoke with personal knowledge of the great amount of work done by the Premier." He introduced Graustein in equally glowing terms, describing him as "one of the great captains of industry in America." Among these laudatory remarks, Robinson also expressed his belief that it was completely appropriate that such a large enterprise should be associated with the province's forest resources, which "were the chief source of wealth of the province."[82]

Robinson's ascendance in the 1920s moved in step with emerging and revitalized resource sectors. Aside from pulp and paper, Robinson was also interested in fisheries, serving on the board of directors of Connors Brothers Ltd., a Blacks Harbour–based company that was re-organized in 1923 and became a world leader in the sardine business.[83] Both Connors Brothers and the forestry sector witnessed the eclipse of direct proprietorship and its unique form of paternalism during the 1920s with the rise of joint-stock ownership; but these corporations could themselves implement their own variety of paternalism.[84] A. Neil McLean, president of Connors Brothers, exercised a form of corporate paternalism in the community of Blacks Harbour and was a prominent Liberal. One Conservative observer claimed that McLean created a "near-autocracy on the coast of Charlotte" County.[85] That Robinson was associated through business connections to prominent Liberals across the province such as A. Neil McLean, G. Percy Burchill, and A.P. Paterson simply provides more evidence of his ability to operate successfully in economic life without having to cultivate specific party loyalties.

Robinson also represented a break within the Saint John business community away from the local industrial economy, which was rooted in an earlier era of paternalistic enterprise. This shift in accumulation strategy synchronized with the increasingly popular Maritime Rights version of regional economic history, which argued that Confederation had caused the decline of the Maritimes and thus ignored the significant industrialization of the National Policy period. New Brunswick, Robinson explained to Lord Beaverbrook in 1929, had "got into the doldrums after Confederation, and suffered so severely through the loss of wooden ship building and, later, of the lumber industry [*sic*] that we, as a people, almost lost the 'will to do.'"[86] "To me," Robinson would reiterate years later, "the golden and heroic age of this province is associated with the building of ships."[87] The experience of urban industrialization did not figure much into Robinson's historical consciousness, nor his accumulation strategy, and his support of Maritime Rights was an articulation of this reimagined political economy during the 1920s. Robinson's support of Maritime Rights was apparent in his personal intervention in favour of sending a "Great Delegation" to Ottawa to voice Maritime concerns, and his sympathy for the movement was also evident in the *Telegraph-Journal*'s role as a Maritime Rights organ; even R.B. Hanson was driven to protest the prominent role given the dyspeptic Maritime Rights crusader A.P. Paterson in the paper's pages.[88] The decline of the partisan press helped facilitate the articulation of nonpartisan regionalism under the rubric of Maritime Rights, and the movement became an updated boosterism embraced by an emerging provincial business elite whose accumulation strategy had moved beyond the localism of the old community-oriented entrepreneur. Robinson adopted the language of Maritime Rights with ease. "Now we are fighting for our rights and we will continue to fight,"

Robinson explained before the Maritime Board of Trade in 1928; he advised "his hearers to forget political prejudices and work in unison and harmony for Maritime welfare."[89] Under such platitudes, Robinson advanced an aggressive pro-business agenda and identified that agenda with the general good of the region.

At around the time of the opening of the Dalhousie mill, a gastric ulcer forced Robinson to withdraw from active business life. "I have been back to work for the last month for the first time in three years," Robinson reported in December 1932, a year after having received treatment at Johns Hopkins Hospital.[90] Indeed, severe periodic illness plagued Robinson throughout his life, a pattern not dissimilar from that observed by Christopher Armstrong and H.V. Nelles among Canadian promoters operating in the Latin American utilities business, namely Max Aitken, James Dunn, and F.S. Pearson; the stress-driven world of business was often more than the body could handle.[91] In Robinson's case, the periods of illness were unusually extended and disruptive; had not another gastric ulcer struck in 1937, Robinson would have served as a commissioner for the Royal Commission on Dominion-Provincial Relations.[92]

The privileges of wealth allowed Robinson to escape the stress-filled world of business with Pearl, his wife. One refuge was Caton's Island, located in the St John River, twenty-one miles from the City of Saint John. Robinson bought the island in 1926 and transformed it into a summer resting place, including a summer cottage and landscaped surroundings, which received attention from a Montreal "tree surgeon." By 1941, he had also built a barn, a chicken coop, and a pig sty. It was a genteel farm, since by that time the property also included a rebuilt summer home named Windemere – with "wings built on both sides together with a back extension" – furnished with "fine antique furniture" and walls lined with "old prints." A small one-room building was erected for the chauffeur.[93] In the winter, Howard and Pearl Robinson fled the cold weather. Since 1927, they had been heading down to Nassau, Bahamas, for a month to six weeks of rest and relaxation during the winter, a practice that was becoming increasingly common among the Canadian bourgeoisie, attracting the likes of Sir Herbert Holt and Sir Frederick Williams-Taylor as well as some wealthy Canadian tax exiles in the 1930s who made it a permanent home.[94]

By the late 1920s Robinson had emerged as a self-assured, well-established businessman. Though his marriage in 1921 did not make Saint John's social pages, by the latter half of the decade Robinson had established himself as a leader of the Saint John elite, even helping collect money for Saint John's elite boys' school, Rothesay Collegiate.[95] However, his social network was much broader than Saint John alone. In 1928, he became a member of Montreal's ultra-exclusive Mount Royal Club, the preserve of capitalists associated with the "CPR-Bank of Montreal group."[96] His appointment to the board of directors of the Royal Bank of Canada, announced by the *Financial Post* in January 1935, further confirmed his important position on St James Street, the centre of Montreal's financial community.[97]

Robinson's ascent, however, was also marked by an ambiguity that arose from the contradiction between his role as a provincial booster in an economically marginalized province and his integration into national business circles. This tension was particularly obvious in Robinson's ongoing involvement in the telephone business. Though the board of directors of New Brunswick Telephone brought together important New Brunswick businessmen, the capital requirements of the telephone business made strict provincially based control highly uncertain.[98] From 1911 to 1921, New Brunswick Telephone's invested capital doubled to more than $2.5 million.[99] During the 1920s Robinson and New Brunswick Telephone officials were forced to make repeated appeals to the Board of Commissioners of Public Utilities for increased capitalization in order to meet financial obligations. In 1920 the company asked for the authority to issue more stock to raise the capital required to pay $300,000 owed its creditor. The financial position of the company was not perilous, however. Robinson emphasized that the issuance of new stock was simply necessary to raise the "working capital" required in the capital-hungry telephone business. The cyclical nature of construction, the collection and payment of debts, as well as payments on bonds created a thin margin of liquidity that required the telephone company to continually raise more capital.[100] New Brunswick Telephone's relationship with the banks was also rather unstable. In 1925 Robinson explained that the company had used three different banks over the previous eight years.[101] The company's growth in the late 1920s made the need for new capital as pressing as ever. "This province is growing and we have quite good evidence of it in

the growth of our business," said Robinson in 1928. He concluded that
"[a]s long as we are in business we are going to find approximately this
same demand for increased facilities which means of course additional
money," noting that the telephone business had been good even in times
marked by depression.[102]

Operating outside of the nation's principal capital markets of Montreal and Toronto, New Brunswick Telephone maintained a provincial
autonomy that was ambiguous from the beginning. Indeed, it had been
affiliated with the Montreal-based Bell Telephone of Canada since
Robinson first became involved with the company before the First
World War. Robinson, however, was largely successful in exercising
a sort of province-based control over New Brunswick Telephone. In
1931, for example, Bell vice-president J.E. Macpherson referred to
his company's policy of "noninterference" in New Brunswick Telephone affairs. Ambiguity reigned even here, though. Macpherson
cited the noninterference policy in response to R.B. Hanson's request
to be considered to serve as legal counsel for New Brunswick Telephone, a position that J.B.M. Baxter resigned in order to take up a
judgeship on the New Brunswick Supreme Court. Hanson expressed
appreciation for Macpherson's "attitude in not interfering," and asked
Macpherson to "have a little private conversation with Howard Robinson" instead.[103] Hanson appears to have thought that he was appealing
to a higher authority by contacting Macpherson; Robinson, ill at the
time, remained a source of considerable authority in the company's
affairs.

The *Financial Post* in April 1935 listed New Brunswick Telephone
as one of several companies interlocked with Bell.[104] That connection
was strengthened as Bell purchased a large bloc of New Brunswick
Telephone stock as a "preventative measure against American interests
who were definitely seeking control." Even though Macpherson emphasized that Bell would continue to respect the fact that New Brunswick Telephone was a "provincial company," this structural control
would, as the forceful Robinson disengaged from active business in
the 1940s, place Bell in a dominant position vis-à-vis the board of directors of New Brunswick Telephone.[105] A decade later R.B. Hanson
wondered to Robinson, "Are we rubber stamps? I feel rather strongly
that we are," he concluded, expressing disgust at the ease with which
the company's board of directors tendered a contract to an "upper

Canadian firm" to dig trenching and lay conduits from Fredericton to Woodstock without considering local firms.[106] Robinson concurred, writing that he was "astonished to find that the Executive Committee had agreed to this thing."[107] Though Robinson later discovered that an effort had been made to tender the contract to a New Brunswick firm, to him the episode revealed a general state of mind governing Bell's relationship with New Brunswick Telephone. Robinson complained that New Brunswick Telephone did not even buy its ladders from a perfectly fine local manufacturer in Hampton – but from Montreal – because someone in the company thought the local ladders were no good. "I have been personally using [the Hampton] ladders at my house in the country ... for over twenty years to the complete safety and satisfaction of all concerned," Robinson explained in outrage. He continued: "Apparently anything that has ever been done in construction work in this Company is now viewed as wrong, careless and a waste of money. I get so damn fed up with this God-awful complex on the part of people in Montreal and Toronto that I feel like very much going to the mat on it." Robinson ended correspondence on this issue with Hanson on a melancholic note:

> However, as no one on the Executive Board seemed to be impressed with anything unusual in what transpired, and as at the general meeting of the Board nobody but yourself and myself seemed to be interested, I do not feel that I will go any further with the matter. Life is too short, and the control of this company is too definitely in other hands; and I am afraid the attitude of at least some people associated with the control is antagonistic to the point of being somewhat unreasonable towards local men, things and events.[108]

Bell's representative on the New Brunswick Telephone board, Paul McFarlane, evinced the mindset that so upset Robinson. In private correspondence that year with newly elected New Brunswick Telephone president G. Percy Burchill, McFarlane wrote that effective work of the directors "will not be curbed and checked by provincial traditions of another age."[109] Burchill had replaced Robinson as president; Robinson moved to chairman of the board. Had things moved too far along for Robinson to effectively intervene?

No, it seems. By the end of the year Bell had relinquished its control of New Brunswick Telephone, and McFarlane had left the board.[110] The exact manner in which Bell relinquished control is not entirely clear; it is clear, however, that Robinson had long been working towards such an outcome. With the detached but friendly relationship between Bell and New Brunswick Telephone transformed during the 1930s as Bell took a more active role in the company, Robinson, as early as 1933, suggested that Bell limit its purchase of New Brunswick Telephone stock.[111] As threat of government takeover became more real during the Second World War, Robinson sought again to repatriate shares to New Brunswick residents. Disagreement, however, surfaced over the purchase price. Bell had, in Robinson's view, paid a "crazy" price for New Brunswick Telephone shares in its earlier drive to secure control of the company from competitors, which had resulted in a bidding war; Robinson did not believe New Brunswick investors should have to pay the same "crazy" price to bail out Bell.[112] Bell president C.F. Sise Jr, unconvinced that his company's control of New Brunswick Telephone would make it vulnerable to government takeover, refused to sell in 1944.[113] New Brunswick Telephone made considerable profit during the war, so much so that in 1945 Bell suggested New Brunswick Telephone increase its dividend payments from 5 to 6 per cent. More in touch with the local political situation, Robinson advised that the dividend remain at 5 per cent for public relations reasons, even though New Brunswick Telephone would "have an embarrassingly large surplus at the end of the year."[114] Meanwhile, the company embarked on a program of rural line extensions, prompting a cabinet member of J.B. McNair's Liberal provincial administration to comment: "It's pretty near G – D – time that you were getting around to it, if you hadn't, somebody else would have done it for you."[115] An overflowing company treasury, the possibility of government control (New Brunswick Power's Saint John plant was expropriated by the New Brunswick government in 1948), and company executives such as Robinson interested in fostering provincial ownership: all appear to have contributed to New Brunswick Telephone's reemergence as a provincially based enterprise.[116] It was an uncertain arrangement. In the 1970s Peter C. Newman would observe that New Brunswick

Telephone "concentrates on its board much of the province's business power" – "[a]lthough it's controlled by Bell Canada."[117]

Empire, Liberalism, and Political Crisis

By the end of the Second World War, Robinson had sold the newspaper business to K.C. Irving – just as quietly as he had acquired it. It was not merely newspapers that Robinson sold to Irving; it was also the CHSJ radio station. Robinson and his associates from the New Brunswick Publishing Company, J.D. McKenna and T.F. Drummie, acquired the radio station from C.F. Monro in 1934, threatening to set up a competing station if Monro did not sell.[118] From a business point of view, the acquisition made sense. Not only was radio growing in importance, but it was a good fit with Robinson's holdings in newspapers and telecommunications: the radio station received feeds from the Canadian Press via the newspaper offices, while radio broadcasts profited from a telephone line devoted exclusively to its purpose.[119] The capital that Robinson wielded was apparent by the fact that Monro's 100-watt CFBO station was transformed "literally overnight" to the modern CHSJ station soon after the New Brunswick Broadcasting Company, in which Robinson was the major shareholder, gained ownership.[120] Both the *Telegraph-Journal* and *Evening Times-Globe* devoted an extended section on the new radio station in their 18 April 1934 issues, advertising programming that included weekly performances by Don Messer and his "old tyme dance radio orchestra" as well as regular broadcasts from the recently formed Canadian Radio Broadcasting Commission; the station's modern facilities, located in the Admiral Beatty Hotel, were also highlighted.[121]

Not mentioned was the fact that the new company had fired the old full-time CFBO staff after they went on strike to protest the dismissal of an engineer who had blown an essential tube. Since the staff consisted of four people, this was far from a weighty labour dispute; they were replaced within twenty-four hours.[122] Nonetheless, the dispute did reflect Robinson's rough-and-ready style of labour management. Robinson, indeed, seems to have prided himself on his lack of sophistication on the topic of labour relations. Asked in 1920 whether he had ever read *Psychology and Industrial Efficiency*, a 1913 tome by German

American psychologist Hugo Münsterberg, he replied no and followed with a story that highlighted his short temper and seemed to poke fun at psychology's application to the workplace: "As far as criticism of the service is concerned, I think Dr. Baxter and myself are probably two of the severest critics. I got mad one time and tore a telephone off the desk and threw it through a wall. There is psychology in that."[123] He was no labour-relations expert, no Mackenzie King. But his aggressive and plain personal style seemed to mirror a broader cultural phenomenon associated with the assertion of meritocratic ideals among the wealthy during the first few decades of the early twentieth century.[124]

Robinson and his political allies had exercised an effective hegemony during the 1920s under the Maritime Rights banner, valorizing development directed by business before everything else. That wealthy capitalists were the natural leaders of society was assumed; Robinson played an active role in advertising this view in 1930 when he organized a ceremony to give Angus McLean the "Freedom of Saint John," where McLean's business and political associates gathered to publicly celebrate his achievements. Typical of the event's tenor, Lieutenant Governor Hugh H. McLean lauded "the beneficent services" Angus McLean had "rendered to the province and city." "To Mr. McLean and men of his caliber," proclaimed Arthur Meighen in obvious celebration of society's presumed meritocratic order, "we must pay the respect due them in their day and generation." Premier Baxter not only lauded McLean's enterprising example but also championed the political spirit that McLean represented. The *Telegraph-Journal* reported: "The old party political idea had pretty well been gotten out of the minds of the people of the Maritimes, Premier Baxter said, and it had got to be known that the best form of government was that which gives good business administration. 'In other words,' he said, 'the business of the country should be the politics of the country.'" At the end of the tributes, Robinson presented McLean with a silver tray to commemorate the event.[125]

But the beneficence of private enterprise came under increasing attack with the onset of the Great Depression of the 1930s, and at the national level a social-democratic political party, the Co-operative Commonwealth Federation (CCF), was formed in 1932, while the Communist Party gained supporters. In this context Robinson's politics became markedly reactionary. In his earlier career Robinson behaved as if organized labour was illegitimate. The attitude of New Brunswick Power while he was a director in the 1921 street railway strike is probably the most obvious indication of this attitude. In an attempt to lower wages and introduce the controversial "one-man car" – to replace the traditional car, operated by two men – the directors rejected conciliation in the belief "that the company must have control of its employees."[126] In Robinson's correspondence from the 1930s and 1940s, these sentiments are voiced repeatedly. As he moved to embrace a militantly individualistic solution to the problems of his province and the rest of the capitalist world, he also backed away from his earlier embrace of regionalism, revealed as his opinions on regional protest diverged from those of regionalist stalwart A.P. Paterson.[127] Robinson's reference to "the average lazy-minded individual who makes this Province his home" in 1944 starkly reflected the limits and ambiguities of his provincial loyalty.[128]

The political victories won by Robinson and his allies in the 1920s were quickly threatened under the weight of the economic crisis of the following decade. Robinson held steadfast to the dictums of fiscal orthodoxy and private enterprise. He believed that fiscal austerity was the path out of the Depression, arguing in 1932 that "Government must do exactly what business men have done, namely, cut down expenses in every way, shape and form. Taxes must be reduced instead of increased, if we are to pull out of this mess."[129] In this respect, Robinson's laissez-faire views accurately voiced the more general position of the business executives whom he joined at the national level, such as CPR president Edward Beatty (see chapter 3).[130] In the context of a capitalist crisis involving widespread unemployment and suffering, the call for reduced government expenditures and pull-yourself-up-by-the-bootstraps rhetoric propounded by these businessmen had little potential to create the class alliances necessary for the creation of a hegemonic movement, especially as politicians and activists to their left seemed to offer more convincing accounts of – and solutions to – the crisis. Robinson voiced what were essentially elitist formulations that were becoming increasingly marginal politically. What Robinson believed true and correct was becoming widely unpopular; this – the unpopularity of their beliefs – was the perennial problem of the Canadian business elite in the 1930s, causing businessmen such as Robinson to question the viability of democratic methods during a period of economic crisis.

"I have seen many cases where a good laborer has been spoiled by too much education," Robinson observed in 1938 while discussing educational developments. After noting that proper inculcation in classical education was beyond the reach of many people and emphasizing the need for more practical educational pursuits, Robinson then turned to the world scene. "Undoubtedly we are entering a period when dictatorships, even though temporary in character, are bound to make tremendous headway," Robinson argued, "due to their temporary efficiency in competition with the stumbling and blundering methods of our democracy." Though Robinson believed that democracy would win in the end, he still saw the possibility of having "to go back to the Dark Ages and gradually creep back again to the Golden Age of Democracy."[131] In the 1930s, J.B.M. Baxter, who, it was reported, had invested $50,000 in Robinson's newspaper business, displayed a similar elitism and aloofness to democracy while discussing world events.[132] In a diary entry written in 1938, Baxter based his hope for Franco's victory in Spain upon the following principle: "I would rather have dictators from the better classes than submit to the dictatorship of those – or in the end – perhaps one [sic], whose outlook is that of the criminal classes."[133] The emerging message was that the moneyed and propertied should govern – those, as Robinson would explain, with "a stake in the community."[134]

But Robinson also had an awareness of tactics and was willing to change with changing circumstances. The same year Baxter hoped for Franco's victory in Spain, R.B. Hanson wrote Robinson to suggest that they protest the provincial government's increased taxation of the telephone company.[135] The most Robinson could do was reassure Hanson that they had friends in the Liberal government of A.A. Dysart who had succeeded in shooting down suggestions for even higher taxation rates. Clearly Robinson maintained important business and political contacts, which he could use to his advantage. But he understood the limitations imposed by the prevailing political climate. He wrote Hanson that "we must realize today that we are living in an age of realizm [sic] when ideas and ideals have got to be kept in cold storage until such a time as a change in public thinking and public sentiment again brings us back to an era of fair-play and encouragement for private enterprise. Until that time arrives I feel that it is wise to more or less compromise with the assassins."[136] Robinson, aware of the continued need to adjust during the Second World War, worked towards the selection of the Manitoba Progressive premier, John Bracken, as leader of the national Conservative Party in 1942. Explaining to Beaverbrook that he had "worked behind the scenes for the selection of Bracken," Robinson elaborated upon his motivations:

> I know him personally and know his political record, and I think through him we will get normal evolution and possibly prevent excesses of a revolutionary character which [is] threatened through the C.C.F. I cannot see how any political party as a party can govern a country through the war such as this and be returned at the first general election after the peace. Therefore it becomes a question of who is going to beat the existing government party; I have feared the C.C.F. I think however the selection of a man of Bracken's type will do a lot to dissipate that fear.[137]

Though Robinson's specific analysis proved incorrect, for the Liberals would return to power after the war, his more general observation about the need to adjust the Conservative Party was astute.

It would be a mistake to read these instances of political adaptation as part of a more general embrace of social reform, however. It was a purely tactical manoeuvre. Robinson, indeed, viewed the early indications of social reform with alarm. Responding to Bennett's "New Deal" radio addresses, Robinson wrote to him to explain that it contributed to a siege atmosphere within the business community. "Unfortunately," Robinson continued, "your remarks are being interpreted, or perhaps I should say misinterpreted, and, through propaganda, it is being made to appear that we are going to have the New Deal, the N.R.A. and all kinds of interference, through despotic bureaucrats, with a normal trend of business." Robinson was firmly committed to what he referred to as the "British method" of dealing with economic depression and claimed to Bennett that "nine men out of ten" in the Maritimes shared this view.[138] The British method meant, in Robinson's usage, a political economy characterized by very limited government interference with "natural" economic trends.

Operating with the British Empire as his essential frame of reference, Robinson viewed the British tradition as inimical to New Deal reforms, and thus valued the imperial connection as a bulwark against encroachments upon individual freedom that – he believed – were being perpetrated by New Dealers south of the border. Fascist aggression and the onset of the Second World War represented a new stage in a continued series of external threats facing the empire. Robinson worried, less than a year after the outbreak of the Second World War: "the stuff that made the British Empire seems to have been civilized out of us." "Our only hope is to become rough, tough and dusty," he claimed, elucidating further: "The British have been slapped, kicked and insulted by practically every nation in the world and it is about time that somebody showed a little bit of the good old British stuff that did not take this sort of back-talk from anybody."[139] Robinson's call for a return to primal tactics and hope for a reinvigorated British Empire articulated an interrelated set of political and cultural objectives that were underpinned by a belief in the superiority of British institutions and people.

He rooted his sense of empire in New Brunswick's Loyalist past, and – from his Loyalist ancestry – felt a special connection with that past. In a 1932 essay intended to advertise the idea of celebrating the 150th anniversary of the arrival of the Loyalists, Robinson proclaimed that "[i]n all the romance of the British Empire, dating back for more than one thousand years, there is nothing to compare with the Loyalists story." Robinson believed that history received through "American channels" had put a partisan spin on events that caused many others to unjustly overlook the story of the Loyalists. His discussion of Loyalist history led to the following reflection:

> At all times and in all revolutions, it is the man without stake in a community, the floater or irresponsible individual, who is the first to demand an appeal to force in settling his difficulties with his fellow men. The more mature brain of the educated individual and his natural desire not to jeopardize his stake in the community by resorting to arms, naturally, puts him in the class of those who favor constitutional methods of correcting wrongs rather than by restoring to arms. The Loyalists were of this latter class.[140]

Characterizing the Loyalists as propertied and educated, Robinson was drawing upon a long-held myth about the elite origins of the Loyalists while at the same time revealing his own class assumptions.[141] The propertied, Robinson believed, were educated and thoughtful; those "without stake in a community," by contrast, were prone to foment social disorder. Robinson also highlighted the unifying impulse and stability of the imperial connection by pointing to the racially diverse support garnered by the Crown, but also defined the Loyalists themselves as racially British.[142] The Loyalist past, in Robinson's view, made New Brunswick – and especially Saint John – unusually British. "I do not think that there is any part of Canada where the British tradition is as deeply ingrained as in the good old city of Saint John," claimed Robinson in private correspondence with Lord Beaverbrook in 1929.[143]

Robinson's keen interest in local and provincial history was more than an arcane pursuit; it was part of an attempt to construct an identity and project political values. He was one among many prominent New Brunswick residents to join the New Brunswick Loyalist Society, which had been reestablished in 1930, and surviving personal papers indicate his avid interest in genealogy, not surprising given his racialist construction of Britishness.[144] Even more noteworthy was his important role in the New Brunswick Museum, established in 1929. As chairman of the museum finance committee, Robinson solicited donations from prominent business associates, such as T.H. Estabrooks and Frank M. Ross, and played a central role in financing the construction of a museum building, which opened in August 1934 in tandem with the 150th anniversary of the founding of New Brunswick.[145] Robinson had advised such a course in March. Writing to John Clarence Webster, a fellow New Brunswick Museum board member, Robinson explained: "if we can organize a celebration of the 150th anniversary of this Province and make the formal opening of the Museum at that time the centre of our activities, it will do a great deal to introduce it to the public."[146] It would, as Robinson clearly realized, help to solidify the museum's connection with the province's Loyalist past, and he was involved in planning the three-day celebration that marked the museum's opening.[147] As Greg Marquis has observed, the museum became "the major edifice that would mark the 150th anniversary of the Loyalist province."[148]

Robinson also sought to use his position in the newspaper business to enhance the imperial connection in Canada. He helped Beaverbrook disseminate material for his Empire Free Trade campaign during the 1930s, and, as director and vice-president of the Canadian Press during the early years of the Second World War, worked to distance the press in Canada from U.S. dominance, specifically its reliance upon the Associated Press (AP) news service for empire news.[149] Robinson suggested to Beaverbrook the establishment of an empire news service to counter the AP's dominance in Canada – to no avail.[150] As a director of Famous Players Canadian Corporation, a subsidiary of Paramount Pictures, Robinson was also aware of – and implicated in – the hegemony of the U.S. film industry, serving as both representative and critic of mass U.S. culture. "I do not know what the solution is in the motion picture industry," he lamely conceded.[151] In the world of business, Robinson's Britishness was ambiguous.[152] This was less the case in the political and cultural realms, where Robinson clung to Britishness in opposition to various challenges facing the old political economy. "I am rapidly coming to the point where I fear I am going to be one of those who believe that the only way of saving the British Empire is for the individual Britisher to get rough and rude and crude again and fight for his own peroperty [sic] as well as for his neighbour's," wrote Robinson in December 1938, explicitly aligning the defence of the Empire with the defence of private property.[153] This sense of Britishness was carried forth in the 1930s and 1940s by moneyed contemporaries such as C. George McCullagh of the *Globe and Mail* and Edward Beatty, and it was briefly resurrected by Arthur Meighen in his unsuccessful attempt to lead the Conservative Party in 1942.[154] Meighen's defeat that year in the York South by-election to the CCF candidate must have been an awful shock to Robinson.

Although Robinson went on to support the party's leftward shift under Bracken, Robinson's *mentalité* was fundamentally reactionary. At the beginning of the Second World War, Robinson perceived "an active Communist campaign" in Canada being carried out through an array of sources – book publishers, clergymen ("in most cases of the United Church, with an occasional Baptist"), college professors, and so on – and anticipated a resumed battle on the home front after the war.[155] As the CCF gained strength and as Ottawa gained extraordinary control

of the wartime economy, Robinson correctly noted the worsening political position of capital. "I am one of those who believe that everyone
who has a stake in the community must do everything in his power
to help stabilize public opinion and employee relationships," he wrote
lumberman Percy Burchill in 1943. Concerned about "the completely
uncontrolled flood of suggestions having to do with after-war affairs,"
Robinson explained: "In my view there has been enough suggestions
made in the last two years to upset and cancel everything that civilization has done since the Birth of Christ. That may be an exaggeration
but, in my opinion, only a minor one. There seems to be a necessity for
someone to rally individuals with a stake in the community and who
know what can be done and what cannot be done without upsetting the
whole apple-cart." Believing those "with a stake in the community"
were tasked with the responsibility of upholding civilization against
the barbarians, Robinson explained that contact with his "newspaper
friends from all parts of Canada" had caused him to conclude that the
Dominion was "rapidly verging on anarchy."

Who were the barbarians? Government bureaucrats "without any responsibility to the citizens" and representatives of the CCF who, in
Robinson's view, were taking advantage of the "spirit of animus" –
"created by the 'controls'" – that had arisen among the general public.
Robinson viewed the administrative state and the CCF as precursors to
fascism. He expressed a firm historical grasp of what Ian McKay has
described as the "liberal order" in presenting his analysis to Burchill
in a fascinating piece of correspondence from 1943.[156] "We seem to
have departed from responsible government as my forebears believed
it to be," wrote Robinson, "because they were among those who opposed dictatorship of the Family Compact." That it was an order moving through a phase of "organic crisis" was revealed in Robinson's
following observation:

> To me Hitler and Mussolini and Stalin were merely the leaders of political
> parties which seize control and then regulate everybody by decree. The
> C.C.F. are merely the forerunners of the same sort of gang in this Domin-
> ion, and I am one of those who are prepared *for possible murder and sud-
> den death for them as a way out* [emphasis my own]. Appeasement will
> not do anything more than appeasement has ever done since the dawn of

civilization. Munich is the best yardstick to measure that sort of thing by. To me it is not a question of either old parties so much as it is a question of preserving our way of life in this Dominion of Canada, and the same as our young men are doing to preserve it for the world by giving their lives on the sea, in the air, in the Mediterranean and in Italy. If we win the battle in these latter places but lose it in Canada, then the sacrifice of these lives has been in vain.[157]

Perceiving individual rights (and rights of property) to be under threat, Robinson was prepared for drastic action. His macabre imaginings of political assassination reveal his siege mentality and suggest a highly contingent commitment to parliamentary democracy. Of course, Robinson was out of step with the emerging economic and political order and rejected the new brand of hegemony that was being constructed around the Liberal Party.[158] He also failed to understand that Canadian soldiers were, in a great many cases, fighting for a freedom radically different from his own: the historical evidence suggests that the soldier vote was weighted towards the CCF.[159]

The postwar world was largely incomprehensible for Robinson. By the end of the Second World War, the "British world" that Robinson imagined was well on its way to collapse. He lamented the continued involvement of the state in Canadian social and economic life after the war; the bureaucracies established to manage the postwar economy, Robinson believed, represented another step towards fascism. He derided the "god-like individuals at Ottawa who are forcing the value of money down" and who, he concluded, had become "our temporary hitlers."[160] In another diatribe against the expanded Ottawa civil service, Robinson concluded that "autocracy and bureaucracy ... are first cousins to each other."[161] On the other hand, to his mind the state was not aggressive enough in fighting organized labour. He wished for more decisive action by the federal government in confronting the 1946 strike wave in Canada, pointing to Harry Truman's high-handed threats south of the border in the national railway strike that year as a praiseworthy tactic.[162] Guided by a sense of Britishness that was not merely symbolic or ceremonial, Robinson was also hostile towards the growth of Quebec nationalism and lamented the willingness of the Mackenzie King Liberals to court that sentiment.[163] Believing that "Canada is

British," Robinson complained about "demands for a Canadian flag, the recognition of Canadian 'nationality' and the obvious attempt to substitute a dirge called 'Oh Canada' for 'The King.'"[164] The barbarians had breached the gates.

Conclusion

The casket was carried down the aisle to choir hymns at the St Paul Valley Church in Saint John. Floral tributes had been received from a veritable who's who of New Brunswick – Lord Beaverbrook, premier J.B. McNair, Sir James Dunn, G. Clifford McAvity, K.C. Irving, and numerous others – as well as moguls of Canadian and North American business life – the presidents of the CPR, the Royal Bank, International Paper, Bell Telephone, and still more. Robinson had died on 23 August 1950 at the Algonquin Hotel in St Andrews, New Brunswick – another favoured vacationing spot of the Canadian bourgeoisie. Suffering from hardening of the arteries (arteriosclerosis) and hypertension, Robinson was inflicted with a stroke (cerebral thrombosis) in July before eventually succumbing to pneumonia.[165] He was seventy-six.

He had outlived Canada's longest-serving prime minister, Mackenzie King, who had passed away one month earlier. But unlike King, who was his exact contemporary, born in 1874 too, Robinson's legacy was not obvious or particularly enduring. Though in the late 1940s Louis Rosenberg of the CCF listed Robinson among the "fifty big shots" who controlled the country's banks and major industries, and Communist Tim Buck placed Robinson among the "finance-capitalist oligarchy of Canada," Robinson was a man who had lost his grip.[166] His ascendance in the 1920s mirrored the political and economic rise of big business, but it was a fleeting victory. Embracing a rigid philosophy that valorized private enterprise and unhindered property rights, Robinson showed a willingness to adapt tactics but was, more broadly, unwilling to adapt his thinking to the new economic order of state-managed capitalism and social-democratic concessions. Connected with St James Street, he represented both its power and its limitations. His appointment to the board of directors of the CPR in 1945 made him the first-ever true Maritime resident to become a CPR director, but the power of the CPR had itself already significantly dissipated by that time (see

chapters 2 and 3).[167] Though he never truly retired and appears to have
contributed to efforts to reassert provincial control of New Brunswick
Telephone after the Second World War, health problems significantly
limited his activities in the late 1940s, by which time he had already relinquished control of the newspaper and radio business to K.C. Irving.
Not having built an identifiable business empire, having fathered no
heirs, and overwhelmed by political change, Robinson's legacy fizzled
out in the anonymity with which he had lived.

Robinson, nonetheless, evinced broader changes in the politics of
business. Under his control, the Saint John *Telegraph-Journal* became
an ardent and leading voice of the Maritime Rights movement in the
1920s. The nonpartisan spirit of Maritime Rights was highly attractive politically for Robinson, whose pro-business politics overrode the
game of partisanship. And though aligned with the provincial Conservative Party after the First World War, Robinson's party loyalties were
flexible and largely determined by his broader political aims, which
were consistently directed towards ameliorating the province's investment climate. Robinson's rise after the First World War, though part of
a specific regional and provincial story, also reflected broader changes
in how the business elite operated in politics; press barons such as Lord
Atholstan of the Montreal *Star* in the 1920s and C. George McCullagh
of the Toronto *Globe and Mail* in the 1930s similarly used their control over daily newspapers to voice business-friendly perspectives irrespective of party loyalty. Though Robinson was much less hands-on
in editorial writing than were Atholstan and McCullagh, the political
style and strategy they pursued were similar: adopting business agen-
das, they sought to dictate public policy to political parties. Robinson
was one of several figures who marked the shift to more direct business control over the press. And, like Atholstan and McCullagh, he was
driven to play a more active role in politics over the issue of government intervention in the economy. But, paradoxically, while businessmen were able to articulate their ideas more directly through the press,
their political effectiveness waned under the strains of economic crisis.

Although Robinson was particularly rigid in his ideological outlook,
his general experience was archetypical of the larger anxieties of the
Canadian bourgeoisie. Embracing a political economy structured by
the old liberalism of the nineteenth century and the experience of the

National Policy period, they viewed the Great Depression of the 1930s through an ideologically narrow lens. Robinson responded especially forcefully to the crisis, motivated by his sense of acting in defence of the British Empire and British traditions. Prioritizing the defence of unfettered property rights as a fundamental aspect of the "British method," his strong and rigid ideological commitment produced a willingness to discard civil liberties in the face of perceived political radicalism. Robinson articulated scepticism about the capacity of a democracy to adequately respond to the economic crisis of the 1930s, a scepticism that spread to many within the higher ranks of the business community. As we shall see in the next chapter, such anxieties signalled a broader ideological divergence between economic liberalism and political democracy after the onset of the Great Depression, as wealthy defenders of the "liberal order," to draw upon Ian McKay's terminology, became increasingly hostile to the influence of popular opinion.

2

Charles A. Dunning:
A Progressive in Business and Politics

Unlike feudal or other traditional societies whose social structures are dependent upon familial succession, liberal capitalist ones allow for a certain level of fluidity in their social structures – including a freedom to fail, as suggested in recent years by a U.S. cultural historian who has noted the widening definition and growing fear of "failure" in nineteenth-century America.[1] Of course, the obverse path – to success – has historically received more attention within public discourse and has played a significant role in legitimizing the social inequalities inherent in liberal capitalist societies. Charles Avery Dunning (1885–1958) represented the latter trajectory and enthusiastically embraced the meritocratic ideal that became central to legitimizing disparities of wealth and power in the twentieth century.[2] Dunning moved from modest social circumstances in Leicestershire, England, to commence farming in Yorkton, in what was soon to become part of Saskatchewan, at the age of seventeen. Upward mobility would characterize much of his adult life in the Dominion. He became: a key figure in Saskatchewan cooperative grain marketing (1911–16); a cabinet member in W.M. Martin's Liberal provincial administration (1916–22); premier of Saskatchewan (1922–6); federal cabinet minister in three Liberal administrations, holding the important portfolios of railways and canals as well as finance (1926–30 and 1935–9); and, during the early 1930s, in between his terms as minister of finance, he also emerged as a mogul of Canadian big business. "Some of his exploits read like a chapter from the pages of Horatio Alger," commented the *Ottawa Journal* upon Dunning's elevation to minister of finance in 1929.[3]

Dunning's mobility was not merely vertical, from poverty to wealth; it was also a regional trajectory associated with the experience of Western Canada during the National Policy period. When the *Ottawa Journal* lauded his ascension from the position of a "penniless immigrant farm hand," it also noted that he was to become the first minister of finance from Western Canada. Indeed, four years earlier, Dunning had been brought into William Lyon Mackenzie King's cabinet as the government's western lieutenant on the basis of his popularity among western farmers, whom King wished so dearly to court. Dunning's popularity in the West stemmed from his association with western Progressives and past activism as a Saskatchewan farmer and member of the Saskatchewan Grain Growers' Association (SGGA) as well as his founding role in the Saskatchewan Co-operative Elevator Company (SCEC). Dunning, like Howard Robinson, represented regional interests. But while Dunning was a more visible representative of regional interests than Robinson had ever been, his turn away from regionalism was more dramatic and complete, as he grew apart from the western agrarian milieu that had made him such a popular figure in Saskatchewan. Dunning underwent a process of socialization that brought about his transformation from a western agrarian progressive – concerned with ideals such as democratic management – to an accepted and influential figure among Montreal's economic elite by the early 1930s, a member of what Eugene Forsey described in 1934 as the "economic cabinet of Canada."[4] He left Saskatchewan to join King's cabinet as minister of railways and canals in 1926, never truly to return to the West.

Dunning displayed many characteristics of what has been described loosely as progressivism: a willingness to move outside the realm of political partisanship, a commitment to efficiency, and a belief that class differences are reconcilable and class politics are unnecessary – indeed harmful to the interests of society. If, as Shelton Stromquist has argued, U.S. progressives were obsessed with class even as they denied its existence, Dunning suggests something similar in the Canadian context. But whereas Stromquist's progressives were urban, encouraged state intervention, and played a major role in shaping twentieth-century liberalism, Dunning emerged from rural Canada, was largely inimical to the idea of an interventionist state, and embraced a classical liberalism that appeared increasingly reactionary and became increasingly marginal in the context of the Great Depression.[5] Dunning's political path was similar to that travelled by T.A. Crerar.[6] Like Dunning, Crerar was, as president of Manitoba's Grain Growers' Company, a leading figure in cooperative grain marketing and, as leader of the Progressive Party in the 1921 federal election, a critic of the protective tariff and a lead figure of moderate progressivism in the West – as opposed to radical-democratic progressives such as Henry Wise Wood, who represented the Alberta wing of the Progressive Party. In the 1930s Dunning and Crerar became Liberal federal cabinet ministers and remained unusually resistant to government intervention and the unorthodox fiscal theories of John Maynard Keynes. Their smooth entry into the corridors of power and shared resistance to government intervention suggests their ideological framework was easily assimilated into elite circles: Crerar's advocacy for the mining industry hinted at it, but Dunning's experience suggested it even more so.[7] As he became associated with Canadian big business, including the CPR, during the early 1930s, Dunning became the subject of numerous upper-class machinations – which he seemed to encourage – to clean up an overly slow-moving and corrupted political world.[8] His reputation as a nonpartisan politician was attractive to moneyed interests in search of strong political leadership, not susceptible to the day-to-day political pandering characteristic of the party system.

Straddling the realms of business and politics like few others of his time, Dunning's progressive style presented opportunities to the elite social class he decisively joined in the 1930s. But, ultimately, Dunning failed to transform politics and shore up the old economic order as his allies at the commanding heights of the economy wished. The super-rich were not popular during the 1930s, and Dunning, widely seen as their politician, could not expect considerable popular support. Appointed as minister of finance following the 1935 general election, Dunning was nonetheless placed in a position to protect the interests of big business. Indeed, Dunning received the appointment from King specifically to steady the frayed nerves of capitalists, who actively supported Dunning's appointment. In the final analysis, however,

Mackenzie King's hands were steering the ship as the Liberal Party began to consolidate its position as the "Government Party."

From an immigrant farm hand on the western prairies to minister of finance to director of an array of large Canadian corporations, Dunning's life provides evidence of individual opportunity just as it provides clues as to the resilience of the liberal-capitalist order in Canada. Of central importance to the present study, Dunning's case reveals the significant political limitations that were imposed upon the Canadian bourgeoisie during the Great Depression of the 1930s. As the legitimacy of big business came in for attack under the strains of the economic crisis, the ability of businessmen to shape public policy was limited to a greater extent than has been commonly acknowledged. While scholars have regularly emphasized the conservative nature of social reform during the 1930s and the business elite's ability to manage the reform process, they have tended to underestimate the importance of the right-wing alternatives that were embraced by leading businessmen and politicians who acted to shore up the old political economy.[9] The failure of these alternatives was by no means certain to Dunning and other moguls, who continued to believe in the necessity of balanced budgets and retrenchment in the context of the Depression. Maintaining a worldview based upon the experience of the National Policy period and narrowed by their insular social world, they knew not the future that awaited them.

The Making of a Western Progressive

> A square-shouldered, solidly built chap with [a] round, rather handsome face, keen, steel gray eyes with a humourous glint in them, a short clipped brown mustache, under it during most of his waking hours a short briar pipe, a singularly alert look and that mysterious emanation of power and confidence which some call a dominating personality, others, personal magnetism, is going down to Ottawa from Saskatchewan shortly to be Canada's Minister of Railways. His name is Charles Avery Dunning.[10]

So went the description of an admiring observer in March 1926. Such admiration was not unusual at that particular moment. Dunning was widely viewed as a dynamic westerner whose ambition, talent, and vitality had not only accounted for his remarkable ascent in public life but had bestowed the government of Saskatchewan with economical and efficient management for the past four years. His arrival in Ottawa was an important event.

Dunning had come a long way from the tenant farm in the hamlet of Croft, a few miles from Leicestershire, England, on which he was born, 31 July 1885. At the age of fourteen, after having worked as an office boy in a patent office, Dunning began an apprenticeship at a local foundry. Three years later, after losing consciousness at the end of a swimming competition, doctors advised that the restoration of his health required he move out of the city and do only light work for the time being. Dunning, as a result, decided to move to "the colonies." He reminisced years later: "I obtained employment with a farmer in the Yorkton district [of Saskatchewan] and sent what money I could home, with the result that Dad came out and we each entered for a quarter section, which gave us three hundred and twenty acres."[11] With his health restored, and having been joined by his family, prospects looked relatively bright. Before long, however, he was to realize that hard work alone could not guarantee success.[12] As a contemporary agrarian writer noted, the price offered farmers for their grain by the elevator companies sapped the "Englishman's new feeling of 'independence,'" and before long Dunning became an active member of the Beaverdale local chapter of the SGGA.[13]

The local SGGA became the centre of social and political life in Beaverdale, observed western Liberal and soon-to-be secretary of the Canadian Council of Agriculture, Norman Lambert, in 1917.[14] Within this cradle of agrarian populism, Dunning developed his talents for clear thinking as well as a formidable oratorical style. In 1910 he was sent as Beaverdale's first-ever delegate to the SGGA's annual meeting at Prince Albert, the association's ninth annual meeting. Helping to resolve a potentially divisive resolution on hail insurance at the February 1910 meeting, Dunning so impressed the other delegates that he was elected district director.[15] Perhaps equally beneficial for Dunning's public reputation was the story that later emerged regarding the financing of his trip; as Moorhouse explained, the Beaverdale local could raise only $17.50 for his expenses, and Dunning "figured by making friends with the furnace man of one of the hotels he might be allowed to sleep in the cellar for the week," thus staying within his meagre budget. It was later reported that he came back from Prince Albert with money in his pocket.[16]

Dunning was elected vice-president of the SGGA the following year and became secretary-treasurer of the newly formed SCEC, having drafted its bylaws. The rise of cooperative grain marketing in Saskatchewan during the next five years was a testament to Dunning's managerial abilities and the collective economic power of Saskatchewan farmers. It also represented a political victory for the more business-minded SGGA representatives, such as Dunning, who opposed more radical experimentation with government intervention.[17] Using an older cooperative farming company to act as a selling agent for the SGGA in 1911, Dunning was "looked on as a green kid from the farm and laughed at" by representatives of the private elevator companies at the Winnipeg Grain Exchange. Not long after, Dunning, worried that the attitude of the private elevator companies had moved from amusement to purposeful fear, poured more capital into elevator construction to avoid possibly being squeezed out of the field by the private companies. With 137 elevators built by the end of 1912, the future of the SCEC was secured. When Dunning retired from the company in 1916, it had become the "largest single grain handling company in the world," profits exceeded $750,000, and progress was being made on the construction of a new terminal at Port Arthur, Ontario, which was being built by the engineering firm of C.D. Howe – who would join Dunning in Mackenzie King's cabinet in 1935.[18]

Dunning had also reached a transitional period in his public and private life. In 1913 he was appointed to a royal commission on agricultural credit and another on grain marketing in Europe, leaving that summer for Europe to collect data. While in England he met "a charming girl who still remembered him."[19] Charles Dunning married Ada Rowlett of Nassington, Northants, in England on 3 July 1913.[20] The young couple would have two children, a girl before the close of the decade and later a boy. With home life thus establishing itself, Dunning's reputation for competence in business affairs spread beyond the farming community, evidenced in the summer of 1916, when he was invited to join the board of directors of the fledgling Grand Trunk Pacific. Dunning's retirement from the SCEC that year marked the end of his formal association with Saskatchewan farmers, for he had already in 1914 refused the nomination to continue as vice-president of the SGGA. In October 1916 Dunning entered W.M. Martin's Liberal administration as provincial treasurer. Coming into an administration that had been rocked by a series of recent scandals, historian J. William Brennan has observed that Dunning was wanted by the Liberals as much for his business ability as for his connection with the SGGA.[21]

Dunning had behaved in a nonpartisan fashion to that point. His only "political" involvement prior to his entry into government was with the Direct Legislation League, a nonpartisan organization supported by the SGGA, which sought greater control of the legislative process for the electorate.[22] Dunning's aloofness from party politics was not due to a lack of concern, but reflected his view that the SGGA best served the farmers as a nonpartisan organization; and, indeed, the leaders of the SGGA supported the association's involvement with the Direct Legislation League to "ward off what they considered the greater threat of converting the Grain Growers into a political party."[23] Dunning believed the formation of a farmers' party would divide and weaken the political strength of farmers; he thought it best to operate within the established parties. This strategy made particular sense in Saskatchewan, where the provincial Liberal Party had governed in close alliance with farmers' representatives. The Liberals had governed the province since its formation in 1905 and had developed a close relationship with the SGGA, which was consolidated early on by figures such as W.R. Motherwell and J.A. Calder.[24]

As a farmers' advocate before his entry into political life, Dunning embraced a democratic, small-proprietor outlook, which was revealed in his proposed plan to consolidate the cooperative grain marketing of the prairie provinces along the lines of England's cooperative wholesale societies. George F. Chipman, editor and manager of the Winnipeg-based *Grain Growers' Guide*, lauded Dunning's plan as "the most democratic and best suited to secure a uniformity of policy and control."[25] Prioritizing the preservation of the small producer's economic autonomy, Dunning embraced an outlook rooted in what C.B. Macpherson has described as "possessive individualism," an ideology that continued to assume popular, democratic dimensions in the Prairie West of the early twentieth century, evidenced by the political success of individuals such as Dunning himself.[26] Writing to Chipman in 1914 in response to a proposal to pool the resources of the three provincial grain companies by John Kennedy, vice-president of Manitoba's grain growers association, Dunning explained,

> I am afraid we are still apart on the fundamental question as to whether the control should be from the top down or from the bottom up. You know my ideas on the subject fairly well, and I think your own coincide as to which is the most democratic and at the same time feasible form of capitalization and control. Kennedy's method of control, apparently, is from the top, but he proposes to regulate it by means of direct legislation. To tell the truth, it rather reminds me of R.L. Richardson's phrase that "the best form of government for this country would be a beneficent autocracy tempered by assassination." Needless to say, I do not think that form of government applied to our farmers' business institutions would prove practicable.[27]

Contrasting his views with the apparently antidemocratic suggestions of the *Winnipeg Tribune*'s managing director, R.L. Richardson, Dunning aligned himself with the ideals of democratization and economic progress.[28] That said, his refusal to consider the formation of a centralized purchasing and retailing agency as part of any consolidation of the three provincial grain cooperatives proved to be an irreconcilable stumbling block rooted in more pragmatic considerations; as the largest grain cooperative, the SCEC would be forced to share its advantages of size if such a plan came to fruition.[29]

Dunning harboured a considerable ambition and an ego to match. His contemporaries said as much in private correspondence on numerous occasions, and one must take this into consideration when assessing his career trajectory. His politics changed in step with his changing political allegiances, which were not always clear. The famously partisan Saskatchewan Liberal Jimmy Gardiner "could never free his mind of the suspicion that Dunning was not a Liberal at all, but an opportunist who saw a more secure future for himself in the Liberal party than in any other."[30] His political style differed from older colleagues who became deeply integrated into the party apparatus. Unlike figures such as Motherwell and Gardiner, who came to identify deeply with the Liberal Party and pursued advancement within the party itself,

Dunning was not so wedded. Dunning publicly stated that he joined the Liberals to "fight for the principles of the [SGGA]."[31] The conscription crisis in 1917 revealed this divergence, as Dunning and Gardiner bolted to opposing camps. Gardiner, loyal to Laurier, sided with the Motherwell camp and Dunning with the Unionist Martin camp.[32] The crisis provided a basis for nonpartisan action, which prefigured the establishment of a Progressive Party in the West, and all three Liberal administrations in the Prairie West severed ties with the federal party.[33] Dunning, then, was following the cue of the Saskatchewan administration in 1917 in defying Laurier and became, as historian John Herd Thompson has observed, "a particular favourite [of Unionist Liberals] because of his close connection with the farm movement."[34] Serving as chairman of the Saskatchewan Victory Loan Committee and director of the Canada Food Board's drive to encourage greater production, Dunning's public role in supporting the war effort expanded, as did his role in the cabinet of the Saskatchewan government.[35]

The exigencies of war made Union government possible; but in peacetime continued cooperation between western progressives and the Conservative Party proved impossible, especially given their divergent views on the protective tariff. J.A. Calder, an influential founder of Saskatchewan's Liberal Party and, somewhat ironically, a former mentor to Jimmy Gardiner, joined the Union government as minister of immigration and colonization in October 1917 and was broadly on the same page as Dunning regarding political strategy at war's end. "What you say is true," wrote Calder to Dunning in early 1919. "There is every possibility of a strong agrarian movement in the near future. Personally I doubt very much if anything can stop it. To me it appears that the time is now ripe throughout the whole of Canada for a movement of this kind. Instead of opposing it or running counter to it, there is a possibility that your wisest course would be to join it."[36] Dunning would eventually land the premiership by following such a strategy.

Friction between Premier Martin and the Progressive Party would pave the way for Dunning's ascension to the premier's chair. The 1921 Saskatchewan election witnessed another Liberal victory, but one that was much less decisive than in years past. Progressive and Independent candidates won a total of twenty-one seats, as Liberal supremacy continued to rest upon a strategy of cooperating with the SGGA;

J.A. Maharg, having served as president of the SGGA for eleven years, was brought into the government as minister of agriculture by Premier Martin the previous year. Yet soon after securing this mandate, Martin campaigned against the Progressives in the 1921 federal election, prompting Maharg's resignation and the widespread scorn of Saskatchewan farmers.[37] Martin had, in the words of J.W. Dafoe, "cooked his goose."[38] He had to go. Dunning was the obvious successor.

In April 1922, Dunning succeeded Martin as premier of Saskatchewan and proceeded to maintain a distant relationship with the federal Liberals while extending an olive branch to the Progressives. Norman Ward and David Smith have noted that "had [Dunning] been clearly partisan, ... he would almost certainly not have attained the premiership in 1922."[39] Grant Dexter, of the *Winnipeg Free Press*, described Dunning as a "sort of half Progressive – doesn't see anything wrong with a Progressive."[40] "On accepting office," Dunning explained his position with apparent pleasure to Kirk Cameron, a Montreal industrialist and free-trade Liberal: "I made a flat-footed declaration of Liberalism, which, of course, has stirred up a hornet's nest, and which was, evidently, not as much appreciated by our friends in Ottawa as it might have been."[41] The tariff lay at the centre of tensions between Dunning and King's federal administration. Dunning complained of the federal party's failure to abide by its 1919 platform; King's finance minister, W.S. Fielding, the Nova Scotian who had served as Laurier's minister of finance, appeared to Dunning and other westerners as uninterested in western calls for tariff reductions. The Progressives, Dunning warned Mackenzie King in 1923, were capitalizing on the Liberal Party's evident inconsistency in this area. "I am not one of those who believe that this country can get to a free trade basis but I do believe that in order to remain a factor in Canada," argued Dunning, "and particularly in Western Canada with its growing electoral power, the Liberal party must demonstrate that it is sincerely a low-tariff party and give evidence of that by performance when in power." Dunning noted that his provincial constituency of Moose Jaw County was almost entirely contained within the federal riding of Moose Jaw; in the last federal by-election, he explained to King, "more than one-half of the Provincial Liberal Executive of my Constituency supported the Progressive." He continued:

I do not attach much importance to the present Federal Progressive members as such. They are simply the puppets of a sentiment, – puppets which
that sentiment is just as likely to discard at the next Progressive nom-
inating conventions as it discarded several of their predecessors. I am
not concerned with the puppets but I am concerned with the sentiment.
Progressive sentiment in the main, – divested of its extreme radical man-
ifestations in some quarters, is really Liberal sentiment.[42]

The natural home of Progressives, Dunning believed, was with the Liberals; they needed merely to harness Progressive sentiment and ride
it to electoral victory. It was not so simple. King was in a difficult
situation since Liberal support in Quebec was, as Reginald Whitaker
has observed, "precisely the wing of the party dominated by high-tariff
big business interests most inimical to the kind of policies required to
attract farmers back into the Liberal flock."[43] With the exit of Lomer
Gouin and Fielding from the Dominion government in 1924, however,
King was freed to court western progressives more aggressively.[44]

Meanwhile, Dunning had been forging a reputation as a successful
administrator in Saskatchewan. He had, before rising to the premiership, acquired a range of experience in government. Coincident with
serving as provincial treasurer from 1916 to 1922, he held the portfolios
of railways, telephones, agriculture, and municipal affairs at separate
occasions. The business community generally approved of Dunning's
management of the Saskatchewan government. Monte Black, of the
Winnipeg financial and insurance firm Black & Armstrong and grandfather of one of Canada's most famous capitalist buccaneers, Conrad
Black, wrote Dunning in 1924 that "I should almost have to elevate
you to the Peerage, following the announcement made by you in the
House with regard to savings effected during the past two years."[45] T.R.
Deacon, the Winnipeg manufacturer whose intransigent attitude towards unions helped spark the 1919 Winnipeg General Strike, believed
that if Dunning were not "such a ferocious free trader," he "would
be about the most popular public man in Canada."[46] H.M. Peacock,
of the investment house of A.E. Ames & Company and brother of the
Canadian-born London banker E.R. Peacock, reported to Dunning that
his brother, who chatted with Dunning in London, England, "was much

impressed with your grasp of the various problems of the West, particularly the railroad problem and your attitude towards them." Peacock
hoped that Dunning would eventually become prime minister of Canada, believing that with Dunning at the helm, "this country will receive
a very good administration."[47] Erastus S. Miller, manager of the Imperial Life Assurance Company's Ottawa office, assured Dunning in early
1925 that he commanded "the confidence of the business interests of
the country in a very marked degree." "I think it would be a great thing
for the country if you," Miller beckoned Dunning, "or any other strong
man, could come and clean up the situation [in Ottawa]."[48] Dunning occupied a fortunate position. The business community saw in Dunning a
relatively safe version of progressivism that was prepared to appear in
Liberal clothing – similar to that put into practice in Manitoba by John
Bracken, although Bracken would choose Conservative clothing in his
transition to the federal stage.[49] They appreciated Dunning's fiscally
conservative management of Saskatchewan's affairs. The Dunning
government, as J. William Brennan has observed, "adopted a policy of
retrenchment." New taxes were avoided and capital expenditures kept
low; Dunning left the Saskatchewan government with a balanced budget in 1925.[50]

Dunning could pursue this policy and remain popular, observed
Brennan, because the overwhelmingly rural population base of Saskatchewan prioritized low taxation – even to a greater degree than
the somewhat more urbanized provinces of Manitoba and Alberta,
where the provincial administrations expanded taxation.[51] Moreover,
Dunning's farming background and past involvement with the SGGA
were assets in meeting the provincial challenge of the Progressives:
"Dunning ... alone could attack the farmers' political movement without appearing to criticize its foster parent, the S.G.G.A."[52] The SGGA,
however, was itself in decline, "a reflection perhaps of Dunning's own
personal popularity among Saskatchewan farmers," but also the result of schisms within the farmers' movement.[53] In 1921 the Farmers'
Union was established, a group that organized itself along the lines of
an industrial union, emphasizing class position and collective action
and adopting the rituals of fraternal societies.[54] Clifford Sifton reported
a conversation with Dunning on the subject to J.W. Dafoe, the influential editor of the *Winnipeg Free Press*:

[The Farmers' Union] is an out and out radical deadbeat organization, appealing to the impecunious and those who are so loaded with debt that they do not ever expect to get out of debt. [Dunning] says they are a secret organization, oath bound with grips and pass-words and such like, and he says there are *six hundred* lodges in Saskatchewan. His view is that they are rapidly eating up the Grain Growers' organization in Saskatchewan. Their platform is practical repudiation of debt of all kinds. He says they are spreading like the measles. He is not afraid that they can beat him, but he looks with alarm on the organization of the Tory party in Saskatchewan, because it may absorb a certain number of the saner and more level-headed farmers and endanger his chances in three-cornered contests. He did not complain to me, but I think he rather feels that the [Winnipeg] Free Press is giving too unlimited support to the Progressives and tending to create a radical off-shot in the West, which may get under the control of the extreme radicals.[55]

Agrarian protest had moved beyond the liberal individualist ideology of the SGGA in many places, most significantly in Alberta, where H.W. Wood advanced the idea of "group government," which advocated political organization along the lines of occupational blocs.[56] This radical-democratic variant of the progressive movement was associated with the Alberta wing of the Progressive Party and laid the basis for the entry of the United Farmers of Alberta (UFA) into politics in 1919. Two years later, the UFA formed government in Alberta; and though Wood and the UFA government proved a disappointment to a leftward-moving base, UFA members would play a key role in founding the Co-operative Commonwealth Federation (CCF) in 1932, a socialist party that united farmers and industrial workers, which was presaged by the alliance of labour representatives and advanced agrarian progressives who had formed a "ginger group" in parliament in the 1920s.[57] The ideological milieu of Dunning's pre-political activities was being eclipsed as Western Canadian progressivism hit a forked road – one path socialist, the other liberal.

Dunning's experience in government, too, had transformed his outlook. Always at heart a liberal individualist, Dunning loathed class politics. He embraced cooperative marketing and even for a time as premier pressed for a grain board, which had been established by the

Dominion government during the First World War only to be disman-
tled immediately after; but these were not ends in themselves. Rather,
they were for Dunning means for the farmer to achieve the ultimate
goal of economic independence. John Evans, Progressive Saskatchewan MP, wrote Dunning in March 1925 to urge him to head up a national party that "could elect a government that has been free from the
corruption of the past 40 years." "There's a great future for some one
with ability such as you have, to lead a peoples [sic] party of which the
Progressives form a very good foundation," but, Evans suggestively
concluded, "[w]e are short a leader."[58] Dunning did not want to lead
that party, and his reasoning is telling. He explained to Evans:

> I do not readily forget associations of long ago, although I do feel at times
> that in your relationship to me you tend to forget the wide difference in
> experience which must occur between men when one of them is free to
> pursue a more or less free lance mode of life while the other has been for
> many years charged with very heavy public responsibilities.
>
> I look back rather wistfully sometimes to that portion of my life which
> was devoted to advocacy because I have had the same experience which
> other advocates had had especially among old country public men, that
> when one is actually charged with a responsibility, it appears that the
> wheels of progress move most painfully slowly in spite of one's efforts.

Quite plainly, Dunning's experience in government had changed his
perspective. His priorities, too, had changed. Once concerned with
exploitation from above, his concern now turned to radicalism from
below, a shift indicative of the wider reaction against the left in Canada
during and after the First World War.[59] The rise of the British Labour
Party and political developments in continental Europe (i.e., the rise of
broad-based socialist parties) presented, to Dunning's mind, instructive
lessons:

> My study of the situation in the old country last year and my observations
> of the conditions in the House of Commons as well as what I read with
> regard to the Continental countries, [sic] impresses me with the idea that
> new parties constantly breed other new parties; that the formation of a

group to the left of existing groups tends to cause still further subdivision and still further movement to the left.[60]

He was not about to leave the Liberal fold.[61]

Entering the Federal Scene

Later that year a progressive-Liberal group based in Winnipeg began to seriously consider Dunning as a potential successor to Prime Minister Mackenzie King. As S. Peter Regenstreif has documented, "The Winnipeg Sanhedrin," which included J.W. Dafoe, former Progressive Party leader T.A. Crerar, independent Liberal A.B. Hudson, former Winnipeg mayor Frank O. Fowler, and lawyer H.J. Symington, explored this possibility near the end of 1925. Having kept aloof from the federal party as premier of Saskatchewan, Dunning remained so in responding to King's entreaties to join the federal cabinet in the summer of 1925, preferring not to involve himself in a government whose near future was uncertain.[62] Following the disappointing results of the October federal election – as the Liberals fell short of majority government status for the second time under King's leadership – Dunning, in a telephone conversation with H.J. Symington on 7 November 1925, expressed the view that King should be replaced – but, he emphasized, the decisive move should come from "the East, Lapointe, Cardin, etc." Symington reported that Dunning "thought C[rerar] and all of us ought to be most careful about appearing to be plotting, leave it entirely to the Frenchmen."[63] However, the "Frenchmen" would not serve Dunning's end, and Lapointe remained loyal to King. Moreover, would-be kingmakers within the Montreal wing of the party looked to former Nova Scotia premier George Murray and later J.A. Robb to replace King, never Dunning.[64] The episode illustrates Robert A. Wardhaugh's view that "Dunning was a deceivingly straightforward type of politician whose emphasis on sound and efficient administration often disguised a powerful ambition."[65] The whole affair was more fantasy than serious plotting.

But as the mock intrigue proceeded behind the scenes, Dunning's public profile was growing more impressive. His provincial electoral victory in the summer confirmed his public appeal and ability to court the Progressive vote. Following a Liberal meeting in October at Toronto's Massey Hall, at which he shared the podium with King, Ernest Lapointe, and Vincent Massey, one admirer claimed that the audience was "simply amazed" by Dunning's performance.[66] Dunning was an impressive orator and cultivated a public image of vitality and strength despite shaky personal health. The vitality Dunning projected aligned closely with the cultural reconstruction of the ruling class as described by Jackson Lears in the U.S. context. Lears has argued that the first three decades of the twentieth century witnessed the emergence of a revitalized upper class in popular imaginings, wherein the wealthy were represented as more active and sleeker than the archetypal nineteenth-century plutocrat. In mannerisms and appearances, of course, Mackenzie King was more of the latter mould – a stodgy intellectual from the east; the younger Dunning who made good in the West – "a well-known site of regeneration for eastern dudes" in the United States – compared rather favourably.[67]

This popular image, bolstered by a record of fiscal conservatism and administrative efficiency, made Dunning popular beyond his home province even before he made the decisive move to Ottawa. "We have always felt that Saskatchewan was a particularly well governed Province, and in our own minds have placed most of the credit for this desirable condition on you," wrote A.H. Williamson, of the investment banking firm Wood, Gundy Limited, to Dunning in February 1926.[68] Earlier, in November 1925 while rumours that Dunning might succeed King were still in circulation, W. Rupert Davies pledged to Dunning his "whole-hearted support" as well as the support of his daily newspaper, the Kingston *British Whig*.[69] J. Vernon McKenzie, editor of the national magazine *Maclean's*, upon hearing news that Dunning would leave Saskatchewan to become minister of railways and canals in the Dominion government, maintained hope that Dunning would eventually replace King. "When you succeed to the leadership of the Liberal party," McKenzie wrote Dunning early in 1926, "as you no doubt will within the next few years, I shall return to Canada and to the Liberal fold with great pleasure."[70] Closer to home, Winnipeg's George W. Allan – director of Great-West Life and the Canadian Bank of Commerce, member of the Canadian Committee of the Hudson's Bay Company, and former Unionist MP for Winnipeg South – lauded Dunning for having given "Saskatchewan strong, honest and efficient Government." Despite being a Conservative himself, Allan expressed to Dunning the view that "[w]hen it comes down to my friends, I don't care a damn which side of politics they belong to, ... the only thing with me in this connection which is worth while, is to know that they are white all through and that their hearts work overtime for their friends."[71] Allan's suggestively racist metaphor for pure intentions – "white all through" – not only reminds us of the centrality of "whiteness" in structuring social relations in the Prairie West, whose settler society was in most cases only a generation old, but it also articulates the progressive belief that virtuous action could overcome the degraded, partisan world of politics. Another Winnipeg mogul, W.A. Matheson, president of Monarch Life Assurance Company, similarly invoked the themes of strength, youth, and character in his message to Dunning:

> If ever a country required strong men[,] Canada does today, and I believe it is the young men and young women that should step out and help this country. The west is to be congratulated and in fact the whole Dominion that they have a man like yourself that is willing to step out and take hold and do his share in putting this country back to where we were before the war.[72]

National revitalization was to come from the West – in the form of Charles Dunning.

Dunning's image – both real and imagined – had won him considerable support from the nation's business community by the time he made his way to Ottawa and served as a testament to how easily businessmen assimilated progressive sentiments in their thinking. His reputation as a progressive stemmed more from a businesslike record of administration than from exemplary political morality, however. Dafoe, a well-informed observer of western affairs, considered Dunning's reign in Saskatchewan "rather small-minded and tyrannical" and hoped he would "get away from his small-town ideas of political manipulation"; in particular, Dafoe cited deals made between newspaper proprietor George M. Bell, whose interests included four Regina and Saskatoon newspapers, "with Dunning in which newspaper support figured."[73] For the moment, nonetheless, Dunning's political support reflected the moderate progressive ideal, uniting farmers and businessmen into a formidable political bloc. He stood to legitimize the King administration in the West. And, after months of encouragement from King and his emissaries, Dunning finally expressed his willingness to join the Dominion government in November 1925, palace intrigue being put to rest for the time being.[74] He was sworn in as minister of railways and canals on 1 March 1926, and a seat soon after opened up for him in Regina, which he won by acclamation.[75]

King, in retrospect, may have gained more than Dunning: he neutralized a potential competitor by bringing Dunning into government; moved Dunning away from the Saskatchewan Liberal Party and replaced him with a more reliable party stalwart, Jimmy Gardiner; and, of course, shored up support in the West. Dunning was, as Robert Wardhaugh has documented, at the centre of Mackenzie King's political designs in the West.[76] King's decision to undertake construction of the Hudson Bay Railway – which passed through the cabinet in the summer of 1925 – was a specific concession to Dunning and broader western Liberal and Progressive sentiment that demanded the line's construction.[77] King was also able to move some way in accommodating Dunning's request that the personnel of the cabinet signal low-tariff intentions, since the high-tariff forces within the cabinet had already been weakened.[78] King, indeed, was about to embark upon a sort of western honeymoon. Having lost his own seat in the recent election, one was opened for him in Prince Albert, Saskatchewan, in early 1926, just as word of Dunning's impending entry in the government began to spread. King arrived in Saskatchewan in early February 1926 and was nominated at Prince Albert. The experience impressed upon him the organization and good spirit of the Saskatchewan Liberals as well as the personal charm of Dunning and his family. King wrote Dunning in appreciation of the "generous and kindly introduction" Dunning gave him at meetings in "all the important centres of the constituency." From King's perspective the future looked bright: "I look forward with delight to the growth of a friendship which has its roots in the public service of our country."[79]

As Dunning had been warned, however, Progressive support for the government remained precarious.[80] This support failed, and a nonconfidence vote passed following revelations concerning the corrupt dealings of certain Liberal supporters in the Customs Department, particularly in Montreal. When King asked for a dissolution of parliament, Governor General Byng refused and called upon Arthur Meighen to form government. Thus arrived the King-Byng affair, an event King used to his political advantage, styling himself as a defender of Canadian autonomy.[81] Meighen's government did not last through the summer, leaving King and the Liberals more emboldened than before and with an issue upon which to campaign. The election, held on 14 September, resulted in a resounding Liberal victory. Meighen, having lost his own seat in Portage la Prairie, Manitoba, retired. Dunning won in Regina in the face of a reportedly well-financed Conservative mud-slinging campaign.[82] More importantly, with Dunning's help, King had mastered the Progressive challenge; and T.A. Crerar entered the administration as minister of agriculture.

Cultivating a "National" Perspective

Dunning arrived in Ottawa already socialized to life in government. His new role as minister of railways and canals would make him much more intimately involved with the upper echelons of Canadian business. The portfolio had acquired additional significance since the Canadian government's expansion in the railway business. Having taken over the bankrupt Mackenzie and Mann interests during the First World War, and the Grand Trunk and the Grand Trunk Pacific soon after the war, Borden's Conservative administration set a policy course that resulted in the establishment of the Canadian National Railways (CNR), completed by 1923.[83] Encompassing also the Intercolonial system in the Maritimes, the CNR spanned the continent, representing direct competition to the privately owned CPR. As minister of railways, Dunning was charged with the responsibility of not only overseeing CNR operations but also negotiating between the two systems. In such cases, Dunning observed in 1928, his role was to protect the interests of the public, who were served by both systems.[84] Widely lampooned in the

Prairie West as the epitome of protected eastern interests, the CPR and its representatives might have been concerned about the newly minted western cabinet minister. Tellingly, they were not. "For a great many reasons, some of them personal," wrote CPR president Edward Beatty to Dunning following the 1926 election, "I should be very sorry if you consented to any other portfolio in the new administration than that of Railways." Beatty's tone – accepting another portfolio would "damage your own prestige" – indicated sincerity. "Good administration" is all Beatty claimed to want from Dunning, who Beatty suggested was "the strongest man in Canada."[85] And though the CNR's president, Sir Henry Thornton, had already expressed similarly positive views of Dunning, over time in this ministerial position Dunning would gain a reputation for pro-CPR leanings.[86] For a supposed representative of the West, this presented a political conundrum.

The ongoing hostility between Thornton and Beatty, rooted in competition between the railway systems each served, heightened the importance of Dunning's intermediary role. But a thriving railway business fuelled by good crops in the West and an expanding resource frontier – most evident in northern Ontario and Quebec – made the task somewhat easier. Within this context of relative prosperity – the final expansionary period of the nation's railways – Dunning was charged with the responsibility of managing competition, not the much more troubling questions of solvency and retrenchment that would dominate railway debates throughout the Depression of the 1930s. J.W. Dafoe believed Dunning managed in favour of the CPR, pointing to Dunning's interventions in northern Alberta and line extensions to Flin Flon and the Sheritt-Gordon mines. Dafoe claimed that while the CPR gained a strategic hold in northern Alberta, Dunning stood idle, stalling CNR line extensions where profits were a near certainty. These reflections, coming from Dafoe in January 1929, were distilled into some broader conclusions:

> the popular impression undoubtedly is that Dunning has been and probably still is sympathetic to the Canadian Pacific Railway. The Canadian Pacific Railway, I should say, are so to speak, capitalizing this sympathy or friendship by putting themselves into a strategically strong position for the future ... I am a little afraid that not only Mr. Dunning's

temperamental attitude towards questions as public ownership but also his sympathies, due perhaps to past associations and future expectations, will make him a discreet but effective partizan of the Canadian Pacific Railway. If so, the situation will be serious for the Canadian National; and, I should think, serious also for the Liberal party ... I don't think the trouble is with the Canadian National directors. It is right in Ottawa and I fear a large proportion of the trouble can be located in Mr. Dunning's office.[87]

Even Frank Fowler, "originally an ardent Dunning partisan" and Winnipeg Sanhedrin member, was driven to the belief "that Dunning is in the cabinet to do a chore for the Canadian Pacific Railway and the Power trust whenever opportunity offers," as Dunning presented legislation in opposition to recommendations received from CNR officials.[88] Another Winnipegger, George W. Allan, would, after Dunning had moved on to become minister of finance, congratulate him for having given the privately owned railway "fair-play" and "a square deal"; but Allan, who had ascended to the presidency of Great West Life, more represented the perspective of big business.[89] Though progress in the construction of the Hudson Bay Railway would continue to advertise Dunning's western roots, his commitment to western interests seemed to buckle under the weight of his ambition.[90]

Living and governing in Ottawa had distanced Dunning from his political base in Saskatchewan.[91] Relations between Dunning and his successor as Saskatchewan premier, Jimmy Gardiner, were frosty, and Tory adversaries spread rumours of Dunning-Gardiner infighting in the press.[92] This took a toll on Dunning's public image in the West. Discussions at the 1927 convention of the United Grain Growers held in Winnipeg prompted one delegate to later ask Dunning: "Have you really changed?"[93] "It seems that whenever a Western man comes to Ottawa to live," Dunning answered,

as he must in order to discharge his responsibilities to the country as a Minister, subterranean forces are immediately put to work to undermine the respect in which he is held by the people generally and especially by the people in the part of the country from which he comes. Without the support of the Western people which has been given to me so generously through all my public life, it would be impossible for me to retain the influence in Dominion affairs which will enable me to fight successfully for the policies for which the Western people stand. It seems to me sometimes that our Western people have a lesson to learn yet with regard to standing by their public men in the Federal arena.[94]

Increasingly, however, the West had less and less reason to stand by Dunning.

He had become more settled in Ottawa and the surrounding area. Mackenzie King in May 1927 saw the new house Dunning purchased in Ottawa on Range Road for $25,000 – "a good investment," reported King.[95] Lunches, planned social events, and speaking dates: these all brought Dunning into the same social world as the nation's bourgeoisie and would provide new career opportunities for him in business, and one suspects that he may have already been anticipating those opportunities as he cultivated friendly relations with the CPR. Meanwhile, a new opportunity in Ottawa was about to open up. Following the death of Minister of Finance J.A. Robb in late 1929, Dunning was moved to that portfolio. Tariff and budgetary decisions were thus placed under his control, making it even more difficult for him to appear as an advocate of the West.

As was the case with his earlier portfolio, Dunning was the first westerner to take charge of finance. Differing from Tory economic nationalism, which centred upon the protected manufacturing sector of Central Canada, Dunning was more oriented towards fostering economic growth through foreign trade, an unsurprising view for someone whose experience was in the wheat business, which was utterly dependent upon export markets. But his appointment to finance signalled a very limited political victory for the West, for it also indicated that Dunning's views on the tariff had become sufficiently moderate to warrant the appointment; downward revisions were desirable, but drastic change was not. Tariff policy, Dunning realized, was a negotiated settlement between differing groups. In Regina in March 1930, Dunning explained: "As is well known I am a low tariff man. That means that I believe that the tariff of this country should be set as low as possible having due regard to the interest of producers, consumers and industry generally." Believing freer trade to be the recipe for increased employment and a generally robust economy, Dunning accepted that tariff revisions required "due regard" for differing interests.[96] Embracing the "relative autonomy" required of him as an agent of the state, Dunning also became more closely associated with big business.[97]

Dunning's move into the finance portfolio was welcomed by Canada's economic elite, and he was invited into their exclusive circle. From Montreal hearty congratulations were extended from such luminaries as: M.W. Wilson and Jackson Dodds, general managers of the Royal Bank of Canada and the Bank of Montreal, respectively; John Bassett, newspaperman and mining magnate; A.W. Currie, principal of McGill University; and Senator Raoul Dandurand, who assured Dunning that "all our friends in Montreal are most happy to see you at the head of the Finances of the Dominion." Quebec premier Louis-Alexandre Taschereau, who was well respected by Montreal's Anglo-establishment, similarly assured Dunning "his appointment was popular throughout the Province of Quebec."[98] The appointment also promised Dunning closer social interaction with the world of high finance. Smeaton White invited Dunning to the exclusive Mount Royal Club to facilitate his social interaction with the city's big bourgeoisie:

> I had the honour of entertaining the late Mr. Robb when he was appointed Minister of Finance, and would feel honoured if you will accept an invitation to dine with me some time during December, at the Mount Royal Club, to meet some of the Montreal men. I consider it important, in your new position, that you should be acquainted with the people in this city who represent financial and other interests, and I do not think anyone will accuse either you or myself of introducing political atmosphere into the entertainment, as it will be a purely social one, with the idea of enabling you to meet some of the Montreal business community in this way. If you will suggest what date would be convenient, I would endeavour to have one, or possibly two, of your colleagues join you, as I feel our people in Montreal do not frequent enough opportunity of getting personally acquainted with the Members of the Government which, in my opinion, is a handicap to both sides.[99]

Dunning could not commit to White's invitation; he had already received a similar invitation from his "old friend, Mr. E.W. Beatty,

President, Canadian Pacific Railway."[100] Toronto financial magnates E.R. Wood, A.E. Ames, and Joseph Flavelle also expressed their approval; so did Sam McLaughlin, president of General Motors of Canada in Oshawa; and favourable words were even received from that famous expatriate New Brunswicker overseas, Lord Beaverbrook. Tories and Liberals alike, commanding figures of the national economy collectively signalled an attitude of real confidence in Dunning; though, no doubt, they were also aware that something might be gained by doing so.

Electoral support was another matter. Thoughtful commentators realized that, as finance minister, Dunning would not be able to implement the level of tariff reductions many in the West wanted, and his stock in the West waned after he accepted the portfolio.[101] King campaigned upon the "Dunning Budget," which promised prosperity through increased world trade, especially with Britain. However, R.B. Bennett, the leader of the opposition and another figure who had made good in the West before entering federal politics, claimed the budget, by its use of countervailing duties, accepted the principles of Tory protectionism in all but name. "One is not permitted in parliamentary debate to use the expression hypocrisy," Bennett proclaimed following Dunning's budget speech, "but it is always a matter of satisfaction to see sinners turn from their sins ... to see those who have erred converted to the light."[102] Even more important in bringing about the political defeat of Dunning and the King government in the 1930 Dominion election was the onset of the Great Depression and failure of the Liberal government to deal with – or even recognize the seriousness of – the crisis. With a capitalist world in disarray, Canadians were more compelled by R.B. Bennett's promise to "blast" into new markets and eliminate unemployment.[103] Added to this unfortunate mix of factors, growing xenophobic sentiment in Saskatchewan bolstered the strength of the Conservative Party, as it had in the New Brunswick provincial election of 1925. J.T.M. Anderson and his Conservatives defeated the Liberal administration of Jimmy Gardiner in the 1929 provincial election.[104] Similar forces helped to defeat Dunning in the summer of 1930. He claimed the combination of Ku Klux Klan influence and 3,000 unemployed in Regina made his defeat unsurprising.[105] When, claimed Dunning, on election night the Klan paraded through Regina "by the thousands with banners and crosses flying I knew that my instinct was correct."[106]

St James Street

The year 1930 was a topsy-turvy one: the Dunning Budget had received much acclaim in the spring, but, before the leaves had fallen, Dunning's electoral fortunes had as well.[107] It was also, in Dunning's mind, a watershed year: the question was whether to remain in active politics or apply his skills to the business world. "I feel sometimes that I am at the cross-roads of life," wrote Dunning to J.A. Cross, "deciding whether to definitely abandon politics for a business career or to accept some arrangement of an indefinite character (and on a basis suspiciously close to charity in my view) to enable me to remain in public life."[108] Being a politician out of government did not look particularly attractive to Dunning. Money was an issue: his wife was sick with cancer, and his children's educations had become more costly. Within a few years, Dunning would report that he was also supporting his parents and two widowed sisters and their families.[109] There were laudable motives driving him into the business world, though Dunning's past activities had already revealed a personal ambition that was likely to land him in moneyed corridors. Dunning had been successful in attracting money to the Liberal Party too, and when he left active politics, so too did money donated to the party for his continuance in politics.[110] King hoped that Dunning would act as party organizer.[111] Dunning concluded that he simply could not financially afford to remain in public life.

It did not take long before offers came his way. Winnipeg Liberal H.A. Robson advised Dunning before the end of August that a grain-dealing firm was considering him for a management position.[112] In early October, Dunning became vice-president of Ontario Equitable Life, an insurance firm based in Waterloo, Ontario. The position, Dunning explained, was especially attractive because it was the only offer among many that did not require his "retirement from public life."[113] Later that month, Dunning was named vice-president of Lucerne-in-Quebec, a CPR company that operated the Seigniory Club, an exclusive resort on the Ottawa River in Montebello, Quebec. Describing Dunning's new duties, Harry Sifton explained: "He builds roads, excavates for swimming pools, sells land and has a great time, getting $25,000.00 a year for doing it."[114] "I am in the happy position of having more work than I can comfortably handle," Dunning explained to a friend, "which always represents a condition of real happiness for me."[115] From a western regional perspective, little ambiguity remained: Dunning had "become an easterner."[116] Suspicion of Dunning's pro-CPR leanings seemed confirmed. A CPR lobbyist claimed Dunning was "going into the CPR organization for keeps" as the company's next treasurer.[117] But his political aspirations remained. The next five years, as he became a well-known face of big business, would dramatically change the way in which the public perceived him. New political opportunities emerged as Dunning became entrenched in the national business community, but his status as a bigwig would also prove limiting.[118]

The Lucerne-in-Quebec Seigniory Club at Montebello was not merely a moneymaking project; it was also a project of class consolidation. Taken over by the CPR from a U.S. syndicate, it was seventy-five miles west of Montreal and forty-five miles east of Ottawa, conveniently located between Canada's centres of economic and political power and "easily accessible by Canadian Pacific Railway, or by Montreal-Hull-Ottawa highway, Quebec Route 8."[119] Dunning was, in a sense, ideal to manage the project, since he was already familiar with the Montreal-Ottawa axis that the Seigniory Club served and helped consolidate. Encompassing an area of 80,000 acres stretching into the Laurentian Mountains, the club was a planned community that offered exclusive hunting and fishing rights to its members, golf, an array of seasonal activities, and an exclusive club atmosphere. Beatty encouraged Prime Minister Bennett to treat "Lucerne as a suburb of Ottawa" during the Imperial Economic Conference in 1932 and argued it was a "convenient ... place for the residence of delegates or advisers while the Conference is proceeding."[120] During the Second World War, Algoma Steel president Sir James Dunn spent much of his time at Montebello to stay close to Ottawa, where the steel controller and minister of munitions and supply, C.D. Howe, became "[a]nnoyed by the steel president's frequent, unannounced appearances at his office."[121] This moneyed preserve had been a seigneury, as the club's name suggested – that of Louis-Joseph Papineau, the famous *patriote* of the Lower Canadian Rebellion whose descendants could no longer afford the manor's upkeep and auctioned it in 1929. Resold to the Lucerne-in-Quebec Community Association Limited, Papineau's chateau was converted into a clubhouse with a large ballroom, a billiards room, and a mock-Elizabethan tavern. A promotional booklet emphasized Papineau's role as a parliamentary reformer and reimagined the organic structure and aristocratic tenor of life on the seigneury; the property was thus not only legally appropriated but intellectually appropriated as well.[122]

Moneymaking and the maintenance of social exclusivity: one reinforced the other, since attracting the "right" people would make membership more desirable for others. Beatty encouraged CPR directors to join the club for that reason. "I have already told Mr. Dunning to send application forms to Sir Herbert Holt, Sir Charles Gordon, Mr. Tilley and myself," explained Beatty to Stelco president Ross H. McMaster, also a CPR director. "He has already received an application from Senator Beique," continued Beatty, "and applications for membership will also be sent to Mr. R.S. McLaughlin, Colonel Frank Meighen, Colonel Cockshutt and other members of our directorate. As you will appreciate this support should be of great value in the sale of lots, and if you feel free to take a lot, I would naturally be very glad."[123] Jews, meanwhile, were excluded, a policy that reflected the ubiquity of upper-class anti-Semitism during the period, and the procedure to gain membership ensured that only those with the requisite wealth and social standing would gain admittance.[124] "Membership in the Seigniory Club and Lucerne-in-Quebec community is both selective and exclusive," proclaimed a promotional booklet.[125]

Though Dunning was far removed from his former social milieu in Saskatchewan, his activities were still subject to the same market forces. This happened to work against the business success of the planned snobbery he was charged with overseeing at Montebello. Between 1 January and 31 May 1931, Lucerne-in-Quebec had run an operating deficit of $741,000 and was on its way to losing well over $1 million that year; Beatty lamented: "at this rate the Association will be swamped without hope of recovery in a few years."[126] He pressed Dunning to cut operating expenses by implementing the same economies that were being applied to railway operations.[127] It was an about-face for Lucerne-in-Quebec's optimistic philosophy, evidenced in the enormous log chateau – purportedly the largest in the world – that had been built in 1930 to serve as a hotel for members while they constructed their mansions in the woods.[128] Dunning inherited this problem. He was about to tackle one of far greater magnitude, but born of the same forces.

On the eve of the Great Depression, pulp and paper was Canada's leading industry.[129] The great majority of the industry's production – 85 per cent in 1929 – was newsprint.[130] Dominating this vast economic activity at the national level were three companies, the "Big Three": Canadian International Paper, the Canadian subsidiary of New York-based International Paper, whose presence, as we have seen, had been greatly felt in New Brunswick (see chapter 1); the Abitibi Power and Paper Company; and Canada Power and Paper. The last two companies were forged during the consolidation wave of the late 1920s. The unthinking spirit of optimism so characteristic of capitalistic endeavours in boom times and efforts to stem diminishing rates of profit had fuelled the industry's merger wave and had produced unwieldy capital structures.[131] The onset of economic depression was like a cold shower for industry grandees who were forced to confront the consequences of their unrestrained methods. Nowhere was this truer than with Canada Power and Paper.

In March 1931, Charles Dunning was appointed chairman of a "protective committee for the security holders," which also became known as the Dunning Committee, charged with the task of reorganizing Canada Power and Paper's capital structure. The *Financial Post* reported Dunning's appointment "was understood to have been made at the suggestion of E.W. Beatty."[132] The company had been established only a few years earlier, in 1928, by a group led by Royal Bank of Canada president Sir Herbert Holt and Toronto investment banker J.H. Gundy that orchestrated the gradual merger of five separate operating companies under Canada Power and Paper control.[133] In so doing, the Holt-Gundy group positioned itself at the helm of the country's newsprint industry, controlling the largest bloc of productive capacity in Canada. Linked through money and personnel to the country's two largest banks and the CPR as well as major life insurance companies, Canada Power and Paper represented a group that was among the country's most powerful and well-established capitalist interests.[134] Having already revealed the company's financial standing upon the request of the Montreal Stock Exchange and deferred dividend payments in February, company president J.H. Gundy painted the expected dire picture at April's annual meeting: operating at 43 per cent capacity, the company's properties were in no way capable of generating the profits required to meet interest and debenture charges. Reorganization was necessary. The banks, which had loaned Canada Power $14,558,000 by the end of 1930, would have a significant hand in the reorganization.[135]

Dunning, the self-described practitioner of "business statesmanship," was thus called to intervene: "I am certainly finding plenty of demand for the kind of service which people appear to think I am qualified to render in the business world," he explained in early May.[136] The newsprint industry bore some resemblance to the wheat business with which Dunning was familiar: both were export oriented and governed by cooperative marketing. The Newsprint Institute of Canada, which sought to regulate newsprint production, however, had become an increasingly impotent agency as U.S. publishers (the *Chicago Tribune* and the *New York Times*) operated their own mills in Canada and successfully drove down the price of newsprint, while Canadian International Paper had, to make matters worse, stopped cooperating with the institute.[137] These problems were made even worse by the fixed payments built into Canada Power's financial structure; this was the central problem Dunning confronted as head of the "protective committee" – to adjust the capital to reflect "current earning power," as opposed to "potential earning power," which had driven past financing. Significantly the investment house of J.H. Gundy – Wood, Gundy & Company – was not represented on the protective committee, whose formation and work remained under a veil of secrecy.[138] The *Financial Post* observed that, even though the committee claimed to represent the interest of security holders, "no meeting of the shareholders or bondholders of parent or subsidiary companies was ever held duly to elect these representatives. Nor has the committee ever made a public statement as to the interests primarily responsible for bringing the committee into being."[139] The personnel of the committee indicated the dominant presence of high finance, led by Montreal interests, including eminent members of the Canadian legal profession such as future Liberal cabinet minister J.L. Ralston, as well as representatives of London and New York.[140]

On 3 June, the committee announced a reorganization plan – soon coined the Dunning Plan – that was supported by the Royal Bank of Canada and the Bank of Montreal. It proposed the formation of a new company to take over Canada Power's assets and, significantly, cutting the former capitalization by half; stocks, bonds, and debentures formerly valued at $103,832,266 were to be reduced to $52,627,596.[141] Investors, naturally, were not uniformly supportive. A week after the plan was announced, the *Financial Post* reported that opinion was divided on its merits, and its execution remained uncertain. A sufficient proportion of the old securities needed to be deposited in exchange for new ones in order to validate the plan, and some reticence remained among security holders, especially since the committee had not named the new board of directors.[142] The strongest resistance came from representatives of the Belgo-Canadian Paper Company, who claimed the proposed stock swap offered insufficient compensation for Belgo security holders. At a Belgo security holders' meeting in mid-June in Montreal, former company president Hubert Biermans and former general manager John Stadler advised shareholders to demand better terms, and a committee was organized to protect preferred shareholders.[143] The Belgo representatives were dispatched to meet with the protective committee headed by Dunning, but at the ensuing meeting a dispute arose over the ownership of two new machines recently installed at Belgo's plant at Shawinigan Falls, Quebec; the protective committee was not about to offer better terms.[144] Biermans urged Belgo security holders not to surrender shares to the protective committee in early July.[145]

The protests from Bierman and Belgo had the greatest effect, since they were the most organized. Indeed, the reorganization, which was originally slated to come into effect 15 July, was pushed back again and again until November, when Belgo finally capitulated, giving formal approval to the Dunning plan.[146] In the summer, while the banks, the CPR, and the insurance companies called for support of the plan, Dunning sounded a call for calm, warning "that liquidation and litigation would demoralize the whole situation and might spell disaster to one of Canada's greatest industries."[147] Belgo was not the only aggrieved party. The chairman of a committee representing holders of Canada Power and Paper Laurentide series debentures wrote Prime Minister R.B. Bennett to report "the heavy loss that has been sustained by investors, from poor people as well as person of means," and to demand government action: "this scandal is even worse than ... Beauharnois." Bennett's secretary of state, C.H. Cahan, later claimed that no investigation was possible since Canada Power was incorporated under Quebec law and not the Dominion Companies Act.[148] The formation of a new board of directors was meant to signal the company's liberation "from old influences" that had created the mess; and the new and unimaginatively named Consolidated Paper Corporation was free from any direct association with Gundy's financial recklessness, as U.S. corporate executive LaMonte J. Belnap, whose experience had been "largely along the lines of an industrial engineer," was named president.[149] Nonetheless, the "old forces" remained well represented on the new board of directors, and Cahan and Bennett, both of whom had worked as corporate lawyers, were not about to launch an investigation that would have touched the upper stratum of St James Street. The businessman who received the brunt of the Beauharnois scandal, W.L. McDougald, was considered an outsider by Montreal's upper class and was thus apparently more vulnerable to reprisal.[150] The wealthiest and most powerful insiders seemed to enjoy special immunities – but not entirely. W.E.J. Luther, the president of the Montreal Stock Exchange and partner in the brokerage house of Luther, Craig & Company, lost a lot of money in Holt securities. And after Holt instructed the Royal Bank to no longer carry Luther's brokerage house, a distraught Luther travelled to Holt's Stanley Street house in May 1932 and shot him. He then went home and started up the car in his shut-up garage; Luther killed himself, mistakenly thinking he had killed Holt. Luther's firm was petitioned into bankruptcy the following day, while Consolidated Paper went on to flounder, not paying dividends until after the Second World War.[151]

By early 1933, Mackenzie King saw in Dunning a bloated plutocrat. "He had got to look very fat & heavy," King wrote of Dunning after meeting with him for two and a half hours in January. He further explained: "His face sinks down into his cheeks, he has become member of the board of financiers, including Sir Charles Gordon, Borden & others, a great mistake if he has any further thoughts of public life, which I am beginning to doubt."[152] Though Dunning liked to think of himself as "the Western iconoclast of St. James Street," most people did not.[153] The appearance of vitality was gone, replaced by the stodginess of big money. Montreal Liberal manufacturer Kirk Cameron, a low-tariff political ally from the 1920s, wrote Dunning in 1934 to complain about unfair punishment meted out – by the big newsprint producers and Taschereau's Quebec administration – to a small pulp and paper company in which he was interested that had been accused of violating its production quota:

> We hesitate to believe that your association with St. James Street during the past three years has contaminated your otherwise sound principles of freedom of trade, freedom of operation and freedom from government interference. It is true ... you daily associate with those who exercise very often coercive and subversive powers. Does it mean in the words of Scripture "Evil communications corrupt good manners or in other words re-actionary association corrupt sound thinking"[?][154]

It seemed, indeed, that Dunning had become "contaminated" by his close association with big business.

Mackenzie King went even further in August 1932, claiming that Dunning "is now acting pretty much as an agent for Beatty & the C.P.R."[155] This, King believed, was evidenced by Dunning's position on the railway question, one of the most debated public policy issues in the 1930s: as both national railways fell into financial difficulty under the strain of economic depression, Beatty and his Montreal allies argued vigorously that "amalgamation" or "unified management" of the two railways was needed to stabilize the economy and protect the nation's credit (see chapter 3). Railway unification was not popular, however, especially in the West, where farmers almost universally feared the prospect of a railway monopoly. A similar view obtained throughout most of the country; railway workers quite reasonably worried that layoffs would result from the rationalization inevitably to follow unification; there also existed a general concern among many commentators about the prospect of deteriorating railway services as well as concern about railway assets – paid for by the Canadian government – being turned over to the CPR. Though railway unification was not popular, Dunning thought it a possibility in the early 1930s and criticized Mackenzie King for "the positive nature of his remarks on the railway

situation" in the course of a "fighting speech" King delivered in Winnipeg. Dunning thought, rather than committing himself to defend the
"integrity" of the CNR, King "would have been better advised to remain in a watching position, so far as this problem is concerned, rather
than to take a positive attitude, which hard facts later may make it impossible for him to maintain."[156]

In late 1931, not long before Tories assailed Sir Henry Thornton's
public reputation in the House of Commons, Dunning publicly suggested the possibility of railway unification in an address before the
Commercial Travelers' annual banquet in Toronto. The Toronto *Globe*
commented on Dunning's statement, "there has been a very vital
change in his convictions regarding railway monopoly. Mr. Dunning
as Minister of Railways and Mr. Dunning as executive of the Canadian Pacific Railway would seem to have diametrically different views
on this outstanding issue."[157] Soon after Thornton's resignation, Dunning expressed the belief to Mackenzie King that he expected to be
appointed as Thornton's replacement. King elaborated further upon his
conversation with Dunning in his diary:

> Believes he can do the job better than any one with experience he has had.
> He says Tommy Russell [a Montreal industrialist] & present Presdt. of
> Montreal Harbor Board have declined the position. He does not count on
> politics at once. I can see that. Says Mrs. Dunning suffering effects of ra-
> dium. I cannot blame him for seeking ways & means to live. We had a very
> pleasant talk – but clearly it was as an emissary of Beatty's & to soften the
> expression "integrity" of Nat'l Railways, he had come, & possibly to sound
> me out on his own acceptance of the presidency of the C.N.R.[158]

As familial responsibilities pressed, so also Dunning sought to expand
his responsibilities in public life. But King exaggerated the extent to
which Dunning was acting on Beatty's cue. In January 1933, Dunning
reported to Floyd S. Chalmers, editor of the *Financial Post*, that he had
been feeding Beatty arguments for his amalgamation plan but lamented
that the Bennett government would not have the courage to carry the
plan out. Asked by Chalmers whether a "National Government" – a coalition of the Conservatives and Liberals – could be established, Dunning concluded the two party leaders, Bennett and King, stood in the

way. But, nonetheless, he thought the idea had considerable potential and might allow the implementation of unpopular, but necessary, policies: with Bennett and King out of the way, he believed, "a group of loyal citizens could organize a suicide club and go into office and clean up a lot of serious situations that could be cleaned up no other way. They would have to go into office prepared to kill themselves off politically in order to do unpopular and unpleasant things." Unpleasant things such as the railway unification plan Dunning sketched out to Chalmers.[159] Dunning told Norman Lambert, another former western figure who had become deeply integrated into national political life during the 1930s as president of the National Liberal Federation, that joint management of the two railways by a holding company to facilitate "rationalization of shops + terminals as well as unnecessary parts of main lines" could solve the railway question.[160] Such solutions were exactly what many Canadians feared.

It would be an oversimplification to portray Dunning as Beatty's emissary in this period. Life in this charmed Montreal-Ottawa world – spent at the Ritz-Carlton in Montreal and his home in Ottawa – allowed Dunning to view the human consequences of the Depression with considerable equanimity.[161] As he joined the ranks of the business elite, Dunning embraced their outlook – an outlook he had already been moving towards in the 1920s. Moreover, the progressive style he represented was one which seemed to offer big business significant opportunities to overcome the morass of partisan politics, its party machines, and its inefficiencies. More than opportunism or blind ambition, Dunning embraced a *mentalité* typical of his new social peers. Gone was Dunning's belief, from his days in Saskatchewan's cooperative movement, that sound economic development easily dovetailed with democratic principles. Increasingly, the two appeared to be in conflict. Dunning believed that history recommended growing demands for immediate action by the state or other drastic measures be resisted. In 1932 he explained,

Personally, I take a great deal of pleasure in these times reading history. It tends to comfort one to know that while things are very bad, they have been very bad before. Also, reading history tends to disprove the idea one gets occasionally that we are all going crazy, because one learns that always in such periods there have been technocrats, currency renovators, commonwealth fadists [*sic*], and endless other "ists" and "isms," each one with a potent remedy for the condition then prevailing. Astonishing as it may seem, always in the past humanity appears to have survived, without having applied any one of the amazing remedies then proposed.

I doubt very much personally whether it is wise to make basic, fundamental changes in either our economic or our political structure when humanity is under the kind of stress which it labours under at the present time, and I am afraid that basic changes adopted for the purpose of meeting the present condition would not stand the test of time, for the reason that our eyes are glued to [*sic*] closely upon getting out of the present condition quickly somehow, and we have not a clear conception of the effect of some of the remedies proposed upon our future well-being as individuals or as nations.

He argued the "wheat pool" had circulated false ideas about the dawn of a new economic order; and, displaying a measure of upper-class anti-Semitism, Dunning grouped "eminent New York Jews" among the false prophets.[162] It was, to his mind, the violation of immutable laws that had created the crisis. Humanity was doing necessary penance. Dunning's words reveal much about his state of mind:

I have profound belief that the immutable laws of economics are working. For a time humanity defied them, and we were told by the Wheat Pool and by some eminent New York Jews that the old economic law had past away and that we were living under a new economic dispensation. All the time these same old immutable laws kept grinding on, and what we are suffering today is the inevitable result of defying them. I think we sometimes forget in this time of trouble that these laws work for us. Humanity is now doing penance in an economic sense for infraction of the laws of sound economics. This very penance is bringing us daily back more and more closely into harmony with economic law. The process is very painful, but I have faith that 1932 will be known in future as the most painful year through which we have past.[163]

Dunning's prediction was not entirely incorrect: 1932 was the nadir of the Depression. But the recovery was slower than he expected, and its ultimate solution would come through the very things he feared would create even greater problems: aggressive government intervention, deficit spending, and, last and most importantly, war. Dunning was ideologically incapable of accepting such ideas.

Dunning embraced a residual ideology of a "liberal order" in crisis. The individualism and fiscal orthodoxy of nineteenth-century liberalism had always been part of Dunning's mental universe, and in the early twentieth century those ideals had been compatible with agrarian protest and the cooperative movement of which he was a part. This changed after the First World War, as Canada's liberal order fell into a period of crisis: agrarian protest moved towards more radical alternatives in some quarters, the Farmers' Union in Saskatchewan being one example, and the onset of the Great Depression encouraged a more widespread questioning of the old liberal ideals and created the conditions for a general resurgence of the left.[164] Having been repressed on the heels of the First World War, evidence of the left's political revitalization in Canada was apparent with the formation of the CCF in 1932 and the increased activism of the Communist Party of Canada, whose followers saw revolutionary potential in the economic crisis. With the Communist Party's adoption of the popular front strategy of cooperating with the social-democratic left in 1935, a formidable left-wing oppositional political bloc was forged, which would make itself felt in a resurgent labour movement during the latter half of the 1930s (see chapter 4). And, significantly, even individuals within the two major political parties began to seriously question the liberal orthodoxy of the old political economy. Dunning was out of step with this broader trend as he continued to hold on to an ideology that was proving remarkably durable among the nation's economic elite.[165]

Dunning defended a specific notion of freedom, just as he embraced antidemocratic ideas and political tactics. Reading books such as *The New Despotism* and *Our Wonderland of Bureaucracy* – both studies arguing the rise of government bureaucracies were undercutting law and individual freedom, the first, a British study, the second, an American one – Dunning believed an interventionist state would restrict freedom.[166] Widely seen within the business community as a figure to lead a political movement to defend against unwise government intervention, which threatened classical liberal notions of freedom embraced by numerous moneyed Canadians, Dunning's name continued to arise in National Government speculation. But the prospects of such a government seemed less and less likely. Dunning began to gravitate back towards the Liberal fold. He told Lambert in October 1933 that there was no chance for National Government, as the "necessary elements are not present in political situation."[167] "It is clear he sees how the wind is blowing," reported King following a dinner conversation with Dunning in November. Though King believed him "anxious to be back in the Government," Dunning remained fairly noncommittal up until 1935.[168] More than that, there is evidence to suggest that Dunning was becoming involved in another episode of mock palace intrigue, but this time with the support of Montreal courtiers. Gordon Ross warned King that Dunning was not to be trusted because he had spoken "in a deprecatory manner."[169] And indeed Dunning described King as a "charming, polite, hospitable + inert mass" that stood in the way of real accomplishment.[170] Within the Montreal wing of the party there existed enough discontent with King's leadership to spark rumours that Dunning or J.L. Ralston, Liberal finance critic and Montreal corporate lawyer who travelled in many of the same circles as Dunning, were prospective candidates to replace King.[171]

Business life in Montreal proved difficult for Dunning. Lucerne-in-Quebec continued to hemorrhage money. "I am a little disappointed in the lack of original suggestions to improve the situation," lamented Beatty to Dunning in April 1934.[172] Late in the year Dunning left Montreal for Toronto to head up the Maple Leaf Milling Company, and was sent off by a gathering of friends at the Mount Royal Club in November.[173] Maple Leaf suffered from the same ills as had Canada Power and Paper. "He liked the idea of being a physician to a sick business," reported Lambert. "But he soon discovered that he had taken on the job of being physician to an incurable." Worse still, he did not like Toronto; "Montreal was his atmosphere," but top positions in Montreal were closed off to him because he had "queered himself with Beatty" when he left the CPR for Toronto. With a general election looming in 1935, a return to politics was possible.[174] J.L. Ralston advised him to get back into politics "at once" if "he wished to be in running for leadership later on."[175]

Dunning also continued to politely entertain the suggestion that he lead a National Government – for example, the idea suggested to him in

January that he form a coalition with Conservative renegade H.H. Stevens.[176] But that changed with the sensationalist story published in the 12 March 1935 issue of the Toronto *Globe*. The *Globe* placed Dunning at the head of a St James Street campaign to form a coalition government in the interests of big business and, in particular, to push through a policy of railway amalgamation. Dunning, "much put out about it," responded quickly to the *Globe* via telephone to emphatically deny the story, predicting as well that Mackenzie King would be Canada's next prime minister; his rebuttal was published the following day on the front page of the *Globe*.[177] This signalled the end of Dunning's willingness to entertain further National Government machinations. T.A. Crerar reported to Lambert, just over a week after the *Globe*–National Government episode, that Dunning wanted back in government.[178] If so, he would have to travel through traditional party channels.

The Limits of the Party System

Those channels were certainly open to Dunning once again. The always politically savvy King, who was already assuming victory in the upcoming Dominion election, realized Dunning would be an asset to his cabinet as a signal to the country's business community. Indeed, in April, King worried about the prospect of losing J.L. Ralston and Dunning and the resultant weakness it would inflict upon his cabinet.[179] Ralston was in fact King's preference for minister of finance, but it was unclear whether he would be willing to join, in which case, Lambert mused, Dunning "would undoubtedly have to face certain pressure to go into the Cabinet."[180] When Ralston expressed his unwillingness to join the cabinet, Dunning was next in line. In June, King was discussing "cabinet formation" with him, and in the following months Dunning became actively involved in the Liberal campaign, though he did not run in the federal general election, set for 14 October.[181] Indicative of Dunning's high-powered support, former prime minister Robert Borden wrote Quebec premier Louis-Alexandre Taschereau three days after the Liberal electoral victory to press for Dunning's entry in the cabinet as minister of finance. Borden was troubled by a recent conversation with Dunning in which the latter indicated he did not know whether he would receive the appointment. Borden wrote to Taschereau: "May I venture to express the hope that you will write to Dunning and that you will use your powerful influence to see that he does enter the Administration under the conditions indicated." "If he should be invited," Borden went on to explain the conditions, "he would be disposed to put aside his personal interests and undertake the Ministry of Finance if assured that the new Administration will stand for stability, non-interference with legitimate business, sanctity of governmental contracts and prevention of provincial raids upon the Federal Treasury."[182] As Robert Craig Brown has observed, "Dunning sought Borden's advice and, after a long conference, agreed to accept 'if assured of sane policies and support by colleagues.'"[183]

King did not need to be pressed or convinced, for his own economic thinking was rather close to Dunning's. Indeed, in the end Dunning ended up basically representing King's views within the cabinet and, as a result, received the brunt of a considerable amount of caucus infighting from more leftward-leaning colleagues. Dunning was to take many proverbial bullets for King, perhaps poetic justice for Dunning's past transgressions against him but more a testament to King's wiliness and instinct for self-preservation. That was yet to come. For the moment, as Blair Neatby has observed, "King wanted Dunning as Minister of Finance because he represented fiscal conservatism."[184] As such, Dunning served a double purpose for King: to bolster his own outlook within the cabinet and to "reassure industrialists and manufacturers" of the government's conservative intentions.[185]

Of course, the outcome was not a plain victory for big business, especially for those who had been hanging their political hopes upon National Government possibilities. Still, one is impressed by the non-partisan approval that Dunning's appointment received at the upper levels of the two major parties. After King had handed him the finance portfolio, the next issue became finding an appropriate seat. The West was out. Dunning and party leaders considered seats in Ontario and Quebec, and for a time it looked as if Dunning would run in the Eastern Townships, in J.A. Robb's old riding.[186] Eventually Queens County, Prince Edward Island, was chosen as a sufficiently safe riding. J. James Larabee, having won the seat in the recent federal election, vacated the seat in exchange for an appointment as "Inspector of Rents at $3500." "Got seat arranged for [Dunning] in Queens Co. P.E.I. through Walter

Jones," reported Lambert in typical laconic fashion in mid-December.[187] However, local Conservatives who hoped to contest the seat put hopes of Dunning's election by acclamation in jeopardy. Having lost the riding in the recent general election, W. Chester S. McClure wrote to R.B. Bennett to say the seat could be won if the Conservative Party wished to contest it. "The general feeling is against an outsider being brought in here," wrote McClure to Bennett, "because he could not get a seat anywhere else. Dunning is not popular."[188] Bennett's secretary, R.D. Finlayson, told Lambert a few days later that McClure seemed set on contesting the seat, and "RB would have to go there + and speak for him."[189] McClure was advised by an emissary of the Ottawa perspective that "leading Conservatives in Ottawa were not anxious to oppose Dunning," and that it was in his long-term interests not to contest the seat. Leading members of both parties were "unanimous" in this view. This nonpartisan agreement at the upper levels of both parties upset McClure's partisan sensibilities, and he voiced his protest by reciting the dictum "Liberals are always Liberals."[190] In the end, the threat of a moneyed Liberal campaign encouraged McClure to accept "the verdict of the higher ups." McClure lamented that an "advance guard" representing the perspective of the Conservative Party's national leadership turned the tables on local resistance, "and both Liberals and Conservatives banqueted Mr. Dunning."[191]

The difficulties that surrounded Liberal – and, indeed, Conservative – efforts to assure Dunning's election are a compelling testament to his diminished popularity. No longer the dynamic westerner, the farmer representative whose appeal defied class divisions, Dunning was now decidedly aligned with the "big interests." On the other hand, in leading business circles, Dunning was widely regarded as a reliable finance minister sufficiently committed to financial orthodoxy. King, too, was impressed by Dunning's business expertise and even his acquired social refinement. "I confess, as I talked with him," reflected King, "I realized more than ever the knowledge that he can bring to bear on public matters and his quite exceptional ability. I noticed, too, a considerable improvement in his general style of address and manner, as a result of his associations in Montreal and Toronto."[192]

Dunning was more than a representative of Canadian big business. He was one of its elite members, and his ideological predispositions reflected a wider social and cultural experience. Only reluctantly and in a limited way did he begin to adapt his ideas. Dunning had even before the election expressed reservations about what King's pronouncements on public policy would cost the treasury; though he admitted they may have been sound politically, Dunning also wondered "how the country is going to stand it all economically." He claimed no particular opposition to social reform itself, except that he thought it useless without resting on "a sound economic base."[193]

When he did take his views to the public on the campaign trail, in a national radio address delivered on 25 September in support of the Liberal Party, Dunning propounded a nineteenth-century liberal doctrine that ran counter to the growing body of thought emphasizing the need for economic planning and social reform; indeed, he positively opposed such notions. In Dunning's intellectual universe, no doubt tainted by partisan calculation, only the Liberal Party offered to protect the freedom of Canada's citizens. The following quotation, taken from Dunning's 25 September radio address, reveals much:

To me the decision on principle is simple, because Conservatives, Reconstructionists and C.C.F.'s are all standing for various methods of applying socialism and regimentation to the Canadian people and their problems. I do not care whether it is the Fascism of the Conservatives and Reconstructionists or the Marxian Socialism of the C.F.F. To me both mean tyranny. They mean the gradual setting up of an army of bureaucrats who would direct ultimately all our actions as individuals, – what we should produce, what we should sell and at what price, what we should buy + at what price, what we should do and how we should live, move and have our being.

The present Government have gone a long way on this road and so far have demonstrated that this form of tyranny, as applied by the Marketing Act for instance, is unsound, inefficient, and contrary to the independent spirit of our people, ... give them five years more of power and they will create such a bureaucratic tyranny as will take years to overcome. The Reconstructionist Party and the C.C.F. programs mean the same thing but with a different tyrant. Of course, we are told that the tyranny will be good ... that it will be beneficial. It would certainly involve jobs for a very large number of us, to regulate and regiment the rest of us.[194]

In this somewhat hyperbolic argument, only "liberalism" could protect Canadians from bureaucratic tyranny, by which Dunning meant
the term in a double sense, referring to both the Liberal Party and the
classic ideology. Indeed, Dunning went on to argue that the fundamental economic problems of the day were all traceable to the Great War
"and its destructive cost in men and material."[195] The economy was,
for Dunning, an organism that had been disrupted by the cataclysmic
shock of war. This notion – of economy as organism, most effectively
able to recover without "outside" interference – remained the common
sense of many elite Canadians in this period. In his first budget speech,
Dunning proclaimed economic law to be on Canada's side again, but
worried that war might once again disrupt progress.[196]

The public policies of the King government have been examined
elsewhere in great detail. There is, then, no need to catalogue Dunning's activities as finance minister here. Rather, it is best to pursue two
broad observations. First, Dunning failed in his objectives to curb government spending and revitalize private enterprise. "There have been
heavy deficits in the public accounts of each year, since we assumed
office, and, unfortunately," lamented Dunning in January 1938, "there
will be a deficit of a considerable amount for the present fiscal year."
He was still hoping that the Liberal administration would be in a future position before the next election to "show a surplus of receipts
over expenditures" and to reduce the "present high rate of taxation."[197]
Only months after that statement, Dunning collapsed in the government lobby of the House of Commons, evidently succumbing to the
hot weather as well as the stress of resisting calls for increased social
spending from more left-leaning colleagues.[198] Not coincidentally, that
year marked "the first time a government had consciously decided to
spend money to counteract a low in the business cycle."[199] Weakened by
the heart attack and a "minor stroke," Dunning's influence in the cabinet waned and he was forced to accommodate.[200] In his budget speech
the following year, Dunning proclaimed that the "old days of complete laissez-faire ... have gone forever."[201] It was Canada's first truly
Keynesian budget.[202] Second, in joining the cabinet, Dunning became
involved in a mechanism that imposed a limited range of policy alternatives upon him. A new tension between Dunning as finance minister
and the business community was revealed in his final budget speech.

He pointed to the "ironical" position in which he found himself, having to appear "to argue for high debt and high taxes." He could not but voice disappointment in "the lack of imaginative business leadership in recent years" for having contributed to making the interventionist state a necessity: "When private investment expands, not only will we find our need for Government expenditure less but also our revenue receipts will be so much increased that debts can be reduced and taxes lowered."[203]

Major realignments had occurred, and the political effectiveness of Canadian big business had diminished in significant ways. In bridging the worlds of business and politics during the Great Depression, Dunning served as an important political activist of the country's economic elite; but, unable to harmonize political life to the outlook and interests of big business, he exited politics physically broken and ideologically compromised. His accomplishments must be viewed in terms of his role in containing radical alternatives: the federal government's reassertion of authority in banking and finance, evidenced by the disallowance legislation that voided the attempts of William Aberhart's Social Credit government in Alberta to annul massive amounts of personal debt; its stewardship in the area of public finance, which, having become a major portion of the financial sector's business since the First World War, had emerged as a major element in the overall structure of Canadian capitalism; and, finally, the general restraint that Dunning and King imposed upon government spending.[204] Meanwhile, the contingencies of the ongoing Depression encouraged the federal state's further entry, under Dunning's oversight, into Canada's economic life, in wheat marketing, banking (i.e., the federal government's purchase of all Bank of Canada shares), transportation (i.e., the establishment of Trans-Canada Air Lines and the state's continued control of the CNR), and other areas.[205]

Conclusion

Dunning's progressive style of politics bore considerable fruit in the 1920s, especially during the first half of the decade, when he was widely perceived as a western agrarian representative. His regional identification waned in the 1920s after he moved to Ottawa to become minister of railways and canals; it waned further after he took charge of the finance portfolio; and it was eclipsed when he became a St James Street executive, where his efforts as a "physician" to sick businesses never turned out as well as he hoped – though he did succeed in safeguarding the capital of the banks. Like Robinson, Dunning had moved into a national elite whose power was faltering.

It was believed by many influential figures that Dunning's progressive, nonpartisan political style could be deployed to shore up the old political economy through retrenchment and balanced budgets. Dunning's identification with the "big interests" made such a drive politically difficult, if not impossible. Ironically, Dunning, who found the idea of class politics repugnant, became one of its most widely identified practitioners. Dunning entered King's cabinet as minister of finance after the 1935 general election through the activism of big business figures and because King wished to signal his administration's conservative intentions in those quarters. But Dunning was no longer a popular figure. His hope to succeed King as leader of the Liberal Party came to naught, and his tenure as finance minister proved a disappointment.

The *mentalité* that Dunning evinced throughout the 1930s revealed a stubborn attachment to the ideals of classical liberalism. But these ideals were uniquely structured by his social ascent into the upper stratum of Canada's business community. Thus, while Dunning clung fiercely to individualism and economic freedom during the 1930s, he had also come to accept the protective tariff, which, after all, served a fundamental role in protecting the economic interests of St James Street.[206] The apparent shift in his position on the tariff was a crucial aspect of his political estrangement from the Prairie West. Dunning's outlook came to reflect the general interests of the established industrial-financial nexus of St James Street. But, with the onset of the Depression and the concomitant decline of the old political economy, St James Street experienced a political crisis for which its representatives, such as Dunning, had no easy answer. Political failure had to be felt before capital-rich Canadians acquiesced to further accommodation: Dunning's experience was a part of this historical trajectory.

Dunning left a political world in which he had little room to operate. Reflecting the ease with which the Canadian bourgeoisie continued to travel between the private sector and the state, after Dunning left government he was recruited by Montreal business mogul J.W. McConnell to serve as president of Ogilvie Flour Mills Company in Montreal, where Dunning acquired directorships with companies such as the CPR, Stelco, Consolidated Paper, and the Bank of Montreal.[207] In 1940 Dunning also became chancellor of Queen's University, a position once held by CPR president Sir Edward Beatty; and Dunning resumed his activities within the state during the war as chairman of a crown corporation, the Allied War Supplies Corporation.[208] Moreover, he would return to politics through the back door in 1943, establishing a secret think tank that brought together leading Canadian business executives to defend free-enterprise ideals against the threat of socialism; the group financed the work of Gilbert Jackson, a Toronto-based economist and business consultant, who became their public face. It was politically innovative, but also evidence that the traditional political techniques had been failing.[209]

Dunning's smooth transition between politics and business was, for some, a model to emulate. "I should like to make some such business connections as Charlie Dunning did when he also was sent about his business"; so wrote Robert J. Manion, former minister of railways after losing his seat in the 1935 general election, to Sir Thomas White, vice-president of the Canadian Bank of Commerce – and a former minister of finance himself.[210] Though they moved between business and government easily, the power Canada's business elite exercised was increasingly limited by popular opinion in a new era in which the political entitlement of big business was challenged and its beneficence doubted. As we shall see, business leaders sought to overcome this dilemma by weakening the influence of democratic pressures upon the state.

3

The Dilemma of Democracy:
Sir Edward Beatty, the Railway
Question, and National Government

On 20 November 1931, the Royal Commission to Inquire into Railways and Transportation in Canada was established amid widespread concern about the viability of the nation's railway systems and growing worry about Canada's credit after the onset of the Great Depression. More widely known as the Duff Commission, after its chairman, Lyman Duff, commission members were mandated to "inquire into the whole problem of transportation in Canada, particularly in relation to railways, shipping and communication facilities therein, having regard to present conditions and the probable future developments of the country."[1] After conducting hearings that included people of varied political stripes across the country, the commissioners – consisting of numerous important business figures – tabled their report in the House of Commons the following year. The report concluded that economical management of the public system required it to be insulated "from political interference and community pressure," evidencing a keen awareness of – and even an aversion to – the pressures of popular opinion.[2] In addition, the report made clear that while amalgamation of the two systems under private ownership may have provided a theoretical solution to the financial difficulties of the country's railways, such a solution was a nonstarter because of its obvious unpopularity with the public. Edward Wentworth Beatty (1877–1943), president of the privately owned Canadian Pacific Railway (CPR), had argued in favour of amalgamation before the Duff Commission; he was duly disappointed by the report. "[W]hen politics comes in the door," lamented Beatty, "courage goes out the window."[3]

Beatty's lament reflected a more general concern within the business elite about the viability of democratic government during the 1930s, a concern that regularly arose in tandem with discussion of the railway question. The historic importance of railways generally and the CPR specifically is hard to deny. Responsible for building a line along an East–West axis, linking the West with Quebec, Ontario, and the Maritimes, the CPR built the transportation infrastructure that simultaneously consolidated the Canadian nation-state and expanded the scope of the British Empire. The capitalists represented in the CPR positioned their enterprise at the centre of this imperialist nation-building project during the nineteenth century by cultivating relationships with politicians to profitable ends. This economic elite, operating mostly from a Montreal base, was formed in step with the National Policy, accumulating capital in the process of forging the economic structure of a nation. Westward expansion and settlement, abundant British capital, large influxes of immigrants and – of immeasurable importance – a close relationship with the Canadian state, all worked to assure the CPR large and continued profits during the National Policy period.[4] As Richard White has recently written of nineteenth-century western North America, "railroads and the modern state were coproductions."[5] Beatty, appointed president of the CPR in 1918, was thus cast in a leadership position of an economic elite that had dominated the national scene economically and politically for some time. As he would discover, developments over the next two decades would challenge that dominance; by the 1930s Beatty and moneyed allies had come to argue in favour of the formation of another coalition government, a "National Government," to address the contingencies of economic crisis.

The storm had been brewing for some time. In the heady days of the "Laurier boom" prior to the First World War, railway competition emerged from the Canadian Northern, which was promoted by the famously optimistic duo of William Mackenzie and Donald Mann and supported by Western Canadian political figures interested in lowering freight rates and who shared Mackenzie and Mann's unbounded expectations of western growth.[6] The Grand Trunk also expanded westward through the Grand Trunk Pacific to compete with the CPR.[7] After these competing interests fell into financial disrepair, they were consolidated into a nationalized railway system. The state was thus cast by the 1920s as a competitor to the CPR – the very corporation it had historically nurtured. More than this, the basis of the political economy from which the CPR had grown had been eroded since the First World War. Immigration dried up, as did British capital, and railways began to encounter competition from trucking. The Great Depression did even more to upset the situation; the collapse of the wheat economy significantly decreased railway traffic, farmers vacated marginal lands, and overall retrenchment made it difficult to raise the capital necessary for the operation of railway facilities. As this financial strain was placed upon both railway systems, Beatty discovered that "politics," which had been so skillfully managed by the CPR in the past, had become a significant hindrance to its aims. Unable to wield the desired influence through the traditional channels of the party system, Beatty sought alternatives.

This chapter offers a case study of Beatty and his activism surrounding the railway question as well as his broader efforts to shape public opinion on important questions concerning the role of the state in society. More broadly, it is a case study of St James Street's attempt to shore up the old political economy of the National Policy period, in which the CPR had played a central role, expanding the British Empire and consolidating a transcontinental nation. It takes us into the smoke-filled rooms of elite social clubs, the at-home meetings between political and business leaders, the luxurious train cars in which Beatty and others of comparable standing travelled: it was in these sites of class exclusion where political initiatives were hatched to create a world more friendly to private enterprise. The fundamental failure of these initiatives throws light upon the waning political effectiveness of the Canadian bourgeoisie during the Great Depression. Moreover, it was part of a broader political failure that signalled the decline and eventual fall of the old political economy of the National Policy period, and the relative decline of the CPR itself; although, the railway's political clout remained sufficient to ensure that it not become too seriously targeted for nationalization. After the First World War, the presidency of the CPR retained a commanding social prestige that came with the virtual assurance of a lordship or knighthood – along with commensurate economic power. Beatty, as one commentator noted in the late 1920s, "was the man with the world's biggest job."[8] Despite this, Beatty's political efforts during the interwar period failed to come to fruition, and he embraced a *mentalité* that evinced growing ideological isolation and hostility to the prevailing currents of political change. Given his commanding position on St James Street, Beatty's political failure was of central importance to the restructuring of the nation's economic elite; the presidency of the CPR would never regain the prestige it lost during these years. The dominion of capital was undergoing a historic change.

Born into the CPR

Edward Beatty was born in Thorold, Ontario in 1877. His father, Henry, who emigrated from Northern Ireland to join his brothers in southern Ontario at the age of ten, had made a small fortune in the 1860s while still in his thirties by operating a hardware store in California during the Gold Rush and later staking claim to a gold deposit in Cariboo, British Columbia. Henry Beatty returned to Thorold in 1864 with $40,000 and joined his brother's steamship line operating on the Great Lakes and later formed a separate line for himself. In 1869 Henry wed Harriet M. Powell, a relative of the Massey family, already well-known manufacturers of farm implements; three children were born of the couple before Edward, the youngest, arrived. By the time the second CPR syndicate was formed in 1880, Henry Beatty had established himself as the preeminent shipper on Lake Superior and was contracted to ship equipment for the CPR while construction of the railway proceeded. He eventually sold his shipping fleet to the CPR and joined its ranks as manager of lake transportation, gaining 1,000 shares in the process. Some commentators have claimed that Beatty, a lifelong bachelor, married the CPR; but one could just as easily have said that he was born into it.[9]

Accounts of Beatty's early life suggest a rigid, quintessentially Victorian upbringing. Beatty's strict father moved the family to Toronto in 1887 apparently to allow his children access to better educational opportunities. (His sister was one of the University of Toronto's earliest female graduates.) Beatty attended that bastion of educational elitism, Upper Canada College, as well as the Model School, Harbord

Collegiate, Parkdale Collegiate Institute, and for a time he studied under the instruction of a private tutor. D.H. Miller-Bartow, author of the only book-length biography on Beatty, published in 1951, wrote that "the variety of schooling was, in at least one instance, encouraged by the polite suggestion from a principal that 'he might do better elsewhere.'"[10] Fonder of physical play than book reading, Beatty achieved mediocre academic standing at the University of Toronto but managed to graduate with a degree in political science in 1898. Beatty was more at home on the rugby field, where he relished rough-and-tumble competition and the male camaraderie of team play; it was here where Beatty met John Hobbs, who became "his closest friend in life" – and an important Toronto business figure.[11] Beatty's athleticism became more legendary with his later success in the business world, and he admitted in 1939 that it was greatly exaggerated: "Honesty compels me to admit ... quite frankly that my athletic career at Toronto – when it was in the making – was far from being a distinguished one."[12] Nonetheless, Beatty continued to devote attention to his physical fitness in later life, running one hour every day, thus paying heed to the physical ideal of the emerging meritocratic style of the wealthy.[13] Obeying his father's injunction that he pursue a career in law or medicine, Beatty trained in the eminent Toronto law offices of McCarthy, Osler, Hoskin and Creelman, one of whose major clients was the CPR, and graduated from Osgoode Hall. Called to the bar in 1901, Beatty left Toronto with one of the partners, A.R. Creelman, to work as his assistant in the legal department of the CPR in Montreal. Beatty worked hard and advanced rapidly within the company, becoming: general solicitor, 1910; general counsel, 1913; vice-president, 1914; and member of the executive committee, 1916. By this time, the aged CPR president Thomas Shaughnessy realized a successor would soon need to be chosen. Passing over general manager and vice-president George Bury, who by seniority and position was the heir apparent, Shaughnessy chose the less senior Beatty, who only a few years earlier was thus described by a friend: "a man who just the other day was a boy, and who still regards life as a game of Rugby."[14] At forty-one years of age Beatty became the youngest president in the CPR's history.[15]

Beatty's rise within the CPR, though a snub to Bury, might have been expected. When Beatty sought to leave the CPR in 1912 to become a partner in W.N. Tilley's prominent Toronto law firm, Shaughnessy asked Beatty into his office. "Beatty," quipped Shaughnessy, "do you want to be an ordinary lawyer all your life, or do you want to be President of the C.P.R.?"[16] Beatty was persuaded to stay. Though he worked his way up the corporate hierarchy through hard work, the path to the presidency had already been cleared by a privileged upbringing and his father's connections with the company. Beatty, indeed, was the last CPR president to control a significant holding in the company itself, courtesy of a multimillion-dollar estate willed to him by his father.[17] He also became connected with an array of institutions that solidified his leadership role within Montreal's economic elite. He was, of course, a member of elite social clubs, such as the exclusive preserve of Montreal's big bourgeoisie, the Mount Royal Club. Founded in 1899 by leading figures of the Bank of Montreal-CPR group who felt "the St. James Club membership had become too broadly inclusive for their tastes, and desired a new and more selective association," the Mount Royal Club, located on Sherbrooke Street, was near the mansions of its capital-rich members in Montreal's "Square Mile," a well-defined elite enclave.[18] Beatty was also appointed chancellor of Queen's University in 1919 before being appointed chancellor of McGill the following year; though he did not perceive a conflict of interest in remaining chancellor of both universities, he resigned from Queen's and would become an unusually active chancellor at McGill, especially in combating academic radicalism during the 1930s.[19] Ideologically, Beatty was much more at home as president of the Boy Scouts of Canada, an organization whose sense of empire and martial spirit resonated with his worldview.

Beatty regarded his rise to prominence through the lens of a worldview that was both meritocratic and elitist. In an interview with journalist Charles Vining in 1927, Beatty reflected upon his rise within the CPR. Claiming he had not entered the CPR with any particular ambition, Beatty explained: "I just kept on working hard at whatever came my way because I liked it. In the first ten years I took ten days' holidays." Failure, Beatty claimed, was most often caused by "grouching" – a negative attitude towards work, a feeling that one's work is not remunerative, "that the men above him are no good." Beatty explained to Vining that success flowed from "intelligent work," but not merely intelligence:

I think personality is more important than brains. A great deal of business in this world depends on personal relations and the man who can meet another man with frankness, and with a personality that the other man likes and trusts has advantage over a man who is merely clever. A man who views business as a poker game is wrong from the start. While poker hands – poker faces – are not lacking in some transactions, the poker days of business generally speaking are past. Big business is done now by laying all the cards on the table, and the more open a man can be the better are his chances of getting what he wants.[20]

One succeeded on the basis of "character," that ill-defined marker of social worth, which spawned a surveillance regime in nineteenth-century North America as credit agencies sought to uncover the "real" character of individuals, "recordable by objective, not subjective, means."[21] Beatty believed success generally – and also his personal success – to be the result of vigorous work and a certain élan indicative of "character," which sorted the social order according to merit. "The breaks of the game always go to the better team," Beatty claimed, "and they go also to the better man. Some men seem to start in better circumstances than others, but it is effort which takes advantage of these circumstances, or creates them."[22] He embraced the meritocratic ideals of the period, which explained merit in ill-defined terms of vigour, action, character, and fair play, casting it more as a style than a particular set of skills, and thus portraying the upper class as deserving but also decidedly exclusive, beyond the reach and capacity of those below. In his portrait of Beatty, Vining wrote of no stodgy plutocrat, but a human dynamo. Vining described entering the CPR's head office at Windsor Station to meet Beatty:

you go up in the elevator to the second floor and walk along a city block of corridor to the south side until you see a door numbered 215, with "President" printed on it in plain black letters. At a table beside the door is a young man and you explain yourself ... [W]hen the clock on the wall ticks the hour of your appointment, the young man takes you through the door into a small room where typewriters are nattering politely. There is a second door, and you walk into a large, long room, with portraits on the

walls, high windows, semi-circle big black chairs, [and] thick rug ... Toward the far end of the room, beside a window, is a wide desk.

   ... [S]tanding out in the middle of the door near the desk when I walked
in ... was a man of medium height with slim legs ... and heavy shoul-
ders. He was dressed in plain gray suit and plain white shirt, and he was
standing with feet apart, hands shoved in his pockets, square chin thrust
forward ... appraisal in his eyes. He was ready for me. As he watched me
come into the room to shake hands I felt him say ... "Now, what's this
one like?"

Rather than being entrenched behind a desk like most, explained Vining, Beatty is ready and "eager for things. He goes out to meet them":

Before one gets across the room to him one knows that here is a man
intensely alive, supremely on top of whatever he has to do. Anyone who
goes inside that door must immediately be aware of it.

   Poise of body and challenge of eye are the outward expression of this
vitality. Whether standing or sitting there is a curious hint of alertness
about Mr. Beatty. He does not move quickly, but one feels always he is
ready to do so and in his face is the same readiness and purpose.[23]

Not merely a man, Beatty was emblematic of a new breed of capitalist.[24]

The Challenge of Public Enterprise

He faced new challenges as well. His career as CPR president coincided with the government's expansion into the railway business. The
overbuilt infrastructure of Canada's railway system had been laid before the First World War by aggressive capitalists able to secure financing from mostly British sources. The economic dislocation of the Great
War was substantial: immigration dwindled, capital suddenly dried up,
and revenues fell.[25] Having already forwarded loans to the financially
strapped Canadian Northern and Grand Trunk Pacific systems in 1914,
Prime Minister Robert Borden announced the appointment of a royal
commission to study the problem. The commission's majority report,
authored by Henry Drayton of the Board of Railway Commissioners

and British railway economist W.M. Acworth, was released in May 1917 and, observed historian Ken Cruikshank, "shaped and legitimated the subsequent railway policy of Prime Minister Borden."[26] Coming to fruition in the period between 1917 and 1923, the plans implemented by the Canadian government included nationalization of the Canadian Northern, the Grand Trunk, and the Grand Trunk Pacific, and their consolidation into a larger system, the CNR, which also included the Intercolonial. Two competing national systems thus remained – one publicly owned and the other held by private interests.

The creation of the CNR emerged out a context of significant political realignment, which was felt during the war but was prefigured by changes within the Conservative Party under Robert Borden, party leader since 1901. As John English has shown, Borden sought to reduce the party's traditional dependence upon the CPR by courting party outsiders from Toronto's business elite, including former Liberals who vigorously supported Borden during the decisive "reciprocity election" of 1911.[27] The formation of a Union government in 1917 further disrupted traditional party loyalties, as members of the two main political parties – Conservatives and pro-conscription Liberals – joined hands to form government. Conservative Party stalwart Robert Rogers of Winnipeg, skilled practitioner of "machine politics" and important party organizer, lamented the breakdown of old party loyalties and drew upon his Montreal connections, cultivated "in his long years as principal party organizer," to oppose Borden; the CPR was an eager ally, its executives already made dyspeptic by Borden's railway policy. The Canadian Northern Acquisition Bill was introduced on 1 August 1917 amid objections and threats emanating from CPR quarters; and Lord Shaughnessy reportedly favoured a Liberal victory in the 1917 election.[28] As English has argued, these developments emerged from Borden's broader effort to move Canadian politics beyond localism and slavish partisanship. Furthermore, as John Eagle has shown, Borden's policy of railway nationalization was not merely forced by the contingencies of the time, but had in fact been articulated as early as 1904, and was animated by progressive ideas that advocated a more active, efficient, and nonpartisan state role in the economy.[29] With the contingencies of war pushing Borden forward, the historic link between the Conservative Party and the CPR was profoundly disrupted.

Arthur Meighen, who succeeded Borden as Conservative Party leader in 1920, had been instrumental in carrying forth the government's railway policy and thus made the rift between the CPR and the Conservative Party more lasting.[30] Meighen's "sin" would not be forgiven in Montreal; during the 1921 federal election, Lord Atholstan's Montreal *Star* embarked on an anti-Meighen campaign, including false reports that Meighen planned to move CNR headquarters from Montreal to Toronto. The Montreal "tycoons," associated with the CPR and whose views were articulated by the Montreal *Star*, shifted their strategy and, as political historian Roger Graham noted, "counted on conservative Liberals like [Lomer] Gouin and [Walter G.] Mitchell to dominate the situation at Ottawa"; J.W. Dafoe claimed, following the Liberal victory in the 1921 general election, that Montreal Liberals had worked out a deal with the city's "corporation interests" to press for a settlement of the railway question favourable to the CPR.[31] Beatty's involvement in the anti-Meighen campaign remains unclear, and Meighen later doubted Beatty's active involvement.[32] However, Beatty did publicly attack the government's railway policy at a gathering for British Columbia's lieutenant governor in Victoria in September 1921, and following the Liberal victory, Beatty predictably remained open to working with Prime Minister Mackenzie King.[33]

Conflict over the railway question unfolded during the 1920s, in part as a conflict between competing factions within the national bourgeoisie. Lord Shaughnessy had strenuously opposed railway nationalization as CPR president, and his objections were publicized in 1921, following his retirement. He advanced a plan – which took his name – that presented a scheme whereby the CPR would pool its railway properties with those of the government, while leaving the Grand Trunk as a separate, privately owned system, and also leaving the CPR's non-railway properties (mines, hotels, and so on) out of the pooling agreement. In making his case, Shaughnessy claimed the CNR, as a government-run enterprise, would place a grave financial strain upon the public purse and would lend itself to the perils of "political interference."[34] Government-appointed chairman of the Grand Trunk and stalwart of Toronto's business community, Sir Joseph Flavelle, harboured similar concerns regarding "political interference" in railway management and shared Shaughnessy's general distaste for public enterprise. But the

Shaughnessy plan was even less attractive to him; indeed, Flavelle, as his biographer Michael Bliss has written, "agreed with every Western farmer and every radical politician that a CPR monopoly would be a threat to Canadian democracy."[35] More concretely, Flavelle levelled the criticism that the CPR would inevitably favour its own lines in managing pooled government lines, leaving the government in a perilous situation.[36] In publicly opposing the Shaughnessy plan in 1921, Flavelle was snubbed at the Mount Royal Club and later in the year came under attack from Atholstan in the *Star*'s infamous campaign against Meighen.[37] The attacks were dishonest, rooted in deeper animosities between Montreal and Toronto. In Toronto, figures such as Flavelle and others connected with institutions such as the National Trust Company and the Canadian Bank of Commerce had supported competition to the CPR in the form of the Canadian Northern, which was heavily financed by the Canadian Bank of Commerce. Operating within the Cox family of companies, the financial empire established by Senator George Albertus Cox (1840–1914) in Toronto around the turn of the century, Flavelle and his business associates rivalled the political and economic dominance of the older CPR-led group in Montreal. And, indeed, when the Canadian Northern moved towards the financial abyss and put the Bank of Commerce in a vulnerable situation due to its loans to Mackenzie and Mann and holdings of Canadian Northern stock, it was the Borden government that intervened to steady a situation that otherwise might have threatened to destabilize the bank.[38]

Beatty, aware of this tension, expressed concern to Meighen in 1920 that a portion of the West and Toronto wanted the government to use "every weapon in its power against the Canadian Pacific."[39] The extent to which Borden cultivated support in Toronto had been an annoyance to Montreal's business elite and had been made tangible with the appointment of Thomas White, of National Trust, to the finance portfolio following the Conservative electoral triumph in 1911.[40] Support for the CNR was much greater in Toronto than in Montreal. That a government-run railway was safeguarding Canada from a private monopoly was not the ideal for many Toronto businessmen, but state ownership was not foreign to them either and was, indeed, more advanced in their province, where power generation was government run, than in Quebec, where Sir Herbert Holt sat atop the field.[41]

With Meighen still leader of the Conservatives and the 1925 general election approaching, St James Street continued to hope to influence public policy through the Liberals. At Beatty's Montreal home in July, King met with Beatty, Royal Bank president Sir Herbert Holt, and Bank of Montreal president Sir Vincent Meredith. After dinner the group adjourned to the verandah room to discuss "the Rys & when & how to deal with the situation." Beatty and King agreed it best to remain noncommittal on railway matters until after the election, and Beatty suggested the spectre of railway "amalgamation" be avoided in public discussion. Beatty believed King "needed a majority to tackle the subject." King gratified his hosts by asserting his resolve not to allow "cut throat or reckless competition" to persist in the face of mounting deficits. King also agreed that some form of "unified control" might be implemented and seemed to please the powerful Montreal trio. Heading back to his hotel after the meeting, King asked Holt if he could count on their support. King recorded Holt's response: "He said that he cld not get into active political arena tho' ... I had 'sympathy' in full measure. I shall be greatly surprised if the C.P.R., Bank of Montreal & Royal Bank do not use their influence to see we gain a majority."[42] Masterful politicking it was, rich with the carefully deployed ambiguity and subtle misrepresentation that was to make King such an effective politician.

King's administration, however, had not shown any sign of bending much in the CPR's direction. Indeed, his government implemented Borden's railway legislation, passing the Canadian National Railways Act of 1919, and appointed an outstanding executive, Sir Henry Thornton, to the helm of the CNR in 1922. Thornton was a U.S.-born railway executive and engineer by background who had moved up the corporate hierarchy of the Pennsylvania Railroad before taking a general manager's position with the Great Eastern Railway in England, at the time the world's largest commuter system. After the outbreak of war, Thornton's technical knowledge was drawn upon in the British war effort as he was cast into the role of inspector-general for the British Expeditionary Forces and made "responsible for operation of the whole intricate system upon which the existence of the British line depended."[43] Embracing advanced views on unions and labour relations, Thornton was respected by Great Eastern Railway employees and was a personal friend of J.H. Thomas, a major figure within Britain's national railway union. It was Thomas who mentioned the CNR position to Thornton – a position that had opened up following the resignation of D.B. Hanna, who resigned in protest over "political interference" in CNR affairs exercised by the recently elected Liberal administration of Mackenzie King. Knighted for his war services, the affable Thornton had gained a reputation as a railway "superman," though his position with the Great Eastern had been extinguished after the government passed legislation to reorganize the British railway system. Thornton was quick to charm the Canadian public as well as CNR employees.[44] Thornton "has quite won the hearts of all who have met him," exclaimed Flavelle.[45] More troubling to Flavelle and moderate progressives such as Dafoe, however, were Mackenzie King's blatant political appointments to the CNR board.[46] This was a departure from Borden's ideal of nonpartisan, businesslike operation. Nonetheless, with Thornton at the helm, the CNR had behind it a power of incalculable importance: popular opinion.

Beatty was quick to see public relations as the most significant challenge facing the CPR.[47] In 1923, encouraged by Beatty's recent public pronouncements, Lord Atholstan commenced his "Whisper of Death" campaign in the Montreal *Star*, which forecast an oncoming deluge resulting from a mounting national debt, made intolerable by costs associated with the CNR.[48] Beatty considered Thornton nothing more than a "showman," and sought to meet his challenge and correct "political misrepresentation" about the railways through an institutional advertising campaign.[49] (Thornton, for his part, considered Beatty "a lawyer [and] not a railway man."[50]) Indicative of this public relations drive, Dafoe reported in the summer of 1925 that "unfair competition invariably comes up" in discussions with high CPR officials; "[t]hey hope for the Shaughnessy plan or a merger."[51] In April, Clifford Sifton reported: "I do not think the Canadian Pacific has ever been as active in propaganda as it is now. Their intrigues and efforts to influence official opinion are in evidence everywhere." Sifton asked Dafoe to have the *Winnipeg Free Press* "declare war on the scheme and fight it out."[52]

This drive had its effect in Ottawa, where a Senate committee was established to investigate the railway question in 1925. At the committee's closed-door hearings, Beatty and Sir Herbert Holt presented cases for railway amalgamation so similar that a summary of the proceedings described their presentations as one position.[53] The Senate proved particularly responsive to CPR influence, and the committee's report presented an opinion generally in line with Beatty's case, which Beatty himself would reference in arguing for railway unification in the future.[54] Beatty and Holt, as we have seen, met with King the same summer to discuss railway policy, and Beatty continued to press King to leave the door open for railway unification later in the year. But the political bagmen who inhabited the Senate found it easier to embrace railway consolidation than the MPs who counted on popular support in their constituencies. This was somewhat stifling to the aspirations of Beatty and his moneyed allies. With neither major political party embracing his position on the railway question, Beatty remained "neutral" in the 1926 federal election, preferring to support favoured individuals in both major parties.[55]

While Beatty finessed his way around Ottawa, much of the railway battle was being waged in direct business competition, made more lucrative by the boom at the end of the 1920s as the two companies engaged in competition through line extensions, hotel construction, expansion of shipping fleets, and improvements in commuter services. While Beatty advocated consolidation of the two competing systems under private ownership, economic expansion during the 1920s made competition a viable option.[56] Indeed, Beatty reported that $353,346,450 in dividend payments were distributed to common and preferred shareholders during the period from 1918 to 1930, representing 85 per cent of the company's total earnings "after deducting fixed charges and pension fund appropriations."[57] Thornton, meanwhile, modernized the CNR and emerged as a national icon of sorts, emblematic of the possibilities of public enterprise and cooperation between the state, capital, and labour, culminating in Thornton's address at the American Federation of Labor's international convention in 1929 in Toronto, where Thornton proclaimed the beginning of "a new labor era." The "very particular conjunctures of context, character, and circumstance" that underpinned Thornton's rise, as Allen Seager has observed, disintegrated with the arrival of the Great Depression.[58] Thornton would be one of its first and most public victims, a public sacrifice encouraged by Beatty as he moved even deeper into political activism.

The Duff Commission and "the Tragedy of Henry Thornton"

Meighen, Roger Graham has written, "was not spared the intrigues of the Montreal tycoons" as talk that R.B. Bennett would be his successor emerged in early 1926; Bennett was "known to hold more 'business-like' opinions about railway matters" than Meighen, whom Bennett once famously described as "the gramophone of Mackenzie and Mann."[59] Bennett's election as leader of the Conservative Party in 1927 was an encouraging sign and a small victory for Beatty and St James Street. They respected the independently wealthy Bennett, believing him to be above petty politics; they shared his deep sense of loyalty to the British Empire; and they felt assured about his protectionist tariff policies. "St. James Street favours Bennett because of his protectionist policies," wrote Prime Minister King pessimistically before the 1930 election. King also learned that "Beatty was favourable to Bennett's views."[60] The list of Montreal donors to Bennett's campaign, observed historian Larry Glassford, "read like a Who's Who of the Montreal financial and industrial establishment."[61] Formerly the chief western solicitor of the CPR and a major shareholder in the Royal Bank, Bennett's immersion in business and his history with the CPR certainly helped to make him a more reliable candidate for wealthy Montreal residents – but on the campaign trail such connections were a potential liability. With his proclamation "Amalgamation never, competition ever" in a campaign speech, Bennett sounded publicly his independence from Beatty in an attempt to assure western voters that he would not cede a railway monopoly to the CPR.[62] Popular appeal again seemed to trump Beatty's long-term goals. The seeds of future conflict between Bennett and Beatty were planted even before the electoral triumph of the Bennett Conservatives in 1930.[63]

Canada had more railway mileage per capita than any other nation by the 1930s.[64] The financial strain of maintaining two competing national lines had seemingly resolved itself during the boom years of the late 1920s, only to reemerge as a sudden crisis once the economic slump set in. The financial position of the CPR worsened: in the first half of 1931, the CPR reduced dividend payments and soon after suspended payments altogether.[65] Worse still was the position of the CNR, which was already weighed down by an unwieldy capital structure that included old debts accumulated by Mackenzie and Mann and the Grand Trunk. Company earnings fell by $46,249,000, and Thornton attempted cost-cutting measures without implementing wholesale layoffs.[66]

Philosophically opposed to public enterprise, Bennett viewed Thornton as a creature of the King government; and he supported a campaign that conflated Thornton's lavish private lifestyle with his management of the CNR. While in London, England, in October 1930, Prime Minister Bennett wrote his minister of railways and canals, R.J. Manion, about the shopping activities of Thornton's wife: "President's wife here purchasing furniture. President cabled her improvements would cost eighteen thousand dollars and she must spend less for furniture. She says building requires improvements. Whatever action you take entirely satisfactory. I was only desirous [to] communicate casual information."[67] The CNR directors had approved funds for Lady Thornton to furnish their Pine Avenue home "in a manner appropriate for the residence of a president." But, having received this "casual information" from Bennett, Manion reneged on the agreement. Thereupon Sir Henry perceived that "a concerted plot to ruin his personal reputation" was in the works.[68] He pressed Manion in December to honour the agreement that $20,000 in CNR funds be made available for renovations to his house, explaining that he was "very hard up, stock losses, etc." Manion did not bend and described his reply to Bennett: "I told him that if the case came up in the House I wanted to be able to say that we had nothing to do with the matter – that the whole arrangement had been made under the previous administration."[69] Thornton would serve as a sacrificial lamb for the supposed improprieties of the King administration.

The following year the Railway Committee of the House of Commons provided new opportunities to undermine Thornton's public reputation and associate him with the supposedly spendthrift ways of the Liberals. Manion, R.B. Hanson of New Brunswick, and Dr Peter McGibbon, MP for Muskoka-Ontario, were among the most active Conservative members to tar Thornton in the House, citing imprudent company expenditures on hotels, suggesting (falsely) exorbitant company salaries, and drawing attention to Thornton's salary and personal expense account.[70] Though Beatty admitted the unfairness of some of the attacks levelled against Thornton, he also recognized new political opportunities on the horizon.[71]

Upon Beatty's suggestion, a beleaguered Thornton called for the formation of a royal commission to study the railway question.[72] And though Beatty and Holt complained about delays in getting the commission established, the Duff Commission was finally formed in November.[73] Before the commencement of the commission's hearings, Beatty was "very hopeful that something constructive" could be achieved and lauded its personnel as "really outstanding."[74] Chaired by Supreme Court Judge Lyman Duff, the commission included six other prominent figures with weighty business – and some academic – credentials: Joseph Flavelle; Beaudry Leman of Montreal, general manager of the Banque Canadienne Nationale and president of the Canadian Bankers' Association; U.S. railway executive Leonor Fresnel Loree, president of the Delaware and Hudson Railway Company; Lord Ashfield, head of London's underground system, the Metropolitan Railways; Walter Charles Murray, president of the University of Saskatchewan; and the Shediac, New Brunswick, physician John Clarence Webster, a respected Conservative, museum patron, and personal friend of Howard P. Robinson. From his office in Winnipeg, Dafoe reflected upon the significance of the commission's establishment. "Perhaps I am getting too suspicious in my old age," he wrote *Free Press* correspondent John A. Stevenson, "but I have a most decided 'hunch' that this Commission was appointed to do a particular chore, and that with perhaps two exceptions its members know what the chore is to be. I think the linked money powers in Canada and the United States, with all their subordinate and associate interests, have decided that the time is opportune to oblige Canada to remove her desire to own and operate her own railways." Dafoe believed that – as part of this plot to gut the CNR – the same tactic deployed in England to dislodge the Labour government might be deployed in Canada: "National Government."[75]

Had Dafoe become "too suspicious" in old age? Not entirely. The ever-domineering Bennett had taken a personal interest in the formation of the commission and appeared to be in closer contact with St James Street than the responsible minister, Manion. *Winnipeg Free Press* correspondent Grant Dexter reported on 15 November that Manion was in "complete ignorance" about the commission's personnel, but two weeks earlier a private memorandum written by Floyd Chalmers of the *Financial Post* revealed that Sir Herbert Holt was up to date

on recent developments in the selection of commission personnel. "I
want to take back anything about believing that amalgamation is off,"
wrote Dexter.[76] Meanwhile, Thornton's experience at the hands of the
Conservatives had led him to an about-face: in a meeting with Dafoe at
Winnipeg's Fort Garry Hotel on 12 October, Thornton lamented that he
had lost faith in the ideal of public enterprise – the CNR, in the interest of its own survival, would have to come under the control of some
form of unified management along with the CPR. He told Dafoe that
he and Beatty had been working on such a plan together, a fact later
confirmed by Lady Thornton.[77] After Thornton's death, his biographer,
D'Arcy Marsh, would write (in 1934) that Thornton had been made
"constitutionally incapable" of opposing Beatty, and Dexter believed
that Thornton had sold out to Beatty to save his job.[78] Dafoe, Marsh,
and Dexter were overly cynical in assessing Thornton's actions. And
though Dafoe's suspicions had some basis, he greatly exaggerated the
level of coordination between Bennett and Beatty.

   The proceedings of the Duff Commission commenced on 4 December 1931 with the commissioners interviewing Sir Henry Thornton in a
session closed to the public – as was the testimony of all senior railway
and government officials. Thornton proposed the establishment of a
ten-person "superboard," consisting of the presidents of each railway
company, two Liberal, two Conservative, and two Progressive representatives, a representative of labour, and a representative of the minister of railways and canals.[79] Though Dafoe and others, not privy to his
testimony at the time, might have considered it something of a sellout,
such judgments are overly harsh.[80] Thornton believed the board, which
would oversee both railways and enforce cooperation, would be able
to conciliate various interest groups, and his plan thus attempted to
establish a mechanism whereby a form of democratic control over the
management of the country's railways would obtain. It was Thornton's
embrace of the principle of democratic control that set him apart from
Beatty – and here Thornton was steadfast. The very goal of exercising
democratic control over Canada's railway systems was thought dubi-
ous by commission members, however. Commissioner Loree asked
CNR vice-president S.J. Hungerford whether "it be a fair statement to
make that a democratic form of government is no competent agency to
carry on the railroad business?" To Hungerford's assertion that "[w]e

are seeking to do it," Loree replied: "But are they doing it? The records do not show they are, because they are going behind every year."[81]

With the questioning at times threatening to transgress the line of gentlemanly decorum, Thornton stressed that management of the CNR was a matter of public policy and thus did not necessarily need to justify itself on the basis of profits and losses. In response to a statement by Joseph Flavelle that such an enterprise should not be maintained, ·Thornton asserted that it was "a matter for the Canadian people to decide."[82] Beatty appeared before the commission the next day and presented a case that was ideologically much easier for the commissioners to appreciate. "If, on one hand, the privately owned system finds it is unable to maintain its credit in an unequal struggle with the long purse of the state," Beatty said before the commission, "a grave injustice will be done to the shareholders of a corporation which has fulfilled its fifty-year old contract with the nation, and which has made its full contribution to the upbuilding [sic] of the Dominion. Such a consummation would cause most serious injury to the reputation of this young country as a field for private capital."[83] The cases of Beatty and Thornton differed at a fundamental level, centring not only on the appropriate role of the state in the nation's economic life but on the appropriate role of public opinion in shaping economic policy. Beatty opposed government intervention, except in a helping role to private capital – steamship subsidies and protective tariffs, for example (which the CPR benefited from). He was also generally dismissive of popular opinion. Thornton, he believed, had succeeded by "showmanship" and "mob appeals."[84] The deluded public, in Beatty's estimation, deserved only a very limited role in deciding public policy, and, as we shall see, he turned to "educational" work to address this issue. Thornton, by contrast, accepted some degree of "political" interference in economic affairs as inevitable under any democratic government. "After all in any form of popular government it must be accepted as axiomatic that the business of government is politics and," Thornton stated before the commission on 4 January 1932, "irrespective of whether one likes it or not, politics is something with which a government must reckon in all its activities."[85]

Though commission members disliked the idea of public influence over railway management, a view that would be plainly expressed in their report, they were at least equally concerned with the prospect of leaving the nation's railways in the hands of a private monopoly. Beatty proposed a "unification" plan of the two systems under CPR management that would maintain separate ownership: CPR personnel would act as trustees of the government's property. Commissioners Flavelle and Loree expressed concern over the de facto monopoly that Beatty's plan would create.[86] (Beatty privately dismissed Flavelle's business philosophy, which stressed the role of competition, as "the Flavelle school of ruthless business brutality."[87]) Commissioner Webster was somewhat less worried about monopoly. "The fear of monopoly did not terrify me, as it so strongly impressed Sir Joseph," he wrote to Meighen in November 1932, "nor did I shrink from submitting the responsibility of conducting so great an undertaking to a single management."[88] Beatty did not try to hide the monopoly implications of his plan but rather defended the principle of monopoly itself, arguing that "some of the most efficient, most widely administered and most public-spirited public corporations on this continent are monopolies." "They are in the main," he continued, "successful, efficient and progressive, and they are administered by men of high character and great ability."[89] For Beatty, who believed business enterprise to be a form of public service, the most important factor was the quality of business leadership. Since management would be composed of "business statesmen of the highest type," he did not believe the "question of autocracy" could arise.[90]

Beatty appeared before the commission again on 19 February and presented a memorandum outlining the benefits of unification, in which he reiterated the need to impose businesslike management over the country's railways. Asked by commissioner Loree whether a board of directors consisting of CPR and government representatives might successfully manage a unified system, Beatty foresaw two problems. First, the government would be exercising too much active influence in railway matters; second, government involvement would render "doubtful the type [of individuals] that would be selected for appointment to the Board."[91] Such an arrangement could only be successful if independence from the government were established; Beatty suggested an independent tribunal might select government representatives from "the Canadian Bankers Association, the Canadian Chamber of Commerce and a Judge of the Supreme Court" and be "certain to get the type of men whose ability would justify the selection."[92] Beatty's formulations were latently elitist and antidemocratic: "quality" leadership was presumed to reside in the upper echelons of the business community, and management of the railway system could not be entrusted to any other segment of the population – indeed, it was necessary to insulate such leadership from the pressures of popular opinion. According to Beatty's beliefs, efficient railway policy required that it not be formulated outside the meritocratic order that decided success or failure in private enterprise; "political" interference was unacceptable. Beatty was not unique in this mindset; the commission's report echoed similar sentiments.

The commission's proceedings prefaced Thornton's final fall from grace in public life. Thornton had been divorced and quickly remarried (to a much younger woman) several years earlier, and he was known to enjoy nightlife. These were not important problems while the CNR was operating at a profit, but once that changed, Thornton's personal life was conflated with his management style to devastating effect. He managed the railway the way he lived, his detractors claimed. Called once again before the House of Commons to testify, the gentlemanly decorum of the commission hearings evaporated, Thornton was subjected to a verbal assault by R.B. Hanson.[93] Thornton's public tarring eroded his political support in the House of Commons. Teetotaller, opposition leader, and political acrobat Mackenzie King acquiesced to this portrayal of Thornton, writing in his diary: "The truth is Thornton has not measured up of late, has drunk too much – far too self-indulgent."[94] Thornton would later write to King that he had departed from Ottawa under the auspices of a "reign of terror," "always 'shadowed' by a detective."[95] "The Canadian Pacific Ry. has ... exercised a sinister influence in Canadian politics – It has never hesitated at bribing + corruption in all its forms and it represents the worst type of predatory capitalism," Thornton wrote to King the following day. "It has ruined men."[96] Undoubtedly, Thornton counted himself among the "ruined men": "I feel fairly certain I might have remained where I was had I cared to go along with Beatty."[97]

The Conservative Party was the real victor, however, and its members were those most active in associating Thornton's supposedly spendthrift ways with King's Liberal administration – although Thornton's reputation was defended publicly by the left-leaning *Canadian*

Forum.[98] The Bennett government advanced its solution to the railway question in a private member's bill, put before the Senate by Arthur Meighen in October, which incorporated the recommendations of the Duff Commission. Beatty was quick to voice disapproval. Meighen, whom Bennett had appointed to the Senate in 1932, delivered a speech on behalf of the Railway Bill that Beatty described as "innocuous." "The Duff Report is nothing more than a futile gesture and the more one visualizes the possibilities of working it out in any justice," Beatty complained to Bennett, "the more discouraged he must be."[99] Beatty's most emphatic objection centred on the third section of the bill, which sought to establish an arbitral tribunal to enforce cooperation between the railways. Beatty claimed this feature of the bill constituted an attack upon the CPR's property rights.[100] In December, Beatty reiterated this position to Wall Street's Ernest Iselin, reassuring Iselin that "our Directors are unanimous that we must take all reasonable means to prevent interference by any tribunal, [*sic*] appointed by the Government." "Of course," explained Beatty, "the only logical solution is unification ... With a little courage on the part of our Government the thing can be arranged without undue delay."[101] Meighen dismissed Beatty's concern about the prospective violation of CPR property rights, but F.C. Goodenough of Barclays Bank warned Beatty in March 1933 that the prospect of a tribunal intervening in the company's affairs would reflect poorly upon the CPR "in the eyes of the London Market."[102] Beatty and the CPR succeeded in having Duff's recommendation for a "statutory duty of cooperation" watered down to a mere recommendation by the time the bill was made into law; but Beatty's intricate plan to use the Senate to fight for amalgamation was resisted by the leader of the Senate and no favourtive of Beatty's – Arthur Meighen.[103]

National Government

Snow flurries were carried through the streets of Toronto by a crisp northeast wind on 16 January 1933, when a well-to-do crowd gathered in the plush interior of the Royal York Hotel under the auspices of the Canadian Club of Toronto to hear Beatty speak. While the substantial means of audience members assured their physical protection from outside elements, a more profound – yet less tangible and puzzling – sort

of storm was making itself felt in the world economy. This was troubling. Beatty proclaimed to his audience that "we ... are faced with a
railway problem more gravely vital to Canada's future than at any other
time." Not only was the country's railway system wasteful, it stood
to undermine Canada's credit and dissuade investment. Public enterprise and government intervention – with the concomitant increase in
taxation – worsened matters further, according to Beatty. Retrenchment, balanced budgets, self-reliance: the old ethics of private enterprise were key to economic recovery. The adjustments necessary with
regard to the railway question, Beatty told his audience, could "only
be attained if we consolidate our two railways into one system with
one management."[104] Beatty effectively assimilated old liberal ethics to
the demands of monopoly capital – and thus began Beatty's renewed
campaign for railway unification, a campaign that was already transforming into a broader drive for National Government. King noted in his
diary four days earlier that Quebec Liberal premier, Louis-Alexandre
Taschereau, had said in private that Beatty had been "sounding him out
on Nat'l Government"; on 14 January, King addressed the Garrison
Club in Quebec City, where he spoke out against the principle of National Government.[105]

Beatty's Toronto speech, observed the Toronto *Globe* several days
later, "has obviously been accepted by leading Canadian newspapers as
the opening gun in a Canadian Pacific Railway Campaign to absorb the
Canadian National."[106] Editorial commentary across the country was
mostly critical of Beatty's speech, though in numerous cases apprecia-
tive of his call for economy in government expenditures. The *Globe*
criticized Beatty's plan because it would leave the liabilities of the
CNR with the government while handing over its assets to the CPR. "It
requires no colorful imagination to conceive the public reaction," noted
the *Globe*, which deemed Beatty's plan to be "politically impossible."
Though perhaps "politically impossible," the *Globe* suggested that Beatty was garnering formidable support; it reported that "[m]any influential men in and out of Parliament are supporting him with a vigor that
suggests the belief that it is 'now or never.'"[107] Senior Liberal strategist
Norman Rogers explained to King on 23 January that "Mr. Beatty is
obviously preparing the public mind of Canada for what he is looking
forward to during the coming session." Rogers believed, however, that

in view of widespread hatred of the CPR among the public, Beatty's best bet would be to lay low.[108] But Beatty had already tried that tactic to less-than-desired effect. He continued to take his message public, to Winnipeg in February. Not only was the pubic unmoved but the wider business community remained sceptical; sawmill operator John F. McMillan of Edmonton was unimpressed by both performances, characterizing them as attempts to "camouflage his stock-holders."[109] The government was also leery. The minister of railways and canals, Manion, expressed the view in late January that "no government could win an election now by supporting the Beatty plan ... There were 200,000 railway workers and their families who would vote to save their jobs." But Manion thought public opinion might shift if the financial situation worsened or was more fully recognized by the public. He also admitted that a National Government might succeed in implementing a "necessary but unpopular" railway plan.[110]

Beatty did not neglect his behind-the-scenes political work either. And he recognized that, in the Bennett government, the prime minister was the centre of power; when Floyd Chalmers asked Manion whether the government had formulated a railway policy, Manion responded that he did not know because he had not spoken with Bennett about it, nor did he know what Bennett really thought.[111] Four days after his Toronto speech, Beatty followed up a telephone conversation with Bennett on the railway situation with a letter explaining his belief "that among the substantial men of Canada, including those who form what we call the business community, the sentiment is rapidly growing that some more drastic remedy than that recommended by the Duff Commission is essential to the wellbeing of the country." Beatty argued that "drastic" measures might carry political rewards: "if we can evolve something which will effect definite economies in the next two or three years, the public re-action to any such system will be good, and if it is attended by no reduction in essential public services and the saving to the country is apparent, we should expect great public support to the Government's policies."[112] Bennett was not convinced; but Beatty remained relatively close to him during this period. Beatty, for example, attempted to help mediate a disagreement between Bennett and the Montreal *Gazette*, which first began when the *Gazette* criticized Bennett's decision to appoint his brother-in-law, W.D. Herridge, as Canada's ambassador in Washington. Though the *Gazette*, controlled by Smeaton White and John W. Bassett, "was anxious to carry on the fight," it was held in check because "[i]mportant financial interests in Montreal," upon which the *Gazette* depended, were "friendly" towards Bennett.[113] Later a dispute arose between Beatty and Bennett, but Beatty could not afford an open breach because the CPR's "directors would not stand for it."[114] Economic and political ties at the upper stratum of Canadian business and political life helped quiet disputes. Bennett's policies were not ideal, but the consensus on St James Street was that he was the best of a bad lot.

Though speculation emerged in late 1931 that Bennett was considering the formation of a National Government, nothing came of it, and the evidence suggests that Bennett distanced himself from such propositions over the next couple of years.[115] Beatty and his moneyed friends took the initiative, signalled by his Toronto speech. By this time, those favouring a National Government included Beatty (CPR), Sir Charles Gordon (Bank of Montreal), Sir Herbert Holt (Royal Bank of Canada), and Ross McMaster (Stelco): the very apex of economic power in Canada, and all CPR directors. H.J. Symington, a CNR executive with experience in both the West and St James Street, attended a dinner in March with the "mighty" in Montreal; conversation swung towards railway amalgamation and National Government, with the likes of Sir Arthur Currie, Ross McMaster, and Jackson Dodds (of the Bank of Montreal) expressing themselves in favour of the idea. "Some remark was made which aroused the couple cocktails which were under my belt and I opened out on the astonished gentlemen," explained Symington in private correspondence. He offered prescient advice: "I told the bankers that they had better stop trying to manage everybodys [*sic*] business except their own, or somebody else was going to manage theirs. I told them that amalgamation of the railways was at present impossible and it was time they read the signs; that a national government was extremely unlikely and for railway purposes impossible."[116]

Sir Arthur Currie, who at the time was serving under Beatty as principal of McGill University, was not dissuaded. He came out in favour of National Government on 1 March in a speech in Hull.[117] Mackenzie King viewed Currie's speech as "part of a CPR & Bank of Montreal plan, [*sic*] to help in the Railway situation."[118] Prime Minister Bennett was also not impressed, complaining to party bagman (and former Unionist Liberal) Senator C.C. Ballantyne that Sir Arthur's speech, published in the Montreal *Gazette*, was being interpreted in the United States as a sign of the inevitability of a Conservative defeat in the next election.[119] Later in March, Beatty broached the idea with King in a telephone conversation, where he "spoke about building up nat'l govt around a few men." Beatty said to King, "financial conditions were such as to make great reduct'ns necessary" and explained, "change wd have to come in a year or two." King responded that combining the two major parties would only make matters worse by immediately giving official opposition status to the recently formed CCF; but Beatty viewed National Government as a bulwark against the unchecked spread of socialism.[120] Beatty worked flexibly between the two parties, though ideologically he was closer to Bennett. Dafoe, no friend of Bennett, hit the mark when he explained: "Bennett is no chore boy of the big interests though the cast of his mind makes him do things which strengthen this estimate of him."[121]

Beatty became a more strident advocate of railway unification as the CPR's position worsened and as it became apparent that no political party was willing to embrace the policies he believed were required to solve the nation's transportation and financial problems. His New Year's message to Bennett for 1934 encouraged the prime minister to disregard a public that remained suspicious of CPR influence over the government.[122] Beatty saw new political opportunity in the crisis: "There is no gratitude in an easily misled hoi polloi but it may be that the weight of the country's obligations, for which you are not responsible, will ultimately enable you to take drastic actions with the full support of our sounder citizens."[123] In a pro-amalgamation speech in Montreal in May 1934, Beatty explained: "Heretofore all our transportation problems have been settled under political or community pressure. The present situation must, I take it, be dealt with from the standpoint of sound national economics and from no other angle."[124] That "political or community pressure" was inimical to "sound national economics" was self-evident to Beatty, who preferred political guidance from those whom he euphemistically described as "our sounder citizens." The belief that sound decision making was beyond the capabilities of the masses was not untypical in North America and Western

Europe, where the propaganda campaigns of the Great War and the ascendance of the advertising industry in the 1920s underscored the belief among political and business leaders that public opinion was irrational and susceptible to manipulation.[125] The public relations problems of the CPR were, of course, aggravated by the fact that, as reported by the *Globe* in 1930, it was "widely known that the largest holding of [CPR] stock [was] in England, [and] the next largest in the U.S." – Canada being only third.[126] The large amount of non-Canadian investment in the CPR was just one of many political hurdles facing Beatty, whose ideas and strategies were shared by many of his social peers.

Already by this time Beatty had come to the belief that government spending needed to be drastically reduced to meet the economic crisis, despite the fact that popular opinion was moving in the opposite direction.[127] Believing quite literally that "what's good for the C.P.R. is good for Canada," Beatty's elitist dismissal of popular opinion was not at all inconsistent with nationalism as he understood it.[128] He regularly used adjectives such as *thinking* and *reliable* to describe Canadians capable of formulating public policy, indicative of the fact that he believed many were not capable of such responsibilities. Beatty pushed for the linked aims of railway amalgamation and National Government to save the nation from itself. National Government would provide the nation with "strong" leadership; a coalition of the two major parties could pass "necessary but unpopular" legislation that no party government interested in re-election would touch. Dunning, as we have seen, thought of a prospective National Government as a sort of suicide pact between eminent citizens willing to pursue policies that would result in their immediate political deaths but that would secure their glory in the long term, once the populace came to appreciate the necessity of the actions it formerly dreaded (see chapter 2). This was the dilemma of democratic governance for an economic elite that felt it knew better than everyone else.

Bennett's falling popularity, an approaching general election, and growing concern about national solvency seemed to renew the political opportunities of National Government advocates. In September 1934, the *Globe* reported the commencement of a National Government campaign led by "Montreal and Toronto financial interests" in anticipation of next year's election. The unnamed supporters of the movement were said to believe "that only a coalition of all the parties in Canada can

clean up the railway mess"; but the *Globe* astutely noted "the difficulty of inducing any prominent Liberal to join a Union Government"
– made worse by Mackenzie King's certainty of a Liberal triumph in
the next election – was the major obstacle facing National Government
supporters. To make matters worse, the demand for railway unification
– "largely [coming] from the big interests of Montreal" – would not
likely receive any support from the Liberals, who were "opposed to any
plan to dispose of the Canadian National Railways."[129]

Though the National Government campaign was a long shot, it was
beginning to receive more serious consideration in Conservative circles. Bennett and C.C. Ballantyne had been offended by Currie's call
for National Government in March 1933; but by November 1934, Bennett had already made inquiries about its viability, and Ballantyne, an
influential Montreal businessman himself, had come around to the belief that King and Lapointe might be convinced to join a national administration if Bennett were to "place the cold hard facts" of "Canada's
serious financial condition" before them.[130] Beatty wrote Bennett later
that month to warn him that the worst of the economic slump might still
be on its way and recommended the formation of National Government
to meet the impending emergency. "I know, of course," explained Beatty, "that thinking men, forming as they do such a small portion of our
population, have little influence in shaping important national policies,
but I feel that at the earliest opportunity I should transmit these views
for your consideration."[131]

The spectre of national insolvency had already been presented to
Bennett in the summer of 1934, when he was in London, England, par-
ticipating in the World Economic Conference. Governor of the Bank of
England, Montagu Norman, reportedly warned Bennett "that Canada
was heading towards national insolvency," and if nothing was done
"about the railway problem it would break the country." Bennett reported his conversation to Ontario's Conservative lieutenant governor,
Herbert A. Bruce, in Toronto upon his return to Canada. Bruce claimed
to have replied: "why don't you do something about the railway problem? You know what ought to be done." Bennett, according to Bruce's
recollection several years later, agreed that something could be done
if a National Government were formed. Bennett authorized Bruce to
convey a message to Mackenzie King offering the position of prime

minister and selection of half the cabinet in a National Government administration with Bennett, "the understanding to be that the first problem to be tackled would be the railway problem."[132] The need to solve
the railway question did not just press upon wealthy Montrealers, but
was also felt in Toronto; and broader political and ideological fault
lines created the basis for the promotion of shared goals between the
two dominant centres of economic power, which would carry into the
formation of the Leadership League, spearheaded by *Globe and Mail*
president and publisher C. George McCullagh in 1939, which Beatty
encouraged and applauded, and with which Bruce was actively associated.[133] In 1934 Bruce approached Liberal organizer Vincent Massey to
convey the National Government scheme to King, but Massey refused,
explaining "King simply would not consider a union government when
he sees victory staring him in the face."[134] Bennett's sense of operating
within the British Empire seemed to recommend the formation of a
National Government: "We are the only part of the Empire without a
National Government and it well might be that such an administration
would serve a great purpose at this time," observed Bennett in December. Then Bennett asked rhetorically, "is it feasible?" No, Bennett
concluded – not "with the Liberal Party in its present state of mind."[135]

As rumblings for National Government began to reach the public, Beatty turned his attention to an uncooperative Mackenzie King.
He seemed to hope to ingratiate himself with King. On 29 September, aboard the train from Ottawa to Montreal, Beatty spoke with King
for a couple of hours. King's victory in the upcoming election was a
foregone conclusion, said Beatty, assuring King that he had the confidence of "the business interests" – the same comment and compliment
having been applied by Beatty to Bennett the month before.[136] Beatty
made one request: that King make no pre-election commitment on the
railway question, an obvious attempt to keep the door open for unification, and the same advice he gave King a decade earlier. Arriving in
Montreal, and upon Beatty's invitation, they left Windsor Station to
join Bank of Montreal director Fred Meredith and Canadian-born British banker Sir Edward Peacock for lunch. The results must have been
somewhat disappointing for Beatty. King denounced the principle of
National Government, saying "it only meant two parties doing what
one with a majority would not dare to do & therefore was not right."

"I spoke out against dictatorship in any form," wrote King. Though Beatty agreed the time for National Government had passed, his later activities would prove his comment disingenuous.[137]

Beatty preferred Bennett anyhow. "Bennett continues to stand out, in my judgment," Beatty wrote to Sir Robert Borden in early 1935, "and were it possible for him to get himself into a position where he could tackle our railway problem, I would look forward with a great deal of confidence to the trends of the next five years."[138] Only a month earlier, Grant Dexter claimed that the Bennett government was "unofficially" behind Beatty. Dexter further observed:

> The influence of the whole financial combination – banks, big industrial-ists like Carlyle [Carlisle?], most of the loan and trust coy's etc., has been thrown, unreservedly, behind the Beatty campaign. My contacts lead me to think that most of these people believe that [railway] amalgamation can only be carried out by some national government. The saner of them realize that a national government cannot be put over now.[139]

The pressures of an oncoming election soon intervened, and Bennett was pressured from within the Conservative Party to disassociate him-self from Beatty's railway plans. Conservative MP for Lanark, T.A. Thompson, warned Bennett in February "that the majority of the rail-waymen have the idea that you are backing Mr. Beatty in his amalga-mation programme" – a belief fostered by Liberal party propaganda.[140] Meanwhile, Manion, still minister of railways and canals, pledged late in 1934 to an audience at Smiths Falls, Ontario, that the Conservative Party was in favour of maintaining the CNR and railway competition, prompting Beatty to complain to Bennett: "I cannot understand why Dr. Manion should be permitted to hobble your freedom of action in his treasure hunt for votes – votes which I doubt if he will secure by his method."[141]

The stresses of the Depression were polarizing the left and right wings of the Conservative Party, and a fissure was exposed in the sum-mer, when H.H. Stevens left Conservative ranks to form the Recon-struction Party. On the other side, Meighen – once viewed as akin to a Bolshevik in Montreal financial circles for his role in establishing the CNR – was moving towards Beatty's position.[142] This transformation was also reflected in Borden's private retrospective admission to Beatty regarding the railway question: "I was not sufficiently in touch with conditions, political, economic and otherwise, to form a correct judgment, but it did seem to me that two or three years ago the situation might have been gripped effectively."[143] Borden and Meighen – and other more consistently right-leaning Conservatives such as C.H. Cahan – were sufficiently committed to an old liberal outlook to privilege balanced budgets over other more popular ideas. The drive to preserve the days of small government – through the reduction of democratic constraints in politics – was much more widespread within Canadian big business than has been commonly admitted by Canadian historians.[144]

Beatty conceptualized National Government as a spontaneous, patriotic response to the economic crisis, but it was a campaign politically limited by its close association with the big bourgeoisie.[145] Indeed, Beatty seemed impervious to the widespread unpopularity of railway unification; he delivered numerous addresses on the subject in 1935, and he continued to articulate elitist, antidemocratic sentiments. At an event organized by the Kiwanis Club in Montreal in honour of the recently knighted Sir Charles Lindsay, Beatty defended the dispensation of titles and questioned the spread of democracy. As fascism threatened to spread further in Europe, he oddly explained: "We have a great deal of democracy in the world just now, and some of us are inclined to think we have too much democracy and are losing our sense of dignity and our regard for those things upon which we have been accustomed to rely for steadying influence throughout this country." He continued: "We have a way of saying, quite untruthfully, that all men are equal, and that the appreciation of our fellows is the highest honor that can be offered any man, but unfortunately it is not always expressed, and it is no great satisfaction to a man to have a large funeral. I believe that these things must be done to a man while he is still alive and among his fellows."[146] Months later Beatty also received, upon Bennett's recommendation, a knighthood.

In 1935 National Government became part of the public discourse. The League for National Government was formed by a group of more than 100 businessmen in Toronto, although at its founding meeting in March the organization explicitly distanced itself from St James Street and CPR influence. Meanwhile, in Montreal the *Star* and *Gazette* lauded the National Government idea, and Beatty and Sir Herbert Holt reportedly offered H.H. Stevens $3 million to lead a National Government campaign.[147] Montreal financier Ward Pitfield tried to interest Stevens in heading up a National Government movement in April, and though Stevens expressed some interest, he concluded the movement would not be viable for lack of Liberal support.[148] On 12 March, as we have seen in chapter 2, the *Globe* published a sensational story announcing plans to have Charles Dunning take over for Bennett to form a National Government. "The architects of a Union Administration to save Canada for the big interests have their headquarters on St. James Street," claimed the *Globe*.[149] It was the first thing discussed in Liberal caucus the next day. King reported: "I learned that Beatty, Sir Charles Gordon, Molson & one or two other of the financial magnates of Montreal had asked Tom Ahearn (as Director of the Bank of Montreal) to seek to get me to consent to something of the kind ... There is no doubt that they (Montreal) have been attempting to effect a press campaign towards that end." Although King was certain they would accept him as head of a coalition government, he and the Liberal caucus rejected the idea and decided to remain aloof on the question until calls for National Government blew over.[150]

It was a moot project so long as King remained aloof. Beatty appealed to King to consider National Government once again, in June. As in 1933, King rebuked the idea, believing it to be the cloak of an incipient dictatorship that would result in the formation of "an extreme radical party, which would capture everything in the face of the so-called union of the old political parties."[151] A month and a half later, King publicly opposed the idea of National Government in a radio address carried nationwide by the Canadian Radio Broadcasting Commission. His speech, no doubt, was intended to conjure up Beatty's image in the listener's mind in what was a cogent, though somewhat sensational and undoubtedly opportunist, critique of the National Government idea. "I do not doubt the sincerity of many of those who are its advocates," King conceded before delving into the crux of the matter:

> but, with all due respect, to those who are advocating it, as undoubtedly some are, from ulterior motives, I do doubt their understanding of

government and of the value of freedom of discussion, of argument, and reason, and persuasion, as being of the very essence of our parliamentary system.

Traced to its source – the source that is financing the present movement – it will, I believe, be found that the demand for National Government is a last desperate effort on the part of certain persons, enjoying privileges denied to others, to deal with the railways, the tariffs, and taxation, in a manner which will serve to further their own special interests.

Under the guise of submerging partisanship, and gaining political unity for public service, it would seek to do, by combination of parties, things which no single party would dare ask public approval.

In plain English, national government, if established at this time, would sacrifice democracy to serve the ends of plutocracy.[152]

Thus King styled himself as the upholder of Canada's parliamentary tradition, warding off the plutocrats – Beatty being probably the public figure most associated with the term in Canada during the 1930s – who were intent on having their way.

As Beatty attempted to achieve railway unification through National Government, his opponents recognized that democratic governance was their primary defence. The Mount Royal Division of the Canadian Brotherhood of Railway Employees, for example, proclaimed in March 1935: "Parliament is the chief bulwark of the railway workers and the people of Canada against the proposals which have been made for the amalgamation or unification of the two large railway systems or their component parts."[153] Numerous labour representatives had already spoken before the Duff Commission of "democratic management" of Canada's railways. They refused to accept Beatty's argument that Canada simply could no longer afford it.[154]

During a trip to Vancouver in September, Beatty reported to Senator Smeaton White, owner of the Montreal *Gazette*, that he was pleasantly surprised to find many businessmen hoping for the formation of a National Government.[155] However, Beatty and other likeminded businessmen had largely been reduced to hoping. In September and earlier, Beatty referred numerous times to his hope that the upcoming election would produce a "strong" government. "I am very hopeful," Beatty explained privately, "that a strong Government will emerge from the election, and it even may be a National Government formed from the more conservative elements in our Parliament."[156] By October, the month of the election, hope faded into cynicism. Aghast at the campaign speeches of King and Dunning, Beatty despaired over the continued politicization of the railway question, believing the public discussion of the issue to be biased. "I am afraid the results of the elections will be unsatisfactory and that we will have confusion for the next few months at all events," wrote Beatty in a spirit of resignation just days before the election that would bring the Liberals into power.[157]

An Uncertain Embrace: Beatty, Political Freedom, and Democracy

"Without vanity I think that I can say that I am alleged to be an unusually stupid reactionary," said Beatty in February 1936 before the Canadian Chamber of Commerce in Toronto, "because good or ill fortune has placed me in a business position of some discomfort and some prominence. I am even held up as one of the chief reactionaries." This was no confession. Beatty believed the public to be largely misled. He asked rhetorically: "How many of the unwise measures adopted by governments in connection with business have been the product of demagogues appealing to ignorant voters?" Beatty encouraged his audience to embrace a greater sense of national citizenship: "To my mind our failures have been rather as citizens than as capitalistic exploiters of the people." Too often, he argued, local boards of trade and other business associations had played lead roles in encouraging "governments to do things which governments are not well adapted to do." Local jealousies between business groups had forced government expenditures for the sake of "local conveniences." Greater discipline and unity within the business community was necessary to the attainment of the sort of national citizenship Beatty encouraged within Canada's business community. Citing Franklin Delano Roosevelt's New Deal as evidence of the failings of government intervention, Beatty sought to shore up the old political economy and restore the power of capital.[158]

For Beatty, like Charles Dunning and Howard Robinson, freedom and democracy were rooted in the free-market system that was being challenged by increasing levels of government intervention; but the logic of this thinking created considerable scepticism towards the actual practice of democracy in Canada. "The possible alternatives are fascism and socialism," claimed Beatty in September 1936, which he argued were "both based on the theory of a government which 'runs the country.'" He dismissed both theories without comment because he was convinced "that the people of this country are not seeking to change their historic form of government."[159] For Beatty, society was an organism with which one should not meddle.[160] Ignorance, bias, and emotional appeals all, however, continued to move the populace towards actions that threatened Canada's "historic form of government." Beatty's invocations of freedom and democracy were always abstractions, which dissipated once they were brought down to the material world of living individuals, whom Beatty generally felt to be incapable of responsible action. They needed guidance – "education," in Beatty's idiom – from a beneficent elite. That elite was, in Beatty's mind, a business elite, not the Liberal politicians in power in Ottawa who helped perpetuate troubling national trends.

Some of the most troubling trends were occurring in Beatty's bailiwick, McGill University, where he continued to serve as chancellor. Young McGill professors became a particular problem, in their research, public commentary, and political activity. Beatty believed McGill and Canadian universities as a whole had failed in their role of providing national leadership. In universities only "radical professors," Beatty complained, articulated their views to the wider public.[161] At McGill, Leonard Marsh, Eugene Forsey, and F.R. Scott were among the most prominent of the left-wing professoriate who gained the attention of the university's conservative board of governors, which was composed exclusively of Montreal businessmen who felt a deep sense of proprietorship over the university and its direction. Beatty articulated this feeling when, in delivering a convocation address at Queen's in 1937, he complained: "There has been exhibited from time to time a certain inclination of at least a few academic officers of universities to take the stand that all that is necessary is for someone to raise the money and then leave them free to spend it as they see fit. That theory is contrary to facts as they exist, and an attempt to follow it would almost inevitably lead to a general unwillingness to support these institutions."[162] The point was clear: those who control the purse strings should, naturally, have a considerable hand in directing university affairs.

The Social Science Research Project, as historian Marlene Shore has written, "became the object of the administration's attacks on political radicalism in the 1930s," though its funding came from an outside source, the Rockefeller Foundation.[163] Headed by Leonard Marsh, a graduate of the London School of Economics, the project produced studies that were critical of the social consequences of unfettered capitalism; worse still, Marsh and others involved in the project were also associated with the League for Social Reconstruction (LSR), an organization of socialist intellectuals, established in 1931, that advocated the implementation of a planned economy and later became closely associated with the CCF. Beatty was reasonably suspected of having a hand in criticism of one of the project's studies.[164]

He was hands-on in his role as chancellor. When Principal Sir Arthur Currie died in November 1933, Beatty took over the administration of the university, as he had previously done when Currie was ill.[165] In 1935 Arthur Eustace Morgan was appointed principal. But Morgan, an Englishman whose personal disposition alienated many and whose political sympathies and vision of academic freedom antagonized the board of governors, did not last long. Refusing to police the McGill faculty to Beatty's liking, Morgan was forced out over the issue of budgetary control in 1937.[166] Beatty selected Lewis Williams Douglas as Morgan's replacement. Douglas was an American with experience in business, politics, and academia, an FDR cabinet member–turned–New Deal opponent. Appointed principal and vice-chancellor on 1 January 1938, Douglas was quick to implement economies and, together with Beatty, devised a strategy to counter perceived radicalism within the professoriate. The Douglas-Beatty program, as Stanley Brice Frost has described it in the university's official history, redefined tenure "whereby junior staff were clearly seen not to possess it"; it implemented selective promotion so that "socialist-minded" junior academics "were to be pressured out and replaced by less doctrinaire, 'more competent' exponents of the social sciences"; and it sought to counter "radicals" already too senior to force out by creating new professorships to be filled with prominent conservative scholars. The plan was implemented in its entirety – although the last part of the program ran into some difficulty when Douglas offended the chair of the economics and political science department by making an appointment to a three-year visiting professorship without consultation.[167]

While Beatty proclaimed a belief in freedom of speech, those principles buckled somewhat when it came to socialism and other perceived forms of radicalism. "I have always felt that our professors should keep clear of discussing publicly questions involving atheism, communism and sovietism," explained Beatty to a concerned investment banker in 1932, "all of them being fundamentally antagonistic to the views of the people of this country."[168] Beatty attacked "socialist" and "communist" theories as lacking basis in fact, guided by emotion and inaccurate readings of history and thus inappropriate for the university setting.[169] It was a simplistic and tautological formulation, but nonetheless it animated his general outlook toward education, which held that true education would square with his general worldview. Socialists were beyond the realm of legitimate education – and even, in specific instances, beyond legitimate participation in civil society. Beatty defended Maurice Duplessis's draconian Padlock Law (1937), which made possession of any literature deemed "communist" illegal, by arguing that it was well suited to a province whose population, being overwhelmingly "French-Canadian and Roman Catholic," was illiberal: "The padlock law may be a foolish law in the minds of liberals who do not think that freedom can ever be abused, but the overwhelming sentiment of the people of Quebec is against Communism, and the present Government is only reflecting that sentiment."[170] From the perspective of the LSR in Montreal, as Sean Mills has demonstrated, the passing of the Padlock Act was an important event in the erosion of democracy in Quebec, and caused the group to refocus its efforts upon a more robust definition and defence of democracy.[171] Abstract principles of freedom were not, in Beatty's mind, easily transferable to the material world, and democracy itself emerged as a vital subject of debate.

In public speeches during the last half of the 1930s, Beatty often referred to his faith in democracy and the ability of ordinary individuals to choose wisely. One must conclude that Beatty held to these pronouncements tenuously, and that they were made anticipating that the public would come around to embrace "sound" views. Before the United States Chamber of Commerce in 1937 Beatty proclaimed: "The business world cannot defend itself against demagoguery or reform by trickery, or by conspiracy. The hope of survival of capitalism lies, not in repression, but in education."[172] Here, again, Beatty recognized the problem of public relations. He argued for increased activism before his esteemed U.S. colleagues: "It will not do for us to take refuge in the assertion that economic law is on our side and that economic truth is great and will prevail. Truth will prevail, but before now it has gone into eclipse for long periods ... I appeal to you to realize that it is not enough for business men to be right – they must also prove to the public that they are right."[173] Beatty practised what he preached, continuing to speak out about the railway question. By 1938 he seemed to have convinced himself that railway unification was inevitable.[174] Perhaps it was a public relations strategy, but more likely it was evidence that Beatty was, as Floyd Chalmers observed in a private memorandum, "building up for himself a castle of delusions."[175] Believing that he could sway popular opinion, that democracy was on his side, was a supreme delusion, especially for an individual who privately disparaged "the intellectual level of the masses."[176]

Conclusion

Democracy was not on Beatty's side and would prove insurmountable for the success of his political aims. Nonetheless, as we shall see, the National Government drive lived on in new forms, and Beatty and like-minded businessmen continued to exert considerable influence in political life. Their vision for society was becoming less and less viable, however. Beatty operated in an "imagined community" that was imperial in its scope and, indeed, still rooted in economic relations established by the British Empire. The majority of CPR shares continued to be held in Britain, and Beatty and the CPR appear to have made appeals in Britain to whip the recalcitrant Dominion government in line. CNR officials reported in 1936 that CPR agents were carrying out an organized campaign to damage Canadian credit in London "on the ground of the railway situation in the hope that the Government can thus be intimidated into yielding to Sir Edward Beatty's demands."[177] At almost the exact same time King Edward VIII, a personal friend of Beatty (and a notorious Nazi sympathizer), expressed himself in favour of railway unification to Prime Minister Mackenzie King.[178] This was no basis upon which popular approval could be won in Canada in the late 1930s. Beatty fell ill in December 1939, suffered a severe stroke in 1941, and passed away in 1943; his health permitted him to do relatively little after the onset of the Second World War.

Beatty had embraced a losing political strategy to shore up a declining political economy. Failure does not imply unimportance, however. In the open-ended political context of the times, the failure of railway amalgamation and National Government while Bennett was in office was hardly inevitable. And, as James Overton has shown, economic crisis in Newfoundland did in fact spell "the end of democracy" for a period with the implementation of commission government.[179] Prime Minister Bennett had, indeed, come to seriously consider the formation of a National Government. But, differing from the Union government formed in 1917, the prospective National Government circa 1935 was almost exclusively aligned with big business and, as a result, failed to gain a significantly broader base of support. Its failure attested to the way in which parliamentary democracy provided a framework within which the general public could resist and limit the influence of a formidable business elite during a period of economic crisis.

Beatty had been cast as a dynamic business leader, capable in both cerebral and athletic pursuits, evincing the broader meritocratic ideal that emerged in North America during the early twentieth century to revitalize the image of the upper class – but obviously many people were unconvinced during the Depression. Beatty himself understood his social position, and society generally, within this meritocratic framework. As such, he saw little problem in promoting the political influence of big business; after all, according to his outlook, the country's business executives represented Canada's best and brightest. The antidemocratic implications of this outlook became obvious once popular opinion began to push public policy in directions that Beatty believed unwise. Beatty advanced radical solutions in response to the persisting economic crisis and growing political ferment of the 1930s, a response that hardly signalled a willingness to adapt. As a man who occupied what was widely considered to be the most important position in the Canadian business world, the presidency of the CPR, Beatty's frustrated political efforts signalled a significant political crisis within the Canadian bourgeoisie and evidenced the CPR's relative decline in Canada's political economy.

These developments were related to expansion in other areas that were reshaping the country's economy and its business elite. Nothing more clearly signalled this transition during the interwar period than the automobile industry. But the automobile industry's expansion came with its own contradictions, as we shall see in the next chapter, made especially apparent with the rise of labour militancy among Canadian autoworkers. Conflict with workers provided the basis for renewed political cohesion within Canada's changing business elite, just as it signalled the beginning of change in the broader relationship between capital and labour. As Beatty and the political economy of the National Policy period faded, we shall witness the emergence of a new type of political economy in the coming chapters. This political economy, which was acquiring new momentum in the 1930s and 1940s, was more continental in its geographic nexus and managerial in its ethos and produced a state that was more autonomous from big business than before.

PART TWO

Continentalism and
the Managerial Ethic

4

Stewardship and Dependency: Sam McLaughlin, General Motors, and the Labour Question

In early April 1937 all eyes were on Oshawa. Workers picketed the General Motors plant, while armed forces – including the Royal Canadian Mounted Police (RCMP), the Ontario Provincial Police (OPP), and a special force recruited by Ontario premier Mitch Hepburn, derisively labelled "Sons of Mitch's" and "Hepburn's Hussars" – waited only a few miles away in Toronto. The mood was tense and the threat of violence palpable. Oshawa autoworkers had affiliated with the Committee for Industrial Organization (CIO), drawing inspiration from that organization's recent success south of the border at the General Motors operations in Flint, Michigan, and other centres, where workers had occupied plants in a wave of sit-down strikes that resulted in recognition of their union. A near hysterical Hepburn, ostensibly worried about the spread of communism, declared his resolve to keep the CIO out of Canada. He had recently applauded vigilantism at a foundry near Sarnia, where armed thugs had halted a CIO sit-down strike by breaking through the picket and beating the strikers inside before turning them over to the authorities. As soon as the General Motors strike commenced on 8 April, Hepburn wrote to the Dominion minister of justice, Ernest Lapointe, that the situation in Oshawa had become very "acute" and violence was "anticipated any minute."[1]

The conflict was dramatic evidence of how the political economy of the automobile industry had transformed Oshawa in recent years. Only a decade earlier, the Oshawa Chamber of Commerce had described local labour conditions as "happy" and "pleasant"; "80% of

the residents of Oshawa own their own homes. The workers are conservative, productive and permanent."[2] The 1937 strike represented a
clear break from that past. Oshawa was the Canadian headquarters of
General Motors, and recent transformations there mirrored the stunning rise of the auto industry in Canada generally. From an array of
small factories producing a plethora of brands in the early 1900s, the
auto industry expanded in Canada after the First World War to become
one of the country's most important industries during the 1920s. By
the close of the decade, the corporate contours of the modern industry
were well in place: centralized in southern Ontario, Canada's auto industry was a branch of the U.S. industry, dominated by the Big Three –
Ford, Chrysler, and General Motors.[3] As the emergent industry of the
interwar period in North America, the auto sector became a decisive
site of class conflict. Semiskilled and unskilled workers employed in
auto plants across the continent fought vigorously for union recognition, challenging at once both the industry grandees as well as the conservative trade unions affiliated with the American Federation of Labor
(AFL). As the drama unfolded in Oshawa, General Motors of Canada
president Colonel R.S. McLaughlin (1871–1972) was caught off-guard
vacationing in Bermuda. Several decades earlier, McLaughlin – or "Mr
Sam," as he was often called – had worked as an upholsterer alongside
skilled workers in his father's carriage factory; he was now decidedly
distanced from the workforce.

Sam McLaughlin, the subject of this chapter, embodied an emergent
variety of capital in Canada – that of corporate America. His trajectory reflected the transition in Canada's economic life during the early
twentieth century from an economy whose foreign investment came
primarily from British portfolio investment and was tied to imperial
expansion and nation-building through, as we have seen, corporations
such as the CPR to an economy whose principal foreign investment
came from the United States and was represented mostly in branch
plants. The carriage manufacturing business of his father, begun in
1867, had sprung from local capital in small-town Ontario and by the
turn of the century had purportedly become the largest manufacturer of
carriages in the British Empire. Sam McLaughlin and an elder brother,
George, joined their father in the growing carriage concern. But, as Sam
McLaughlin perceived, the future was with the car. The McLaughlin

brothers briefly attempted to manufacture their own car before buying the rights to manufacture the Buick in Canada in 1907. A decade later they relinquished control of their business to become the Canadian subsidiary of General Motors. It was a profitable arrangement. Always interested in other investments, Sam and George McLaughlin exercised relatively little entrepreneurial initiative within General Motors, and in 1924 George retired and Sam assumed a more hands-off role with the appointment of a general manager to the Oshawa operations. They became *rentier* capitalists of sorts. Through the interwar period Sam McLaughlin became integrated into the Canadian bourgeoisie, gaining directorships in important companies such as the CPR and the International Nickel Company of Canada (Inco), engaging in the typically upper-class pursuits of horse racing and art collecting, and playing an active role in the social life of the nation's economic elite – joining elite social clubs such as the Mount Royal Club, St James Street's choicest club. This process of integration was important to class consolidation, since McLaughlin and the auto industry generally had largely stood outside the social and economic institutions of the Canadian bourgeoisie after the First World War; indeed, during the 1920s numerous businessmen and politicians had questioned the importance of the auto industry within the Canadian economy. As McLaughlin's place within the upper stratum of Canada's economic and social life expanded during the 1920s and 1930s, the place of General Motors of Canada – and the auto industry as a whole – within the new Canadian political economy was further established.

As McLaughlin confirmed his economic and social position within Canadian big business, paradoxically he and his family lost influence in Oshawa. In the 1920s McLaughlin's paternalism remained effective, consolidated around a shared belief in high tariffs and an ethos of community stewardship. Oshawa residents organized a protest against tariff reductions in 1926, and two years later McLaughlin and General Motors of Canada officials helped resolve a strike with conciliatory tactics. When the economic slump of the 1930s ravaged the auto industry and Oshawa generally, however, the McLaughlin discourse of community stewardship became less convincing, as General Motors of Canada implemented massive layoffs and as Sam's brother George tightened the purse strings controlling local relief. Sam McLaughlin's estrangement from the local working class was revealed when he sent out Christmas turkeys to the homes of workers, some of whom did not own ovens; a few of those turkeys were given back, thrown on McLaughlin's lawn.[4] This symbolic gesture of resistance prefigured the 1937 strike, which represented a culmination of McLaughlin's estrangement from a more independent and militant working class. By 1937 the challenge from a reinvigorated left, prominently exemplified by the growing popularity of the CIO among workers in Oshawa and beyond, gave Canadian business leaders and their political brokers a renewed purpose for collective action. McLaughlin himself came to embrace the idea of National Government, like Beatty and Dunning, just as Hepburn, C. George McCullagh, and Conservative Party organizer George Drew plotted to form a coalition government in Ontario to fight the CIO. Although the Mackenzie King government assumed a conciliatory role during the strike, McLaughlin's private opposition to the CIO mounted and General Motors of Canada refused to recognize the union.[5] During the 1920s and 1930s McLaughlin grew into a changing Canadian bourgeoisie that was able to unite politically around certain key issues – railways, public debt, industrial unionism. Though McLaughlin's small-town origins and self-styled folksiness have caused some observers to view him as an outsider, never truly able to gain acceptance in high society, such views not only underestimate McLaughlin's social success but fail to appreciate the common political and ideological outlook that united McLaughlin and other business leaders, which was of far greater political import than high-society cliquishness.[6] As autoworkers picketed the General Motors plant in Oshawa, businessmen, politicians, professionals, and others worked to halt the CIO's "invasion" into Canada.

The Making and Transformation of an Industrial Enterprise

The McLaughlin carriage business that was eventually to become General Motors of Canada had emerged out of the transition to industrial capitalism in the Ontario countryside during the nineteenth century. Robert Samuel McLaughlin was born in the tiny village of Enniskillen, Ontario, on 8 September 1871. Robert McLaughlin, his father, had built a shop there two years earlier, where he designed and painted wagons and sleighs, known as "cutters," constructed by a small staff, which had

been expanded to eight around the time Sam was born.[7] Having wed
Mary Scott, a neighbour, Robert built a family home on a plot of land
purchased from his father near Tyrone, Ontario, and constructed an ac-
companying driving shed and workshop, where he began to construct
sleighs and buggies in 1867.[8] Initial production in the Tyrone shop was
dependent upon journeymen whose work habits reflected the rhythm of
preindustrial society. It was an arrangement typical of "the dozens of
small carriage shops in Ontario," explained Sam McLaughlin in 1954,
"which used visiting journeyman artisans for important roles in carriage building, with resulting limited production and dependence on
the whims of a very independent bunch of men." Robert nearly failed
to deliver on his first contract because of the tardiness of a blacksmith,
and soon after he built his own blacksmith shop to alleviate this dependency. Within two years the Tyrone shop had become too small. Robert
moved his nascent enterprise and family to Enniskillen. By 1878, following the death of his first wife and a quick remarriage, he had moved
it again, this time to Oshawa, a small commercial and industrial centre
on the main line of the Grand Trunk Railway, more than thirty miles
east of Toronto, a town not unlike a dozen other aspirant towns in the
southern Ontario countryside.[9]

Robert's outlook combined the sensibilities of craft production
with a "mechanical turn" that would transform the McLaughlin Carriage Company into an enterprise of national scope. The breakthrough
came when Robert invented and patented a gear that made carriages
more steady and manoeuvrable.[10] The popularity of the McLaughlin
gear spread and, as Robert McLaughlin later recalled, "brought the
name 'McLaughlin' before the many carriage builders ... and before
the general buggy-using public." Some carriage manufacturers became
sales agents for the entire McLaughlin carriage. Before, sales had been
"almost entirely local," but now orders for the McLaughlin gear and
carriage poured in from "far beyond Ontario in eastern and western
Canada." Robert hired travelling salesmen to peddle his wares across
the country as the McLaughlin Carriage Company captured markets
only recently made accessible by the implementation of the National
Policy.[11]

Sam was not particularly interested in entering the family business, though his brother, George, had already been apprenticed in the

carriage works. In 1887 Sam graduated from high school and worked five months in a local hardware store. He was contemplating the possibility of becoming a lawyer and was also an avid cyclist. An apprenticeship under his father's direction would surely limit his opportunities to cycle. His eldest brother, Jack, convinced him otherwise, however.[12] Sam began a three-year apprenticeship in the upholstery shop that year.[13] An adventurer of sorts, Sam left the McLaughlin works at the end of his apprenticeship in 1890 to prove himself as a journeyman upholsterer in New York State. In Watertown, he gained a position with the firm of H.H. Babcock, where the factory superintendent hailed from the village of Brooklin, Ontario, near Enniskillen. Sam was given the run of the plant: "I absorbed a lot of ideas about plant management, design and quality control. I stayed with the Babcock Company for two months and was sorry to leave." Working briefly in Syracuse and Binghampton, McLaughlin ended the trip in New York City, where he spent his savings and "did the town."[14] He returned to Oshawa to become foreman in the upholstery shop and carriage designer. In 1892 Sam and George were made partners in the firm; Sam's work would centre on factory operations, while George's efforts would focus upon sales. Sam McLaughlin was barely in his twenties.

Sam became a town councillor in 1897, but it proved unfulfilling. "I really wasn't interested in politics, municipal or any other kind," he reminisced.[15] His father continued to fulfil the more weighty tasks of business and political leadership. Robert's reputation as a solid, religious man secured credit for the company locally, and when the carriage works was destroyed by fire in December 1899, Robert turned apparent disaster to his advantage.[16] Renegotiating better terms on freight rates from the Grand Trunk, he stepped down as mayor to secure a $50,000 interest-free loan from town council.[17] The Oshawa factory was rebuilt as an enlarged, modern factory. As the "Laurier boom" set in, output at the McLaughlin Carriage Company Limited expanded greatly.[18] By 1911, one observer marvelled at the carriage factory in the northeast section of Oshawa, a bustling industrial centre of more than 7,000 residents, which had come to call itself the "Manchester of Canada": "Their factory ... is the largest of its kind under the British flag ... They employ from six to seven hundred men, most of whom are well-to-do, contented artizans who make their employer's interest their own." One carriage was being turned out for every ten minutes of production.[19]

As production soared at the McLaughlin factory, a Walkerville carriage manufacturer, Gordon M. McGregor, convinced Henry Ford to extend his modest auto manufacturing business to Canada. Ford Motors was incorporated in Canada in August 1904; the parent company in Michigan retained a controlling interest in the Canadian branch.[20] Sam McLaughlin soon became interested in establishing an agreement with a U.S. automaker as well. Automakers, like carriage manufacturers, received tariff protection of 35 per cent in Canada, and thus U.S. firms were encouraged to establish branch plants in Canada to jump the protective tariff.[21] Sam visited with numerous U.S. automakers in 1905 before entering negotiations in 1907 with William C. "Billy" Durant, a friend of ten years whom he knew from the carriage business.[22] Durant had taken over a fledgling automaker, the Buick Motor Car Company, in 1904. Within a few years he had helped turn it into a successful enterprise based in Flint, Michigan.[23] McLaughlin was impressed by the Buick engine and wanted to use it on a Canadian-made chassis, but he could not reach an agreement with Durant. Returning to Oshawa, Sam conferred with his father and brother and the decision was made to build an engine in Oshawa, but McLaughlin, as he later explained in 1933, "discovered the futility of trying to manufacture automobiles upon a small scale." McLaughlin was soon again in touch with Durant.[24] The McLaughlins experienced significant financial pressure when they first entered the automobile business, and Sam and George spoke with the Oshawa manager of the Dominion Bank, Clarence E. Bogart, to describe a "tale of woe as to [their] poverty and desire for financial help." Bogart proved sympathetic.[25] Durant, too, was likely encouraged to reach an accommodation in a tightening financial environment.[26] On 20 November 1907, the McLaughlin Motor Car Company was created to assemble Buicks in Canada. Nearly everything, except the wooden bodies, was shipped from the United States and assembled in Oshawa.[27]

Carriage manufacturers or dealers established eleven of twenty-five automobile companies initiated by Canadian capital that succeeded in making more than twenty-five cars.[28] Sam McLaughlin's early path in the auto industry revealed another familiar pattern: the industry's striking dependency upon U.S. technology. Canadian manufacturers such as the Canada Cycle and Motor Company (CCM) had some early success manufacturing automobiles, and thirty-five automobile firms began production in Canada between 1908 and 1915 – but only two survived.[29] U.S. automakers were quick to develop marketing strategies and financial controls that solidified U.S. hegemony over the industry and revealed structural factors – a larger population base and capital market, a more mature industrial structure, and a national state that was committed to domestic industrialization – that worked against the success of independent Canadian firms. Though it has been argued that the failure of independent Canadian firms was the result of Canada's comparatively less dynamic business class, it must be admitted that Durant and McLaughlin were rather similar entrepreneurial types: both had begun in the carriage business, and both sought to partake in the automobile business by harnessing technologies developed by others – and both became close friends and business allies.[30] All things considered, no one explanation can account for why the Canadian automobile industry developed as it did. Most obvious, however, was the role of the tariff in encouraging the migration of U.S. operations to Canada.

Sam had also established a family by this time. In 1899 he married Adelaide Mowbray, a woman of a respectable middle-class family who had attended normal school with his younger sister. Adelaide gave birth to their fifth and last child in 1908. All five children were girls, and Sam insisted on calling Eleanor, the fifth child, "Billie." In 1915 he contracted Canada's most prominent architectural firm of the day, Darling and Pearson of Toronto, to coordinate the design of a family home in Oshawa. It was a mansion of the most ostentatious proportions to be built on a twelve-acre property, formerly the site of a public park. Darling and Pearson had designed Holwood, Joseph Flavelle's Toronto mansion; one senses that McLaughlin's Parkwood was an attempt to buy his way past or into Toronto's establishment. Blueprints for the fifty-five-room mansion were completed in March 1916, and by the following year the mansion was completed for a sum of $1 million. It was the most expensive house in Canada. Adorned with intricate wood panelling and marble; containing a bowling alley, heated pool, and built-in organ; and staffed by a veritable army of live-in servants, the mansion made a commanding statement about the wealth of "Mr

Sam" and would provide a venue for continued displays of conspicu-
ous consumption in the future.[31]

Not everyone was impressed with Sam's achievements. Indeed, Mc-
Laughlin's political sway remained tenuous outside of Oshawa. He felt
slighted when Joseph Flavelle failed to deliver the munitions contracts
he expected during the war.[32] McLaughlin was just beginning to truly
emerge as a figure of national importance in business, being elected
director of the Toronto-based Dominion Bank in 1917. Flavelle, of
course, was associated with a different group of capitalists, concentrated on the boards of the Bank of Commerce and National Trust, and
remained involved in an array of national business enterprises. Furthermore, as director of the Imperial Munitions Board, Flavelle controlled a
direct link to the British market and patronage. By contrast, McLaughlin's early and most important business associations flowed through
a North–South axis. McLaughlin's U.S. connections were important
for other investments, too. A considerable portion of McLaughlin's
wealth came not, as one source reported, from carriages or automobiles but originated from a nest egg passed down from his father,
which McLaughlin used to invest in "sundry successful speculative
ventures in the United States, made possible by his wide connections
with industrial enterprises in that country."[33] McLaughlin's accumulation strategy was thus tied in numerous ways to the United States,
even though he espoused an unabashed commitment to the British
Empire – a contradiction, as we have seen, not unusual among capital-
rich Canadians.

More interested in status than politics, McLaughlin was not a business leader in the manner of Beatty or Flavelle, individuals who regularly articulated views on pressing issues of the day and engaged in
political activism.[34] Before having reached the age of fifty, McLaughlin
had already stamped himself as a man of leisure. One contemporary
observer wrote in 1917:

> Keen as Mr. McLaughlin is as a business man, he is by no means a slave
> to work. As a matter of fact, there are few, if any, among Canadian busi-
> ness men who enjoy life more than he does. Motoring is a keen pastime
> of his. But it is by no means his only one. In the summer time he is fre-
> quently to be seen on the links of one or other of the three clubs of which
> he is a member. In the fall he spends a week or two deer-hunting, and in

the winter, when the ice permits, he will be found curling with his home club. Consequently he is all the time "as fit as a fiddle."[35]

Though McLaughlin's lifestyle reflected in many ways the "leisure class" critiqued by Thorstein Veblen in the United States and targeted by Stephen Leacock's satire in Canada, McLaughlin represented a sleeker version of wealth than the widely lampooned "plutocrat."[36] Writing to his daughter Isabel in 1924, McLaughlin reported that he was on a diet and had lost about five to six pounds. He hoped to take off twelve pounds to achieve, as he explained, "what physicians call a 'perfect figure' – not that I have bulged in any one spot, no, no, but I have been just a little too fat."[37] He paid close attention to physical fitness, was at ease among workers on the shop floor, and had achieved success in business – all of which enabled him to project a meritocratic élan, a projection that emphasized McLaughlin's individual agency and achievement. It was a social projection that combined the illusion and reality of meritocratic achievement and worked to revitalize and renew the entitlement of the super-rich.[38] In McLaughlin's case, legitimacy was also tied tightly to his paternalism as an employer and Oshawa booster.[39]

Joining GM

In the first half of the 1910s, before the First World War, the automobile was still only a sideline to the carriage business, and the shape of the auto industry remained highly fluid and uncertain.[40] But Sam McLaughlin was coming to appreciate the coming transition. "By 1915 carriage sales were declining steadily," McLaughlin reflected, "[and] automobile sales were rocketing. I calculated that there would only be three or four years in which carriage production would show a profit."[41] McLaughlin had a fortuitous encounter with Billy Durant while visiting New York City that year. Durant had established General Motors in 1908, but in two years he lost control as the company became dependent upon financial backers who believed his methods too reckless. The Boston and New York bankers appointed five trustees to the GM board, forcing Durant's supporters to retire. Sam McLaughlin was among the Durant allies removed from GM's board.[42] Durant mounted a comeback by having an expert mechanic named Louis Chevrolet design a car for him; though Chevrolet quit the company in 1913, the following year the Chevrolet Motor Company came out with two models that achieved instant success.[43] By the time he met McLaughlin at Pabst's Restaurant in 1915, Chevrolet was a successful enterprise with a very saleable product – and looking to expand into Canada. Durant offered the rights to manufacture the Chevrolet in Canada to the McLaughlins, familiar and trusted business partners. A tentative agreement was made, and the McLaughlin brothers travelled back to Oshawa to convince their father, whom they affectionately referred to as "the Governor" out of continued respect for his patriarchal stature in the family enterprise.[44]

If the McLaughlins wanted the Chevrolet contract, the manufacture of automobiles would consume their factory; they would be forced to sell the carriage business. As historian David Roberts has noted, Robert McLaughlin had been carefully following the decline of the carriage business during the past three years as well as "Sam's ongoing pains to attract the attention and respect of kingpins in the fast-moving American auto industry."[45] Robert agreed to abide by the decision of his sons, accepting the passing of an era.[46] A 1924 article in *Maclean's* described Sam as "a typical go-getter," "the impulsive type, the business-builder, always 'on his toes,' as modern sales managers want men under them to be." George, by contrast, was described as "his brother's antithesis, conservative, slow, perhaps, to decision – a balance wheel." Sam, "the talker and 'mixer' of the brothers," hastened the move into the automobile business.[47] The McLaughlins sold the carriage business to a provincial competitor three days after the Chevrolet agreement was settled and converted operations for the sole purpose of manufacturing automobiles. The first Chevrolet rolled off the assembly line within two months.[48]

Before the end of 1918 the McLaughlins formalized this dependent but profitable relationship by selling their Canadian operations to General Motors, which had again come under the control of Billy Durant, with the aid of interested Wall Street moguls Pierre S. du Pont, of the famed explosives-making company, and Louis G. Kaufman.[49] George, as Sam recalled, was looking forward to retirement; Sam had no male heirs to eventually take the reins; and the expiration of the Buick contract was approaching. On 1 November 1918, the McLaughlins agreed to sell their automobile business to General Motors. Realizing that they were not merely selling property but the well-regarded McLaughlin name, the McLaughlins drove a hard bargain with GM.[50] Sam Mc-Laughlin would later justify the sale in terms of community stewardship: "I had in mind the fact that Oshawa had to carry on and our best workmen had to have jobs. This was the best way to get jobs for them."[51] Though Sam would also claim years later that he approached GM about the sale, the reality was that GM had approached the Mc-Laughlins. General Motors bought out the McLaughlins as part of a general expansion program, which the company's chairman, Jacob J. Raskob, a trusted lieutenant of Pierre du Pont, presented to the board of directors on 12 December 1918.[52] Durant along with du Pont and Raskob – who, together, were the new masters of GM – imposed one condition upon the sale: the McLaughlins would continue to run the business.[53] Sam was appointed president of General Motors of Canada and regained his directorship with the parent company, and George became vice-president of the Canadian subsidiary. Durant had been the U.S. connection for their previous car-making contracts, with Buick in 1907 and Chevrolet in 1915, and thus the sale to GM signalled the continuation of a familiar and friendly cross-border business relationship.

In two years Durant, an affable capitalist buccaneer more successful at creating companies than administering them, would be forced to resign from the board of General Motors. Durant proved himself out of step with the procedures of the modern corporation; he made decisions arbitrarily with little appreciation for oversight or organized planning, and his refusal to delegate responsibility caused the resignation of one of the company's most competent executives, Walter P. Chrysler, and generally made the functioning of the business inexpedient. But, ultimately, it was the onset of an international economic recession in 1920 that caused Durant's downfall; having independently begun to purchase large amounts of stock with borrowed money, Durant sought to counteract plummeting valuations by purchasing even more GM stock. In the end, the financial giant J.P. Morgan & Company became involved, with the encouragement of du Pont, and bought up Durant's stock and underwrote a new offering through a new holding company. A potential financial catastrophe was thus avoided, but with the departure of Durant, the McLaughlins lost their most important connection to the parent company.[54] Sam exercised little influence over the grand policies of the company, never serving on the all-important finance and executive committees.[55]

Within this corporate structure, Sam McLaughlin became the public face of General Motors of Canada, imbuing it with a potent brand of paternalism rooted in notions of Britishness and community booster-ism. Robert McLaughlin, too, remained an important figure in shaping the company's image. His motto, "one grade only, and that the best," continued to be used by Sam and other company officials in advertis-ing automobiles that rolled off Oshawa's assembly lines, even after his death in 1921 as he "underwent a kind of corporate sanctification."[56] While still alive, an elderly Robert McLaughlin expressed the opinion that the Canadian consumer embraced "old British ideas" of quality production, differing from U.S. consumers, who tended to "buy any-thing so long as it was a low cost."[57] Before a gathering to celebrate the company's long-serving employees in 1928, Sam McLaughlin argued a similar thesis, stating that the devotion of General Motors of Canada workers made true another company motto: "It's better because it's Canadian."[58] Though a wholly-owned subsidiary of one of the world's largest corporations, firmly within the grasp of Wall Street grandees, the corporate image of General Motors of Canada remained tightly tied to the McLaughlin family and their ideas concerning the unique nature of the Canadian market and Oshawa workforce. Sam McLaughlin had ceded his business autonomy but had ensured the survival of the Os-hawa factory. Increasingly, his power was symbolic.

The Politics of the Tariff

As the long-established political and economic power of the CPR began to dissipate after the First World War, the rise of the automobile helped refashion Canada's political economy and signalled the ascent of southern Ontario vis-à-vis Montreal, where the automobile industry had very little impact. More broadly, the industry's rise was part of Canada's "Second Industrial Revolution" during the first three decades of the twentieth century, which witnessed dramatic corporate consoli-dation and centralization, the growth of U.S. branch plants, and the rise of other mass production and consumer goods industries. Moreover, the expansion of U.S. corporations into the Canadian economy during this period meant that new ideas of "scientific" management and welfare capitalism were further introduced into factories.[59] General Motors of Canada well reflected these broader developments, just as it demonstrated the peculiar nature of Canada's industrial development in the twentieth century: as U.S. influence expanded during the interwar period, economic historians William Marr and Donald Paterson have written, "the fundamental switch took place as manufacturing became a more important source of income than primary production."[60]

Though the Canadian automobile industry revealed various forms of economic dependency, it was also the product of an effectively functioning state policy designed to lure industrial investment to Canada. In the 1920s Canada became the world's second largest automobile producer – well behind the United States, of course, which was the source of 93 per cent of the world's automobile production in 1926. U.S. manufacturers were encouraged to locate facilities in Canada not merely to gain access to the country's domestic market but also to gain access to the British Empire market. The Canadian government refunded duties for components used in cars made in Canadian factories destined for other parts of the British Empire, so as to allow Canadian factories to take full advantage of imperial preference. The effect of the policy was readily apparent. In 1924, for example, the number of automobiles exported from Canada represented 31 per cent of total U.S. exports, even though U.S. makers produced nearly twenty-four times as many automobiles as their Canadian counterparts. General Motors of Canada was a significant beneficiary of this policy; 40 per cent of its production was destined for the export market. The initial growth of the Canadian industry was, therefore, very much connected to Canada's place within the British Empire, as the Dominion served as intermediary between U.S. producers and empire consumers, sending more than 72 per cent of all its exports to within the British Empire.[61] Historian Tom Traves has correctly observed: "By the 1920s the automobile industry was a creature of the tariff."[62]

Under these conditions, General Motors of Canada expanded considerably. Already by 1918 more than 20,000 units were produced by GM in Canada. The recession of the early 1920s was felt as production dipped to 15,544 in 1921 before quickly accelerating again. By 1925 production reached nearly 45,000.[63] At the end of the year, rumblings of downward tariff revisions began to reach the press. As we have seen, the pressure for tariff reduction was most concentrated in the West among farmers who protested having to pay for manufactured goods made more expensive by the tariff while raising crops that received no such protection. The discussion of downward tariff revisions emerged as the King Liberals courted western Liberals with progressive sympathies – most notably, Charles Dunning (see chapter 2). Industrial Oshawa was another world. Sam McLaughlin wrote minister of finance J.A. Robb to ask for clarification, pointing to the unsettled atmosphere that had been created by public speculation.[64] The community of Oshawa, McLaughlin suggested, was under grave threat.

In his public pronouncements, McLaughlin highlighted the flowering mutual relationship between the company, its employees, and Oshawa generally. At his brother's retirement celebration in 1924, he "declared himself a worker not as he did one time in the factory, but as an executive," and he "wished he could spend time in the trimming shops where he learned his trade, hammering in the tacks."[65] McLaughlin's work as an executive was further reduced that year, nonetheless. With the view of "easing off," before George's retirement he asked the head office to appoint K.T. Keller, "formerly connected with the Buick and Chevrolet Company in the United States," as general manager of the Oshawa operations. The request was approved by the new president, Alfred Sloan Jr.[66] Sam remained distant from the centres of power at GM after Durant's departure, and he appears to have been unenthusiastic about active involvement in the corporation's affairs; when he reported that Oshawa would be assuming responsibility for GM's entire export business in 1921, he described it as an imposition.[67] By 1929, McLaughlin's working day was quite short. "I get down in the morning about nine," he reported, "leave about twelve thirty for lunch, back about two and leave about four thirty. Then I go riding – ride in the afternoon, not the morning."[68] This did not diminish his political importance within Oshawa, however. Like their father, Sam and George were community leaders, filling top positions in a plethora of local organizations, from the Rotary Club to the Oshawa Curling Club, the Masonic temple, local hospital and St Andrew's Church. In 1920 McLaughlin gained the title of lieutenant-colonel, an honorary position in the Ontario Regiment, which was improved to colonel in 1936; Sam was a much-appreciated patron of the local militia.[69] He cast a large net in the community's social, political, and cultural life, well beyond the parameters of General Motors of Canada alone.

Protected by the tariff, in the 1920s Oshawa developed as a unique outpost of the British world within the North American auto industry, wherein McLaughlin's discourse of mutuality remained plausible. Differing from the ethnically diverse workforce at the Ford plant in Windsor, in Oshawa GM recruited its workers from the surrounding countryside, resulting in a relatively homogeneous workforce, which was reinforced by the company's practice of hiring relatives of employees.[70] McLaughlin proudly advertised the homogeneity of the Oshawa workforce, asking an interviewer in 1928 to "please mark this – over 98 per cent of our men are British."[71] Like many other capital-rich Canadians, he was particularly distrustful of eastern Europeans. He felt compelled to warn his daughter Isabel, who befriended a group of Russians abroad in 1922, to "not allow these people to make too great an impression on you." Russians, McLaughlin explained to his daughter, "are a very peculiar race" and "not to be trusted": "As a rule they are very thriftless and impecunious."[72] Sam could take comfort in the fact that Oshawa remained overwhelmingly British.[73]

To McLaughlin's mind, downward tariff revisions were scandalous, threatening General Motors of Canada and the sturdy, home-owning British subjects it sustained. Oshawa's Dr T.E. Kaiser, Conservative MP, argued at length in the House of Commons against proposed reductions to the automobile tariff early in April 1926, emphasizing how the whole fabric of Oshawa's economic life would be affected. Having witnessed Oshawa grow from a "village of 3,500 people to a city of 20,000," Kaiser also pointed to the municipality's large investment in infrastructure to meet the requirements created by the city's recent industrial expansion: Oshawa's bond debt had expanded from just over $600,000 in 1918 to nearly $3.5 million by 1925. "Let me say that in Oshawa we are undertaking greater obligations to-day in maintaining this industry than the assistance that is being asked to complete the Hudson Bay railway," thundered Kaiser in a backhanded attack upon the Progressives who were assailing the tariff. Much was at stake.[74]

The King Liberals revealed their western sympathies within a few weeks. On 15 April, Robb announced tariff reductions of 15 per cent on automobiles selling at $1,200 or less, and 7½ per cent for automobiles over $1,200.[75] McLaughlin responded immediately the following day by shutting down the Oshawa plant, and within two days the *Oshawa Daily Reformer*'s headline proclaimed: "AUTO INDUSTRY WRECKED."[76] McLaughlin claimed the shutdown was necessary for company officials to calculate the implications of the tariff revision, but it was undoubtedly motivated by political aims. The plant, McLaughlin explained, would reopen in a few days to clear inventories and fulfil agreements with suppliers, which, he lamely claimed, would go on for about two months "at a heavy loss to ourselves." After two months, McLaughlin forecast, the plant would likely be significantly reduced.[77] Protest was also led by T.A. Russell of Automotive Industries of Canada (AIC), a trade organization in which McLaughlin exercised considerable influence. AIC directors met with motor manufacturers and parts makers to voice their collective opposition to the tariff revisions.[78]

As Tom Traves has observed, Robb's reduction of the automobile tariff revealed the industry's political weakness. Canadian automakers were, Traves has suggested, "isolated from the country's major centres of political power" because "politically powerful financiers, brokers, and bankers had no significant stake in [the industry's] fortunes." Leading financiers such as J.H. Gundy, Liberal bagman W.E. Rundle of National Trust, and Sir Clifford Sifton were all in favour of a lower automobile tariff.[79] Indeed, in May the provincial treasurer of Ontario, William H. Price, prepared a memorandum for Conservative premier Howard Ferguson based on interviews with a number of lifelong Conservative businessmen. The memo reported "a total lack of sympathy with auto manufacturers," although it also stated that those interviewed tended to be sympathetic to parts makers. The opposition to automakers was based on two beliefs: first, automakers were using the tariff to put "illegitimate profits in their pockets"; second, the industry "was sucking the lifeblood of every other industry" by absorbing huge amounts of consumer spending, made possible by installment payment plans, which allowed individuals to purchase automobiles, who, "on a true economic basis, could not afford to do so." That said, the memo actually advocated increased duties on imported automobiles and parts, so as to stimulate the manufacture of car parts while curtailing the mass marketing of inexpensive automobiles, which were thought to be beyond the real means of many Canadians.[80] In the 1920s, then, a significant portion of the business community did not acknowledge the auto industry as a cornerstone of the Canadian economy, reflecting the fact that the industry – though already a leading sector by the mid-1920s – was still young and not politically entrenched. However, as the memo revealed, businessmen who opposed automakers did not necessarily embrace lower tariffs.

Moreover, automakers were not completely isolated from the banks. McLaughlin, of course, had been a director of the Dominion Bank for a decade by 1926. Also, for example, the Prosperity League of Canada, a business organization that counted an array of powerful financiers and industrialists on its board of directors, railed against the tariff reduction. Among the directors of the Prosperity League were Bank of Montreal president Sir Charles Gordon, Montreal jeweller William Birks, textile magnate A.O. Dawson, and brewer Colonel Herbert Molson – all leading figures of St James Street.[81] Indeed, McLaughlin became a member of St James Street's most exclusive social club, the Mount Royal Club, in 1926. Thus, the auto industry was not without powerful allies, and McLaughlin's connections with St James Street would expand over the next decade. Nonetheless, Traves's argument can stand: numerous businessmen, some connected to the leading financial institutions of "Old Toronto" (the Cox family of companies, including the Bank of Commerce and National Trust), rejected the political claims of automakers.

As the Oshawa plant reopened on 19 April, community leaders made plans to send a delegation to Ottawa to protest the tariff revisions, and various members of the Oshawa business community came forward to oppose the revisions, from parts makers to piano makers.[82] The following day, McLaughlin, former Oshawa mayor Gordon D. Conant, and others addressed an audience of 2,000 people at the Armories.[83] "Never in the history of many of the old timers of this city have so many crowded into the Armories," reported the *Oshawa Daily Reformer*. Addressing the audience as "fellow citizens and fellow workers," McLaughlin launched into an attack of the tariff revisions. Emphasizing his desire to provide local employment, McLaughlin drew heavily upon the themes of economic nationalism and British fair play in presenting his wish that Oshawa workers would not be forced to move "across the line" to the United States in search of employment: "All we want is a chance and that is British fair play."[84] McLaughlin thus styled himself the defender of local workers, interested in the expansion of local employment and economic growth. By the end of the day, a group of local businessmen had organized committees to arrange the Oshawa delegation's trip to Ottawa.[85]

In Ottawa, Mackenzie King was unconvinced, describing the two-day shutdown in his diaries as "all a bluff."[86] King did not have much regard for the general aura and style of car makers, once describing a deputation from Windsor as "the hardest looking lot of manufacturers' promoters I have seen, a genuinely brute force gang from Fords and other concerns."[87] McLaughlin's comportment was similarly crude. Indeed, in a meeting with Robb and other automakers in 1925, McLaughlin reportedly "flew off the handle" when Robb requested to see the financial statements of General Motors of Canada – which would have revealed massive profits. Even worse, McLaughlin "practically challenged the Government to alter the tariff." Robb responded by saying that "he would shew [sic] him." J.A. McGibbon, a member of the Oshawa delegation to Ottawa, had received this information from, as he explained, "one of our leading Liberals" who spoke with Robb while in Ottawa. Surely the government's tariff policy had not become a matter of "[s]pite pure and simple," as McGibbon believed.[88] But it may have played a role. Robb's statement that "we will stand by our guns" before the Oshawa delegation at Keith's Theatre in Ottawa revealed, perhaps, the articulation of male bravado rooted in a dispute with a gruff and arrogant opponent insufficiently schooled in the diplomatic niceties of the inner chambers of political power.[89]

Publicly, McLaughlin styled himself an observer, claiming to have had nothing to do with organizing the delegation that arrived in Ottawa on 23 April. It was, he called the Toronto *Globe* to explain, a "spontaneous" expression "and altogether independent of any impetus from the company."[90] Though perhaps technically correct, the ubiquity of McLaughlin and GM in Oshawa was well known, and the signal sent by the plant closure well understood. Discussion had taken place in city council the day before over a proposal to spend $3,000 to send 200 workers to Ottawa for the protest. Though one dissenting councillor argued that the employers should pay for the trip, describing the proposal as a "misappropriation of civic funds" and a "capitalistic move to continue the princely margins enjoyed by the manufacturers," the motion passed.[91] This protest went unrecorded in the local paper, which claimed that 1,700 people had left Oshawa as part of the delegation to Ottawa, 70 to 80 per cent of whom were reportedly ex-soldiers.[92] Of course, McLaughlin was one of the paper's principal shareholders; his presence was felt, even where it was not apparent.

The "on-to-Ottawa delegation," as it was dubbed, invoked patriotism and brought considerable military pomp to Ottawa as ex-servicemen paraded through the streets, carrying banners with slogans such as "Our Home and Our Living Are at Stake."[93] The delegation numbered in total about 3,000 – just under half had come from other centres, particularly Toronto.[94] Of the delegation, 500 met with the cabinet in the railway committee room, where several representatives of the delegation delivered addresses. Oshawa's mayor, R.D. Preston, referred to McLaughlin in all but name: "In our city we have some manufacturers whom we know and trust, who have suffered with us in our sorrows and rejoiced with us in our joys. We have found them not to be bluffers and when it was announced that these industries would have to close their doors and cease to operate we feel that they are perfectly sincere."[95] Kaiser was later more direct in the House of Commons: "The people at the head of General Motors have never deceived the people of Oshawa in their lives."[96] The display revealed the extent to which McLaughlin's interests had come to represent the greater good in Oshawa.[97]

Sam McLaughlin tended to remain aloof from partisanship, typical of the political tendencies of large corporations operating above the limited realm of political partisanship. The McLaughlins remained close to local Liberals such as Gordon D. Conant and supported a Liberal candidate in the 1925 federal election, but George also shared a platform with Conservative leader Arthur Meighen.[98] Obviously, however, their influence within the federal Liberal Party was tenuous.

But the automakers could not be cast aside, and the Liberal administration negotiated a settlement. The excise tax base was adjusted to give the industry additional protection, provided that a quota of 50 per cent Canadian content was met. King and the Progressives accepted this adjustment after automakers publicly promised to pass the tax reductions on to the consumer – 5 per cent on cars priced up to $1,200 and 10 per cent for those above that figure.[99] The policy promoted the expansion of Canadian parts making and encouraged General Motors of Canada to increase the Canadian content in its automobiles. Though the Oshawa operations maintained parts-making operations locally as well as in Windsor, the major components were mostly imported from the United States, including motors, transmissions, and some bodies. This was typical of the Canadian industry, which assembled rather than manufactured automobiles. The most important exception was Ford, which manufactured the entire automobile except for the carburetor.[100] McLaughlin and Ford agreed to the adjustments before other dissenting manufacturers succeeded in having the content requirement reduced to 40 per cent until April 1927, when the 50 per cent requirement would come into effect.[101] General Motors of Canada turned out over 91,000 units in 1927, having captured a larger share of the market than its chief competitor, Ford.[102]

The Politics of Paternalism

The Ford Model T was introduced in 1908, and the Ford Highland Park plant was completed two years later. In 1908, 425 workers produced 10,607 automobiles at Ford. Six years later the Highland Park plant employed nearly 13,000 workers and churned out nearly 250,000 Model Ts. The technical and managerial innovations that underpinned Ford's expanding production revolutionized the automobile industry and factory production generally. With standardized designs, the implementation of recent machine-tool technology and progressive assembly, as well as the rationalization and reorganization of work tasks following the ideas of scientific management guru Frederick W. Taylor, Ford engineers and managers realized the explosive potential of mass-production techniques. Henry Ford offered workers higher wages in exchange for obedience at the factory and sobriety and thrift at home. By the end of the First World War, Ford's paternalism had failed, as the company retreated to the coercive and corrupt labour management techniques for which Highland Park became famous.[103] Though General Motors was slower to fully develop mass-production techniques, by the 1920s it wed mass production with innovative marketing strategies to fully exploit the business opportunities of a flowering mass consumer society. GM introduced yearly models, numerous makes, and financing plans that made car ownership a possibility for a larger cross-section of the population. In 1927, the Model T having become anachronistic, Highland Park was shut down and retooled to produce the new Model A.[104]

GM also implemented a "progressive" industrial relations program after the First World War, introducing group insurance, home financing, and savings plans, which encouraged GM employees to invest in the company's stock and thus, as company executive John J. Raskob argued, allow every employee the opportunity to become a "partner."[105] In Oshawa, H.L. Broomfield served as director of the Industrial Relations Department, which administered the company's paternalist initiatives. Wages were deposited directly into workers' savings accounts to "stimulate thrift," and employees could bank up to $300 per year with the company at 30 per cent interest – a "thrift bonus." The company also initiated a housing scheme, which housed 100 workers by 1927, and an employees' association was established to handle "petty grievance" and provide workers a forum to express views on production matters. This industrial relations work also percolated down to sporting activities, including company hockey and softball teams, and the sponsorship of choir, an orchestra, and theatre. Thus the company strove "to bring added happiness and prosperity to all members of the General Motors family."[106]

McLaughlin family lore was combined with these carefully planned industrial relations strategies to give General Motors of Canada a particularly strong paternalist tone in Oshawa. Sam McLaughlin liked to emphasize the loyalty of long-serving employees, and dinners were organized periodically to acknowledge the contributions of veteran workers. "There never was a happier industrial family than ours," claimed McLaughlin in 1928. Linking the modern Oshawa plant with an older artisanal tradition, he continued: "It's the old employes that keep me here. You ask Jack Gibson. I used to go and gaze with boyish wonder at the sparks in Jack's blacksmith shop. He's been with us 43 years. Ask Jack how we get along."[107] McLaughlin enacted his symbolic authority at annual company picnics held at Lakeview Park, which had been donated to Oshawa by his father. At the 1926 picnic, McLaughlin climbed atop the bandstand to announce that, with the passing of the recent instability, GM would, "with the hearty co-operation of [its] loyal staff," enter a "new era." The local press claimed that 12,000 people attended the day-long picnic; two years later the press reported an attendance of over 30,000.[108] McLaughlin partook in the planned events, presenting awards to prizewinners with his wife and in 1928 making an appearance as a softball pitcher.[109] That year, employees attending a company reception for individuals who had served over ten years sang "for he's a jolly good fellow" after McLaughlin's address.[110]

McLaughlin's paternalism, however, was little felt at the point of production. Though associating General Motors of Canada with a tradition of craft production and quality in his public pronouncements, McLaughlin encouraged a quickened pace in the Oshawa factory, which transgressed the norms of craft production and offended the sensibilities of workers.[111] McLaughlin reminisced years later about an episode that caused several local workers to leave Oshawa for Detroit: "Old man Keddie and the Coady boys made the tops until I brought in an outside man from Brockville. He could make five tops a day whereas the Coadys and Mr. Keddie would average about one and a half. He was so disgusted they could not keep up with him that they left us and went over to Detroit."[112] Beneath the public rhetoric, a different picture existed within the General Motors Oshawa operations. In March 1928, shortly after GM shares had achieved stunning gains, Oshawa trimmers working on the Chevrolet and Pontiac lines were handed a 30 per cent wage reduction, the third reduction in six months. In response, on 26 March, 300 trimmers walked off the job.[113]

By the following day, the remaining trimmers, the entire Chevrolet and Pontiac assembly lines, and many from the Buick assembly line joined the strike. H.A. Brown, plant general manager, responded sternly to the outbreak of the strike, which had created a bottleneck in production, declaring the ease with which striking workers could be replaced. Indeed, management's refusal to bargain with a delegation representing the trimmers – which had offered to accept half the pay cut announced by management – had sparked the walkout. By 28 March, 80 replacement workers had been hired, but the number of strikers rose to 1,800, including 100 women sewing machine operators from the trimming room. H.A. Brown published the rates paid trimmers, apparently with the hope of capturing sympathy for the company; Robert McLaughlin had successfully disarmed a strike over twenty years earlier by using exactly such a tactic. Brown claimed the workers already had representation through the employees' association and pointed to the company's employee programs in claiming "there is not a plant in Canada which surrounds its employees with more ideal working conditions than exists in our institution." A parade of 3,000 strikers and strike supporters through the streets of Oshawa on 29 March dramatically suggested otherwise, as workers voiced displeasure with recent production speed-ups and protested treatment meted out by particular superintendents and foremen.[114]

McLaughlin was vacationing in Florida when the strike broke out, but, as Heather Robertson has observed, he appears to have forced Brown to back down and thus "reinforced his personal authority at the plant."[115] Brown's public rhetoric was quieted, and McLaughlin attributed the trouble to "agitators" – from the United States. M.S. Campbell, chief conciliation officer of the federal Department of Labour, met with the strike committee and company on 29 March, and within two days the strike was ended, both sides having agreed to arbitration. "Oshawa has seen the last of the worst industrial crisis in its history," reported the *Oshawa Daily Times*.[116]

However, a larger contest was initiated when the striking workers declared their intention to form a union on 30 March. A.C. "Slim" Phillips was appointed chairman of a committee charged with the task of arranging union affiliation. Phillips favoured affiliation with the new All-Canadian Congress of Labour (ACCL), a national trade union federation formed in 1926 and headed by Canadian Brotherhood of Railway Employees president A.R. Mosher. But the autoworkers voted to affiliate with the more conservative and established Trades and Labour Congress of Canada (TLC) upon the understanding that they would be able to organize the plant along industrial lines, not according to craft; TLC vice-president James Simpson was appointed to represent the workers on the conciliation board, and the new union was granted a charter from the AFL.[117] The dispute was finally settled a month later. The company agreed to pay wages in effect prior to the March reduction until 1929 models were introduced and also agreed not to discriminate against union members; however, the agreement stated that efforts would be made to close the gap between the Oshawa plant and GM operations in the United States with higher production ratios.[118] McLaughlin, now back in Oshawa, described the dispute as a "misunderstanding" and reiterated the company's intention to operate its plants "on the principle of the Open Shop, which," he argued, "is ... the only practical method under which our particular business can operate."[119]

Emerging tenuously, the union's effectiveness was quickly eroded. Slim Phillips relinquished the leadership of the local in order to become a foreman; financial troubles surfaced amid evidence that the secretary had committed fraud; and by the end of the year a competing industrial union, the Automobile Workers' Industrial Union of Canada (AWIUC), was formed – and affiliated with the ACCL. Meanwhile, the TLC-AFL organizers proved too wedded to craft-based organization, and support for their union collapsed by the end of the year. The AWIUC, too, achieved limited success; in early 1929 the union's Windsor branch had discovered in its ranks two spies whose reports had resulted in the discharge of twenty union activists at Ford and Chrysler, and by the end of 1929 the union was no longer functioning.[120] Thus, autoworkers' efforts to organize the Oshawa plant were cannibalized by the AFL-TLC's rigid adherence to craft distinction and the organizational frailty of the industrial union drive. Of course, the widely attended company picnic in the summer of 1928 demonstrated that, under the auspices of a beneficent Sam McLaughlin, General Motors of Canada continued to play a significant role in structuring the public life of Oshawa autoworkers; indeed, James Pendergest has written that "the company killed the union with kindness."[121] Conflict at the workplace persisted, nonetheless, and in 1929 Winnipeg Labour MP A.A. Heaps read correspondence in parliament from GM workers claiming that wage cuts, speed-ups, and intimidation had returned to the Oshawa plant.[122]

Community and Class in the Great Depression

Autoworkers in Oshawa during the late 1920s perceived the striking contradiction between GM's windfall profits and rising stock prices on the one hand, and production speed-ups and wage cuts on the other.[123]

They often worked at a breakneck pace to a monotonous, deadening rhythm. And the strains of the job exacted a heavy toll, aging workers quickly. Often by the age of forty an autoworker was deemed too old for employment by plant management.[124] Though management paid lip service to its "partnership" with labour, workers who raised concerns about unfair or unsafe work practices "were either let go or forgotten at the start of a new production season." Favouritism was also rampant, as employees were forced to "look after the boss" to secure their place in the factory. One GM employee from the 1920s reported that workers brought baskets of vegetables for the foreman and cut lawns and performed household chores for the bosses. For women, as Pamela Sugiman has observed, "favouritism had a sexual undercurrent."[125] Moreover, workers' yearly earnings were drastically reduced by the seasonal nature of the industry, which picked up in the spring and tapered off again in the fall. The shell of paternalism and community stewardship obscured various forms of exploitation structuring day-to-day plant operations.

The Great Depression of the 1930s put a decisive end to the automobile industry's spectacular phase of development. The industry's contraction was particularly severe. It has been estimated that the auto industry was running at only 15 per cent capacity in Canada in 1932; and, indeed, the output of General Motors of Canada that year was less than 20 per cent of its 1929 total.[126] Not unlike in the rest of the country, unemployment struck hard in Oshawa; the immediate effect was to make autoworkers even more dependent upon GM, as workers competed for a precious few jobs. Municipal revenues also declined as taxes went unpaid, and more and more Oshawa residents were driven to the relief rolls. Oral testimony collected by Christine McLaughlin in her community study of Oshawa indicates that working-class Oshawa residents not only resented having to request relief but were often angered by demeaning treatment received at the hands of the city's welfare agencies.[127]

Members of the local elite headed these agencies. Sam McLaughlin's wife and brother were particularly active in relief and other philanthropic work. Adelaide had helped found the Oshawa Women's Hospital Auxiliary in 1907; served as national president of the Canadian Federation of Home and School Associations throughout the

1930s; and held memberships in many other organizations, including the Girl Guides, the Canadian Red Cross, and the Young Women's Christian Association.[128] George exercised considerable control over the administration of local relief during the 1930s, serving as first chairman of Oshawa's welfare board and playing an active role in raising money for Oshawa's Welfare Fund.[129]

He also took an active role in politics, being one of a handful of prominent Oshawa residents to stand for municipal election in 1933 under the banner of the newly formed Civic Improvement League. George McLaughlin was the leading vote-getter of the new council, which consisted of "three lawyers, three industrialists, three retail merchants, and a physician."[130] As chairman of the welfare board and the finance committee, he oversaw "drastic cuts in civic expenditure."[131] And though he significantly reduced Oshawa's financial liabilities, he did so at a significant political cost, "and meetings of the public Welfare Board more than once required police protection."[132] After the 1935 municipal election, the Civic Improvement League was left in a minority position in the council.[133] George McLaughlin bitterly lamented finishing the 1935 electoral contest "as a tail-ender with the 'Also Rans.'" "Such, too often," he concluded, "are the rewards of public service."[134]

As unemployment mounted, the claims of Sam McLaughlin and General Motors of Canada to community stewardship appeared less and less convincing, indicative of a more widespread suspicion of the supposed beneficence of elite-led public service, which, as we have seen, haunted powerful business executives such as Edward Beatty. Of course, Oshawa itself had undergone a sustained transformation with the auto industry's expansion; and the city's working class became an increasingly unknown entity for McLaughlin as Oshawa, the town, grew into a city. Workers arrived from beyond the surrounding countryside, bringing with them politics and union traditions learned in other parts of the globe, particularity Britain. Meanwhile, Communist Party organizers made inroads, as the persisting crisis radicalized many unemployed as well as some autoworkers.[135] The old mutuality was being undermined.

Sam McLaughlin remained aloof from the active political work of his brother. His world was more about entertaining, leisure, and displays of wealth. McLaughlin's social reach extended well beyond the institutions of the local elite – such as the Thirty Club, the Oshawa Golf

Club, and the Oshawa Curling Club – but he nonetheless remained a stalwart of local high society. Beginning in the late 1920s, the McLaughlins hosted an annual "chrysanthemum tea" every fall, where their prizewinning chrysanthemums were displayed in Parkwood's greenhouse before as many as 800 guests.[136] "Sam recognized everyone as they came in," later reported Floyd Chalmers, "he put his arms warmly around all the ladies and shook hands so vigorously with the men that their fingers ached for the next week or two."[137] Local Oshawans might also run into Sam McLaughlin at the Masonic hall or at a Rotary Club meeting. Other events, such as the marriage of his youngest daughter, provided a venue for McLaughlin to display his family's prominence: *Mayfair* and the Toronto *Globe* covered the lavish celebrations surrounding the marriage of Eleanor, an accomplished equestrian, to Lieutenant Churchill Mann in 1930.[138]

His daughters were, indeed, all accomplished riders and had helped capture many awards for Parkwood stables, and McLaughlin himself had begun to learn to ride in the early 1920s.[139] McLaughlin's horses went on to win the King's Plate in 1934, and later again in 1946 and 1947 – reflective of the fact that McLaughlin was said to have spent more money on horse racing than charity during the Great Depression.[140] McLaughlin's taste for quasi-aristocratic pursuits was also evidenced in his yachting endeavours. In 1926 his yacht – *Eleanor*, named after his daughter – represented the Royal Canadian Yacht Club at the Richardson's Cup in Toledo and took the title.[141] Art also provided a quick route through which McLaughlin could purchase cultural capital. Whenever time was permitting in New York City, so McLaughlin claimed in 1924, he sought out the city's art galleries. He also benefited from some familial guidance. His daughter, Isabel – who became associated with the Group of Seven, studying under Arthur Lismer in the 1920s, and was a founding member of the Canadian Group of Painters in 1933 – helped advise her father on art purchases; Group of Seven paintings were mounted on the wall beside the bowling alley in Parkwood. From the murals that McLaughlin commissioned to be painted on the walls of his mansion in the 1920s, to the boiserie reportedly shipped in from a war-ruined French chateau to adorn the mansion's French salon, to the gardens built upon the grounds of Parkwood in the 1930s, McLaughlin commissioned leading artists, architects, and artisans to make Parkwood beautiful; he also collected an array of things – valuable furniture, a rare Steinway piano, and a rare snooker table – which projected an opulence fitting an aristocrat.[142] He presided gloriously over Oshawa society.

His social world, of course, in many ways had little to do with Oshawa. In the 1920s and early 1930s, McLaughlin and his wife began to travel to Aiken, South Carolina, for part of the winter; and in 1936 he bought a summer home, Cedar Lodge, in Bermuda, formerly owned by the late Senator Nathaniel Curry, following other moneyed Canadians to winter in the West Indies.[143] Hunting and fishing were among McLaughlin's favoured fair-weather pastimes. He maintained a trout preserve twenty minutes from his office, and in the early 1920s he began to lease a thirty-nine-mile stretch of river at Cap Chat, on the Gaspé Peninsula.[144] In 1932 McLaughlin became a member of the Long Point Company, an exclusive hunting club established in 1866 "by a small group of wealthy Canadian and American businessmen," maintaining a privately owned hunting preserve on a spit of land extending out into Lake Erie, near Port Rowan, Ontario.[145] Here, McLaughlin was able to hobnob with Wall Street moguls such as Junius S. Morgan II and Harry Morgan as well as royalty. The Duke of Windsor, who had relinquished the British Crown in 1936 to marry the American divorcee Wallace Simpson, appears to have visited Long Point with Sam in 1944. "His Excellency is most agreeable to the camp," reported McLaughlin.[146] Clearly he was delighted to belong to a transnational social network that helped solidify business contacts and boost his personal status.[147]

McLaughlin's business connections grew increasingly dense during the 1930s. In 1931 he joined the board of Famous Players Canadian Corporation; in 1932 he became a director of the CPR; he was elected director of the CPR's mining company, Consolidated Mining and Smelting of Canada, the year following, when he also became a director of Inco; in 1934 he gained a directorship with Canadian General Electric; and in 1935 he became a director of the Royal Trust Company.[148] McLaughlin was gravitating towards St James Street: General Motors of Canada was maintaining an account with the Bank of Montreal in the mid-1930s, and McLaughlin was serving as governor of the Seigniory Club, having been invited to join early in the club's existence, near the beginning of the decade.[149] In 1934 and 1935 McLaughlin went on excursions to Western Canada with CPR president Edward Beatty and other Canadian business magnates, including Sir Charles Gordon (Bank of Montreal), C.F. Sise Jr (Bell Telephone of Canada), Ross H. McMaster (Stelco), and Norman Dawes (National Breweries).[150] As McLaughlin's business and social life extended further into the traditional bastions of Canadian economic power on St James Street, and as he became associated with massive corporate empires emanating from south of the border, such as Inco and General Electric, he also developed a keen and broad interest in northern Ontario mining and became associated with the capitalist buccaneers in Toronto who promoted upstart mining enterprises, such as J.P. Bickell. In 1937 McLaughlin assumed a seat on Bickell's company, McIntyre Porcupine Mines Ltd.[151]

McLaughlin was notable for embracing a continental accumulation strategy that defied the old rivalries between Montreal and Toronto. This signalled a more general trend towards consolidation and cooperation in Canadian big business. Investment banker J.H. Gundy, for example, had received his start in the Cox family of companies, centred on Senator George Cox in the early twentieth century, representing Toronto's most powerful financial group and an emerging challenger to Montreal's hegemony. By the late 1920s, Gundy's investment bank was working with Royal Bank of Canada president Sir Herbert Holt in promoting Canada Power and Paper (see chapter 2). Nouveau riche St James Street moguls such as J.W. McConnell also operated above the inter-city rivalry of years past.[152] McLaughlin's free movement between Montreal and Toronto business circles demonstrated the coalescence of Montreal and Toronto capital; but, of course, his business world also embraced Detroit and New York. McLaughlin, if his brother's portfolio can serve as an indicator, invested in many different companies during the 1930s: George owned more than 100,000 shares in the Chrysler Corporation, more than 50,000 in Goodyear Tire, and held lesser amounts in a long list of companies, including shares in numerous northern Ontario mining operations, such as McIntyre Mines, Sherritt Gordon Mines, and Kirkland Lake Gold Mines.[153] Sam, meanwhile, was one of the larger holders of Inco stock, which was publicly revealed in accordance with the American Securities Exchange Act of 1934.[154] Correspondence during the Second World War between McLaughlin and long-time friend and GM director, C.S. Mott, indicates

McLaughlin's considerable interest in Canadian mining companies; Mott sent McLaughlin his portfolio to get his opinion. "Your list is a very good one on the whole and I do not think you will have to worry unduly about its future provided, of course," wrote McLaughlin in 1944, "one believes in Gold Stocks. I am a heavy holder of some of the mines in which you are interested, particularly – of course – McIntyre. I think there is a future for these mines. At any rate, I am going to bank on it and trust to what the future may hold."[155] McLaughlin's economic interests extended into various branches of the North American economy, revealing, as U.S. historian Martin Sklar has observed, the extent to which corporate concentration helped socialize risk among leading capitalists.[156]

McLaughlin had gravitated towards the centre of the Canadian business elite during the interwar period. Immediately after the First World War, McLaughlin had been relatively isolated from Canada's leading business centres. Heading up a U.S. branch, he may have also appeared – and have been – politically vulnerable against Canadian businessmen unconvinced of the auto industry's importance and western farmers angry about the higher price of Canadian automobiles. By the middle of the 1930s, much had changed. McLaughlin had become socially and economically integrated within the Canadian bourgeoisie, from the board of directors of the CPR to the elite social clubs of Toronto and Montreal, but he also operated within a larger North American business environment. The importance of the auto industry, too, was now beyond question in Canada. The rise of the parts industry during the 1930s placed the Big Three in Canada at the centre of a vast industrial complex. In 1929 the manufacture of parts comprised 18 per cent of the value of all vehicle production in Canada; in 1932 that figure had risen to 32 per cent, and by 1939 it reached 36 per cent.[157] By 1938 General Motors was extensively engaged in the manufacture of parts in Canada, making components such as engines, transmissions, generators, spark plugs, gears, axles, electrical equipment, wheel casings, radiators, and fenders, while purchasing products such as tires, floor mats, car radios, and bumpers from other Canadian operations. General Motors of Canada cars achieved a Canadian content as high as 75 per cent, proclaimed the *Financial Post*.[158] And while the sharp rebound of the auto industry in the mid-1930s attested to the industry's dynamism – as production rose nearly threefold at General Motors of Canada between 1933 and 1936 – it also prefigured a new confrontation between capital and labour.[159] McLaughlin's main political opponents were no longer outsiders – politicians, businessmen, and farmers – threatening to meddle with the tariff; rather, he faced an increasingly militant working class in Oshawa, a force which he little knew or understood.

Oshawa 1937

The General Motors strike in Oshawa, involving some 3,700 workers, in April 1937 has long been acknowledged as a watershed moment. McLaughlin's understanding of the events of that month reflected the broader concerns of the business community in Canada about U.S. industrial unionism: the strike, from this perspective, was not a contest between capital and labour but one of British law and order against the lawlessness of U.S. labour bosses. Oshawa's working class had been hoodwinked by slick outsiders, so this interpretation ran. "I didn't think they would do it," McLaughlin lamented. "They must have been promised the moon."[160]

The strike, indeed, developed as part of a transnational conflict. In November and December 1936, workers at GM plants in Kansas City and Atlanta engaged in sit-down strikes before the sit-down wave touched more important GM operations in Cleveland and Flint near the end of December. This grass-roots strike wave flowed from recent developments in the U.S. labour movement. In 1935 John L. Lewis, president of the United Mine Workers of America, had left the AFL to spearhead the formation of the Committee for Industrial Organization, a breakaway organization of affiliated unions committed to industrial unionism.[161] Opposing the craft-based unionism of the AFL, which had proven inadequate in the auto industry and other sites of mass production that were characterized by a wide range of crafts and by large numbers of semiskilled and unskilled labour, the CIO was deeply involved with the United Automobile Workers of America (UAW) organizing drive launched in the middle of 1936. At a meeting of CIO leaders in Pittsburgh in early November, also attended by UAW president Homer Martin, a decision was reached to step up the organizing campaign in the auto industry to take advantage of the favourable political climate created by the recent electoral victories of President Franklin D. Roosevelt and of the populist and pro-labour governor of Michigan, Frank Murphy, who was to assume office 1 January 1937.[162] The organizing drive, meanwhile, also benefited from the Communist Party's embrace of "united front" tactics in 1935, which advocated Communist participation in non-Communist labour organizations and encouraged, more broadly, cooperation with social democrats in an antifascist and anticapitalist coalition.[163] Union recognition was central to the strikers' demands; and on 11 February 1937, in an agreement between UAW representatives and GM officials, the colossal corporation "for the first time agreed to recognize an international union as a party to the collective-bargaining process."[164]

Within two weeks, CIO organizer Hugh Thompson was addressing Oshawa body-shop workers who had downed tools in response to a recent speed-up. Thompson had come up from Detroit likely in response to an invitation from William Gelech, a communist and member of a cell operating clandestinely in the body shop, consisting mostly of Scottish and Welsh immigrants whose political education had been received in the epic class struggles of Britain's coal mines.[165] Thompson delivered a short address outlining the success of the UAW in the United States. All the men in the room voted to join the UAW and returned to work on Thompson's advice. The following day, Thompson established a headquarters for UAW Local 222 in a downtown office.[166]

The UAW-CIO victory in the United States was a source of inspiration for Oshawa autoworkers, but success could also be seen closer to home: parts makers in Oshawa and other centres had signed contracts with unions affiliated with the CIO in the months preceding the GM strike in Oshawa.[167] Ontario premier Mitch Hepburn, nonetheless, was proving to be a particularly strenuous opponent. When vigilantes violently suppressed a CIO sit-down at the Holmes Foundry near Sarnia, Hepburn unequivocally supported the action, thundering in the Ontario legislature: "There will be no sit-downs in Ontario!"[168] Hepburn not only considered the sit-down tactic an illegal trespass on private property, but he also viewed the CIO in terms of a communist scheme designed to subvert social order. Hepburn was also closely aligned with a coterie of Toronto mining magnates who were worried about the possibility of the CIO making inroads in northern Ontario mines.

McLaughlin was not a regular at the King Edward Hotel, the watering hole of Hepburn and his mining associates, but he was certainly associated economically – through J.P. Bickell and McIntyre-Porcupine, as well as Inco. As negotiations between union and company representatives broke down over the question of union recognition in late March, the possibility of a strike loomed. On the morning of 8 April, upon Thompson's direction, the shop stewards ordered the plant vacated. The strike had begun. At the time, McLaughlin was resting in Bermuda, enjoying the salty sea breezes of Hamilton Harbour.

Hepburn, too, had been away but arrived in Toronto from Florida the day before the strike broke out. In his 1974 article on the Oshawa strike, Irving Abella claims that GM had agreed to recognize Local 222 shortly before the strike, only to resume its refusal to recognize the CIO upon the urging of Hepburn, who promised total support from the government.[169] John T. Saywell, in his 1991 biography of Mitch Hepburn, points out that such an account is not sustained by the contemporary evidence and argues that Abella relied too heavily upon the unreliable remembrances of David Croll, Ontario minister of labour at the time, and Croll's secretary, Roger Irwin. Heather Robertson, who had access to GM's archives in Oshawa, presents an account that not only tends to confirm Saywell's assertion but claims that General Motors of Canada had anticipated a strike since the beginning of 1937, stockpiling cars since January. Robertson also speculates that GM may have thought it possible to weaken the UAW in the United States by beating the union in Canada. In addition to this, McLaughlin's private and public pronouncements consistently indicated that he remained set in the belief that the CIO was not a legitimate labour organization.[170] All of this suggests, of course, that the Ontario government did not exercise as much autonomy during the strike as previously presumed. Becoming the most vocal public opponent of the CIO during the strike, Hepburn backed up GM's refusal to recognize the CIO in Oshawa – but he was by no means the author of the company's policy.

Hepburn quickly sought to ready a police force to suppress anticipated "disorder," cabling Dominion minister of justice Ernest Lapointe to request reinforcements from the RCMP. That day, 8 April, Hepburn's initial request was granted: "100 men are being dispatched today to Toronto to support the Ontario Provincial Police," reported

RCMP commissioner J.H. MacBrien.[171] However, Mackenzie King instructed the RCMP to act as support to provincial and municipal forces
should violence arise; they were not to "initiate" action but should be
"kept in the background as much as possible."[172] Furthermore, later
in the afternoon Hepburn requested another 100 RCMP officers to
ready for the "main crisis," which he expected in two or three days.[173]
No more officers were sent. All the same, Hepburn put the OPP on
twenty-four-hour alert and mobilized 100 officers in the Oshawa area
while ordering the Department of Welfare to deny relief to strikers.[174]
At a press conference on the day of the strike's outbreak, Hepburn
lamented that GM workers had followed the lead of "CIO-paid propagandists from the USA to desert their posts at a time when both employees and the industry itself were in a position to enjoy a prosperity
not known since 1929."[175] The *Globe and Mail*, meanwhile, under the
direction of mining magnate–turned–newspaperman C. George Mc-
Cullagh, the paper's president and publisher, railed against the CIO
and hit a similar chord as Hepburn – which might not be surprising
considering McCullagh's later boast suggesting that he was the brains
behind Hepburn's anti-CIO crusade.[176] "Time will show that the trouble at Oshawa has been engineered from the United States to serve the
purpose of the Lewis program," editorialized the *Globe and Mail* on 13
April, "and did not originate with the workers in that city." The paper
suggested a Bolshevik conspiracy.[177]

The views of Hepburn and McCullagh sharply contrasted with the
realities in Oshawa. The strikers conducted an orderly picket outside
the plant. When picketers began to rock company trucks attempting to
move through the plant gates on 10 April, Hugh Thompson arrived on
the scene and warned the strikers that GM was looking for an excuse
to call in the Mounties. The trucks, after being checked for machine
guns, were allowed to pass. Contrasting with this discipline, Hepburn's
unrestrained public blustering and vacillating attitude during negotiations with union representatives seemed to anticipate and welcome
confrontation. After meeting with union representative C.H. Millard on
9 April, Hepburn expressed hope that the strike could be concluded, but
soon after he descended into a rage, pointing to CIO organizing initiatives in northern Ontario and promising to, if necessary, raise an army
to fight the CIO. On 16 April, Hepburn again proved volatile, ending

negotiations with union representative and labour lawyer J.L. Cohen. Hepburn abruptly ended negotiations after Cohen made a long-distance call to UAW president Martin, claiming that he would not submit to negotiations by "remote control." Cohen was perplexed. Hepburn had agreed to Cohen's consultations with Martin beforehand. His "remote control" allegation was an excuse to halt negotiations. While Hepburn engaged in theatrics at Queen's Park, union officials enforced public order in Oshawa with the help of local police. Striking workers received bread, meat, and cheese from local grocers and fuel from coal dealers – and provincial liquor vendors remained closed, with the consent of the union. Mayor Alex Hall attested to the orderliness of local affairs and protested Hepburn's efforts to bring in outside police.[178]

On 13 April, 200 special constables were sworn in "for possible emergency duty," joining a combined force of 165 RCMP and OPP officers stationed in Toronto. And Hepburn looked to the Dominion government again for another 100 RCMP officers, but his request was refused on 14 April. The refusal reflected mounting tensions between the Dominion government and Hepburn. Norman Rogers, King's minister of labour, had upset Hepburn when he offered to mediate the dispute. Mayor Hall had invited Rogers's intervention, and the union was also agreeable to mediation by Dominion government officials. However, GM released a statement at midnight on 12 April rejecting the offer. The following day, Hepburn publicly blamed the federal government for letting CIO organizers into Canada over his objections six weeks earlier. He also issued a statement calling for unity within his own cabinet in the Ontario government's "fight against the forces of John L. Lewis and Communism which are now marching hand-in-hand"; the next day he secured the resignations of two dissenting cabinet ministers, attorney general Arthur Roebuck and David Croll, who held the public welfare, labour, and municipal affairs portfolios. Hepburn received encouragement early, on 9 April, from Noranda Mines president James Y. Murdoch, who congratulated him on his "brave and splendid action in immediately stepping into the strike situation in Oshawa." And after further hardening his stance, Hepburn was congratulated by Robert H. Bryce, president of Macassa Mines, for his "constructive actions." Hepburn received many such words of encouragement from businessmen, and he captured broader support based on concerns about outside influence and the spread of communism.[179]

Commanding Heights: St James Street during the 1920s. Montreal's St James
Street remained the preeminent centre of Canadian capitalism after the First
World War. The headquarters of the Bank of Montreal is on the immediate
left, imposing pillars across the front of the building. *St James Street,
Montreal, Quebec, about 1925*, McCord Museum: MP-0000.25.222.

Canada's "Second Industrial Revolution": General Motors of Canada, circa 1918. The automobile industry was a transformative force in Canadian economic and political life after the First World War, hastening the relative ascent of southern Ontario and the increasingly continental orientation of Canadian economic life. Oshawa Public Libraries: LH1037.

Harvesting Wheat: The National Policy in the Prairie West. Export-oriented wheat production was a central plank of the National Policy, but farmers often felt marginalized by the resulting economic and political outcomes. During the 1920s and 1930s, agrarian protest was much less amenable to the classical liberalism that the Canadian bourgeoisie espoused. *Harvesting an extensive wheat field near Saskatoon, Saskatchewan, about 1920*, McCord Museum: MP-0000.25.423.

Western Progressive: Charles Dunning (1885–1958). Dunning embraced a progressivism that was viewed favourably by the business community, but which would lose its popular resonance as Dunning joined the ranks of Canadian big business during the Great Depression of the 1930s. Queen's University Archives: V28 P-59.3.

Party Politics: Mackenzie King and his cabinet, 1930. Though big business sought to transcend party politics through various nonpartisan initiatives from the 1920s to the 1940s, party politics remained crucial to the exercise of power, and the influence of Canadian big business within the major national political parties was in decline during the Great Depression of the 1930s. The failure of Charles Dunning (third on the right from Mackenzie King at the centre) as minister of finance to restore classical liberal ideals during the Depression underlined the political dilemma that the Canadian business elite faced. *Cabinet Meeting, Privy Council Chamber, East Block*, 1930, Library and Archives Canada: C-009060.

Provincial Man of Mystery: Howard P. Robinson (1874–1950). Robinson became a leading figure of New Brunswick's business community, developing important national and international business connections. This contributed to his emergence as an important political actor after the First World War, though by choice he remained out of the public spotlight. *Howard P. Robinson* by Miller Gore Brittain, 1941, New Brunswick Museum, Saint John, New Brunswick: W4641.

Big Capital in the Countryside: International Paper's newsprint mill and pulpwood loom over Dalhousie, New Brunswick, 1936. The pulp and paper industry soaked up large amounts of capital during the 1920s. Provincial Archives of New Brunswick: P93-RI-2.

The Bourgeoisie Dining: Sir Frederick Williams-Taylor hosts a dinner, Montreal, 1923. Williams-Taylor, general manager of the Bank of Montreal and president of the Canadian Bankers' Association, is seated at the end of the table (to the right side of the centrepiece), and next to him is Sir Charles Blair Gordon, vice-president of the Bank of Montreal and president of the Dominion Textile Company. *Sir Frederick Williams-Taylor's dinner, Montreal, Quebec, 1923*, McCord Museum: II-252180.3.

Capital's Crisis of Legitimacy: Oshawa 1937. War veterans and clergymen in
Oshawa protest the recruitment of 200 war veterans for a special police force
during the General Motors strike in April 1937. The auto industry became
the epicentre of the industrial union drive in North America during the 1930s.
Walter P. Reuther Library, Wayne State University.

Consumer of Culture: Sam McLaughlin (1871–1972) with his favourite horse, Punch, circa 1928. From horses to yachts and art, General Motors of Canada president R.S. McLaughlin was a voracious consumer of culture. City of Toronto Archives, Fonds 1244, Item 1307.

EDWARD WENTWORTH BEATTY, B.A., K.C.

President, Canadian Pacific Railway

Wealth Revitalized: Edward Beatty (1877–1943). Beatty projected a sleeker and more vibrant representation of the wealthy, which became more typical during the first few decades of the twentieth century in what U.S. historian Jackson Lears has described as the "managerial revitalization of the rich." *Edward Wentworth Beatty, BA, KC, President, Canadian Pacific Railway* by Arthur George Racey, 1922, McCord Museum: M20111.9.

The Bourgeoisie Socializing: Aboard a yacht, Sir Edward Beatty (second from left) is flanked by Sir Herbert Holt (right) and Herbert Molson (left, at the end). *On board yacht* Curlew. *Left to right: Herbert Molson, Sir Edward Beatty, Sir H.S. Holt, N.L.C. Mather Sr, D. Forbes Angus, H. Joseph, A.D. MacTier, and W. Morrice*, ca1936, Library and Archives Canada: PA-149052.

Residence of R.S. MᶜLaughlin
Oshawa, Ont.

Displaying Wealth: Parkwood, circa 1920s. Sam McLaughlin's mansion
Parkwood was built during the First World War, an imposing monument to
his wealth and social and cultural ambitions. Oshawa Publics Libraries:
LH1054.

Engineer of Capital: C.D. Howe (1886–1960). As minister of transport and later as minister of munitions and supply, Howe championed a more active and autonomous state role in Canada's political economy, a stance that was intensely resisted by leading members of the Canadian bourgeoisie. *The Hon. C.D. Howe inspects an aircraft being built at an aircraft factory*, March 1941, Fort William, Ontario, National Film Board of Canada/Library and Archives Canada.

A radically different understanding of the situation was voiced in the streets of Oshawa. On the morning of 14 April, war veterans met at Memorial Park to protest Hepburn's efforts to recruit veterans into his special police force. Dr T.E. Kaiser addressed the crowd of 500 veterans and as many spectators. Kaiser had, as the local Conservative MP, supported McLaughlin in 1926 when much of Oshawa had rallied behind GM in protesting the King government's auto tariff revisions. Now, he voiced opposition to the company: "Insofar as citizens of Oshawa are concerned, what I am complaining of and what I think men have a right to protest against was the first invasion of Americanism into the city in the nature of what is called 'efficiency.' The poison of efficiency is that a man shouldn't have a job after the age of 45. I oppose it emphatically." The crowd roared with approval. "Where a poison goes," the doctor continued, "and where a poison spreads, there is nearly always close by an antidote. If American organizers come in as antidote to oppose American efficiency, I'm not going to oppose their coming here." He concluded by aligning the strike with loyalty to the British Crown: "I'm not worried about us becoming Bolsheviks. We're loyal British subjects and loyal to our King, but we can eradicate the sins of industrialism."[180] Such views indicated that public opinion was shifting. Sam McLaughlin was now viewed as a representative of an element foreign and opposed to the well-being of the community. Indeed, local UAW leader C.H. Millard was a veteran of the First World War and a prominent layman in the King Street United Church; he may have seemed a natural ideological ally of McLaughlin during the 1920s as a budding small businessman, but the harsh experience of the Great Depression changed his outlook and caused his transformation into a labour activist.[181] McLaughlin's local base of political support had been drastically eroded by the economic crisis.

Hepburn's call for police reinforcements coincided with the arrival of OPP reports that indicated the effectiveness of the pickets. On 12 April, OPP constable Alex Wilson reported that the picket line had tightened and appeared to be having the desired effect – "that is to shame those who are working into quitting."[182] The union ensured that the strike remained orderly throughout its duration, as workers well understood that an outbreak of violence would benefit the company; indeed, Millard claimed to have "definite proof" of a GM attempt to incite disorder.[183] Eric Havelock, a Victoria College classics professor who voiced his public support for the workers at a strike meeting, years later recalled the nightly mass meetings of strikers held in the auditorium of the local collegiate institute. A contingent of war veterans filled the first four rows and enforced order:

> Quite a few were wearing medals and wound stripes; many were accompanied by wives; the whole assembly had something of the atmosphere of a huge family party; the auditorium was jammed; more veterans parading the aisles, keeping watchful order; the balconies overflowing with men young and old, the feet of those in front hanging through the balustrade; the whole assembly tense but attentive. At the first sign of any disturbance, however minor, even a question asked of some small movement or interruption, the ushers swiftly closed in on the culprit and escorted him from the hall. There was a good reason for these precautions.[184]

The spectre of violence was always present, laying bare capital's crisis of legitimacy in Oshawa.

Despite Hepburn's consistently provocative rhetoric, J.L. Cohen succeeded in negotiating a settlement with GM officials and Hepburn on 22 April, which provided for recognition of the local union without any reference to the CIO. The agreement was ratified by vote the following day. It was timely for the union, since rank-and-file support waned as it became apparent that no immediate support – in the form of strike pay or a solidarity strike – would be coming from UAW members south of the border, contrary to earlier promises.[185] Both sides claimed victory. Hepburn claimed that the CIO had been defeated in Canada, since the agreement only acknowledged the local union, not the CIO. Meanwhile, UAW Local 222 president C.H. Millard claimed victory. It remained an ambiguous conclusion. The Oshawa settlement became, as labour historian Laurel Sefton MacDowell has observed, "a model for corporations, whereby managements granted de facto recognition to a union, dealt with a local union committee, but withheld formal recognition."[186] A new entente had been achieved, but the future of industrial unionism was far from assured.

On 12 April, as tensions mounted in Oshawa, Sam McLaughlin said that he had no plans to return to Oshawa and no comment to make on the strike.[187] This aloofness was a great contrast to the 1928 strike, when McLaughlin supposedly rushed back immediately to Oshawa to help resolve the dispute. As the stewardship associated with the McLaughlin Carriage Company morphed into dependency with GM and combined with the economic crisis of the 1930s, McLaughlin's claims to community leadership became compromised. Sam arrived back in Oshawa on 23 April, unconvinced of the union's legitimacy: "We have letters from dozens who were threatened into joining the union and of others who did so because they didn't want to be bothered any more." And he expressed approval of Hepburn's attitude during the strike, as well as Ernest Lapointe's public pronouncements against the sit-down tactic. "I'm glad they would not tolerate the iniquitous condition that exists in the United States where they step right in and take possession of your property and will not move out even at the request of the state police," explained Sam. "If such a condition ever developed here I would move right out of the country. But I don't think it can ever happen in Canada."[188] These barely veiled threats revealed his frustration. George was also bitter, lashing out at "alleged evangelical church workers" who, he believed, supported the "foreign agitators of the type of the C.I.O. Lewis gang" and "whose salaries are being paid in a large measure by the very people whom they attack."[189]

The rule of money and its apparent influence in the Hepburn government had only limited effect upon events in Oshawa. The UAW's success in Flint was made possible, as labour historian Nelson Lichtenstein has observed, "because General Motors was temporarily denied recourse to the police power of the state."[190] In Ontario, Hepburn was only too eager to deploy the police in Oshawa, though Mackenzie King was not willing to throw the Dominion government behind Hepburn's crusade. Had a sit-down been attempted, perhaps another outcome would have resulted. As it was, there was no need for a sit-down in Oshawa. Unlike Flint, there was not a hostile local police force and veritable army of company police to assault picketing workers in Oshawa – one considerable advantage of the sit-down, after all, was the fact that it physically insulated strikers from these threats. No such insulation was needed in Oshawa, where local support was decidedly behind the workers and where the union had considerably displaced Sam McLaughlin as the source of working-class loyalties.

McLaughlin did not view these developments with equanimity. After the strike, he came to believe that national political efforts should be concentrated on battling the CIO. The issue, McLaughlin believed, crossed party lines: "It is about time the people in this country waked up and instead of squabbling as to whether they are Liberals or Conservatives, they should have a National Government in order to fight the almost intolerable conditions which are about to arise if something is not done to stop the progress of the communistic C.I.O."[191] Years later, George McCullagh reminded McLaughlin of their early opposition to the CIO: "I saw it early and, in company with you, took the bold step of opposing the C.I.O."[192] Bold steps, indeed, had been attempted.

Hepburn and McCullagh had tried to orchestrate an anti-CIO coalition government in Ontario during and after the strike, and McLaughlin was undoubtedly sympathetic to, if not involved with, this effort. Hepburn first raised the possibility of a coalition with the Conservatives on 12 April, when he approached Conservative leader Earl Rowe with the offer. On 16 April, Rowe mentioned Hepburn's offer to Conservative Party organizer George Drew, who became a strong advocate for the coalition. While Rowe remained aloof, McCullagh made contact with Drew on behalf of Hepburn on 23 April, at a St George's Society dinner at which Drew gave a speech. Agreeing to meet with McCullagh, Drew found in McCullagh someone who presented "a definite vision for the future" and who "could speak his own language." McCullagh thus presented Hepburn's offer: a fifty-fifty split in cabinet postings, six Liberals and six Conservatives; the position of attorney general for Drew; and, if Drew and Rowe wished, Hepburn would step down as premier. Drew sounded out Lieutenant Governor Dr Herbert A. Bruce on the CIO two days later; the following day, Hepburn approached Bruce to discuss the coalition. Both Bruce and Drew tried to convince Rowe to accept Hepburn's offer, but Rowe, viewing Hepburn's anti-CIO campaign as alarmist and contrary to liberal principles, refused. On 30 April, Drew offered his resignation as Conservative Party organizer to Rowe, in an apparent effort to pressure Rowe into entering the coalition government with Hepburn. Rowe refused again and accepted Drew's resignation. On 1 May the coalition proposal was aired publicly in the press – both Hepburn and Rowe denied it.[193] "The great 'putsch' for the establishment of an anti-C.I.O. Government in Ontario has come to a somewhat inglorious end," reported *Saturday Night* on 13 May.[194]

Following the strike, McLaughlin was also associated with the group who sought to use imperial loyalty and the mounting threat of Nazi aggression as a rallying point upon which to advance a right-wing agenda. Speculation appeared in the press that the group centred around Hepburn, Drew, and McCullagh also hoped to achieve railway unification.[195] It was a plausible claim. Strident British imperialists committed to fighting the growing scope of government intervention, these wealthy individuals coalesced around broad ideological goals as the threats of increasing government debt and government interventionism mounted. After the Oshawa strike, the CIO was another issue around which these individuals rallied. This sentiment was to culminate in the emergence of George McCullagh's Leadership League in 1939 and Arthur Meighen's failed attempt to lead the Conservative Party in 1942. Mackenzie King reported a conversation with Governor General Lord Tweedsmuir in February 1939, shortly after the Leadership League was formed: King said to Tweedsmuir that McCullagh and John Bassett of the Montreal *Gazette* were "trying to work out a Fascist party in Canada" and "were prepared to use Hepburn, Drew and others, to further their ends." King named McLaughlin as one of the plotters, stating that he wanted to "protect his millions against the C.I.O." Shortly after war was declared on Germany, King worried about McLaughlin, McCullagh, and others – whom he collectively described as "a body of gangsters" – "who have been using the Canadian Army Corps ... seeking to get possession of the Government of Canada at this period of war."[196] Allowing for the hyperbole of King's diary entries, these statements confirm a perceived drift to the right among a number of the country's leading big business figures at this time.

McLaughlin's visceral reaction to the CIO and the political associations he cultivated revealed a stubborn ideological and political commitment. McLaughlin and his vice-president, H.J. Carmichael, insisted that the company not rehire William Gelech, the employee who had originally contacted the CIO and had been dismissed by the company prior to the strike. Meeting with a union deputation arguing on Gelech's behalf, personnel manager J.B. Highfield admitted that nothing was wrong with Gelech's work, but he noted that Gelech had broken a "solemn promise" not to engage in agitation or radical activities. High-field then produced an RCMP file on Gelech's political activities prior to arriving at General Motors.[197] McLaughlin assuredly embraced a right-wing brand of politics that had won considerable support within the country's business elite by the late 1930s. But the aura of benef-icence was now gone, as the stewardship of the McLaughlin family was overwhelmed by the economic crisis of the Depression and Sam McLaughlin's dependent accumulation strategy, which not only intro-duced a new form of industrial development to Oshawa but also intro-duced a new level of conflict between employer and employee.

Conclusion

"What about the future?" asked journalist Gordon Sinclair in 1943. McLaughlin had entered his father's business when he was just "a gaf-fer in short pants and the business had eight workers"; now he presided over a business with 14,000 workers. "Could a young man starting out now," probed Sinclair, "in these days of restrictions, ever get where you have got?" Yes, McLaughlin believed. Success required the conquest of obstacles, and though the managed wartime economy had created new "fences," opportunities for ambitious young men – as he was fifty years earlier – still existed. "I agree with Mr. Churchill that the nation which destroys initiative can't live," McLaughlin concluded. "I believe that with all my heart and I see no prospect of the country going backward. It will forever go forward."[198] Initiative and enterprise were, naturally, the cornerstones of society to McLaughlin's mind; he looked forward to their flowering in the postwar world. Though the older paternalism with which he had grown up had been dissolved by new conditions, including the rise of labour unionism, and although the political initia-tives with which he became associated in the 1930s did not succeed as he would have liked, he expected "enterprise" to flower in the postwar world in new forms and that General Motors of Canada would assume an even more central position in the nation's political economy. Sir Ed-ward Beatty dismissed the preaching of, as he called him in a private letter, the "Reverend Sam McLaughlin" on the demise of the steam engine.[199] But McLaughlin was, in a sense, essentially correct; the po-litical economy of the automobile would shape and reshape Canada

– touching business life and politics, culture and social life – while railways assumed a position of lesser importance.

As we have seen, the story of General Motors of Canada and Sam McLaughlin reflected broader trends of growing U.S. involvement in the Canadian economy and the related shift in economic orientation of Canadian big business towards the emerging continental political economy. Since the auto industry was centred almost entirely in southern Ontario, it also reflected the rise of southern Ontario during the Second Industrial Revolution. And underlying these conceptual and spatial changes was a trend towards heightened class struggle.

During the interwar period, Oshawa autoworkers acquired a political consciousness that was no longer dependent on Sam McLaughlin and General Motors of Canada. McLaughlin continued to exercise an indirect form of political leadership in the community during the 1920s, based upon community stewardship and protectionist politics. Continued exploitation at the workplace combined with the political, economic, and social effects of capitalist crisis during the 1930s, however, worked to undermine the sense of mutuality that formerly united McLaughlin with his workers. In step with these changes, McLaughlin acquired new directorships that solidified his position within Canadian big business, as the auto industry itself gained a more central position in the nation's economic and political life. McLaughlin's estrangement from Oshawa's working class found its most dramatic expression in the 1937 strike, which also signalled the newfound political effectiveness of the city's autoworkers. In important ways he was no longer a player on this stage, and this perhaps helps explain why he remained in Bermuda during the most decisive weeks of the conflict. And though McLaughlin refrained from public activity against the union, his private and public utterances reveal his political and ideological association with right-wing business and political leaders in Ontario, such as George McCullagh, Herbert Bruce, and George Drew. On the shop floor, too, McLaughlin appeared to oppose concessions; a few months after the strike, he and Carmichael apparently vetoed a wage increase for tool and die makers that J.B. Highfield had agreed to.[200] More broadly, McLaughlin became a participant in a new phase of class conflict, which Mackenzie King's Liberal administration struggled to manage as the Hepburn Liberals encouraged outright confrontation. But the Canadian bourgeoisie would be forced to live with political and economic change during the 1930s and 1940s, while from within King's cabinet a brash engineering contractor–turned–politician, C.D. Howe, paved the path towards a new, but similar, postwar society.

McLaughlin was a transitional figure. His accumulation strategy helped create the framework of Canada's increasingly continental economy during the twentieth century, but his sentimental attachment to the British Empire remained strong. He strived to gain social status through the traditional avenues of bourgeois culture, such as art collecting; but he also embraced the emergent meritocratic style of the wealthy, and, like Beatty, he projected an image of vitality and sought to stay physically fit. In the 1930s and 1940s, C.D. Howe would champion an emergent capitalist ideology that would point even more clearly to the new direction of Canadian capitalism. We turn to him next.

5

Engineering Canada:
C.D. Howe and
Canadian Big Business

In late December 1946 Canada's minister of reconstruction, Clarence Decatur Howe, left Montreal with a party of distinguished gentlemen. Humming through the sky on a Trans-Canada Air Lines (TCA) plane bound for Nassau, the small party looked forward to golf, bridge, and male camaraderie in comfortable surroundings. Howe had secured use of the plane from TCA president H.J. Symington, or, as he called him, "Herbie." The men joining Howe in the crown corporation plane were a distinguished group: Dr T.H. Hogg of Ontario Hydro; C.F. Sise Jr of Bell Telephone; senator and former National Liberal Federation president Norman Lambert; and Nova Scotia premier Angus Mac-donald, a fellow cabinet minister with Howe during the war. Howe's good friend, R.E. Powell, or "Rip," as Howe affectionately called him, was also invited, but his responsibilities as president of the Aluminum Company of Canada Limited required he forego the trip (but perhaps Powell consoled himself with memories of the stunning golf game he played, in the company of the Duke of Windsor, on a similar trip with Howe two years earlier). Although C.D. Howe (1886–1960) presided over unprecedented state intervention into the economy, he did so in the context of a social world that was much wider than the formal chambers of political and economic activity and included social forays such as leisurely trips to Nassau or fishing at Sam McLaughlin's lodge at Cap Chat, Quebec. As the use of names such as Herbie and Rip suggest, Howe cultivated relationships within the business community that were of more than a professional or formal character. "Beyond the formalized channels of interaction," observed business historian Duncan McDowall, "the real crucible of new industrial strategies was the system of personal friendships centred around Howe himself."[1]

This might be viewed as a considerable feat for a man who only five years earlier had accused the nation's leading business journal, the *Financial Post*, of being the "number one saboteur in Canada" of the war effort. Indeed, not long after he became a member of Mackenzie King's cabinet following the 1935 federal election, Howe, as minister of transport, made powerful enemies, most notably Sir Edward Beatty of the Canadian Pacific Railway. Howe entered the House of Commons and King's cabinet a wealthy man, the proprietor of a successful Port Arthur engineering firm, especially noted for construction of terminal grain elevators in Western Canada. But unlike Charles Dunning, who also joined the King administration, Howe could not be considered a member of the national bourgeoisie. And where Dunning sought to guide the government towards balanced budgets and fiscal prudence in an attempt to restore financial order and limit government expansion, Howe guided the government towards new activities and responsibilities. Howe would help forge a new relationship between government and big business, contrary to the wishes of many leading business executives who wanted the old political economy restored. Indeed, Howe's ascent to the commanding heights of the Canadian economy during the period of the Great Depression and the Second World War was evidence of the bourgeoisie's inability to defend and reinstate the old political economy of the National Policy period.

In popular and academic writing Howe has often been cast as a fairly straightforward representative of big business.[2] Such depictions tend to oversimplify and misrepresent Howe's changing historic role. The few scholarly biographical treatments that exist have offered more nuanced understandings of Howe, but they tend to place too heavy an emphasis upon his personality. Indeed, a peculiar feature of the scholarly literature is the view that Howe operated basically without an ideology.[3] David Noble's influential analysis, which posits that the engineering profession provided the logic for the emergence of corporate capitalism as well as for the reproduction of capitalist social relations in the United States, offers a framework that can be used to understand Howe in terms of a broader social process.[4] Howe was trained as an engineer at the

Massachusetts Institute of Technology (MIT) before coming to Canada to teach civil engineering at Dalhousie University and, later, work as a contracting engineer. Howe arrived in the country during a period in the early twentieth century when the engineering profession was emerging in Canada.[5] And he would continue to ascribe considerable importance to his own professional credentials throughout his political career. Howe's hostility to labour unions and his domineering style, accompanied by his willingness to defer to experts in specific fields, all bespeak characteristics that synchronize closely with ideological developments within professional engineering circles analysed by Noble.

By drawing upon Noble's insights one can begin to appreciate the ideological nature of Howe's beliefs and activities in government. In so doing, we can begin to historicize Howe's activities and ideas within a broader "passive revolution" that would ultimately work to restore the legitimacy of capital during a period of crisis. Howe's basic answer to calls for social-democratic reform was this: through increases in productivity and efficiency, encouraged by state intervention where necessary, higher wages could be achieved. Significantly, big business was, to a considerable degree, among the "passive" agents in this historic process of change. The new managerialism that Howe brought to bear upon the state and its involvement in the Canadian economy upset business conservatives who, unlike Howe, continued to embrace the laissez-faire ideal of a self-correcting market economy. Thus, even though Howe was decidedly pro-business and projected the meritocratic and gendered image of a changing elite, the acceptance of his outlook within big business circles remained highly uneven after the Second World War.[6] Howe championed a brand of capitalism more managerial in its ethos, more state-centric in its operation, and more continental in its geographic orientation than what had existed before.[7] His efforts emerged not merely from his professional and ideological formation as an engineer but from popular demands that were forcing political parties to accommodate social-democratic reform and engage in more aggressive forms of state intervention. As old liberal ideals and the British Empire waned in national economic and political life, big business entered an unfamiliar and uncomfortable postwar world, in which Howe operated at the centre of a transforming government-business nexus.

Early Life and Business Career

Born in Waltham, Massachusetts, in 1886, Clarence Decatur Howe grew up in prosperous middle-class circumstances. His father, a carpenter, built houses, served on the local board of aldermen, and spent one term in Congress as a Republican member of the House of Representatives. His mother was a beacon of middle-class respectability, active in hospital and charity work. He had one sibling, a younger sister, with whom he got along well. The family lived in a Victorian bungalow on a large, treed lot along the Charles River. The neighbourhood consisted mainly of skilled factory workers and craftsmen; the Howes were better off than their neighbours, but not ostentatiously so. Howe spent his summers at his grandfather's homestead in Maine until he left for Boston to attend MIT. Propertied respectability and the ideal of social mobility were everywhere apparent in Howe's upbringing. An avid reader in his youth, Howe was particularly fond of the rags-to-riches Horatio Alger books. As a boy, Howe was always near the top of his class, a focused, but not brilliant, student. He was also a sports enthusiast who loved baseball and was an oarsman of considerable quality. His was an upbringing of relative comfort and contentment.[8]

He began his studies at MIT in 1903, where he achieved high grades, joined a fraternity, managed the baseball team, and in 1907 received a degree in civil engineering.[9] During the summers he apprenticed as a draftsman for Joseph Worcester's engineering firm, noted for its important role in planning the construction of Boston's subway system. MIT was an academically and socially successful endeavour for Howe. Upon graduation, however, he found employment prospects were poor because of a brief recession. Howe remained at MIT as a teaching assistant until the summer of 1908, when he left for Halifax to teach civil engineering at Dalhousie University. Nova Scotia's historical connections with New England made Howe's transition to life in Halifax fairly smooth. Only a couple of years older than most of his students, Howe was assigned heavy teaching responsibilities, but nonetheless succeeded in gaining the respect of his students. He particularly liked fieldwork. On trips outside Halifax he and his students would plan the construction of imaginary railways – an ironically appropriate activity for Howe, who, as E.R. Forbes has shown, would do little to promote industrial development in the Maritimes during and after the Second World War.[10]

In 1913 Howe left Dalhousie to take up a position as chief engineer of the Board of Grain Commissioners. A former colleague of Howe at Dalhousie, Robert Magill, a professor of philosophy, had been appointed chairman of the young agency headquartered in Fort William, Ontario. Magill decided the board should construct grain terminal elevators of its own, and he needed someone with engineering expertise to advise on construction; he asked Howe. Howe applied to become a British subject and arrived in northern Ontario to begin a twenty-year odyssey in western business; he returned to the United States in 1915 to wed Alice Worcester, the daughter of Joseph Worcester (in whose engineering firm Howe had apprenticed), but Canada had become Howe's adopted country. Magill chose to build the first elevator in Port Arthur, Fort William's twin city, but the Board of Grain Commissioners would build many more across the West. Howe was able to get in on the ground floor of this business, forming a consulting engineering firm in 1916 and maintaining an important friendship with the ambitious general manager of the Saskatchewan Cooperative Elevator Company (SCEC), Charles Dunning.[11] The success of Howe's firm, unimaginatively named C.D. Howe & Company, hung in the balance early on, when in 1916 gale force winds destroyed a terminal being built by Howe's company for the SCEC. As a result, Howe's ability to complete the contract on time was called into question, but he worked out arrangements to complete the elevator on schedule and succeeded in completing it in time to receive the 1917 crop. As Howe had lost money on the contract, the SCEC voted to cover his losses, which totalled $400,000.[12] His company would plan the construction of 85 per cent of Western Canada's terminal grain elevators as well as design bridges, docks, flour mills, and industrial buildings across the West and the United States. Howe also developed a method of concrete pouring that drastically reduced construction costs and time and built elevators designed to save time in the loading and unloading of grain. He operated with the understanding that the ledger book was at the end of every engineering equation. Having developed an international reputation as

an expert in the construction of terminal grain elevators, in 1932 Howe
was hired by the Baring Brothers, the storied London financial firm,
to oversee the construction of massive grain elevators on the Buenos
Aires waterfront. Howe spent eighteen months in Argentina, reportedly
picking up some facility in Spanish and Italian. One estimate put the
cumulative business transactions of C.D. Howe & Company at some-
where in the order of $100 million between 1916 and 1935. Howe was
reportedly a millionaire by the time he was forty, though he later dismissed the claim. Domestic life was similarly fruitful. By the end of the
1920s, Alice Howe had borne five children. Howe lived with his family
in a three-storey house in a "comfortable middle-class neighborhood"
in Port Arthur, completing a trajectory reminiscent of the Horatio Alger
books of his youth.[13]

An Engineer in Politics

Howe believed an engineer's line of work to be "wholly inconsistent
with political partisanship" and, moreover, that partisanship put the
engineer's livelihood in jeopardy.[14] This conclusion was born out of
Howe's own experience. The business he received from the cooperative grain companies was substantial, yet he did not receive one contract from the private dealers for elevator construction at the Lakehead
between 1917 and 1931; Howe's business appeared to be intertwined
with politics and thus raised the stakes for his own political activity.[15]
However, Howe's nonpartisanship was also rooted in his sense of professional ethics, which privileged expertise and efficiency above political favouritism. During his term as chairman of the Port Arthur board
of education in 1924–5, Howe, as historian Anthony Rasporich has
written, introduced "[m]odern management techniques and progressive
innovations." Under Howe's watch, the board resolved to take advantage of provincial grants for technical education, centralized school records, initiated a building program to cope with population growth,
and transferred the responsibility for personnel decisions from the
school board to principals. The last reform was a response to an earlier
conflict between women teachers and the school board. The teachers
protested low pay and harassment received from the board supervi-
sor and threatened mass resignation in response to the unfair dismissal

of a schoolmistress. Pro-labour board members defended the Women Teachers' Association, but Howe was among the conservative trustees and "openly demonstrated his contempt both for the issues raised and the way in which they were exploited by the women teachers, who crowded into the board meeting, hissing and hurling insults at their employers." By removing personnel decisions from the hands of elected board members, Howe clearly hoped that future confrontations would be unnecessary.[16] An early example of Howe's management of public affairs, his time in the school board reveals not only his belief in administrative efficiency but his hostility towards labour unionism as well as his gendered vision of professionalism, which marginalized women teachers.

Norman Lambert knew Howe through his involvement in the grain business, and both men had experienced business setbacks as the economic slump devastated the grain trade. Lambert moved into politics, taking up the presidency of the National Liberal Federation in 1932, and encouraged Howe to make a similar move. Following a Liberal gathering at Chateau Laurier, Howe told Lambert "he would consider running in Port Arthur."[17] Though interested, Howe remained aloof. He impressed Mackenzie King in a meeting the following year, but, again, no firm commitment was forthcoming, causing Lambert to think Howe was holding out for a guaranteed cabinet position.[18] Prospects of a snap election in late 1934 brought the matter to a head, and Howe accepted the nomination to stand as the candidate for Port Arthur. The story was often later repeated that Mackenzie King secured Howe by convincing Alice that her husband would be able to spend more time at home if he left business for politics.[19]

Nearly six feet tall, stocky, olive-skinned, and with thin grayish-black hair and a thick brow, Howe wore suits seldom properly pressed and as old as they looked. He did not carry himself with the polish of a Charles Dunning, nor did he possess Dunning's oratorical abilities. Nonetheless, Howe's reputation as an upstanding local businessman carried him far in Port Arthur, and his victory in the fall federal election of 1935 was as decisive as the Liberal Party's overall national triumph. Even the Liberal candidate in Fort William, Dan McIvor, whom Howe helped to put in place, was elected in an upset over the Conservative minister of railways and canals, R.J. Manion. Once elected, King gave Manion's portfolio to Howe. This displeased Ontario's Liberal premier, Mitch Hepburn, and would help generate the King–Hepburn feud that would boil over a few years later. Hepburn felt slighted that a greenhorn politician such as Howe should receive a cabinet appointment while his seasoned ally, Arthur Slaight, was left out of the shuffle. Howe was, in King's estimation, a better pick: superior in character, familiar with the West, and more independent from narrow political and business interests than Slaight, who, King believed, "would really be a Toronto minister representing Algoma." This was made all the worse since Howe helped pry control of the Fort William Liberal Association from a small group of Hepburn Liberals to secure McIvor's candidacy. The moneyed provincial Liberal machine, moreover, had helped in the federal election. While Hepburn chafed at the ingratitude, King felt justified in the belief that "we owe Toronto very little."[20]

    Much later in his career, Howe admitted that he could have just as easily become a Conservative as a Liberal.[21] He did not embrace any particular tradition or ideological commitment that would guide him into either the Conservative or Liberal camp. Having grown up outside the British Empire, he did not have a visceral attachment to things British; and, having prospered in a line of business significantly bolstered by government intervention, he was not rendered dyspeptic by the presence of state intervention. Lacking these ideological fetters, Howe introduced a new form of businesslike efficiency to the operation of government. From the beginning of his political career, Howe was primarily identified as a businessman, progressive in spirit, and above partisan excess.[22] Even the Tory *Mail and Empire* of Toronto observed "a good augury of [Howe's] non-political intentions by the appointment of J.H. MacDougall – a Maritime Conservative – to the C.N.R. board."[23] Howe's pragmatism and apparently apolitical style were not the result of any special ability to overcome ideology, but were evidence of Howe's efforts to apply a managerial ethic to the operation of the state, which privileged efficiency within the framework of a capitalist economy and followed the trends of modern business enterprise, especially in the United States, where the new business bureaucracies of giant corporations administered long-term corporate strategies in what Alfred Chandler described as "the managerial revolution in American business."[24]

Howe answered the call for a more businesslike administration of government affairs, but in a manner that ran against some widely held assumptions among conservative businessmen, who were also demanding the application of business principles to government. Early on, Howe made clear his intent to make government operations more efficient, but, significantly, for Howe this did not imply retrenchment. One area in which Howe's eye for efficiency became apparent was in the amalgamation of the Marine Department with the Department of Railways and Canals. The idea of amalgamating the two departments had emerged from the Bennett administration, but Howe pressed further, arguing that sought-after efficiencies required the drafting departments to be amalgamated under one roof into a "space properly laid out"; Howe suggested that the department be located in the newly constructed building on Wellington Street and that the decision be made early enough for architects to properly design the space.[25] Howe did not hesitate to bring engineering principles to bear upon the functioning of government departments and enterprises. Lauding his administrative efforts with the newly formed Department of Transport, the *Globe and Mail* claimed that Howe "proved the value and the need of practical business methods in the changing functions of government."[26] As cabinet colleague Charles Gavin "Chubby" Power recalled, Howe "emerged quickly as a good administrator."[27]

Howe's attempts to apply these methods were apparent on several fronts. First, there were the Harbours Commissions, which Howe came very quickly to view as "perfect sink holes of waste of public money."[28] Created in 1927, the system provided Dominion government funds for seven boards to administer their respective local ports. The set-up allowed for a degree of local control in port administration, but a government-commissioned report, completed by Sir Alexander Gibb in 1932, concluded that this was wasteful. The Gibb Report argued for centralized control to overcome the administrative problems of the commission system. Howe proposed legislation to abolish the local boards and to replace them with one centralized harbours board. "The best interests of Canada seem to have been lost sight of in favour of purely sectional view," argued Howe, believing "cut-throat" competition between Canadian ports should be put to an end.[29] The Harbours Board Bill was given royal assent on 19 June 1936 after considerable debate in the House. That resistance to the bill surprised Howe said something of his political naiveté; stripping local elites of control over patronage was no easy task, and opposition was voiced by both Liberal and Conservative members whose constituencies were being affected by the legislation: Saint John, Trois-Rivières, Montreal, Vancouver, and so on. Conservatives also voiced concern that too much authority was being vested in one body, and C.H. Cahan argued that Howe was creating a patronage monster. Howe saw no merit in these charges, pointing out that the creation of a centralized board in Ottawa would produce long-term savings and better engineering work.[30] Howe had earlier voiced his displeasure with the squandering of engineering expertise in Ottawa, noting that some of "the most important problems" were being handled by "small local staffs." At a dinner held in his honour by the Canadian Engineers' Institute in December 1935, Howe expressed his intention to confine local offices to maintenance problems, leaving new projects to be handled by a central staff in Ottawa, thus ensuring "the best engineering skill and experience of public service can be brought to bear on each problem."[31] Administrative centralization became a theme of Howe's record in government and caused one of his early biographers in the late 1950s to wonder whether demands for administrative efficiency would eventually compromise the functioning of democratic institutions.[32]

Such worries about Howe's tendencies were not as widespread in the 1930s, particularly on the left, where his willingness to advance state enterprise was a welcome change from the Bennett administration's policies of retrenchment. Indeed, it was the citadel of big business that was most troubled by Howe's policies: St James Street and particularly Sir Edward Beatty. Howe was a relative unknown on the national stage in 1935, and Beatty was anxious to meet him. "As I have never had the privilege of meeting you," Beatty wrote the recently minted cabinet minister, "and am anxious to do so and pay my respects to you, I would like very much to have a short chat with you." Beatty claimed to have no particular business to take up with Howe, but merely wanted to shake hands.[33] He had succeeded with past ministers of railways and canals in cultivating social niceties and a general mood of cooperation; he hoped to do the same with Howe.[34] And, indeed, within a year Mackenzie King complained that Howe was talking too much to

Beatty about railway matters.[35] Howe was different from past ministers, however, unfamiliar with the politician's skills at ingratiation, as
well as holding a worldview that was open to the state's managerial
intervention in economic life.

As minister of transport, Howe set out to run the CNR on a basis
more akin to a functioning private business. One of his first moves was
to abolish the board of trustees established by the Bennett administration to oversee the CNR. The board had been established on the basis
of the Duff Commission's findings in an attempt to impose more strict
financial oversight – to remove it from spendthrift political pressures –
and to bring about savings through increased cooperation with the CPR.
Howe believed the cooperative savings hitherto achieved could have
just as easily been achieved without the board of trustees. But, more
importantly, the Bennett government had vested "supreme authority"
in the chairman of trustees, C.P. Fullerton, "inexperienced in railway
operation and management," giving him the authority to interfere with
public policy and overrule the experienced railway officials below him.
In so subordinating the company's seasoned officials to an inexperienced board of trustees, contended Howe, the Bennett government had
compromised "executive authority and the esprit du [sic] corps of the
workers." In a telling analogy, Howe argued that the CNR needed the
same unity of leadership that was required on the battlefield:

> The field service regulations of the Canadian Army contain with some-
> what appropriate reference, at this time entirely applicable to the Canadian
> National situation, so far as direction and management are concerned:
>   Unity of control is essential to unity of effort. This condition can be
> assured only by providing him with the means of exerting the required
> influence over the work and action of every individual.
>   The same might well be said of a railway organization such as the Ca-
> nadian National.[36]

The experts needed the autonomy to exercise managerial authority in
order to influence the "work and action of every individual." Fullerton
was no expert.

Howe also thought Bennett's attempt to remove the CNR from
government interference ill advised, resulting in a form of "absentee

landlordism." "We cannot escape the fact that the railway is owned by the people of Canada, that taxes collected from the people of Canada pay its deficit, and that the prosperity of every citizen in thousands of communities from coast to coast can be affected by its managerial policies," Howe stated before the Toronto Railway Club's annual dinner in December 1935.[37] With the government being both the owner and creditor of the railway, the principle of trusteeship applied to bankrupt private firms – which the Conservatives had applied to the CNR – was unjustified.[38] Howe insisted his role as the responsible minister be more than a rubber stamp, making clear that he had "no objection to accepting complete responsibility for ministerial and departmental policies in the making of which I have a voice."[39] Howe put the legislation before the House in March 1936 to replace the trustee board with a regular board of directors, arguing his case before the House in the following months. Some fireworks naturally ensued, as Bennett sought to defend his policy in an effort to save face. The bill passed in the summer, and Howe urged it be proclaimed effective "July 1st in order to dispose of the present Board of Trustees before they can do harm."[40] His recommendations for the new board included both Liberals and Conservatives and, consisting mainly of big business figures, signalled his intention to avoid partisan controversy as well as his faith in businessmen.

In line with his effort to transform the executive set-up of the company, Howe set out to revamp the CNR's capital structure to place it on a more businesslike foundation. Since its formation in 1922, the CNR had been saddled with the debts of the defunct private roads it took over. Interest charges accumulated on ancient debts – from the Canadian Northern and Grand Trunk – were carried over onto the CNR books as net losses. These debts would have been wiped out by bankruptcy proceedings had the government not intervened. Sir Henry Thornton had earlier pointed to the unfairness of including such charges and pressed the government "to provide a balance sheet which will accurately reflect conditions."[41] Moreover, following Thornton's departure, the accounting firm of Touche & Company completed an audit of the CNR's books and reached a conclusion similar to Thornton's. In a report submitted to government, it advised that Grand Trunk debt be written off and Canadian Northern debt be cut to a fraction of its former amount; it further advised that government advances to service the CNR debt prior to 1931 also be written off – "because it represents nothing but a contribution by shareholders to replace their impaired capital." These and other reforms to the capital structure were necessary to correct the Dominion government's consolidated financial position, Touche & Company concluded, which, if not corrected, might lead to "weakening of Canada's credit in foreign financial markets."[42] Bennett refused to accept the recommendations, describing the report's findings as "wholly at variance with the views entertained by the Government." "As representing proprietors of the undertaking," Bennett told CNR trustee C.P. Fullerton, "we must insist that the Railway Company's reports shall give a true picture of the real situation and that the annual report as issued will enable anyone pursuing it to understand exactly what the Dominion of Canada has invested in its railway enterprises." Bennett believed the public of Canada needed a true picture of what it was spending on railways.[43] Howe signalled his intention to reverse Bennett's policy, and Beatty took notice.

The Bennett administration had emphasized retrenchment and cost-cutting in the affairs of the CNR by placing the railway under the control of a board of trustees to oversee expenditures. Though not fulfilling Beatty's wish for amalgamation, this was at least an indication that government policy was moving – however stubbornly – in Beatty's direction. Bennett's insistence that the CNR carry debts on its books originally created by the follies of overly zealous railway entrepreneurs seemed to indicate a decided hostility towards the CNR, if not public enterprise generally. Bennett broadly shared Beatty's general sentiment that the state's role was to encourage private enterprise without interfering directly in the economy. Howe was more willing to engage the state itself as a capitalist and, as such, adopted the Touche & Company report rejected by Bennett. Beatty was quick to protest, arguing that the CPR would suffer from unfair competition. Beatty objected to the proposed accounting scheme for defining interest-bearing loans, secured through public credit, as working capital and argued that the CNR's ability to raise money through the Dominion government would give the company an unfair advantage in securing low-interest loans.[44] Beatty engaged the services of a different accounting company, Price, Waterhouse & Company of New York, and sent its analysis of the CNR picture – much more commensurate with his own views – to Howe. Howe heard Beatty out. Believing he had come close to reaching an understanding with Howe, Beatty was aghast when he received a draft copy of the proposed legislation; Howe had gone further than even the Touche & Company report. Beatty asked St James Street's inside man, Dunning, for help in the matter.[45] When that failed, he went to King himself, but to no avail. King showed Howe the vituperative letter he had received from Beatty; Howe composed a response for King's consideration. Beatty, try as he might, could not sidestep Howe.[46] Moreover, as Beatty toured Canada to raise concerns over what the CNR was costing taxpayers and to make his case for unification under CPR control, Howe dispatched a team of speakers to counter Beatty's claims.[47] They would soon be fighting to control the sky.

Howe became minister of transport at a decisive moment in the development of civil aviation. Following the First World War, civil aviation was carried out by numerous small enterprises, one-man companies better known for aeronautical daring than profitability: there were twenty-two companies operating aircraft in 1922. The entry of prominent Winnipeg grain dealer and financier, James A. Richardson, into the aviation business in 1926 signalled the beginning of change. As was the case with others in the field, Richardson's interest in aviation emerged initially from his desire to "open up" the mineral wealth of the Canadian Shield. His company, Western Canadian Airways, could transport prospectors, engineers, and geologists by plane to remote locations – that formerly took weeks to reach – in hours. By the time the Depression hit, his company controlled 80 per cent of the nation's commercial air transport and in 1930 won a lucrative contract with the post office. Meanwhile, the railways became interested in the firm, whose name was changed to Canadian Airways Limited (CAL). Sir Henry Thornton approached Richardson to invest in the company in 1929, and, wanting to avoid the ruinous competition that had plagued the railways, Richardson asked Beatty to come on board as well. Beatty agreed. Both railways invested $250,000 in CAL, and Beatty and Thornton served as vice-presidents under Richardson.[48]

The hope – indeed, expectation – of Richardson and Beatty was that civil aviation would remain in the hands of private enterprise. The government funded the Trans Canada Airway in 1929, a series of stations linking up airports from Toronto to Vancouver by radio; and in 1933 a committee appointed by Bennett recommended that CAL be made the airway's sole operator. When Bennett, looking to reduce government expenditures, cancelled CAL's mail contracts in March 1932, the company quickly became unprofitable. Richardson explained in 1934 that the company's decision to remain in business was made in the hopes "that ultimately we would be accorded some recognition for our accomplishments in opening up the country."[49] When Howe took office, the Trans Canada Airway was near completion. Important decisions would soon have to be made, and, with aviation moved from the Department of Defence to Transport, it all fell into Howe's lap.

As the King government moved to consider the direction of civil aviation, intense lobbying ensued. Richardson as well as a group of Toronto capitalists centred on financier J.H. Gundy competed for the government blessing to run the national airline. Howe assured Richardson early in 1936 that Canadian Airways would form the "backbone" of the national aviation system, but he also sent encouraging signals to the Toronto group. Howe's assurances to Richardson seemed to come into further question that fall. Richardson observed in November that the aviation situation had changed since Dunning began "playing with the Toronto group." Later in the month, Howe and King met with a cabinet committee – consisting of Dunning, Lapointe, Ilsley, and Crerar – to determine the government's general direction in the matter. It was decided that legislation should be enacted at the upcoming parliamentary session to establish a national airline as a joint venture with private capital. Howe told Beatty in the new year that 10 per cent of the company would "go to Gundy's group composed of J.H. Gundy; R. Lawson, Gen. Odlum, F. Cameron, Geo McCullagh, Chas. Burns, J.L. Ralston; + this was to offset too much C.P.R. interest." Beatty believed Howe was simply trying to save face with the Toronto group and did not expect them to enter on the proposed basis. This belief was proven correct less than two weeks later, when Howe suggested to Richardson that "Beatty get everybody together + rule distribution to others on a basis which will be refused." Richardson himself, by that time, had come to feel he would not be part of the airways set-up. On 1 February, Howe was approached by one of Gundy's emissaries, but it was already too late: a draft bill had been completed. Howe had grown tired of all the lobbying.[50] The bill provided for the two railway companies to subscribe equally to the aviation company's $5 million in shares, each investing $2.5 million.[51]

Howe and Beatty had different ideas about how the prospective company should be run. The draft bill was unusual in that it effectively made the company's general manager also its chief executive officer. Moreover, it included provisions designed to allow the direct intervention by the minister in the case of stock transactions deemed to be unscrupulous, and it included a stipulation that would allow the government to buy up all shares at book value. The proposed bill, as such, restricted the authority of the board of directors and regulated their autonomy, closing avenues of financial inducement normally available through the buying and selling of stock. Put another way, the administrative stratum of the company was given more power, while its owners were stripped of their normal prerogatives. Representation on the board of directors – that is, effective control of the company – was the most fundamental point of disagreement. The board was to consist of nine directors: the railway companies were allowed to nominate four each, with one place remaining for a ministerial representative. Since, Beatty reasoned, the CNR was essentially a department of government, the CPR would be placed in the position of minority shareholder but owner of half the stock. Beatty believed "the two interests represented should have an equal voice in determining policies" and assumed that the most desirable course of action for the government was for it to minimize its own responsibilities; "otherwise," pontificated Beatty in what seemed a bluff, "it would seem logical that the Government should undertake to conduct the services directly, without intervention from third parties or corporations."[52]

Howe called Beatty's bluff. In a provocative move, which Howe certainly expected would cause Beatty to back out of the undertaking, the bill was changed in the cabinet to reduce the CPR's seats on the board from four of nine to three of nine, with the remaining seats going to the CNR and the government. In addition, a provision was added to allow unsubscribed shares to be sold to other parties, clearly in anticipation of the CPR withdrawal. The revised bill made clear that the CPR would be nothing more than a junior partner. Beatty, clearly aggravated, responded to Howe on 16 March; he asked that their communication on the matter cease and reference to the CPR in the bill be deleted.[53]

The Trans-Canada Air Lines Bill was put before the House of Commons on 22 March. It proposed to establish a private aviation company, wholly run by the CNR. "The set-up is such that the company will be protected against loss," explained Howe, "but its profits will be very strictly limited."[54] Three days later the bill went through a second reading. The Conservative member from Vancouver South and future minister of external affairs for John Diefenbaker, Howard Green, argued that the government should instead subsidize a private aviation firm already in operation and complained that "there is small incentive to a privately owned air company to furnish capital for the new company."[55] On the other hand, the "grim experience" of the railways caused R.B. Bennett to support the principle of government control of aviation; indeed, he said Howe did not go far enough and argued in favour of direct government control, as opposed to indirect control through the CNR.[56] "I think we are getting the best features of government ownership without the obligation of direct government operation," later rebutted Howe.[57] Ideological consistency thrown thus into confusion, the bill, which ensured CNR ownership of no less than 51 per cent of Trans-Canada Air Lines, passed on 2 April.

Private capital was still in the picture, and Howe persisted in trying to bring James Richardson into the company. Richardson proposed CAL be contracted to run the trans-Canada route from Winnipeg to Vancouver, but this was too much for Howe, and Richardson refused to become a TCA director. Richardson's aviation firm was taken over by the CPR after his death in 1939. The main point of contention throughout was the issue of control. Howe invited capitalists to invest in TCA as junior partners. Beatty and Richardson rejected this relationship; however, under Howe, it would become a more common relationship between the state and the private sector. The onset of the Second World War was decisive in shaping this outcome, which would result in Howe exercising hitherto unimagined control over the Canadian economy.

Howe and Beatty represented different priorities and embraced different capitalist ideologies. Beatty, of course, represented the more narrow interests of the CPR and embraced classic liberal ideals, rooted in past expansion during the National Policy period. Incubated in the world of ledger books and stock valuations, Beatty's view of economic activity tended towards the realm of abstraction and was based upon the assumption of a self-correcting market economy – even though the CPR itself operated contrary to that ideal. Howe, by contrast, was an engineer – as had been Beatty's previous opponent, Sir Henry Thornton – trained to address problems of the material world: Howe was interested in the efficient (though also profitable) functioning of organizations and was willing to limit the standard rights of shareholders to ensure that stock speculation and the like not interfere with efficiency and growth. Howe viewed the economy more like a machine, subject to manipulation, than a perfect organism. Howe's thinking thus made considerable allowance for strategic state intervention. As Howe declared in December 1936, he intended to develop air services "along sound lines unhampered by competitive activities and duplications which have marked the older form of transport," namely railways.[58] Of course, fundamentally, he and Beatty were both believers in the free market and the profit motive, and thus their ideological differences should not be exaggerated. J.W. Dafoe observed as early as 1937, for example, that "Howe is at heart a private ownership man."[59] As a representative of the state, however, Howe's outlook was not limited to the interests of a specific corporation, and his managerial outlook introduced a form of businesslike governance that sought to achieve more than retrenchment.

St James Street, the Leadership League, and the Conservative Party

Many business grandees of Montreal and Toronto remained significantly opposed to Howe during the late 1930s and early years of the war. The railway question persisted as a central issue in the politics of big business. Indeed, its importance expanded further in Toronto, where it became enmeshed in C. George McCullagh's sweeping arguments about the need for lowered taxation and less government, which were especially apparent in his radio addresses in early 1939 that prefigured the formation of the Leadership League. Arthur Meighen, too, who had been widely perceived as favouring Toronto over CPR interests in the 1920s, became one of the loudest spokesmen for railway unification as Conservative leader of the Senate. This coalescence of conservative forces was further encouraged by the growth of imperialist sentiment as the threat of war loomed. Conservative political and business leaders such as McCullagh and Sam McLaughlin were troubled by what they perceived as Mackenzie King's overly partisan response to German aggression and questionable loyalty to the British Empire. And, as we have seen in the previous chapter, the challenge of industrial unionism had already helped to consolidate this conservative bloc.

But these business conservatives struggled to regain lost influence in national politics. The split between the Conservative Party and the CPR, which began in the early twentieth century under Borden and continued under Meighen before being shored up somewhat by Bennett during the 1930s, became wider than ever after R.J. Manion, Bennett's minister of railways and canals, was elected party leader in the summer of 1938. On railways, empire, and radicalism, Manion was out of step with the big business wing of the party: Manion was Catholic, married to a French Canadian, and willing to accommodate nationalist sentiment in Quebec, compromising on imperial solidarity in foreign relations; he was against railway unification; and he was critical of Mitch Hepburn's hysterical anti-CIO rhetoric. Moreover, some may have suspected his Conservative credentials; after all, he had been a Liberal before joining the Unionists in the First World War and eventually finding his way into the Conservative Party.[60] Collectively, these policies and characteristics ran counter to the outlook of the party's moneyed patrons, resulting in in-fighting and fundraising problems and encouraging the elite's experimentation with nonpartisan alternatives.

The 1938 Conservative convention, at which Manion was selected leader, revealed the CPR's faltering political influence, just as George McCullagh's decision to form the Leadership League articulated the frustrated political ambitions of conservative business leaders. Big business spoke with a diminished voice within both parties, and Beatty encouraged and applauded McCullagh's radio speeches that led to the creation of the Leadership League.[61] The League also won support from former Ontario lieutenant governor Dr Herbert A. Bruce and Dr Frederick Banting, the famed discoverer of insulin, both of whom were handed the reins of the League by McCullagh in March 1939. Meanwhile, George McLaughlin, brother of the General Motors of Canada president, and Mrs Wallace Campbell, the wife of the president of Ford Motors of Canada, sat on the League's advisory board. Led by Mc-Cullagh and Bruce, and with apparent support coming from George McLaughlin, the League, in many ways, represented an attempted political movement of the anti-CIO crowd (see chapter 4). This association was further evidenced by the fact that George Drew moved his office to Leadership League headquarters; moreover, James Y. Murdoch, Noranda Mines president, was also connected to the League.[62]

Murdoch's drift towards the Leadership League coincided with his disenchantment as a director of the CNR. C.D. Howe had appointed him on the company's board in 1936.[63] But, by early 1939, Murdoch had become disillusioned by what he viewed as the sluggish leadership of the company's septuagenarian president, S.J. Hungerford. More specifically, Murdoch's attitude likely stemmed from the recent announcement, in late 1938, that the CNR intended to recommence plans to build a terminal station in Montreal, which had been scrapped earlier in the decade under Manion and Bennett. Murdoch believed more should be done to introduce savings to CNR operations, but it is important to note that he was not siding with Beatty's unification proposal; in fact, one of Murdoch's complaints was that the government was not doing enough to counter Beatty's propaganda. When the CNR directors met on 10 February, the majority did not agree with Murdoch's belief that Hungerford should be relieved from his duties as president. Howe offered to talk with the directors individually or collectively on Murdoch's behalf, but Howe refused to directly intervene, citing 1933 legislation that gave the directors the power to select the president.[64] Murdoch tendered his resignation on 15 February. "His grounds for resignation are not good enough," later complained Beatty, who obviously hoped the event would give the CPR more political traction.[65] Nonetheless, Murdoch shared the more general concern about the state's growing role in Canadian society; McCullagh reported in April that Murdoch "would work with the League in a very active capacity" since "he believes we are heading for state socialism."[66]

As the responsible minister in charge of the Canadian Broadcasting Corporation (CBC), Howe also became embroiled in controversy with McCullagh when the broadcasting corporation refused to sell him time to broadcast his addresses on the government-owned network.

Howe defended the CBC's autonomy to decide the matter, and he accepted the company's explanation that it was only following its mandate in not selling airtime to McCullagh or others wishing to propound personal views.[67] In his final radio address, in which he announced the formation of the Leadership League, McCullagh attacked the administration of the CBC as "a dangerously irresponsible and bureaucratic method of conducting any free country's affairs."[68] Soon after the outbreak of war, Howe and the CBC's general manager, Gladstone Murray, brokered a truce with McCullagh by allowing him to deliver a series of radio addresses on the CBC. Typifying Howe's penchant for personal dealings and willingness to make decisions quickly and beyond the bureaucratic structures of government, Howe and Murray made the deal without consulting the CBC's board of governors.[69] Through such decisive methods, Howe would establish his reputation and capture the respect of businessmen, but he operated substantially beyond their influence.

And with Manion as leader of the Conservative Party, there existed no party to adopt the conservative business agenda of Beatty, McCullagh, and their allies.[70] Nonetheless, well-connected Conservatives such as C.H. Cahan and Toronto businessman J.M. Macdonnell privately urged Manion to back away from his anti-unification stance, while Arthur Meighen emerged as a lead voice in the railway debate from within the Senate, where concerns about government finances were heightened and old loyalties to the CPR appeared to stand firm.[71] With Beatty's encouragement, Meighen authored a Senate committee report recommending railway unification, which was supported by all but six Conservative members of the Senate but opposed by all the voting Liberal members.[72] The pro-unification sentiment expressed by Conservative senators advertised the division within the Conservative Party and, as Manion recognized, undermined his ability to lead the party.[73] The open breach between Manion and Meighen that summer made matters even worse.[74] Howe and the Liberals exploited this opportunity to suggest that the Conservatives, despite Manion's claims to the contrary, really wanted to discard the CNR.[75] While public association with St James Street was political poison, its persisting political clout could not be ignored, and Manion continued to try to establish a "working arrangement" with Montreal.[76]

Mobilizing Business for War and the Politics
of Wartime Production

Neville Chamberlain and Mackenzie King were proven wrong on 1
September 1939, as German tanks rolled into Poland. Hitler, they had
earlier believed, could be bargained with. Having already acquiesced
to the Nazi takeover of Czechoslovakia in 1938, Chamberlain's policy
of "appeasement" was immediately discredited.[77] And in Canada figures such as McCullagh were far removed from the memories of 1938,
when they had supported Chamberlain's policy.[78] Britain would have
to fight, and – in a deft political move – Mackenzie King secured Canada's declaration of war with the consent of parliament on 12 September. Monuments commemorating soldiers of the First World War had
been recently erected; the societal consciousness of the previous war's
price was still fresh, and so too were reports of great sums amassed
through profiteering. It was later reported that during the first month
of the Second World War sales of cigars and champagne at the Chateau Laurier outstripped total sales of the previous twelve months, as
company representatives positioned themselves to win lucrative government contracts. Howe ignored them, so the story goes, and put out
a press release stating that many contracts would be tendered – but the
government would initiate contact.[79] With Howe as minister of munitions and supply, wartime production was tightly controlled by the
government, profits were regulated, and, where private capital did not
or could not invest, crown corporations were formed, resulting in the
formation of twenty-eight such government-owned companies. The
capacity of the state to intervene in the economy had expanded significantly since the First World War, when Joseph Flavelle headed the
Imperial Munitions Board.[80]

However, before these developments were to unfold, the war gave
new life to the National Government idea among Conservatives and
others who felt the King Liberals too partisan an administration to
conduct the war on its own.[81] On the train from Montreal to Saint
John in late October 1939, R.B. Hanson dined with John Bassett
of the Montreal *Gazette* and Howard P. Robinson of the Saint John
Telegraph-Journal and discovered that National Government had been

a major, but informal, topic of discussion at a recent meeting of the Canadian Press.[82] When, on 25 January 1940, Mackenzie King unexpectedly announced an election for 26 March, Manion was quick to adopt it as part of the Conservative platform: Conservatives would run as National Government candidates.[83] The big business wing of the party, nonetheless, remained unsatisfied with Manion's leadership.

Indications of this were quick to emerge. On 2 February Manion received a letter from mining magnate and important Tory operator Don Hogarth in which was enclosed a memo authored by Arthur Meighen. The memo suggested a course of action that had been recently recommended by Wes Gordon, who had served as minister of mines under Bennett: "I had another letter from Don today incorporating that damn fool suggestion about my retiring in a memo from Arthur," complained Manion.[84] The crux of the memo argued that Manion should remain leader during the election but leave the actual leadership to be determined by some type of caucus of National Government representatives after the election. The proposal, to Manion's mind, was amazingly ill conceived, but it appears to have gained more than a few high-powered proponents in Toronto. Its ostensible political intent was to pursue a vigorous prosecution of the war; since Manion did not favour the immediate implementation of conscription for overseas service, the suggestion that Manion step down after winning a general election was almost certainly a strategy to bring in conscription through the back door. Regardless, Manion disregarded these machinations.[85] His National Government platform aroused limited support within the Toronto business community, and the *Financial Post* formulated an editorial policy during the campaign opposing "union or national governments."[86]

Manion also refused to accommodate Montreal sugar magnate J.W. McConnell, the proprietor of the Montreal *Star* and a close associate of Sir Edward Beatty.[87] McConnell's biographer, William Fong, has observed that "the CPR, the Bank of Montreal, and others in Montreal had contributed $500,000 to the Conservative campaign in the election of 1930, but in 1940 they gave the Conservatives absolutely nothing."[88] St James Street, as Reginald Whitaker has noted, sided with the Liberals in the 1940 contest, including McConnell.[89] And not unexpectedly, former finance minister Charles Dunning remained a supporter of the Liberal Party when he moved back to Montreal to succeed McConnell as president of the Ogilvie Flour Mills Company and become the director of major business institutions such as the Bank of Montreal and Consolidated Paper.[90] Manion's efforts ended in the worst of both worlds: his National Government policy aroused popular suspicion of a moneyed campaign designed to place a Trojan horse in parliament, but, of course, it did not benefit from the actual money and high-powered support. On the campaign trail, Howe attacked Manion's "ghost government," which promised to bring the "so-called best brains" into government rather than "the elected representatives of the people." He suggested that a small group angered by the current administration's "determination to remove profiteering and favouritism from Canada's war effort" was backing Manion: "These men believe that, by a campaign of misrepresentation, they can seize the reins of office and restore the conditions that prevailed during the last war."[91] This seemed to belie the truth, since St James-Street had shifted towards the Liberals. The Conservatives were decisively defeated at the polls on 26 March, and Manion again, as in 1935, lost his own seat in Fort William.

Shortly after the election, the need for "greater freedom of action and authority" resulted in the establishment of the Department of Munitions and Supply, on 9 April 1940.[92] German forces had invaded Denmark and Norway that morning. The predecessor to Munitions and Supply was the War Supply Board, which had achieved only limited success under the direction of Ford Motors of Canada president Wallace R. Campbell. The domineering Campbell had alienated his colleagues, and, though a specialist in his field, he reportedly did "not know Canadian industry."[93] Worse still, Campbell had not been particularly loyal to Howe or the government, and Howe had worked behind the scenes to secure his resignation.[94] With the election decisively won, Howe was able to move Campbell out of the picture by eliminating the War Supply Board and taking charge of the new department himself. As minister of munitions and supply, Howe acquired broad authority that would be expanded even further in later amendments, allowing him to set prices, compel manufacturers and contractors to engage in work deemed necessary for war production, and impose rationing, along with many other powers. Howe also recruited new talent to his team of business executives–turned–government administrators, the "dollar-a-year-men," including a young and wealthy financier from Toronto, E.P. Taylor, who was given command of Canada's war purchasing in the United States. Howe also recruited a dutiful deputy minister, G.K. Sheils. He would carry out the paperwork that Howe tended to shirk, but Sheils would operate without any real power.[95] Howe's position in government put him at the centre of the Canadian economy, but many members of the business community were uncertain about his new role as industrial czar.

Indeed, a persistent criticism was that the Department of Munitions and Supply required a nonpartisan general manager, a business executive of high standing who could devise Canada's overall war production program. The argument, essentially, was that as a cabinet minister in a Liberal government, Howe was too immersed in politics to function effectively as the head of Canadian war production. The deposed Wallace Campbell spoke highly of Howe's "aggressiveness" but believed control should rest in the hands of a "non-political chief." Arthur B. Purvis, the president of Canadian Industries Limited (CIL) and head of the Anglo-French War Supply Board in the United States, was impressed with Howe as "a man of action," but argued that "a first-class industrialist" was needed to take over all of Canada's war buying. Even Sir Edward Beatty admitted that Howe had "done a very able job"; however, like the others, Beatty too called for a nonpolitical figure to take charge of war purchases, arguing that one of the "able men in the country ... should be selected to head up something like an Imperial Munitions Board and be given full authority to get results in his own way."[96] This, too, was the idea propagated publicly by the Canadian Manufacturers' Association and the *Financial Post*.[97] But the *Post* was forced to quiet its criticism of the government prior to the 1940 federal election because its readers and advertisers – influential businessmen – believed it had gone too far in criticizing the government and had descended to the level of a political sheet. For instance, Thurston B. Weatherbee, Montreal general manager of the Bank of Commerce, reported to the paper's editor, Floyd Chalmers, that although "Montreal business leaders had for years regarded The Post as the one paper that stood for their interests in matters of taxation, sound monetary policy, etc.," they now thought the paper too sensational, and some had even become sympathetic to Mackenzie King. The government, they believed, was doing a reasonable job. "[Weatherbee] said he knew this from innumerable conversations with the very top men in that city," reported Chalmers. A few days earlier, on 27 February, Chalmers reported that the *Financial Post*'s relationship with "many loyal followers of the Liberal party who are outside the arena of actual political campaigning had become acute." Chalmers acted to remedy the problem.[98]

The contingencies of the war allowed Howe to use the state more aggressively than would have been imaginable in peacetime, and especially as the Phony War came to an end with the German invasion of France on 10 May; France was out of the war before the end of June and Britain's prospects appeared gloomy. On 24 June, the War Industries Control Board was established to secure and regulate the flow of vital supplies. Hugh Scully, the commissioner of customs, was placed in charge of steel and also served as chairman; H.R. MacMillan, the British Columbia lumber baron was appointed timber controller; George Cottrelle, a banker, was made oil controller; George Bateman, a mining engineer, was appointed metals controller; and, finally, TCA director Herbie Symington was placed in charge of power.[99] Furthermore, the federal government assumed jurisdiction over resources in a time of war, and this meant a considerable shift for resource capitalists who had cultivated friendly relationships with the provincial governments; they would now have to deal with Howe. The government's war production set-up temporarily abolished the free-market system, which had been regulated by provincial jurisdictions; in its place, as Bothwell and Kilbourn have observed, was established "a centrally directed economy regulated by the government's perception of the needs of the war."[100] With the old economic system effectively supplanted, Howe pointed to the exceptional circumstances that war had imposed on the nation. Advertising the sale of war bonds before the Canadian and Empire Clubs in Toronto, Howe noted: "In this time of war ... the emphasis has shifted from the individual to the nation and our whole task of helping to win the war."[101] Old notions about individualism, property, and the free market had to be abandoned, at least temporarily, so that maximum production could be achieved for a national war effort.

Problems, of course, continued to arise. Howe departed for England aboard the *Western Prince* on 6 December 1940 to visit British officials to discuss and better coordinate future production, but on 14 December the ship was torpedoed 300 miles off the coast of Iceland. Howe and two of his party survived, E.P. Taylor and W.C. Woodward. But Montreal financier Gordon Scott did not. Having escaped this ordeal and having made progress with the British, Howe arrived back in January only to encounter unwanted interference. The minister of finance, J.L. Ilsley, and his advisors had appointed H.R. MacMillan to head up the War Requirements Board in November 1940 to examine costing within the Department of Munitions and Supply; Howe was notoriously haphazard with contracts, relying often upon spoken agreements, and the projected spending of his department was elusive. But Mac-Millan interpreted his responsibilities broadly and undertook a general study of the department's efficiency, which he presented to Howe upon his return. Howe did nothing with the report, and a showdown was brewing.[102]

Even before his appointment with the War Requirements Board, MacMillan had anticipated a crisis in war production in about six months because of poor coordination within Munitions and Supply. In private discussion with Chalmers of the *Financial Post* in October 1940, MacMillan argued the necessity of appointing a big industrialist to oversee and coordinate all the department's activities. He also complained that too many of Howe's dollar-a-year men only had experience with small businesses "of the coasts," such as W.C. Woodward (Vancouver) and Howe's president at the Federal Aircraft Company, Ralph P. Bell (Halifax): "the government has to get more of the first-class industrial brains of Ontario and Quebec factories working for it." "His views are almost identical with ours on the matter," concluded Chalmers.[103] By the time Howe arrived back from Britain, not only did he receive the report from MacMillan, but the *Financial Post* was clamouring for the appointment of an "industrial statesman." Howe refused to implement the personnel overhaul that MacMillan wanted, including the removal from command of aircraft production of Ray Lawson and Ralph Bell, who, believed MacMillan, "should be replaced by manufacturers with experience in producing aircraft."[104] Disgruntled, Mac-Millan publicized the report in the 8 February issue of the *Financial Post*. Also, Horace T. Hunter, the paper's president, purchased advertising space in other papers to propagate MacMillan's allegations of disorganization and inefficiency in order "to arouse national sentiment for a 'total war' effort." The revelations contained in the report did not materialize into the political dynamite that MacMillan believed he wielded. When parliament convened on 26 February, Howe declared: "The number one saboteur in Canada since the beginning of the war is the *Financial Post*."[105] It was a coup for the Liberals.

The episode revealed several things. First, it revealed Howe's rather domineering style of management. Campbell had challenged his authority, and next it was MacMillan. Howe's impulse was to get rid of them both, even though they thought rather highly of him personally. He wanted to dismiss MacMillan "out of hand," reported Herbie Symington, who claimed to have talked Howe away from such a rash action.[106] (MacMillan became the Director-General of Shipbuilding in Montreal and resumed cordial relations with Howe.[107]) Second, the episode revealed persisting tensions within the Canadian business community about the organization of war production and the general prosecution of the war. And while Howe and the Liberals remained firmly ensconced in Ottawa, Meighen's resurrection as leader of the Conservative Party became a small, but ultimately unsuccessful, revival of ultra-imperialism and old free-market ideals. The "total war" campaign that Meighen championed attracted support from the old anti-CIO, Leadership League crowd in Toronto – McCullagh and Murdoch, for example – but it was even less effective at mobilizing popular support than the League had been. Meighen's campaign was abysmally unpopular, and he was widely assailed as a stooge of big business.[108] Beatty had encouraged Meighen to contest a by-election to re-enter the House of Commons in the spring of 1940, but only, Beatty maintained, if he was able to run unopposed.[109] This condition was not achieved when Meighen ran in York South in the spring of 1942; the CCF candidate defeated him. Meighen's son, Max, served in the war as a colonel and embraced his father's belief in small government and free enterprise; according to an interview with journalist Peter Newman, Max concluded in 1944 that class war would result in dictatorships worldwide.[110] Though Max Meighen embraced an unusually bleak view of the future, those clinging to the older political economy descended into pessimism as their ideas continued to decline in popularity and as the force of events continued to work against their ends. Howe's vision was different.

Creating the Architecture of a Continental Economy

Addressing the Reform Club in Montreal in November 1943, Howe promised his listeners that the problems of peace could be solved by the solutions used during the war. The conservative Montreal *Gazette* was troubled by this apparent endorsement of continued state intervention: "we ... think he should be a little more cautious in his statements," editorialized the paper.[111] The *Gazette*, however, was not necessarily his intended audience in this instance. A Gallup Poll in September found the CCF to be Canada's most popular national party; Howe's boasts signalled the Liberal Party's reformist intentions in response to the perceived threat of socialism in Canada. Just as Howe promised a postwar future of public enterprise and full employment, he also alerted Canadians to the supposed dangers of the more radical alternative. "We all learn by experience," Howe declared before the Reform Club, "and I am confident that, when the time comes, the people of this country will choose a government with experience rather than a Government dependent on unproven theories and revolutionary proposals."[112]

Of course, elite opinion within the Conservative Party too had come to recognize the need to adapt, as ultra-imperialist political theatrics became unconvincing to even some of its sympathizers.[113] Grant Dexter, the Ottawa correspondent of the Winnipeg *Free Press*, reported in 1942 that moneyed interests supported the ascension of former Manitoba Progressive premier John Bracken to party leader and the party's rechristening as the Progressive Conservative Party; at first Arthur Meighen, C. George McCullagh, and Howard P. Robinson hoped Bracken would lead yet another National Government drive, but a few days later the plan was sunk. Still, they – as well as the CPR – reportedly gave considerable amounts of money to support him. J.W. Dafoe reported Bracken's wealthy supporters – "who think they own the party because they put up the money" – will "want him to put the power at their disposal."[114] Of course, the more consequential developments were closer to Howe, who was developing a commanding profile in the overlapping worlds of business and government.

Howe literally commanded a powerful group of business executives in the dollar-a-year men who served in his department. And he publicly tipped his hat to private enterprise, thanking it for placing "its knowledge of management, technical skills and secret processes at the disposal of the Government and giving freely of its topmost personnel."[115] The shape of the Canadian economy was also changing decisively during the war as Howe further integrated Canada into the continental economy. While the interwar period witnessed considerable expansion of U.S. business in Canada – most notably in the rise of the automobile industry – during the war this tendency became official state policy. After Howe returned from his harrowing trip to England in January 1941, he announced the government's intention to integrate Canadian war production with the United States in order to avoid "unnecessary duplication of facilities by either country," and by April Howe was on his way to Washington with E.P. Taylor, now his executive assistant, to set up "the new economic co-operation between Canada and the United States," which had been recently made official in the Hyde Park Declaration.[116] This signalled a change from the early phase of the war, when Canadian production was synched with British production. In Howe's opinion, cooperation with the Americans was the quickest road to greater efficiency and output, although, as Stanley Russell Howe has observed in his study of Howe's relationship with U.S. business, Howe "was apparently unconcerned with the consequences of this decision."[117] Lacking the reverence for the British Empire maintained by many of his colleagues, and applying an engineer's outlook to the pressing goal of achieving maximum production during a time of war, cooperation and integration with U.S. industry was logical according to Howe's outlook.[118] Indeed, this approach was consistent with Howe's version of Canadian nationalism, which celebrated expertise, efficiency, and productivity as the cornerstones of economic development and the nation itself.

Howe's influence, nonetheless, should not be overemphasized, for Canada's integration into the North American economy stemmed from broader economic forces related to the general decline of British power abroad and the rise of American economic hegemony. For example, Britain's attempts to monetarily reintegrate Canada under its influence in the 1930s not only failed, along with Beaverbrook's Empire Free Trade campaign, but was quickly reversed as a cash-strapped British government struggled to pay the costs of waging war. The Lend-Lease Agreement of 1940 gave the British access to much-needed American supplies, but, in exchange, Britain ceded vast amounts of political leverage to the United States, which the U.S. government would use to open up British markets and recast the postwar world economy under the monetary regime of Bretton Woods – and the Hyde Park Declaration brought Canada's financial relationship with the United States under the terms of the Lend-Lease Agreement. Canada's integration into the North American economy during the Second World War was inextricably tied to the decisive shift in power between Britain and the United States; and while the economic basis of this transition had been, as we have seen, long in the making in Canada, the Second World War solidified Canada's new relationship with the United States.[119]

Howe's relationship with R.E. Powell, president of the Aluminum Company of Canada, the principal operating subsidiary of Alcan Aluminum Limited, was suggestive of the growing U.S. influence during the war. Howe seems to have been first brought in touch with Powell in 1938 or 1939 through Ralph P. Bell, the Halifax industrialist whom Howe later appointed to take charge of aircraft production.[120] Howe and Powell soon became personal friends, particularly evidenced by fishing trips in Quebec. Alcan also enjoyed a rather favourable relationship with the Canadian state during and after the war: the government helped the company expand its aluminum plant in Arvida, Quebec, and build a massive hydroelectric project at Shipshaw during the war, and after the war awarded Alcan major tax write-offs that were highly criticized in the press.[121] When workers struck at the Arvida plant in the summer of 1941, Howe was quick to take Alcan's side. He immediately called for the deployment of mounted police or troops to take the plant back from workers. He claimed the workers were led by "an enemy alien" and pointed to the rippling effect that would arise in war industries generally if aluminum production were not resumed at once.[122] The quick and decisive action Howe demanded did not materialize, while his public comments – implying disloyalty among the workers – were denounced widely in Quebec.[123] A royal commission would soon prove Howe's assumptions unfounded. "Howe has allowed himself to be deceived by the Aluminum Co," reported Ernest Lapointe to Mackenzie King, "and his statements have precipitated a storm in Quebec, after the true facts have been ascertained – Premier Godbout is going to issue a statement, and will ask for an apology."[124] The strike, John Macfarlane has argued, forced the Liberal government, including Howe, to become more tactful in the handling of labour troubles throughout the rest of the war.[125] There was no doubt where his loyalties lay, however.

"Private Enterprise Must Take Over": The Transition to Peace

The United States entered the war at the end of 1941. War production began to hum. And by 1944 an Allied victory began to appear inevitable as the transition to a peacetime economy became a government priority. Howe was appointed minister of reconstruction that year, and he soon voiced his intention to have the private sector take over as much as possible in the postwar period. Notes for a speech Howe delivered in October 1944, at a luncheon given in his honour by a group of Hamilton businessmen, made this clear: "Private Enterprise must take over." The legitimacy of his vision was rooted in the promise of growth and increased production; private industry and workers, Howe believed, could work to achieve high levels of productivity, which would translate into high standards of living as well as high levels of employment. Indeed, in Hamilton, Howe referred to full employment as a government objective, although the government's White Paper, which laid out the economic and social objectives of the government in peacetime, would fall short of such an ambitious proclamation the following year, promising a "high and stable level of employment." And, significantly, Howe assured his Hamilton audience that the state would be there to help.[126] Howe argued, in effect, for a new relationship between the state and private enterprise directed towards creating a new era of business expansionism that would adequately address the widespread calls for greater social security in the postwar period. Although this contravened the old liberalism of limited government intervention, the experience of the war taught even curmudgeons such as Algoma Steel president Sir James Dunn that working with the government could be advantageous.[127]

Nonetheless, the CPR was slow to adapt. Under Beatty and later under the presidency of D.C. Coleman, the railway sought to establish a toehold in the aviation business by buying up feeder lines in the early 1940s.[128] In August 1941 Beatty offered to acquire a minority interest in the TCA and merge the CPR's aviation business with the TCA's, but the TCA board refused the offer to merge its profitable enterprise with the CPR's unprofitable one.[129] By the end of 1943, Canadian Pacific Air Lines (CPA), the CPR's commercial aviation company, which was established in July 1942, had invested nearly $7 million in feeder lines, but Howe remained resistant.[130] That year, as friction between the companies mounted, Howe advised that the government declare the TCA as the government's "chosen instrument" for transcontinental and international air travel; Mackenzie King announced the policy in the House of Commons on 2 April.[131] The following March, Howe announced the government's intention to separate air transport from ground transport within a year of the cessation of the war, in effect barring the CPR from participating in commercial aviation. CPR president D.C. Coleman was quick to argue that an injustice was being inflicted upon the CPR, protesting to Mackenzie King that the government had handed the CPA a "death sentence."[132] He argued in a letter to King that "[a]t no time has the Canadian Pacific shown or entertained an intention of competing in any sense with the T.C.A." The CPA, Coleman suggested, was providing a niche service of North–South routes, in contrast to the national, East–West routes of the TCA; and though the CPA had recently applied for licences on the transcontinental line, Coleman claimed it was "only done for the purpose of providing local service to communities which are not served by the T.C.A."[133] The substance of Coleman's pleading seemed to contradict the general understanding of the CPR's intentions, and certainly Mackenzie King was unconvinced. "I may have been a little more outspoken than I should have been," reported King after meeting with Coleman, "but it seemed to me knowing how the C.P.R. has been lobbying against the Government, supplying funds for Conservative conventions, Bracken's campaigns ... and also realizing that we are right in our policy and that they have been doing what they can to prevent its realization, it was just as well to speak out."[134] And while Howe noted that the government made no official order to break up the CPA, he made it clear that he would not allow competition with the TCA.[135]

Early on, Sir Edward Beatty had believed the war offered an opportunity to finally introduce a railway amalgamation scheme. Beatty anticipated another depression after the war and argued that railway amalgamation should be executed during the busy wartime period,

because in the context of depression – when it would be "urgently necessary" to cut deficits – "the pressure from the labour world would be
too great."[136] In 1944 the CPR had been forced to assume a more defensive posture, as the Liberal administration signalled its intention to
legislate the company out of commercial aviation after the war. According to Howe, "Canada could never have obtained its present position in
aviation through private operation with the profit motive paramount."[137]
Trans-Canada Air Lines fit into Howe's overall economic philosophy
of strategic government intervention, which was also embraced by the
company's president, Herbie Symington. With massive capital expenses
required for the infrastructure to support air traffic in a country as large
and sparsely populated as Canada, Symington argued that the industry
was uniquely fitted to public ownership, though he identified himself as
a "private ownership man"; "I am not one of those who state that black
must be black and white must be white," claimed Symington.[138]

Though the horizon looked bleak for the CPR in 1944, within two
years Howe had backed away from trying to rid the CPR from commercial aviation. He claimed that, with recent changes to CPA management, the two systems had come to work as one integrated system; in
1948 the Liberal administration of Louis St Laurent awarded the fran-
chise for international routes across the Pacific to the CPA.[139] When
twenty-two years of uninterrupted Liberal rule ended with the victory
of John Diefenbaker's Conservatives in 1957, the new government allowed the CPA to break the TCA's transcontinental monopoly, thus
permitting an ironic repeat of the railway rivalry.[140] Howe and the Liberals had, of course, set the stage for these later developments by permitting the limited expansion of a private airline. This was typical of
Howe's performance as minister of reconstruction, which was highly
favourable to private enterprise. Crown corporations and their assets
were quickly liquidated, made especially attractive to the private sector
by the application of accelerated depreciation. The Polymer Corporation, a crown corporation established in 1942 to manufacture synthetic
rubber, was an exception. "Its economic value after the war is doubtful," Howe explained in August 1942, "but I think that operating costs
will be low enough to warrant its peacetime operation as a Government
enterprise."[141] As historian Matthew Bellamy has shown, the crown
corporation had a long and successful afterlife following the war.[142]

The persisting conflict between Howe and the CPR had not been petty politics; it was a conflict involving different visions of the national economy rooted not merely in competing economic or political interests but the product of competing understandings of the Canadian political economy. The old political economy traditionally embraced by the Canadian bourgeoisie, and advanced by Beatty, was rooted in empire and classical liberal notions about the beneficence of private enterprise and the self-correcting market. It was based upon an earlier experience of economic development in which the railways had played a central role, when British capital drove the Canadian economy and the state remained a junior partner. Howe embraced a political economy that allowed for more active state intervention, causing him to view the national economy more like a machine to be fine-tuned than a self-correcting organism to be reified and defended. And he did not subscribe to the older, imperial version of economic nationalism; he looked upon economic integration with the United States favourably, and indeed believed in free trade between the United States and Canada.[143] Howe's overall vision differed markedly from the traditional outlook of big business, which was – somewhat contradictorily – rooted in the economic nationalism of the protective tariff, guarding Canada as a British nation against absorption into the United States – part of what Hugh Aitken long ago described as "defensive expansionism."[144] But, as E.R. Forbes has observed, Howe's economic policies merely consolidated economic disparities that had developed in the Canadian economy since Confederation.[145] The use of the state remained, in many ways, very limited under Howe's oversight, directed towards the narrow goals of efficiency and growth and guided by the outlook of the engineer.

Despite earlier scholarly works on Howe, which have tended to de-emphasize the wider social context in which Howe operated and the ideological nature of his actions and opinions, he felt himself to be a member of a social class. Howe, for example, was explicit in his belief that engineers should work to enhance the "dignity" of their profession, implying that its distance from the trades should be maintained.[146] His interactions with labour were also highly revealing. On numerous occasions, he proved to be particularly uninterested in cultivating relationships with union officials, cancelling a meeting on one occasion because of a press report that incorrectly quoted a union official with whom he was scheduled to meet.[147] This behaviour was rooted in

Howe's general feeling that labour was not entitled to share in industrial decision making in any substantive way: control over production
would remain in the hands of businessmen and professionals. Howe's
reputation as being unsympathetic to labour was well earned; and he
united with big business when it came to industrial disputes, which
grew in frequency and intensity after the war. Standing aloof from organized labour's demands for a role in shaping industrial policy during
the conversion to a peacetime economy, during the 1946 Stelco strike
Howe served as the company's inside man in the cabinet, according
to Mackenzie King.[148] One union official was earlier forced to remind
Howe "that co-operation is a two-way proposition – it cannot be wholly
on one side."[149] Employees from Research Enterprises Limited – one
of the crown corporations he established and which was headed by
Sam McLaughlin's ex-son-in-law, W.E. Phillips – had the audacity to
confront Howe at a Toronto country club, usually a preserve of the
wealthy, about the government's plans for the company. Howe's words
to the workers, as rendered by a union official, were presented to Mackenzie King as follows:

> By the end of September, I do not expect that a wheel will be turning at
> R.E.L. Every person now working will be laid off ...
>
> Let the workers go on strike. What the hell do I care. [*sic*] A little while
> ago I would have been worried, but not now. Now that plants are closing,
> there is no better time to strike. It will suit me fine ...
>
> Workers have been nursed throughout the war. They may well realize
> that the war is over. I don't give a goddamn if they do have to take jobs
> at 25c an hour less. They had better take jobs or they won't be working
> for a long time ...
>
> The plant will be sold to a firm that will employ the most people. The
> Government is not prepared to state to whom. It might scare them off.
> Besides, we have to advertise. We've had many offers. The work will be
> similar to what they are now doing at the plant.

When asked whether seniority rights would transfer over when the
plant was taken over by a private firm, Howe was blunt – "No." He was
no less blunt in ending the encounter: "Now get the Hell out of here!"[150]
Howe claimed he was misrepresented.

The spirit of it seemed to ring true, however. A Winnipeg grain dealer who read the supposedly misrepresenting press reports congratulated Howe for his stand. Howe accepted the congratulations and further explained:

> It is hard for our privileged class in war plants to realize that the atomic bomb killed Santa Claus as far as they are concerned, and they must now go to work. The Minister of Reconstruction will have a very unpleasant time for the next four or five months, but I am convinced that there are jobs for all, which is all that concerns me. After a time, I think that people will become convinced that they must move out of the cities and go back to what they were doing before the war, but they are not going to do so without first raising a clamor.[151]

Workers, according to Howe's professional and class assumptions, would ultimately have to adjust to the resumption of "normal," peacetime conditions, just as he felt they needed to adjust to the heightened production demands during the war without succumbing to the "self-appointed labor dictator" who threatened to disrupt production.[152]

Although he favoured cooperation with conservative trade unionism, Howe opposed ceding any real power to workers and was quite conscious of this objective. The business and professional classes were, according to his view, the ones entitled to make decisions about production. By acquiescing to this arrangement, workers could achieve greater productivity and higher living standards, believed Howe. But he encouraged confrontation of those who failed to conform, as the post–Second World War strike wave became the largest in Canadian history.[153]

Howe's "rough and ready" demeanor was characteristic of an emerging style within wealthy circles during the first half of the twentieth century, and here again we touch upon what has been described in the U.S. context by Jackson Lears as the "managerial revitalization of the rich."[154] Howe's reputation as an uncultured individual, more interested in playing golf and fishing than in attending posh parties, moved in step with the demotic tendencies of the moneyed throughout the twentieth century. Howe also reflected trends observed in Christopher Dummitt's study of masculinity in postwar Canada, in which Dummitt contends that control over nature and the management of risk were central to the consolidation of masculine authority: on fishing trips Howe would not count the number of fish caught but the number of fish "killed," and, indeed, his chosen profession cast the entire natural world at the mercy of the engineer's blueprint. Moreover, Howe's affinity with aviation seems to reflect quite closely Dummitt's concept of "managed risk." Anti-intellectualism, another characteristic trait of the "manly modern," was also always apparent in Howe; though having taught at university, he had very little patience for – or understanding of – philosophical matters.[155] Howe's formation as a member of a national elite was decidedly gendered; he was regularly described by commentators as a "man's man," and his ability as a cabinet minister was often associated with characteristics normatively associated with manliness – decisiveness being the most obvious. Mackenzie King recognized that the unbending Howe would make a terrible party leader and considered him by the end of the war to be "a reactionary Tory influence" within the party. Like Dunning, Howe was something of a political "strongman," whose chances of becoming party leader were limited by his inability to effectively accommodate the competing interests within the Liberal Party as he became more closely associated with the outlook and interests of the national business elite.[156]

Conclusion

Howe's experience helps to explain the ambiguous phenomenon of "change without change," which David Noble sought to understand through the development of the engineering profession in the United States.[157] Howe did not cede ideological terrain to the left, but rather argued that capitalist growth would itself answer all the major social questions of the postwar period. Looking back at the development of Canada, Howe addressed graduating engineers at the University of Toronto in 1952. He argued that

> science, engineering, and industry have had as great, if not greater, part in shaping the destiny and form of this country than have statesmanship and political philosophies. Canada today is a very different country from what it was even fifteen years ago. We are now among the first four industrial nations of the world. Our industries have gained an ability to develop

and manufacture their talents and resources only a few years ago. Today, Canada produces five of every six sheets of newsprint used throughout the entire world. Canada is first in the production of nickel, asbestos, and aluminum. The development of our water powers has made our production per capita outstanding by any comparison.[158]

In Howe's estimation this was a nation made possible by the engineer and, consequently, a nation whose legitimacy was rooted in the efficiency and productivity of the evolving capitalist system. Eventually, it would reveal its own contradictions, too, and Howe's "efficiency" in managing the relationship between government and business would come under question; but at the beginning of the 1950s, Howe had no doubts that the future held an impressive spate of capitalist expansionism.

Of course, Howe's success was made possible by a conjuncture of historical circumstances well beyond his control, which included popular pressures for the expansion of the state and economic planning.[159] Howe was better able to accommodate these pressures than many business executives, who remained deeply sceptical of the state as an economic manger, evidenced in 1943, when Charles Dunning spearheaded the formation of a secret think tank of leading business executives – including Sam McLaughlin and other major industrialists and bank presidents – to defend private enterprise.[160] While business conservatives such as Dunning and Beatty viewed the economy as an organism best left untouched by government intervention, Howe's outlook allowed for a more positive form of state intervention in the nation's economic life. Howe's view was not based upon any ideological preference for state enterprise, but came from his managerial ethic, which privileged efficiency and productivity. As such, in strategic sectors, such as the transportation routes that facilitated the major resource boom, the state could be allowed to assume a more direct role to bolster capitalist enterprise. In many ways Howe signalled the start of a transition to a form of managerial capitalism in Canada. He was an efficient operator within the bureaucratic framework typical of the modern corporation, as Alfred Chandler has famously described it, and with that he accepted a modicum of economic planning.[161] As an agent of the state, however, Howe represented something different than what Chandler described. The economic slump of the 1930s revealed that, even in the United States, the modern corporation could not adequately address the broader problems of a generalized capitalist crisis. And even organizationally advanced companies such as Du Pont could be highly reactionary and conservative in political outlook.[162] Howe introduced a managerial outlook to government, and, encouraged by his introduction to state enterprise as minister of transport and later his immersion in it as minister of munitions and supply, he helped forge a new relationship between the state and the private sector that was guided by the managerial ethic of the engineer. Describing Howe's beliefs in 1955, *Saturday Night* captured the essence of his *mentalité*:

> The acceptance of the engineer in public life and the application of the engineer's "outlook and philosophy" to the highest problems of government are developments which he feels to be altogether fitting and natural – contrasted with the low esteem in which the engineer was held fifty years ago as a mere tradesman.[163]

The contrast that *Saturday Night* invoked between the "engineer" and "a mere tradesman" also reminds us of Howe's meritocratic dimension. Howe paid due heed to merit in his respect for "expertise," and he sought to reinstate meritocratic ideals in the postwar period. But *expertise* was not a neutral term. The dollar-a-year men were, according to Howe's view, uniquely capable of managing the wartime economy, and the nonpartisan makeup of the dollar-a-year men added credibility to Howe's view. That leading businessmen were acting through the state to direct the wartime economy seemed appropriate to Howe in the circumstances. Howe's meritocratic outlook thus offered an explanation for the exclusion of other social groups from wielding similar influence over the state. Howe, in this way, represented a specific example of the "managerial revitalization of the rich," which articulated a logic that limited the democratization of economic life.

For better or worse, Howe's outlook encouraged greater economic integration with the United States and represented a signal change from the old political economy of the National Policy period – which had been framed firmly within the East–West axis of the nation-state and conceived itself as an economic bloc within the British Empire – to a

postwar economy increasingly based upon continental business linkages. This transition witnessed the relative political decline of big capital in Canada, most notably evidenced by the waning political influence
of St James Street and the CPR. Though in some respects, as Alvin
Finkel, James Struthers, and others have shown, the business elite
successfully managed the political crisis that emerged from the Great
Depression of the 1930s, they were also shaped by the crisis in ways
they could not afford.[164] In retrospect, Howe was among the political
operators – of which Mackenzie King was the grand master – who managed various aspects of a "passive revolution" that, ultimately, would
restore the legitimacy of capital; ironically, these political innovations
were also the product of big capital's political weakness and inability
to impose its conservative program upon the state.

Conclusion
Après le déluge

On 28 September 1941, Sir Herbert Holt died. His death was announced on the loudspeaker at a baseball game at Delorimier Stadium in Montreal. An initial hush fell over the crowd – then a cheer. The reaction revealed Holt's personal unpopularity in Montreal, especially as head of the local utility – Montreal Light, Heat & Power Consolidated. Even among colleagues Holt was considered something of "an old cuss," though his personal secretary, Sévère Godin, claimed Holt's steely image was a façade masking shyness and loneliness.[1] Whatever the case, Holt's unpopularity was rooted in a more generalized political and ideological crisis of the Canadian bourgeoisie. Earlier in the year, the Liberal Quebec premier Adélard Godbout had announced his government's intention to expropriate the Beauharnois Company from the Holt power interests. H.J. Symington, Howe's power controller, reported that the move represented a huge blow to Holt and the "power barons," since the financial structure of the interlocked power companies controlled by the Holt group was organized so that "the killing" in profitable returns would be made in Beauharnois common stock.[2] The power barons fought back, but Holt's death, writes Ted Regehr, "expedited nationalization on terms dictated by the provincial government."[3] In 1944 Godbout's administration established a commission to acquire Montreal Power and all its subsidiaries, including Beauharnois. The former Liberal premier of Quebec, Louis-Alexandre Taschereau, had been much more friendly to Holt and his cohorts.[4]

Holt had embodied an older generation of businessmen whose fortunes had risen during the halcyon days of the National Policy period. And though Howard P. Robinson, Charles Dunning, Sir Edward Beatty, and Colonel Sam McLaughlin were much younger than Holt, they all shared similar residual beliefs rooted in the old political economy of the National Policy period. This study has traced the political crisis and defeat of this political economy and, with it, the dissipation of the national business elite's political power. Their capacity to shape the Canadian nation-state had significantly diminished with the decline of the "British world" they once knew, as the "new National Policy" of the postwar period would accommodate social-democratic ideas with which they were not friendly.[5]

In the 1947 edition of *Who Owns Canada?* Louis Rosenberg identified Charles Dunning, Sam McLaughlin, and Howard Robinson among the "fifty big shots" who "owned" the country. Edward Beatty would have made the list too – as he did in the 1935 edition – had he not passed away in 1943. These men had *emerged* as leading members of the Canadian bourgeoisie during the three decades following the First World War. Though their paths were various, connected with different regions and sectors of the economy, their broad political experiences after the onset of the Great Depression of the 1930s conveyed a collective sense of isolation and frustration. National Government, the Leadership League, and Arthur Meighen's attempt to lead the federal Conservatives in 1942 were all symptomatic of the broader political frustrations of Canada's economic elite during the 1930s and 1940s. Embracing a notion of the Canadian political economy as a self-correcting organism operating within the British Empire, leading business executives often remained ideologically committed to classical liberal ideals that significantly limited their political adaptability and diminished their sway in national politics. C.D. Howe did not "own" Canada in the same fashion as Beatty, Dunning, McLaughlin, and Robinson, but the period from the Second World War until Howe's exit from federal politics in 1957 has been described by one business historian as "the years of C.D. Howe"; and after his political defeat, Howe would collect "directorships like medals."[6] That Howe could define the early postwar era speaks to how dramatically the old political economy of the Canadian bourgeoisie was undermined during the 1930s and 1940s. Howe embraced a more managerial and continental logic for capitalist expansion in the postwar period; powerful business executives – notably Sir Edward Beatty – had opposed Howe only to discover their own diminished political stock. Howe's success was their failure.

At the end of the Second World War, as revealed by the composition of Rosenberg's fifty big shots, the country's economic elite remained similar to what it had looked like thirty years before.[7] Twenty-seven individuals of the group resided in Montreal, almost all were of Anglo-Celtic descent, and the Canadian Pacific Railway (CPR) remained a leading corporation.[8] As we have seen, however, significant transformations had been set in motion. Economic momentum was shifting from Montreal towards Toronto's capital market and southern Ontario's branch-plant industries – especially the automobile industry.[9] In Toronto, E.P. Taylor founded Argus Corporation in 1945, and regional capitalists, too, such as K.C. Irving in New Brunswick and H.R. MacMillan in British Columbia, would build upon wartime expansion to construct postwar business empires. And, of course, the CPR exercised a much smaller influence within the emerging continental economy. Indeed, the railway's role had undergone a qualitative shift as the political economy of the National Policy period came to an end. Its nation-building partnership with the state was decidedly in the past, and, though important, the railway was no longer central, as political, economic, and technological change gave rise to a new mix of private and public investment in the new forms of transportation. During the three decades following the First World War, St James Street's command over political and economic life was significantly compromised – and never to be recaptured.

As we have seen, this relative decline occurred as part of a larger political challenge to Canadian big business. While the economic crisis of the 1930s, like an acid, dissolved capital, it also stripped big business of its former legitimacy. As many Canadians went hungry, lost their homes, and suffered humiliation by being made dependent upon charity, the claims of the business elite to community stewardship were eroded. Robinson, Dunning, Beatty, and McLaughlin all viewed the crisis of the Great Depression through the lens of the old liberalism, which recommended further retrenchment. As soon became apparent, this path was unpopular among citizens demanding a more active response from the state to the crisis. In the minds of many elite figures, popular opinion became a stumbling block to economic recovery and raised questions about the efficacy of democratic governance in a period of economic crisis. As the political theorist C.B. Macpherson reminded us more than four decades ago, democracy itself had been a relatively recent and highly contested historical innovation.[10] The response of the Canadian bourgeoisie to the Great Depression belonged to this longer political struggle over the nature of democracy in Canada.

Their beliefs were also often rooted in a general elitism and assumed superiority over the lower orders, which often assumed racialist dimensions. In certain instances, this resulted in a form of paranoia and isolation from mainstream thought; Howard Robinson, for example, felt that the *New York Times* was a fine publication, but he believed also that it was "Bolshevik and Jewish in its propaganda slant."[11] He represented a somewhat more extreme reaction to the crisis, and he also occupied a unique position as a business leader within a declining regional economy; as such, he even came to see Confederation and National Policy expansion in the West as mistakes, but this represented more of a lament for the passing of a supposed pre-Confederation golden age in the Maritimes than anything else.[12] Robinson's sense of political isolation during the 1930s and 1940s was in marked contrast to his political and business advances during the 1920s. His continued involvement in provincial utilities and role in advancing the transition to pulp and paper were indicative of his commanding business presence, which was made all the more impressive by his growing control over Saint John's daily press. Indeed, Robinson emerged as one of several press barons in Canada who brought the daily press under more strict business control, which became especially obvious after the First World War. But while individuals such as Robinson freed newspapers from their formerly close association with political parties, the structural dominance of big business over the daily press proved insufficient to shore up its legitimacy during the Great Depression. Moreover, Robinson's business strategy achieved only limited success. His attempt to carry on the tradition of the "community-oriented entrepreneur" in New Brunswick resulted in ambiguous outcomes, limited by the inherent contradiction of Robinson's role as a participant in the national economy with ties to U.S. capital. Similarly, while Robinson sought to defend Canada as a British nation against the encroachments of U.S. mass culture in the 1930s and 1940s, in the business world, as a director of Famous Players of Canada, he served as a representative of the U.S. entertainment industry. Not unlike his contemporaries in the business community, Robinson's business strategies appeared to contradict the ideals of his worldview.

In contrast to Robinson, Charles Dunning's ascension into the Canadian bourgeoisie involved breaking ties with his Canadian region of origin, the Prairie West. Of course, Dunning's geographic mobility coincided with his social ascent from farmers' spokesman to big business representative, and his trajectory revealed the potential for coalescence between progressive ideals and hard-boiled business objectives. His public image projected the meritocratic ideal of the period. And numerous businessmen were impressed by Dunning, whom they viewed as a political strongman capable of overcoming the limits of political partisanship. But Dunning's meritocratic sheen was lost as he made the transition to Ottawa politics and Montreal business. As minister of finance in 1929 and 1930, his accommodation of the protective tariff caused his stock to decline in Western Canada. And once he became connected with the CPR after losing his seat in the House of Commons in 1930, Dunning's estrangement from the West was virtually sealed. He came to embrace a big business outlook during the 1930s, and some elite figures hoped that Dunning could lead a nonpartisan effort to offer the country stronger leadership during the economic crisis. But this was not to be. Instead, Dunning re-entered the Liberal cabinet as minister of finance following the electoral victory of the King Liberals in 1935. In government, the constraints of popular opinion and the concomitant balance of opinion within the Liberal Party limited Dunning's range of policy alternatives. Ironically, Dunning oversaw the Canadian government's initial experimentation with Keynesian policies. Rather than living up to his former reputation as a political strongman and prospective Liberal leader, Dunning became a pawn in Mackenzie King's deft statecraft, indicative of the larger political difficulties the business elite faced in attempting to shape public policy. Dunning's limited success in politics during the 1930s should not be seen as a personal failure. Rather, it was symptomatic of the diminished legitimacy of big business and the political crisis of the old liberalism, a liberalism that Dunning continued to embrace and that remained important in structuring the worldview of many corporate executives throughout the Great Depression. Dunning left government an embattled man in 1939 to resume his business career in the more politically comfortable environment of St James Street.

No other man represented St James Street more publicly during the 1930s than Canadian Pacific Railway president Sir Edward Beatty. The CPR's political and economic position was seriously eroded during the interwar years, as the political economy of the National Policy period, from which the CPR had emerged, came to a close and as the state emerged as a competitor in the railway business. From the time he became CPR president in 1918, Beatty vigorously opposed direct government involvement in the railway business. On the heels of mounting competition between the CPR and the government-owned Canadian National Railways (CNR), the Great Depression radically worsened the outlook of both railway companies. Disappointed by the recommendations of the royal commission appointed to study the subject in 1931 and 1932, Beatty became a lead proponent of National Government, which meant a nonpartisan administration that would be freed from the constraints of the party system. A key element of such a government for Beatty was its insulation from popular opinion. According to Beatty, the willingness of politicians to mindlessly pander to popular sentiment had stifled a constructive solution to the nation's railway question. He was not alone in this thinking. Numerous businessmen questioned the efficacy of democratic governance in the context of the economic crisis, and they remained deeply suspicious of the wisdom of, to use the parlance of the times, "the man on the street." But Beatty's efforts failed. The political power of the CPR and St James Street was faltering significantly, and signs of broader economic transformation were apparent.

Perhaps nowhere was this more evident than with the rise of the automobile industry. Automobiles represented a key aspect of Canada's economic future, and no one personified the new industry better than Sam McLaughlin, the president of General Motors of Canada. His father's carriage business had been a success story of National Policy industrialization during the late nineteenth and early twentieth centuries.

McLaughlin initiated the transition of the business towards the production of automobiles in 1907 before shifting the company's production entirely to automobiles in 1915. McLaughlin's consistent dependence upon the U.S. automobile industry was formalized when he sold the family business to General Motors in 1918, and he remained in charge as president of GM's Canadian branch. During the 1920s, McLaughlin succeeded in consolidating local support for General Motors in Oshawa, re-creating the paternalism of his father's carriage business; his claims to community stewardship remained effective as he rallied local support to protest the lowering of the automobile tariff in 1926 and as he intervened to resolve a dispute at the Oshawa factory in 1928. But these claims were eroded under the impact of the Great Depression of the 1930s, when GM drastically reduced its Oshawa output in response to the downturn. While the path of dependent industrialization allowed McLaughlin to amass great sums of personal wealth and promoted his integration into the Canadian bourgeoisie, it paradoxically undermined his authority in Oshawa. The epic 1937 strike in Oshawa was evidence of the new militancy among the local working class, as workers transformed Oshawa from a company town into a labour town. In step with his estrangement from Oshawa's working class, McLaughlin retreated to the conservative ideals and solutions that seemed sensible to other business and political leaders in Ontario, such as George Drew and C. George McCullagh, thus following a familiar trajectory among his social peers – of reaction and conservative isolation.

Collectively, these elite figures adopted terms such as *retrenchment* and *economy* in describing the steps towards economic recovery and found the popular clamour for new paths not only distasteful but also often positively frightening. C.D. Howe introduced a new form of business expansionism after the older version – the version of expansion Holt offered in his 1929 address to the board of the Royal Bank of Canada – failed to achieve results. As minister of transport and later as minister of munitions and supply and minister of reconstruction, Howe helped develop a more interventionist state role in certain areas of the economy against significant opposition from the country's economic elite. After the initial transition to a peacetime economy, Howe's former reputation as a government administrator who often clashed with Canadian business titans – most notably, Sir Edward Beatty – began to change. He developed the persona for which he has been more famous within the historiography – a free-enterprise man. At the top of Howe's list of principles guiding the government's industrial development program was this declaration: "Canada is a free enterprise economy and the initiative for industrial expansion rests with private individuals and firms."[13] This principle was one with which Beatty could have heartily agreed; and, indeed, the company with which Beatty had been most connected until his death in 1943, the CPR, prospered in new areas during the postwar period.[14] Howe argued for the appropriateness of state intervention in the pursuit of industrial development, stable employment, and rising wages. Such a policy would also, to his mind, make the social provisions of the welfare state unnecessary. Howe helped replace the pessimistic language of retrenchment from the 1930s with the more positive language of productivity and efficiency, introducing a new managerial ethic to Canadian capitalism in the aftermath of the Canadian bourgeoisie's failure to restore the old political economy.

Of course, Howe was not the definitive embodiment of the new managerial capitalism of the postwar world, which would be taken in directions that went well beyond his rather narrow outlook. By the time of the Pipeline Debate in 1956, Howe had come to assume the role of the old curmudgeon from a bygone era, as politicians and policymakers gained an even greater sense of the state's capacity to intervene in the economy.[15] Later economic nationalists of the 1960s and 1970s were apt to see Howe in terms of his postwar career, viewing him as the man who sold out Canada to the United States. But, as we have seen, he helped create a more active state that was strenuously opposed by powerful figures within Canadian big business. Significantly, although the Great Depression and the experience of the wartime economy had sounded the death knell of the old political economy, the new managerial ethic embraced by Howe held firm to one old and fundamental assumption: that workers would be following orders. While George Grant and the left-nationalists later lamented Canada's apparent failure to produce a truly national bourgeoisie, commentators of the period thought Canada's business class powerful and aggressive enough. "Any attempt to picture Canadian-owned and controlled capital as a domesticated tabby cat as compared with the ravening Bengal tiger of foreign capital should be treated with healthy skepticism," wrote Rosenberg in 1947. "They belong to the same species and have similar claws."[16]

Canada's economic elite survived the crisis, but not in the manner they hoped or expected. The Great Depression of the 1930s presented an unexpected and unprecedented political challenge to the Canadian bourgeoisie. "We didn't even say 'Après nous le déluge,' because we didn't know any deluge was coming," reminisced one wealthy resident of Montreal's Square Mile.[17] The general outlook of the country's economic elite during the Depression – and for much of the three decades following the First World War – was fundamentally shaped by the old assumptions of the National Policy period, when government intervention remained limited to that of a supporting role to private enterprise, and when the Canadian nation-state remained firmly rooted within the economic and cultural sphere of the British Empire: when St James Street ruled and when prime ministers called upon the presidents of the CPR. This world was eroding in the face of increased continental integration, as economic catastrophe seemed imminent, and as social-democratic and socialist alternatives rose. A siege mentality obtained among numerous leading business and political figures in Canada. The vicissitudes of adaptation were anything but smooth. The political failure of these men and the demise of the political economy they embraced were indeed fundamental to the collective experience of the Canadian bourgeoisie, altering the shape of big business and its relationship to the state.

Notes

Introduction

1 *The Canadian Annual Review of Public Affairs, 1928–29* (Toronto: Canadian Review Company, 1929), 671–81; Duncan McDowall, *Quick to the Frontier: Canada's Royal Bank* (Toronto: McClelland & Stewart, 1993), 230; Paul-André Linteau, *Histoire de Montréal depuis la Confédération* (Montréal: Boréal, 1992), 303–6.

2 For the labour revolt, see Craig Heron, ed., *The Workers' Revolt in Canada, 1917–1925* (Toronto: University of Toronto Press, 1998).

3 Richard White, *Railroaded: The Transcontinentals and the Making of Modern America* (New York: W.W. Norton, 2011), 511.

4 See, for example, Gregory P. Marchildon, "'Hands Across the Water': Canadian Industrial Financiers in the City of London, 1905–1920," *Business History* 34, no. 3 (July 1992): 69–95. For a recent study of the broader British connection, examining the role of British businessmen in Confederation, see Andrew Smith, *British Businessmen and Canadian Confederation: Constitution-Making in an Era of Anglo-Globalization* (Montreal and Kingston: McGill-Queen's University Press, 2008). For a recent examination of how empire shaped the calculation of risk among British financiers regarding investment in Canada and Australia during the early twentieth century, see Andrew Richard Dilley, "Empire and Risk: Edwardian Financiers, Australia and Canada, c. 1899–1914," *Business and Economic History Online* 7 (2009), <http://www.thebhc.org/publications/BEHonline/2009/dilley.pdf>.

5 The interpretation in the pages to follow suggests the need to revise the general historiographical tendency emphasizing the successful and orderly adaptation of business leaders to demands for social and economic reform during the 1930s. The successful adaptation of the business community and its ability to control the reform process is argued most explicitly in Alvin Finkel's important study, *Business and Social Reform in the Thirties* (Toronto: James Lorimer, 1979). Finkel's argument, though persuasively argued and broadly correct, tends to overstate the prescience of the nation's business elite. The fundamental conservatism of social reform in the 1930s is also persuasively demonstrated in James Struthers, *No Fault of Their Own: Unemployment and the Canadian Welfare State, 1914–1941* (Toronto: University of Toronto Press, 1981). More recently Struthers has reiterated this general argument about the nature of social reform in "Unequal Citizenship: The Residualist Legacy in the Canadian Welfare State," in *Mackenzie King: Citizenship and Community; Essays Marking the 125th Anniversary of the Birth of William Lyon Mackenzie King*, eds John English, Kenneth McLaughlin, and P. Whitney Lackenbauer (Toronto: Roblin Brass Studio, 2002), 169–85. Numerous monographs have also contributed to the theme of prescient adaptation by emphasizing the role of intellectuals and their growing importance within the expanding government bureaucracy. See, for example, J.L. Granatstein, *The Ottawa Men: The Civil Service Mandarins, 1935–1957* (Toronto: University of Toronto Press, 1998 [1982]); Douglas Owram, *The Government Generation: Canadian Intellectuals and the State, 1900–1945* (Toronto: 1986); Barry Ferguson, *Remaking Liberalism: The Intellectual Legacy of Adam Shortt, O.D. Skelton, W.C. Clark, and W.A. Mackintosh* (Montreal and Kingston: McGill-Queen's University Press, 1993); and Robert A. Wardhaugh, *Behind the Scenes: The Life and Work of William Clifford Clark* (Toronto: University of Toronto Press, 2010).

6 As David Harvey has succinctly noted, "[c]apital is not a thing but a process in which money is perpetually sent in search of more money." See David Harvey, *The Enigma of Capital and the Crises of Capitalism* (New York: Oxford University Press, 2010), 40.

7 See Rudolf Hilferding, *Finance Capital: A Study of the Latest Phase of Capitalist Development*, ed. and intro. Tom Bottomore, trans. Morris Watnick and Sam Gordon (London: Routledge & Kegan Paul, 1981 [1910]).

8   See Eric Hobsbawm, *The Age of Empire, 1875–1914* (London: Abacus, 1994 [1987]).

9   Michael Bliss, *Northern Enterprise: Five Centuries of Canadian Business* (Toronto: McClelland & Stewart, 1987), 225–52 and 285–311; Michael Bliss, "Canadianizing American Business: The Roots of the Branch Plant," in *Close the 49th Parallel Etc: The Americanization of Canada*, ed. Ian Lumsden (Toronto: University of Toronto Press, 1970), 27–42; and T.W. Acheson, "The National Policy and the Industrialization of the Maritimes, 1880–1910," *Acadiensis* 1, no. 2 (Spring 1972): 3–28.

10 For a broad look at the economic activities of the CPR in Western Canada, see John A. Eagle, *The Canadian Pacific Railway and the Development of Western Canada, 1896–1914* (Montreal: McGill-Queen's University Press, 1989). Andy A. den Otter's *Civilizing the West: The Galts and the Development of Western Canada* (Edmonton: University of Alberta Press, 1982) illuminates the business, political, and social networks that allowed a particular family to acquire a privileged share of western development opportunities.

11 Kenneth Norrie, Douglas Owram, and J.C. Herbert Emery, *A History of the Canadian Economy*, 3rd ed. (Scarborough, ON: Thomson Nelson, 2002), 190.

12 For an analysis of this merger wave in international perspective, see Gregory P. Marchildon, *Profits and Politics: Beaverbrook and the Gilded Age of Canadian Finance* (Toronto: University of Toronto Press, 1996), 245–59. See also Gilles Piédalue, "Les groupes financiers au Canada, 1900–1930: Étude préliminaire," *Revue d'histoire de l'Amérique française* 30, no. 1 (June 1976): 3–34. For a broad overview of the role of the financial elite within the business world, see Graham D. Taylor, *The Rise of Canadian Business* (Toronto: Oxford University Press, 2009), 21–34.

13 Robert Craig Brown and Ramsay Cook, *Canada, 1896–1921: A Nation Transformed* (Toronto: McClelland & Stewart, 1974), 2.

14 See especially Adolf A. Berle and Gardiner C. Means, *The Modern Corporation and Private Property*, rev. ed. (New York: Harcourt, Brace & World, 1967 [1932]); and Alfred D. Chandler, Jr., *The Visible Hand: The Managerial Revolution in American Business* (Cambridge, MA: Belknap Press, 1977).

15 See, for example, Sven Beckert, *The Monied Metropolis: New York City and the Consolidation of the American Bourgeoisie, 1850–1896* (Cambridge: Cambridge University Press, 2001); Steve Fraser and Gary Gerstle, eds, *Ruling America: A History of Wealth and Power in a Democracy* (Cambridge, MA: Harvard University Press, 2005); Jeffrey M. Hornstein, *A Nation of Realtors: A Cultural History of the Twentieth-Century American Middle Class* (Durham, NC: Duke University Press, 2005); Jeffrey Haydu, *Citizen Employers: Business Communities and Labor in Cincinnati and San Francisco, 1870–1916* (Ithaca, NY: Cornell University Press, 2008); Kim Phillips-Fein, *Invisible Hands: The Making of the Conservative Movement from the New Deal to Reagan* (New York: W.W. Norton, 2009); Nelson Lichtenstein, *The Retail Revolution: How Wal-Mart Created a Brave New World of Business* (New York: Metropolitan Books, 2009); Julia C. Ott, *When Wall Street Met Main Street: The Quest for an Investors Democracy* (Cambridge, MA: Harvard University Press, 2011); and White, *Railroaded*.

16 Exceptions to this characterization of the literature are: Finkel, *Business and Social Reform*; Reginald Whitaker, *The Government Party: Organizing and Financing the Liberal Party of Canada, 1930–58* (Toronto: University of Toronto Press, 1977); as well as the recent book by Reinhold Kramer and Tom Mitchell, *When the State Trembled: How A.J. Andrews and the Citizens' Committee Broke the Winnipeg General Strike* (Toronto: University of Toronto, 2010), which presents research that significantly alters the standard narrative explaining the suppression of the Winnipeg General Strike by demonstrating the central role played by A.J. Andrews, a lawyer and stalwart of the local elite, in cultivating, directing, and, ultimately, usurping the authority of the state. T.D. Regehr's *The Beauharnois Scandal: A Story of Canadian Entrepreneurship and Politics* (Toronto: University of Toronto Press, 1990) provides insight into the complex patronage relationships between businessmen, politicians, and bureaucrats. The recent book by Andrew Smith, *British Businessmen and Canadian Confederation*, also throws valuable new light upon the politics of business during an earlier period. Duncan McDowall's *Steel at the Sault: Francis H. Clergue, Sir James Dunn, and the Algoma Steel Corporation 1901–1956* (Toronto: University of Toronto Press, 1984) provides insight into the changing relationship between business and government during the

1940s and 1950s. And Michael Bliss, *A Canadian Millionaire: The Life and Business Times of Sir Joseph Flavelle, Bart., 1858–1939* (Toronto: Macmillan of Canada, 1978) reveals a considerable amount about the politics, business and social life, and culture of the Toronto capitalists who grew to rival Montreal's dominance in the early twentieth century. But, nonetheless, a surprisingly small number of historians have sought to examine the ways in which businessmen attempted to rule as a class in the political sphere during the period investigated in this study. The pre-1914 period has received more attention. The works on this earlier period have collectively thrown light upon the broad formation of business elites in Canada from the mid-nineteenth century to the First World War. Sensitive to social and cultural complexities and the historical contingency of social formations, this work has helped to root capitalists within their local contexts as well as in their provincial contexts, but for the most part it examines the national dimensions and class behaviour of businessmen in only a limited and narrow fashion, with the exception perhaps of Brian Young's *George-Etienne Cartier: Montreal Bourgeois* (Montreal and Kingston: McGill-Queen's University Press, 1981). Carman Miller's recent biography of Sir Frederick Borden also provides evidence of class formation at the national level, demonstrating how Borden "was coming to see himself as a member of a national class." Miller also highlights the dense interrelationship between political and business motives. See Carman Miller, *A Knight in Politics: A Biography of Sir Frederick Borden* (Montreal and Kingston: McGill-Queen's University Press, 2010), especially 63 and 273–320. See also T.W. Acheson, "The Social Origins of Canadian Industrialism: A Study in the Structure of Entrepreneurship" (PhD thesis, University of Toronto, 1971); Michael Bliss, *A Living Profit: Studies in the Social History of Canadian Business, 1883–1911* (Toronto: McClelland & Stewart, 1974); Gregory S. Kealey, *Toronto Workers Respond to Industrial Capitalism, 1867–1892* (Toronto: University of Toronto Press, 1980), chapters 1 and 2; Christopher Armstrong and H.V. Nelles, *Southern Exposure: Canadian Promoters in Latin America and the Caribbean, 1896–1930* (Toronto: University of Toronto Press, 1988); Fernande Roy, *Progrés, harmonie, liberté: le libéralisme des milieux d'affaires francophones de Montréal au tournant du siècle* (Montréal: Boréal, 1988); Robert A.J. McDonald, *Making Vancouver:*

Class, Status and Social Boundaries, 1863–1913 (Vancouver: University of British Columbia Press, 1996); Christopher Armstrong, *Blue Skies and Boiler Rooms: Buying and Selling Securities in Canada* (Toronto: University of Toronto Press, 1997). For Peter C. Newman's books on the "establishment," see *The Canadian Establishment*, vol. 1 (Toronto: McClelland & Stewart, 1975); *The Establishment Man* (Toronto: McClelland & Stewart, 1982); and *Titans: How the New Canadian Establishment Seized Power* (Toronto: Viking, 1998).

17 Though their work has been important, the "dependency thesis" argued by an earlier generation of left-nationalists does not offer an entirely convincing characterization of twentieth-century Canada or its bourgeoisie, both of which could more accurately be described as participants within – not outside of – the advanced capitalist world. This is not to deny that dependency is an important theme of Canadian economic development. Indeed, as we shall see, the economic elite's unequal and dependent alliance with U.S. capital grew throughout the period investigated in this study. However, Canada achieved levels of industrialization and affluence during the twentieth century that were characteristic of advanced capitalist societies. This point has been made in Paul Kellogg, "Kari Levitt and the Long Detour of Canadian Political Economy," *Studies in Political Economy* 76 (Autumn 2005): 31–60. The first sustained effort from the left to challenge the left-nationalist characterization of the Canadian bourgeoisie was delivered in Steve Moore and Debi Wells, *Imperialism and the National Question in Canada*, intro. Leo Johnson (Toronto: Moore, 1975). See also Philip Resnick, *The Land of Cain: Class and Nationalism in English Canada, 1945–1975* (Vancouver: New Star Books, 1977). For the left-nationalist position, which drew inspiration from the "staples thesis" of Harold Innis, see: Kari Levitt, *Silent Surrender: The Multinational Corporation in Canada* (Toronto: Macmillan of Canada, 1970); R.T. Naylor, "The Rise and Fall of the Third Commercial Empire of the St. Lawrence," in *Capitalism and the National Question in Canada*, ed. Gary Teeple (Toronto: University of Toronto Press, 1972), 1–41; Daniel Drache, "The Canadian Bourgeoisie and Its National Consciousness," in *Close the 49th Parallel Etc*, 3–25; Mel Watkins, *Staples and Beyond: Selected Writings of Mel Watkins*, eds Hugh Grant and David Wolfe, intro. Wallace Clement (Montreal and Kingston: McGill-Queen's University Press, 2006). Similar interpretations were offered earlier in

L.C. Park and F.W. Park, *Anatomy of Big Business* (Toronto: Progress Books, 1962); and George Grant, *Lament for a Nation: The Defeat of Canadian Nationalism*, intro. Andrew Potter (Montreal and Kingston: McGill-Queen's University Press, 2005 [1965]). Grant, of course, approached the subject as a conservative who lamented the social impact of free-market ideals and the decline of the older version of nation building. Tom Naylor's *The History of Canadian Business, 1867–1914*, 2 vols (Toronto: J. Lorimer, 1975) advanced a particularly ambitious and controversial argument, maintaining that merchant capitalists represented a dominant fraction within the national bourgeoisie and that this fraction had pursued accumulation and political strategies that safeguarded the interests of commerce and finance to the detriment of indigenous manufacturing. Numerous empirical weaknesses of Naylor's argument have since been pointed out. For a useful discussion of these issues, see L.R. MacDonald, "Merchants against Industry: An Idea and Its Origins," *Canadian Historical Review* 56, no. 3 (September 1975): 263–81. Industrialization and industrialists had played a much greater role in Canada's nineteenth- and twentieth-century history than the staples thesis embraced by Naylor and the dependency school suggested. In the 1970s and 1980s, social historians produced numerous community studies that collectively did much to contradict the grand theories of Canadian dependency theorists, demonstrating industrial capital's formidable presence in Canadian communities as early as the middle of the nineteenth century. Among those producing these studies was a group of historians who not only critiqued the work of Naylor and others for being empirically weak but also sought to lay out a different interpretation of Canadian capitalism. Greatly influenced in Canada by the work of Clare Pentland and Stanley Ryerson and internationally by the economic histories of Maurice Dobb and Eric Hobsbawm, this school emphasized the historical importance of the nineteenth-century transition to industrial capitalism in Canada. The scholarship of Gregory S. Kealey and Bryan Palmer, whose interests lay primarily in the history of the working class, became most noticeably associated with this school. See H. Clare Pentland, *Labour and Capital in Canada, 1650–1860* (Toronto: James Lorimer & Company, 1981 [1960]); Stanley Ryerson, *Unequal Union: Confederation and the Roots of Conflict in the Canadas, 1815–1873* (Toronto: Progress Books, 1968), especially chapter 13; Maurice Dobb, *Studies in the Development of Capitalism* (London: Routledge, 1963 [1947]); Eric Hobsbawm, *Labouring Men: Studies in the History of Labour* (London: Weidenfeld and Nicholson, 1964); Kealey, *Toronto Workers Respond to Industrial Capitalism*, especially chapter 1; and Bryan D. Palmer, *A Culture in Conflict: Skilled Workers and Industrial Capitalism in Hamilton, Ontario, 1860–1914* (Montreal: McGill-Queen's University Press, 1979). A lengthier and more complete overview of the literature can be found in Don Nerbas, "The Politics of Capital: The Crisis and Transformation of Canada's Big Bourgeoisie, 1917–1947" (PhD thesis, University of New Brunswick, 2010), 7–23.

18 Canadian historians have in recent years begun to reexamine the cultural dimensions of economic elites. See Thierry Nootens, "'What a Misfortune That Poor Child Should Have Married Such a Being as Joe': Les fils prodiges de la bourgeoisie montréalaise, 1850–1900," *Canadian Historical Review* 86, no. 2 (June 2005): 225–56; Elise Chenier, "Class, Gender, and the Social Standard: The Montreal Junior League, 1912–1939," *Canadian Historical Review* 90, no. 4 (December 2009): 671–710; Keith Walden, "Tea in Toronto and the Liberal Order, 1880–1914," *Canadian Historical Review* 93, no. 1 (March 2012): 1–24. This work enriches our historical understanding of elite culture, but it does so largely without relating cultural activities to capital accumulation and politics.

19 Reinhold Kramer and Tom Mitchell call attention to Perry Anderson's statement on the importance of "history from above" in *When the State Trembled*, 7. Recent work by Kurt Korneski and Andrew Smith, both operating from different intellectual traditions, has also sought to integrate elites into historical narratives within the wider context of the British Empire. See Korneski's "Britishness, Canadianness, Class and Race: Winnipeg and the British World, 1880s–1910s," *Journal of Canadian Studies* 41, no. 2 (Spring 2007): 161–84; "Reform and Empire: The Case of Winnipeg, Manitoba, 1870s–1910s," *Urban History Review/Revue d'histoire urbaine* 37, no. 1 (Fall 2008): 48–62; "Race, Gender, Class, and Colonial Nationalism: Railway Development in Newfoundland," *Labour/Le Travail* 62 (Fall 2008): 79–107. And see Smith's *British Businessmen and Canadian Confederation*; and "Thomas Bassett Macaulay and the Bahamas: Racism, Business and Canadian Sub-imperialism," *Journal of Imperial and Commonwealth History* 37, no. 1 (March 2009): 29–50. Carman Miller's work also shows how Sir Frederick Borden's

outlook and social aspirations were shaped by the imperial context. See Miller, *A Knight in Politics*, especially 273–93. This study, as well, follows the recent literature on the "British world" in recognizing that Canada's historical development, including its social, cultural, and economic history, unfolded within the British Empire until the 1950s or 1960s, when imperial decline, continental integration, and the emergence of new nationalisms finally undercut the older sense of Canada as a British nation. For a recent statement, see Phillip Buckner, "Introduction," in *Canada and the British Empire*, ed. Phillip Buckner (Oxford: Oxford University Press, 2008), 1–21.

20 Watt Hugh McCollum [Louis Rosenberg], *Who Owns Canada? An Examination of the Facts Concerning the Concentration of the Ownership and Control of the Means of Production, Distribution and Exchange in Canada* (Regina: Saskatchewan C.C.F. Research Bureau, 1935), 10; and *Who Owns Canada? An Examination of the Facts Concerning the Concentration of Ownership and Control of the Means of Production, Distribution and Exchange in Canada* (Ottawa: Woodsworth House, 1947), 10–11.

21 Eugene Forsey, "Economic Cabinet of Canada," *The Alarm Clock* (January 1934): 5–8. I thank Kirk Niergarth for drawing my attention to this article.

22 Craig Heron, "Harold, Marg, and the Boys: The Relevance of Class in Canadian History," *Journal of the Canadian Historical Association*, new series, 20, no. 1 (2009): 1–26.

23 E.P. Thompson's classic formulation, in which he described class as not a thing but a historical occurrence related to a wider social experience, remains useful, and the model developed in this study draws upon Thompson's emphasis upon class conflict in shaping the historical development of classes. For E.P. Thompson's well-known theoretical discussion of class, see *The Making of the English Working Class* (London: Penguin Books, 1991 [1963]), 8–13. Sven Beckert has brilliantly drawn upon Thompson's framework of class formation in his examination of New York City's bourgeoisie during the latter half of the nineteenth century. See Beckert, *The Monied Metropolis*.

24 Heron, "Harold, Marg, and the Boys," 4. Although this study analyses the "structural" features that contributed to the formation of the big bourgeoisie, it follows the observation of Geoff Eley and Keith Nield, that

the postulation of "structural regularities" need not entail the "further assumption that these regularities necessarily translate into solidarities and forms of class consciousness that we can then describe as class consciousness traditionally understood, in the canonical and time-honoured way." See Geoff Eley and Keith Nield, *The Future of Class in History: What's Left of the Social?* (Ann Arbor: University of Michigan Press, 2007), 195. An older, sociological categorization of class in Canada is offered in John Porter's classic, *The Vertical Mosaic: An Analysis of Social Class and Power in Canada* (Toronto: University of Toronto Press, 1965).

25 This term is used advisedly as a historiographic concept that builds upon Sven Beckert's influential monograph on the making of New York City's Gilded Age bourgeoisie. See Beckert, *The Monied Metropolis.* See also the essays in Sven Beckert and Julia B. Rosenbaum, eds, *The American Bourgeoisie: Distinction and Identity in the Nineteenth Century.* (New York: Palgrave, 2010), which delve deeply into the cultural construction of the bourgeoisie.

26 Perry Anderson has critiqued Eric Hobsbawm's highly influential *The Age of Extremes: the Short Twentieth Century, 1914–1991* (London: Abacus, 1994) for omitting the bourgeoisie. See Perry Anderson, "The Vanquished Left: Eric Hobsbawm," in *Spectrum* (New York: Verso, 2005), 304–6.

27 C. Wright Mills, *The Power Elite* (New York: Oxford University Press, 1959 [1956]), 147.

28 See Mills, *The Power Elite.*

29 Jackson Lears, "The Managerial Revitalization of the Rich," in *Ruling America*, 181–214.

30 Christopher Dummitt, *The Manly Modern: Masculinity in Postwar Canada* (Vancouver: University of British Columbia Press, 2007).

31 Historians have extensively examined the various racial and ethnic identities of Canada's working classes. For a recent and in-depth historical discussion of race and the political left, see Ian McKay, *Reasoning Otherwise: Leftists and the People's Enlightenment in Canada, 1890–1920* (Toronto: Between the Lines, 2008), 345–415.

32 *Annual Financial Review, Canadian,* vol. 17 (Toronto: Houston's Standard Publications, May 1917); C.W. Parker, ed., *Who's Who and Why: A Biographical Dictionary of Men and Women of Canada and*

Newfoundland (Toronto: International Press, 1916). For an overview of the war's impact upon the Canadian economy, see Norrie, Owram, and Emery, *A History of the Canadian Economy*, 266–8.

33 This is based upon ninety-six individuals whose date of birth was listed in the *Who's Who*.

34 These two were Sir William Price, born in Chile, and Alfred Baumgarten, born in Germany.

35 Only six individuals were Methodist. For the social world of the Toronto Methodists, see Bliss, *Canadian Millionaire*, 53–82.

36 These were Senator Frederic Ligori Beique, Senator Raoul Dandurand, and Sir Rodolphe Forget, Conservative MP.

37 Finkel, *Business and Social Reform*; Arthur Meighen to George McCullagh, 30 January 1939, quoted in Harold A. Naugler, "R.J. Manion and the Conservative Party, 1938–1940" (MA thesis, Queen's University, 1966), 189.

38 Chandler's classic, *The Visible Hand*, describes the rise of big business as an essentially economic phenomenon born of the organizational innovation of the modern corporation.

39 Howard Robinson to W.C. Milner, 29 January 1934, file 7, W.C. Milner Papers, S 11, New Brunswick Museum [NBM].

40 Howard Robinson to R.B. Hanson, 4 May 1938, 31/144, R.B. Hanson Papers, 1247, Provincial Archives of New Brunswick [PANB].

41 George McCullagh, *Marching On – To What? First in Series of Five Radio Addresses Delivered by Mr. George McCullagh, Sunday, January 15, 1939*, 3–4.

42 And, if we move beyond the Forsey-Rosenberg group, other important figures such as Harold Crabtree hold multiple directorships.

43 The data from Rosenberg and Forsey may appear somewhat Montreal-centric, and certainly some important Toronto business figures are not included in their lists. Nonetheless, Montreal remained the centre of Canadian business in the 1930s, and the city's capitalists retained a massive interest in shaping national developments.

44 Much of the national political history from this period is found in old political biographies and party histories, which hardly consider social class as an active force in the period. See Roger Graham, *Arthur Meighen*, 3 vols (Toronto: Clarke, Irwin & Company, 1960, 1963, and 1965 respectively); H. Blair Neatby, *William Lyon Mackenzie King: The Lonely*

Heights, 1924–1932 (Toronto: University of Toronto Press, 1963) and
William Lyon Mackenzie King: The Prism of Unity (Toronto: University
of Toronto Press, 1976); J.L. Granatstein, *The Politics of Survival: The
Conservative Party of Canada, 1939–45* (Toronto: University of Toronto
Press, 1967). A more recent interpretation of Mackenzie King's political
involvement in the Prairie West can be found in Robert A. Wardhaugh,
Mackenzie King and the Prairie West (Toronto: University of Toronto
Press, 2000). See also C.P. Stacey's *A Very Double Life: The Private
World of Mackenzie King* (Toronto: Macmillan of Canada, 1976) for
an exploration of King's private life based upon his diaries. As noted
above, later works by Barry Fergusson, J.L. Granatstein, and Douglas
Owram emphasize the role of intellectuals in supporting and carrying
out the reforms of the 1930s and 1940s. The work of James Struthers
tends to focus more specifically upon the role of politicians, especially
Mackenzie King, but also places a heavy emphasis upon the relationship
between politicians and civil servants. And recently Shirley Tillotson's
*Contributing Citizens: Modern Charitable Fundraising and the Making
of the Welfare State, 1920–66* (Vancouver: UBC Press, 2009) argues that
charity fundraisers helped forge "a common culture of contribution" that
arose out of the discourses and practices surrounding Community Chest
campaigns and hastened the expansion of the welfare state. This study
suggests the bourgeoisie's political decline created the conditions under
which intellectuals, politicians, and bureaucrats could expand their authority in the postwar period. And though, as Finkel has shown, the business elite played an active role in some aspects of the reform process,
their collective ability to rule was greatly reduced during the 1930s and
1940s.

45   Alan Dawley has argued that the rule of "big money" was abortive in
the United States in the 1930s. See Dawley's "The Abortive Rule of Big
Money," in *Ruling America*, 149–80. See also Phillips-Fein, *Invisible
Hands*, 3–15 and 19–25.

1 Provincial Man of Mystery

1   The business lives of Max Aitken (later Lord Beaverbrook) and Sir
James Dunn in Canada have been the subject of two scholarly monographs. For Aitken, see Gregory P. Marchildon, *Profits and Politics:*

Beaverbrook and the Gilded Age of Canadian Finance (Toronto: University of Toronto Press, 1996), and for Dunn, see Duncan McDowall, *Steel at the Sault: Francis H. Clergue, Sir James Dunn, and the Algoma Steel Corporation* (Toronto: University of Toronto Press, 1984). Izaak Killam has largely eluded scholarly attention; there are no personal papers available for researchers to examine. Nonetheless, for a biographical treatment of Killam, see Douglas How's hagiographic commissioned study, *Canada's Mystery Man of High Finance: The Story of Izaak Walton Killam and His Glittering Wife Dorothy* (Hantsport, NS: Lancelot Press, 1986). To date, no biographical study of Ward C. Pitfield exists. Pitfield worked for Max Aitken in the Saint John offices of Royal Securities before moving to Montreal and eventually setting out on his own.

2 D. Murray Young, "Alexander Gibson," *Dictionary of Canadian Biography*, vol. 14 (Toronto: University of Toronto Press, 1998), 400–4; James D. Frost, *Merchant Princes: Halifax's First Family of Finance, Ships and Steel* (Toronto: Lorimer, 2003).

3 For an examination of the earlier brand of community-oriented entrepreneurship, see the classic statement by T.W. Acheson in "The National Policy and the Industrialization of the Maritimes, 1880–1910," *Acadiensis* 1, no. 2 (Spring 1972): 3–28.

4 Monopoly conditions, according to Paul Baran and Paul Sweezy, bring a qualitative transformation to the functioning of capitalism. See Paul Baran and Paul Sweezy, *Monopoly Capital: An Essay on the American Economic and Social Order* (New York: Monthly Review Press, 1966).

5 A number of intellectual trends within Canadian scholarship, including metropolitanism, dependency theory, and the staples thesis, have tended to obscure the continued political importance of regional elites in the first half of the twentieth century. For an overview of the regional literature, see Don Nerbas, "Adapting to Decline: The Changing Business World of the Bourgeoisie in Saint John, NB, in the 1920s," *Canadian Historical Review* 89, no. 2 (June 2008), 152–5. Alfred D. Chandler's classic account of the rise of the modern corporation largely ignores politics. See Chandler, *The Visible Hand: The Managerial Revolution in American Business* (Cambridge, MA: Belknap Press, 1977).

6 See the memo attached to Howard Robinson to W.C. Milner, 25 April 1927, file 6, W.C. Milner Papers, S 11, New Brunswick Museum [NBM].

7 George A. Rawlyk, *Ravaged by the Spirit: Religious Revivals, Baptists and Henry Alline* (Montreal and Kingston: McGill-Queen's University Press, 1984).

8 "Business, Professional Men Gather to Pay Final Tribute at Late Publisher's Funeral," *King's County Record* (Sussex), 31 August 1950, 1; "Howard P. Robinson Dies; Outstanding Business Leader," *Telegraph-Journal* (Saint John), 24 August 1950, 1 and 5; *Census of Canada, 1871*, Albert County, Elgin, Division 2, 5; *Census of Canada, 1881*, Albert County, Elgin, 1.

9 Howard P. Robinson to J.C. Webster, 5 May 1943, file 229, John Clarence Webster Papers, S 194, NBM.

10 "Mrs. R.D. Robinson," *King's County Record*, 6 May 1932, 4; Howard P. Robinson to Lord Beaverbrook, 31 December 1931, 250, Lord Beaverbrook Papers, House of Lords Record Office [HLRO]. Indicative of Robinson's importance in Canada and beyond by the early 1930s, his mother's obituary appeared in the *New York Times*. See "Mrs. Robert D. Robinson," *New York Times*, 2 May 1932, 18.

11 Robinson wrote of his sister's death: "It has upset me and, coming on top of the loss of many near and dear relatives and friends within the last eight months, makes one wonder as to the cause of these terrible occurrences." Robinson to G. Percy Burchill, 18 January 1933, file 21/28/3, box 337, Burchill Papers, MC 1246, Provincial Archives of New Brunswick [PANB].

12 "Last Will and Testament," Howard P. Robinson, 17 July 1949, Letters of Probate, PANB.

13 "Battles Fought and Won by Maritime Publisher," *Financial Post* (Toronto), 16 January 1937, section 2, 2.

14 G.P. Burchill, *The Story of the New Brunswick Telephone Company: As Told to the Writer by One of Its Founders – Mr. Howard P. Robinson* (Nelson-Miramichi, 1974), 2.

15 "Battles Fought and Won," 2; Burchill, *The Story of the New Brunswick Telephone Company*, 2.

16 Nancy Colpitts, "Alma, New Brunswick and the Twentieth Century Crisis of Readjustment: Sawmilling Community to National Park" (MA thesis, Dalhousie University, 1983), 60–1.

17 Howard P. Robinson to R.B. Bennett, 4 January 1933, 421417, vol. 686, R.B. Bennett Papers, MG 26 K, Library and Archives Canada [LAC].

18 Burchill, *The Story of the New Brunswick Telephone Company*, 2; *Daily Gleaner* (Fredericton), 22 August 1906, 1; "Telephone War at End," *Globe* (Saint John), 22 August 1906, 8.

19 "Battles Fought and Won," 2; Howard P. Robinson to R.B. Hanson, 27 October 1913, 14/256, R.B. Hanson Papers, MC 1247, PANB.

20 "Battles Fought and Won," 2.

21 Howard Robinson to J.B.M. Baxter, 4 November 1916, folder: 8 December 1916, box 55, New Brunswick Cabinet Papers, RS 9, PANB. I would like to thank Matt Baglole for drawing my attention to this document.

22 Advertisement, *New York Times*, 9 March 1917, 13.

23 For the government activism of the Foster and Veniot administrations generally, see W.Y. Smith, "Axis of Administration: Saint John Reformers and Bureaucratic Centralization in New Brunswick, 1911–1925" (MA thesis, University of New Brunswick, 1984), 47–115; for road construction and repair policies under Veniot's direction, see Charles Joseph Allain, "The Impact of the Automobile on the Government of New Brunswick, 1897–1932" (MA thesis, University of New Brunswick, 1987), 45–60; for an examination of hydroelectric development and its politics, see Paul-Emile McIntyre, "The Development of Hydro-Electric Power at Grand Falls, New Brunswick: An Issue in Provincial Politics, 1920–1926" (MA thesis, University of New Brunswick, 1974); for the Veniot administration's position on milk pasteurization, see Jane E. Jenkins, "Politics, Pasteurization, and the Naturalizing Myth of Pure Milk in 1920s Saint John, New Brunswick," *Acadiensis* 37, no. 2 (Summer/Autumn 2008): 86–105.

24 "Howard P. Robinson Dies," 5. Information from the *Who's Who in Canada* misleadingly suggests that Robinson was an active combatant: "Served in the First World War as Lieutenant with 3rd Regiment, New Brunswick Garrison Artillery." See B.M. Greene, ed., *Who's Who in Canada, 1947–48* (Toronto: International Press, 1948), 241.

25 William Lyon Mackenzie King, Diaries, 11 August 1937, LAC.

26 New Brunswick Liberal J.E. Michaud reported in 1935 "that since 1917 the Liberals in St. John have not been united, and this breach was about to be healed when some of the non-conformists undertook to speak on behalf of the Liberal party." J.E. Michaud to Norman Lambert, 16 August 1935, file "Ralston, J.L., Correspondence, Political 1935 (July–Nov)," vol. 17, James Layton Ralston Papers, MG 27 III B 11, LAC.

27 John English, *The Decline of Politics: The Conservatives and the Party System, 1901–20* (Toronto: University of Toronto Press, 1977), 175–6.

28 Howard P. Robinson to R.B. Hanson, 19 December 1923, 19/419–21, Hanson Papers, PANB.

29 ? to J.B.M. Baxter, 22 July 1914, J.B.M. Baxter Papers, MC 3153, PANB.

30 Smith, "Axis of Administration," passim; Don Nerbas, "Revisiting the Politics of Maritime Rights: Bourgeois Saint John and Regional Protest in the 1920s," *Acadiensis* 37, no. 1 (Winter/Spring 2008): 114–16; "Public-Capital Divide Opinion Currier Report," 22 March 1919, *Financial Post*, file 13, vol. 35, Financial Post Fonds, MG 28 III 121, LAC.

31 The *Standard* was dyspeptic in its opposition to municipal power development. After the provincial government passed legislation that allowed the City of Saint John to purchase and take over New Brunswick Power's assets, the *Standard* proclaimed: "Never in the history of Canada has such a bare-faced steal been suggested as this is. The Bolsheviks' plans in force now in Russia have nothing on this thing." See "Public Ownership Gone Mad," *Financial Post*, 21 April 1922, file 13, vol. 35, Financial Post Fonds, LAC.

32 "Oppose Setting up Second Plant," *Financial Post*, 13 April 1923, file 13, vol. 35, Financial Post Fonds, LAC.

33 Nerbas, "Adapting to Decline," 176–80.

34 P.J. Veniot to W.L.M. King, 12 May 1923, 81113-4, vol. 95, William Lyon Mackenzie King Papers, MG 26 J1, LAC.

35 P.J. Veniot to W.L.M. King, 12 June 1923, 81115-6, vol. 95, King Papers, LAC.

36 Veniot to King, 12 May 1923, 81113-4, vol. 95, King Papers, LAC.

37 *The Canadian Review of Public Affairs, 1923* (Toronto: Canadian Review Company, 1924), 656.

38 Letters of Patent, B1, 402, PANB; "Howard P. Robinson Dies," 5.

39 "New Companies," *Globe*, 5 July 1923, 9; "Making Progress," *Globe*, 6 July 1923, 4.

40 "The Telegraph-Journal," *Globe*, 16 July 1923, 4. The veneer of provincial and regional solidarity in the paper's public pronouncements also masked considerable behind-the-scenes struggle and intrigue. The recently retired premier W.E. Foster had secured an option on the *Telegraph* and resisted Robinson's plans. In the end, Robinson was able to secure Foster's option

in exchange for a "large block of common stock," which Foster believed
would give him controlling interest when combined with "the other grit
holdings." Foster had miscalculated. The bloc of preferred shares owned
by Robinson gave him control of the newly formed *Telegraph-Journal*.
Foster, for his uncooperative attitude, became a marked enemy; Saint John
Conservative MP J.B.M. Baxter wrote in private correspondence to Arthur Meighen on 10 August that Robinson "is determined to [word here
appears to be *kill*] W.E. Foster when the opportunity is afforded." When
Meighen wrote back to say that he could not read the word between *to*
and *Foster*, Baxter responded: "You can fill that blank with 'beat' 'smash'
'destroy' or any more injurious language which will express annihilation!"
See J.B.M. Baxter to Arthur Meighen, 10 August 1923, 34612-9; Meighen
to Baxter, 14 August 1923, 34620-1; Baxter to Meighen, 20 August 1923,
34622-7, vol. 61, series 3, Meighen Papers, LAC.

41   R. O'Leary to Angus McLean, 11 October 1924, 669143, vol. 118,
Meighen Papers, LAC.

42   J.B.M. Baxter to Arthur Meighen, 10 August 1923, 34612-9; Meighen to
Baxter, 14 August 1923, 34620-1; Baxter to Meighen, 20 August 1923,
34622-7, vol. 61, series 3, Meighen Papers, LAC.

43   J.B.M. Baxter to R.B. Hanson, 12 July 1923, 5/339, Hanson Papers,
PANB.

44   R.B. Hanson to Howard P. Robinson, 17 December 1923, 19/417-8,
Hanson Papers, PANB.

45   Howard P. Robinson to R.B. Hanson, 19 December 1923, 19/419-21,
Hanson Papers, PANB.

46   King Diaries, 12 May 1930, LAC.

47   As Arthur T. Doyle has observed, this transition produced a more quieted form of journalism in New Brunswick, quite different from the
earlier muckraking party journalism. See Doyle's *Front Benches and
Back Rooms: A Story of Muckraking, Corruption, Raw Partisanship and
Intrigue in New Brunswick* (Toronto: Green Tree Publishing, 1976), 276.
In his national survey, Paul Rutherford has written that stricter business
control emerged after 1913. See Rutherford's *The Making of the Cana-
dian Media* (Toronto: McGraw-Hill Ryerson, 1978), 51–2. And Minko
Sotiron's *From Politics to Profit: The Commercialization of Canadian
Daily Newspapers, 1890–1920* (Montreal and Kingston: McGill-Queen's
University Press, 1997) examines this transformation in detail.

48   Howard P. Robinson to R.B. Hanson, 17 November 1922, 19/367, Hanson Papers, PANB.

49   C.E. Neill to R.B. Hanson, 11 January 1921, 16/642-3 and Neill to Hanson, 4 January 1921, 18/638, Hanson Papers, PANB. Neill wrote Hanson in 1921, when Hanson was deciding whether to accept nomination: "The glamour of politics to my personal knowledge has spoiled many good men and wrecked useful careers. If I had the ability and experience to become Prime Minister of Canada, and were offered that position to-morrow, I should decline it, and I think I am as ambitious as most men. The average politician with whom you will come in contact is not a man of high type, and nothing, as far as I have been able to see, in the association is of an elevating character."

50   Howard Robinson to Hanson, 20 August 1934, 28/43, Hanson Papers, PANB. All three were members of the Union Club. See B.M. Greene, ed., *Who's Who in Canada, 1934–35* (Toronto: International Press, 1935), 478 and 991; Greene, ed., *Who's Who in Canada, 1947–48*, 241.

51   Hanson to Baxter, 22 October 1923, 5/342-3, Hanson Papers, PANB.

52   Baxter to Hanson, 1 November 1923, 5/334, Hanson Papers, PANB.

53   "Baxter Declares Veniot Cause of Return to N.B.," *Telegraph-Journal*, 8 August 1925, 1.

54   Roger Graham, *Arthur Meighen: And Fortune Fled*, vol. 2 (Toronto: Clarke, Irwin & Company, 1963), 254–5; Leslie Roberts, *These Be Your Gods* (Toronto: Musson Book Company, 1929), 144.

55   Hanson to George B. Jones, 5 October 1923, 5/509, Hanson Papers, PANB.

56   P.J. Veniot, *The Premier's Manifesto to Electors of New Brunswick* (1925), 11, "Provincial Politics; Election Campaigns, 1912, 1925," 4/1, box 1, J. Leonard O'Brien Papers, MC 299, PANB.

57   A.R. Graustein to R.B. Hanson, 1 July 1925, 6/246; Hanson to Graustein, 6 July 1925, 6/246; Graustein to Hanson, 13 July 1925, 6/252, Hanson Papers, PANB.

58   "Advocate Refuses to Back Baxter," *Telegraph-Journal*, 7 August 1925, 2. The *Advocate*, a northern New Brunswick paper, characterized the Conservative convention held in Newcastle on 24 July as "a Baxter and lumbermen's convention." See "Bolt from the Blue in Northumberland Country," *Globe*, 8 August 1925, 5.

59 Hanson wrote to J.B.M. Baxter less than two weeks before the election: "I got in touch with Howard Robinson and told him to put in the Telegraph a statement contradicting the [Fredericton] Gleaner's roar back of the night before, to the effect that you had made a deal with the big lumbermen at Chatham when there last Friday to give them: (a) The Quebec scale, (b) a reduction in stumpage on the stumpage bills falling due August 11, 1925, and he promised to attend to it." See Hanson to Baxter, 29 July 1925, 6/41, Hanson Papers, PANB.

60 "Opposition Speakers Accuse Government of Imperiling Financial Stability of Province," *Telegraph-Journal*, 8 August 1925, 3.

61 See, for example: Angus McLean, "Second Article from Angus McLean," *Telegraph-Journal*, 5 August 1925, 2; "Baxter Declares He Will Revalue Paper Co. Rights," *Telegraph-Journal*, 7 August 1925, 2; Angus McLean, "Fourth Article from Angus McLean," *Telegraph-Journal*, 7 April 1925, 2; "Candidates Criticise Government Policies," *Telegraph-Journal*, 7 August 1925, 11.

62 "Fifth Article from Angus McLean," *Telegraph-Journal*, 8 August 1925, 2.

63 "M.E. Agar Declares for Public Ownership," *Telegraph-Journal*, 6 August 1925, 12.

64 The Saint John *Globe* believed the Angus McLean wing of the Opposition camp would overtake the pro-public power sentiment within the party articulated by Miles E. Agar. "Politicians Busy in the Evenings," *Globe*, 6 August 1925, 4.

65 Hanson's personal correspondence includes a number of letters from H.H. Morton, who, as the letterhead printed on his letters reveals, was "Grand Scribe" of the KKK in Fredericton. Morton was apparently a local Conservative supporter. He wrote to Hanson in August 1934 on behalf of W.K. MacKenzie of McAdam to see if MacKenzie's son could get a job at the newly constructed McAdam post office. Morton ended his letter thanking Hanson "for past favors." See H.H. Morton to Hanson, 30 August 1934, 10/435, Hanson Papers, PANB. "K.K.K. Member Here," newspaper clipping, n.d., scrapbook, 6/1, box 1, O'Brien Papers, PANB.

66 Calvin A. Woodward, *The History of New Brunswick Provincial Election Campaigns and Platforms, 1866–1974* (Toronto: Micromedia, 1976), 51.

67 Doyle, *Front Benches and Back Rooms*, 258. Reflecting on a conversation with Veniot in Quebec City after the election, King wrote: "listened

to [Veniot's] story re his defeat. There is no doubt U.S. money by predatory interests was used, the lumbermen are a selfish lot. I am beginning
to think Angus McLean, the worst of the lot of them." King Diaries, 23
September 1925, LAC.

68 "New N.B. Premier," *Financial Post*, 14 August 1925, 1.

69 Upon announcement of the election, Robinson was named as an individual
who might be sent to Montreal on behalf of the New Brunswick Conservatives. Fundraising, it seems certain, was the purpose of the prospective
trip. Jones wrote Arthur Meighen: "The election was announced last evening, nomination August 3rd, polling the 10th. Baxter is very busy so am
I. Would you wire Dr. Baxter or myself on receipt of this, if we can send
a man to Montreal. It will be Thomas Bell or H.P. Robinson, both of St.
John. This is very important and I hope that you will give us all the assistance you possibly can." Later, Jones wrote Meighen that he heard "Angus
McLean + H.P. Robinson would meet [him] at the Ritz [in] Montreal."
George B. Jones to Arthur Meighen, 18 July 1925, 68164, and Jones to
Meighen, 23 July 1925, 68165, vol. 116, Meighen Papers, LAC. Angus
McLean served as the New Brunswick envoy to Montreal, though it is
not certain whether Robinson joined him. Meighen reported to Jones on
26 July: "I saw MacLean [*sic* – contemporaries often spelled Angus Mc-
Lean's last name as McLean and MacLean] in Montreal, and no doubt by
this time he will have reported to you." Meighen to George B. Jones, 26
July 1925, 68168, vol. 116, Meighen Papers, LAC. Whether or not Robinson joined McLean in Montreal, the correspondence collectively reveals
Robinson's close association with the inner workings of the Conservative
campaign.

70 King Diaries, 4 September 1925, LAC.

71 Robinson to J.C. Webster, 6 November 1945, file 229, Webster Papers,
NBM.

72 Robinson to J.C. Webster, 18 January 1937, file 228, Webster Papers,
NBM.

73 The Conservatives countered by claiming that public ownership had
nothing to do with creating low power rates in Saint John. "Politicians
Busy in the Evenings," 2.

74 Bill Parenteau, "The Woods Transformed: The Emergence of the Pulp
and Paper Industry in New Brunswick, 1918–1931," *Acadiensis* 22, no. 1
(Autumn 1992): 5–43.

75 Correspondence between Robinson and G. Percy Burchill reveals that
    Robinson was involved in Burchill's efforts to offer an option on tim-
    ber lands and mill properties to Montreal financier Ward Pitfield of the
    Royal Securities Corporation. Pitfield had worked in the Saint John
    office of Royal Securities before the First World War and, no doubt,
    would have been acquainted with Robinson while in Saint John. See file
    21/30/3, box 331, Burchill Papers, PANB.
       Writing from New York on 20 June 1930, Robinson passed this mes-
    sage along to northern New Brunswick lumberman J. Leonard O'Brien:
    "have not had time to take your matter up here yet but will do everything
    possible." See Howard Robinson, New York, to J.L. O'Brien, 20 June
    1930, file 1/2, box 1, O'Brien Papers, PANB. Robinson was likely tak-
    ing up a matter with International Paper. Leonard was doing business
    with International Paper in the 1930s, but later a dispute arose over In-
    ternational Paper's local business practices. O'Brien claimed that local
    International Paper officials had extorted payment from him for rotten
    material and had demanded double payment on some transactions. The
    "racket," as O'Brien described it, was sustained because O'Brien was so
    dependent upon cutting rights on International Paper's "vast public hold-
    ings." See O'Brien to Neill C. Head, assistant to the president, Interna-
    tional Paper, 21 July 1934, file 40/1, box 22, O'Brien Papers, PANB.
76 J.R.H. Wilbur, *The Rise of French New Brunswick* (Halifax: Formac Pub-
    lishing, 1989), 130; Nicole Lang, "De l'entreprise familiale à la compag-
    nie moderne: la Fraser Companies Limited de 1918 à 1974," *Acadiensis*
    25, (no. 2 Spring 1996), 51; *The Financial Post Directory of Canadian
    Directors and Officials 1931 (January)* (Toronto: Maclean Publishing
    Company, 1930), 318–9; Greene, ed., *Who's Who in Canada, 1947-48,*
    241; *The Financial Post Directory of Canadian Directors and Officials,
    1937* (Toronto: Maclean Publishing Company, 1937), 302.
77 A.R. Graustein to J.B.M. Baxter, 5 June 1926, file A2b, Grand Falls
    Power Dam Fonds, RS 196, PANB.
78 See, for example, A.R. Graustein to J.B.M. Baxter, 24 May 1926 and 5
    June 1926, file A2b, Grand Falls Power Dam Fonds, PANB. The pulp
    and paper companies wanted to monopolize control over forest resources
    with very limited conditions. Graustein, for example, complained about
    stipulations in a proposed lease requiring the companies cut at least 6 per
    cent of the forest growth each year – or at least pay the dues that would

have accrued to the government based on such a cut. Graustein and Fraser to Baxter, 23 June 1926, file A2b, Grand Falls Power Dam Fonds, PANB.

79 Robinson to Baxter, 4 June 1926, file A2b, Grand Falls Power Dam Fonds, PANB.

80 "Two papers such as the Gleaner and the Saint John Globe can work infinite mischief by insinuation and suggestion with regard to a thing which is perfectly right in itself," Baxter lamented to A.R. Graustein in 1926. Baxter to Graustein, 3 May 1926, file A2b, Grand Falls Power Dam Fonds, PANB.

81 "Howard P. Robinson Dies," 5.

82 "Formal Opening of Newsprint Mill of N.B. International Paper Company Colorful Event," *Telegraph-Journal*, 15 March 1930, 1 and 5.

83 At his death, Robinson owned 940 class A and twenty class B Connors Brothers shares. Letters of Probate, Howard P. Robinson, PANB.

84 For developments during the interwar period, see Margaret E. McCallum, "Corporate Welfarism in Canada, 1919–39," *Canadian Historical Review* 71, no. 1 (January 1990): 46–74.

85 Neil McLean and his brother Alan were both Liberals and capable of reliably delivering the Liberal vote, claimed R.A. Tweedie, and played an important role in upholding the Liberal government in 1939. See R.A. Tweedie, *On With the Dance: A New Brunswick Memoir, 1935–1960* (Fredericton: New Ireland Press, 1986), 66–7.

86 Robinson to Beaverbrook, 19 October 1929, Beaverbrook Papers, HLRO.

87 Robinson to J.C. Webster, 6 November 1945, file 229, Webster Papers, NBM.

88 Nerbas, "Revisiting the Politics of Maritime Rights," 122; R.B. Hanson to F.X. Jennings, 19 October 1929, 23/319-20, Hanson Papers, PANB.

89 *Busy East* (January 1928), 8.

90 Robinson to Beaverbrook, 10 December 1932, 31 December 1932, and 20 January 1932, Beaverbrook Papers, HLRO.

91 Christopher Armstrong and H.V. Nelles, *Southern Exposure: Canadian Promoters in Latin America and the Caribbean, 1896–1930* (Toronto: University of Toronto Press, 1988), 274.

92 King Diaries, 13 August 1937, LAC: "Took up the Domin. Prov. Commn. Howard Robinson had come on but was in too bad shape (ulcer

in stomach) to take on work. I had told Illesley [*sic*] of this in advance & stressed need for younger man." Maritime Liberals, J.E. Michaud of New Brunswick and J.L. Ilsley of Nova Scotia, had recommended Robinson's appointment. See King Diaries, 11 August 1937, LAC. CPR president Edward Beatty wrote to Robinson later in August: "I imagined that something such as you describe had arisen to prevent you from assuming your duties of a Royal Commissioner." See Beatty to Robinson, 30 August 1937, 197, vol. 165, box 23-008, President's Letter-Books, RG 23, Canadian Pacific Railway Archives [CPRA].

93 James J. Fraser, *A History of Caton's Island* (Chatham: Miramichi Historical Society, 1967), 40–7.

94 Howard Robinson to Lord Beaverbrook, 20 January 1947, 28585–7, case 46(a), R / file 1(c), Lord Beaverbrook Papers, University of New Brunswick Archives [UNBA]; "Maximum Property Tax of $192.50 and Freedom from Income Levy Attracts Canadians to Nassau," *Financial Post*, 24 July 1937, 9.

95 Howard Robinson to Percy Burchill, 29 December 1927, file 21/30/3, box 331, Burchill Papers, PANB.

96 H. Heward Stikeman, *The Mount Royal Club, 1899–1999* (Montreal: Price-Patterson, 1999), 204. This source appears to attribute an incorrect first-name – "Harold P." – to Robinson.

97 "Elected to Board of Royal Bank of Canada," *Financial Post*, 19 January 1935, 17.

98 Sitting on the company's board of directors were: W.C. Allison, Dr A.P. Barnhill, Howard Robinson, J.M. Robinson, and Lt.-Col. J.L. McAvity, all from Saint John; F.B. Black of Sackville, New Brunswick; Archibald Fraser and R.B. Hanson from Fredericton; E.W. Mair of Woodstock; J.E. Macpherson of Montreal; Angus McLean of Bathurst; Richard O'Leary of Richibucto; E.H. Sinclair of Newcastle, New Brunswick; E.R. Sumner of Moncton; and I.R. Todd of Milltown, New Brunswick. *The Financial Post Survey of Corporate Securities, 1929, April* (Toronto: Maclean Publishing Company, 1929), 77

99 Application, New Brunswick Telephone Company, 27 July 1921, 3, file "N.B. Telephone – General Documents, 1921," B 1/2, 27a, RG 3, Public Utilities Board of Commissioners Records, RS 18, PANB.

100 *New Brunswick Board of Public Utilities Commissioners, In the Matter of the New Brunswick Telephone Company, Proceedings at Hearing,*

26 October 1920, 3–4, 7, 10, file "N.B. Telephone General Documents, 1920," B/27a, RG 3, Public Utilities Board of Commissioners Records, PANB.

101 *Before the New Brunswick Board of Public Utilities, in the Matter of the Application of the New Brunswick Telephone Company for Leave to Issue $500,000 Additional Stock*, 25 November 1925, 20, file "General N.B. Telephone Co., 1925," B1/27a, RG 3, Public Utilities Board of Commissioners Records, PANB.

102 *New Brunswick Board of Public Utilities, in the Matter of the New Brunswick Telephone Company, Limited*, 24 October 1928, 6, file "General N.B. Telephone Co., 1928," B1/27a, RG 3, Public Utilities Board of Commissioners Records, PANB.

103 J.E. Macpherson to R.B. Hanson, 5 May 1931, 24/716; Hanson to Macpherson, 30 April 1931, 24/715; Hanson to Macpherson, 6 May 1931, 24/717, Hanson Papers, PANB.

104 "Communications Grow," *Financial Post*, 27 April 1935, 4.

105 J.E. Macpherson to R.B. Hanson, 20 September 1937, 29/551, Hanson Papers, PANB. Robinson reported having been approached by "outside interests" hoping to build a national telephone system in competition with Bell. Robinson refused their offers, explaining that New Brunswick Telephone directors would only sell to the Bell Telephone Company of Canada. Later, "an individual broker with connections in Montreal and Saint John" began to buy New Brunswick Telephone stock and sold stock to shareholders in another, unrelated telephone company. These activities eventually aroused Robinson's suspicion that a takeover was afoot. In Robinson's account of these events, names and dates are omitted. Robinson refers to the individual broker as "an intimate personal friend" – perhaps Ward Pitfield. A bidding war later took place between Bell and the interests backing the "individual broker with connections in Montreal and Saint John." See Howard Robinson to George B. Jones, 19 November 1943, file 21/56/3, box 347, Burchill Papers, PANB.

106 Hanson to Howard Robinson, 21 May 1947, 35/174, Hanson Papers, PANB.

107 Robinson to Hanson, 26 May 1947, 35/175, Hanson Papers, PANB.

108 Robinson to Hanson, 30 May 1947, 35/177-6, Hanson Papers, PANB.

109 Paul McFarlane, Fort Lauderdale, Florida, to G. Percy Burchill, 27 February 1947, file 21/65/7, box 353, Burchill Papers, PANB.

110 G.M. McKiel to G.P. Burchill, 28 November 1947, file 21/65/7, box 353, Burchill Papers, PANB.

111 Robinson to Burchill, 23 February 1933, file 21/28/3, box 337, Burchill Papers, PANB.

112 Robinson to Senator George B. Jones, 19 November 1943, file 21/56/3, box 347, Burchill Papers, PANB.

113 C.F. Sise to F.B. Black, 23 February 1944, file 21/56/3, box 347, Burchill Papers, PANB. F.B. Black, president of New Brunswick Telephone at the time, reported to Sise that he was "disappointed" that the Bell directors "did not look favorably upon the request made by the New Brunswick Telephone Company." He elaborated: "I fear that they have failed to appreciate the main point of our presentation, namely that a Company outside the Province of New Brunswick holds 55% of our stock. This fact stands out conspicuously for demagogues and sensation seeking politicians to shoot at." A central concern for Sise was that New Brunswick Telephone would – should Bell relinquish control – possibly come under the control of an outside competitor. Black suggested that steps be taken to hide its control from the public: "I suggest that since your board had not approved of our first plan that if a considerable block of your holdings in our Company were distributed among twenty or so of your stockholders, it might help the situation if and when an attempt was made to take over the New Brunswick Telephone Company because of the fact of outside corporation control. This, of course, would be more or less of a substitute but the fact that the Bell would not show in publications as the major stockholder would be some advantage in case of difficulties." See F.B. Black to C.F. Sise, 29 February 1944, file 21/56/3, box 347, Burchill Papers, PANB.

114 Fred Johnson, president, Bell Company of Canada, to Howard Robinson, 30 November 1945, and Robinson to Burchill, 6 December 1945, file 21/62/6, box 350, Burchill Papers, PANB.

115 Burchill to Robinson, 21 March 1945, file 21/62/6, box 350, Burchill Papers, PANB.

116 R.A. Young, "Planning for Power: The New Brunswick Electric Power Commission in the 1950s," *Acadiensis* 12, no. 1 (Autumn 1982): 76.

117 Peter C. Newman, *The Canadian Establishment*, vol. 1 (Toronto: Mc-
    Clelland & Stewart, 1975), 227.

118 Jo Anne Claus, *On Air in the Maritimes since 1928* (Saint John: Acadia
    Broadcasting, 2007), 3.

119 Ibid., 5 and 8.

120 Ibid., 3–4.

121 *Telegraph-Journal* and *Evening Times-Globe*, Radio Supplement, 18
    April 1934, 2–6.

122 Claus, *On Air in the Maritimes since 1928*, 3–4.

123 New Brunswick Board of Commissioners of Public Utilities, Proceed-
    ings at Hearing, 26 October 1920, 4, "General – NB Tel General Docu-
    ments, 1920," B1/27a, RG 3, Public Utilities Board of Commissioners,
    PANB.

124 This development has been examined in the U.S. context by Jackson
    Lears in "The Managerial Revitalization of the Rich," in *Ruling Amer-
    ica: A History of Wealth and Power in a Democracy*, eds Steve Fraser
    and Gary Gerstle (Cambridge, MA: Harvard University Press, 2005),
    181–214.

125 "Angus M'Lean to Receive Freedom of Saint John," *Telegraph-Journal*,
    20 November 1930, 5.

126 The quotation is from an unnamed company director. See Nerbas, "Re-
    visiting the Politics of Maritime Rights," 115–16.

127 A.P. Paterson to Howard Robinson, 10 January 1937, file 12, A.P. Pater-
    son Papers, S 69A, NBM.

128 Robinson to J.C. Webster, 30 December 1944, file 229, Webster Papers,
    NBM.

129 Robinson to George B. Jones, 18 April 1932, 300545, vol. 479, Bennett
    Papers, LAC.

130 The friendly nature of relations between Robinson and Beatty can be
    gleaned from Beatty's letter-book. Reflecting the interlocking char-
    acteristics of personal and business relationships, Beatty, in 1931,
    thanked Robinson for sending him a box of Cortland apples and pro-
    ceeded to ask that they have a "chat" when Robinson was next in
    Montreal about "harbour matters." See Beatty to Robinson, 21 Janu-
    ary 1931, 193, box 23-005, President's Letter-Books, CPRA. See also
    Beatty to Robinson, 25 November 1931, 338, vol. 141, box 23-006;
    Beatty to Robinson, 22 September 1934, 72, vol. 150, box 23-007;

and Beatty to Robinson, 7 February 1936, 240, vol. 156, box 23-008, President's Letter-Books, CPRA. In 1940 Robinson indicated his wish to relinquish his directorship in Canadian Airways, the CPR's airline. Beatty asked that he remain for another year, explaining "I am satisfied that the Canadian Pacific's interests in air services should be extended and that is one reason why I should like the support of men such as yourself in putting these plans into effect." See Beatty to Robinson, 7 March 1940, 81, vol. 192, box 23-013, President's Letter-Books, CPRA. For Robinson's club affiliations see Greene, ed., *Who's Who in Canada, 1947–48*, 241.

131 Robinson to J.C. Webster, 4 January 1938, file 228, Webster Papers, NBM.

132 Lambert Diaries, 31 August 1932, box 9, Norman Lambert Papers, 2130, Queen's University Archives [QUA]: Saint John Liberal W.E. Scully reported to Norman Lambert that "Baxter has 50 thousand in McKenna's papers."

133 J.B.M. Baxter Diary, 50, MC 2990, PANB. Support for fascists abroad was considerable among some political and economic elites in Britain and the United States. For Britain, see Clement Leibovitz and Alvin Finkel, *In Our Time: The Chamberlain-Hitler Collusion* (New York: Monthly Review Press, 1997); and for the United States, see Jacques R. Pauwels, *The Myth of the Good War: America in the Second World War* (Toronto: James Lorimer, 2002).

134 Robinson to Burchill, 24 September 1943, file 21/56/3, box 347, Burchill Papers, PANB. See below for the context in which Robinson used this phrase.

135 Hanson to Robinson, 23 April 1938, 31/142, Hanson Papers, PANB.

136 Robinson to Hanson, 4 May 1938, 31/144, Hanson Papers, PANB.

137 Robinson to Beaverbrook, 9 December 1942, Beaverbrook Papers, HLRO.

138 Robinson to Bennett, 7 January 1935, 439096-7, vol. 715, Bennett Papers, LAC.

139 Robinson to J.C. Webster, 4 July 1940, file 229, Webster Papers, NBM.

140 H.P. Robinson, "The United Empire Loyalists," 18 May 1932, 3, 5, and 14, file 8, Howard P. Robinson and J.E. Humphrey Papers, S 78-1, NBM. The essay was read by Lieutenant Governor Hugh H. McLean before the Loyalist Society of New Brunswick in Saint John on Loyalist

Day (18 May) in 1932. See "Loyalist Meeting 4 p.m. to Be Close of Celebrations," *Telegraph-Journal*, 18 May 1932, 14; "History of Loyalists for Use in Schools Suggested by Dr. White," *Telegraph-Journal*, 19 May 1932, 1, 5, and 11.

141 Murray Barkley, "The Loyalist Tradition in New Brunswick: The Growth and Evolution of an Historical Myth, 1825–1914," *Acadiensis* 4, no. 2 (Spring 1975): 5.

142 Robinson, "United Empire Loyalists," 13–16.

143 Robinson to Beaverbrook, 23 August 1929, Beaverbrook Papers, HLRO.

144 Don Nerbas, "The Changing World of the Bourgeoisie in Saint John, New Brunswick in the 1920s" (MA thesis, University of New Brunswick, 2006), 89. See Robinson and Humphreys Fonds, NBM. Robinson, indeed, had actively sought to establish his Loyalist ancestry. See Robinson to W.C. Milner, 25 April 1927, file 6, Milner Papers, NBM.

145 Howard Robinson to J.C. Webster, 3 February 1930, file 228, Webster Papers, NBM; Robinson to Beaverbrook, 26 September 1929, Beaverbrook Papers, HLRO; W. Austin Squires, *The History and Development of the New Brunswick Museum (1842–1945)*, intro. by Dr J.C. Webster (Saint John: New Brunswick Museum, 1945), 17 and 19. Robinson was also a local art patron. See Kirk Niergarth, "Art and Democracy: New Brunswick Artists and Canadian Culture between the Great Depression and the Cold War" (PhD thesis, University of New Brunswick, 2007), 220.

146 Robinson to Webster, 26 March 1934, file 228, Webster Papers, NBM.

147 Robinson to Webster, 12 April 1934, 9 April 1934 and 21 June 1934, file 228, Webster Papers, NBM.

148 Greg Marquis, "Commemorating the Loyalists in the Loyalist City: Saint John, New Brunswick, 1883–1934," *Urban History Review* 33, no. 1 (Fall 2004): 30.

149 Beaverbrook to Robinson, 20 January 1932; Robinson to Beaverbrook, 31 December 1931, 9 and 24 May and 5 June 1939, Beaverbrook Papers, HLRO. Robinson served as director of the Canadian Press from 1926 to 1942 and vice president from 1939 to 1941.

150 Robinson to Beaverbrook, 6 May 1940, Beaverbrook Papers, HLRO.

151 Robinson to Beaverbrook, 27 October 1944, Beaverbrook Papers, HLRO.

152 His position against the proposed pulpwood embargo in the 1920s, for ex-
ample, seemed to encourage economic integration with the United States.
Angus McLean, who owned mills on both sides of the border, took the same
position. Arthur Meighen to Robinson, 18 February 1924, 71303-5, vol. 121,
Meighen Papers, LAC. For the pulpwood debate in New Brunswick and
Nova Scotia, see Bill Parenteau and L. Anders Sandberg, "Conservation and
the Gospel of Economic Nationalism: The Canadian Pulpwood Question in
Nova Scotia and New Brunswick, 1918–1925," *Environmental History Review* 19, no. 2 (Summer 1995): 55–83.

153 Robinson to Beaverbrook, 2 December 1938, Beaverbrook Papers,
HLRO.

154 J.L. Granatstein, *The Politics of Survival: The Conservative Party of
Canada, 1939–1945* (Toronto: University of Toronto Press, 1967), 82–
112; Roger Graham, *Arthur Meighen: A Biography: No Surrender*, vol. 3
(Toronto: Clarke, Irwin, 1965), 130.

155 Robinson to Beaverbrook, 17 November 1939, Beaverbrook Papers,
HLRO.

156 See Ian McKay, "The Liberal Order Framework: A Prospectus for a Re-
connaissance of Canadian History," *Canadian Historical Review* 81, no.
4 (December 2000): 617–45.

157 Robinson to Burchill, 24 September 1943, file 21/56/3, box 347, Burchill
Papers, PANB.

158 See Reginald Whitaker, *The Government Party: Organizing and Financing the Liberal Party of Canada, 1930–58* (Toronto: University of Toronto Press, 1977).

159 Jeffrey A. Keshen, *Saints, Sinners, and Soldiers: Canada's Second World
War* (Vancouver: UBC Press, 2004), 261.

160 Robinson to Webster, 18 February 1946, Webster Papers, NBM.

161 Robinson to Webster, 29 March 1946, Webster Papers, NBM.

162 Robinson to Beaverbrook, 18 May 1946, Beaverbrook Papers, HLRO.

163 Robinson to Beaverbrook, 7 July 1942, Beaverbrook Papers, HLRO.
Robinson, in 1950, lamented: "we are living in an age when all political values, public or private morals, all the old virtues are thrown into
the discard and we accept the theory that minorities, decadent races or
races not sufficiently schooled in the ethics of civilization should be the
masters of those whose background has come through the fiery furnace

of experience." Robinson was referring primarily to Francophone Que-
becers in this passage's reference to "races." See Robinson to Webster, 3
January 1950, Webster Papers, NBM.
164 Robinson to Beaverbrook, 17 May 1945 and 23 October 1945, Beaverbrook Papers, HLRO.
165 Registration of Death, 4089, vol. 194, PANB.
166 Watt Hugh McCollum [Louis Rosenberg], *Who Owns Canada? An Examination of the Facts Concerning the Concentration of Ownership and
Control of the Means of Production, Distribution and Exchange in Canada* (Ottawa: Woodsworth House, 1947), 10–11; Tim Buck, *Canada:
The Communist Viewpoint* (Toronto: Progress Books, 1948), 270.
167 Robinson to Beaverbrook, 20 January 1945, Beaverbrook Papers,
HLRO.

2 Charles A. Dunning

1 Scott A. Sandage, *Born Losers: A History of Failure in America* (Cambridge, MA: Harvard University Press, 2005).
2 See Jackson Lears, "The Managerial Revitalization of the Rich," in *Ruling America: A History of Wealth and Power in a Democracy*, eds Steve
Fraser and Gary Gerstle (Cambridge, MA: Harvard University Press,
2005), 181–214.
3 *Ottawa Journal*, 26 November 1929.
4 Eugene Forsey, "Economic Cabinet of Canada," *The Alarm Clock* (January 1934): 5–8.
5 Shelton Stromquist, *Reinventing "The People": The Progressive Movement, the Class Problem, and the Origins of Modern Liberalism* (Urbana
and Chicago: University of Illinois Press, 2006).
6 David Laycock has characterized the ideological beliefs shared by Crerar and Dunning in the Prairie West as "crypto-Liberalism," including
a commitment to economic liberalism and efficiency in government
and distaste for partisanship. See Laycock, *Populism and Democratic
Thought in the Canadian Prairies, 1910 to 1945* (Toronto: University of
Toronto Press, 1990), 23–68.
7 J.E. Rea, *T.A. Crerar: A Political Life* (Montreal and Kingston: McGill-
Queen's University Press, 1997), 27–8, 137–9, and 179–81.

8 Relations between Dunning and Crerar were strained in the 1930s. Crerar felt Dunning was too sympathetic towards the CPR. See Rea, *T.A. Crerar*, 171–2.

9 See endnote 5 from the Introduction.

10 17 March 1926, 1, file 203, box 21, Charles Avery Dunning Papers, 2121, Queen's University Archives [QUA]. Published in *Western Home Monthly* in April.

11 Dunning to W. Rupert Davies, 5 November 1928, file 63, box 7, Dunning Papers, QUA.

12 J. William Brennan, "The Public Career of Charles Avery Dunning in Saskatchewan" (MA thesis, University of Saskatchewan, Regina campus, 1968), 2–3.

13 Hopkins Moorhouse, *Deep Furrows* (Toronto: George J. McLeod, 1918), 226.

14 Norman Lambert, "Dunning Came up Through," *The Courier*, 17 February 1917, box 11, Norman Lambert Papers, 2130, QUA.

15 Brennan, "Public Career of Charles Avery Dunning," 4–7.

16 Moorhouse, *Deep Furrows*, 227.

17 For an analysis of the SGGA's decision to abandon the more radical "Partridge Plan," which called for direct government intervention, see Robert Irwin, "'The Better Sense of the Farm Population': The Partridge Plan and Grain Marketing in Saskatchewan," *Prairie Forum* 18, no. 1 (Spring 1993): 35–52.

18 Brennan, "Public Career of Charles Avery Dunning," 12, 14–16, and 24–5.

19 Untitled manuscript, 17 March 1926, 5, file 203, box 21, Dunning Papers, QUA.

20 B.M. Greene, ed., *Who's Who in Canada, 1934–35* (Toronto: International Press, 1935), 1424.

21 J. William Brennan, "Charles A. Dunning, 1922–1926," in *Saskatchewan Premiers of the Twentieth Century*, ed. Gordon L. Barnhart (Regina: Canadian Plains Research Center, 2004), 70.

22 Brennan, "Public Career of Charles Avery Dunning," 30–1; David E. Smith, *Prairie Liberalism: The Liberal Party in Saskatchewan, 1905–71* (Toronto: University of Toronto Press, 1975), 70.

23 Smith, *Prairie Liberalism*, 70.

24 As Brennan has noted, in 1916 "Dunning was the third prominent Grain
    Grower to enter the cabinet, joining W.R. Motherwell and George Lang-
    ley as spokesmen for farmers in the councils of the government. An
    interlocking of personnel between the leadership of the Saskatchewan
    Grain Growers' association ... and the leadership of the government at
    Regina had long been a feature of Saskatchewan politics, and over the
    years it had proven to be a mutually beneficial arrangement." See J.
    William Brennan, "C.A. Dunning, 1916–1930: The Rise and Fall of a
    Western Agrarian Liberal," in *The Developing West: Essays on Canadian
    History in Honor of Lewis H. Thomas*, ed. John E. Foster (Edmonton:
    University of Alberta Press, 1983), 247.
25 George F. Chipman to C.A. Dunning, 16 December 1914, file 2, box 1,
    Dunning Papers, QUA.
26 C.B. Macpherson, *The Political Theory of Possessive Individualism:
    Hobbes to Locke* (Oxford: Oxford University Press, 1962). Dunning ar-
    gued that "[t]o consolidate the various units now in existence along the
    lines so successfully adopted in England, it is necessary that the local
    field of collection and distribution of whatever commodities are han-
    dled should be left entirely to the local concerns whenever possible, and
    that also, wherever possible, the gathering and distribution by provinces
    should be left to provincial organizations." See Dunning, Memo, n.d.,
    file 2, box 1, Dunning Papers, QUA.
27 Dunning to Chipman, 19 December 1914, file 2, box 1, Dunning Papers,
    QUA.
28 C.W. Parker, ed., *Who's Who in Western Canada, 1911*, vol. 1 (Vancou-
    ver: Canadian Press Association, 1911), 322.
29 Robert Michael Hugh Dixon, "Charles Avery Dunning and the Western
    Wheat Marketing Problem" (MA thesis, Queen's University, 1974), 83–
    91. See also Dunning to T.A. Crerar, 12 December 1914, file "Dunning,
    Hon. Charles A., October 1912–December 1914," box 105, T.A. Crerar
    Papers, 2117, QUA, with the article written by John Kennedy, entitled
    "Co-operation," attached.
30 Norman Ward and David Smith, *Jimmy Gardiner: Relentless Liberal*
    (Toronto: University of Toronto Press, 1990), 41.
31 Brennan, "Public Career of Charles Avery Dunning," 31.
32 Robert A. Wardhaugh, "Cogs in the Machine: The Charles Dunning–
    Jimmy Gardiner Feud," *Saskatchewan History* 48, no. 1 (Spring 1996):
    21–2.

33 W.L. Morton, *The Progressive Party in Canada* (Toronto: University of Toronto Press, 1950), 55.

34 John Herd Thompson, *The Harvests of War: The Prairie West, 1914–1918* (Toronto: McClelland & Stewart, 1978), 135.

35 *Who's Who in Canada, 1934–35*, 1424; Thompson, *Harvests of War*, 159; Brennan, "Charles A. Dunning," 71.

36 J.A. Calder to Dunning, 14 January 1919, file 2, box 1, Dunning Papers, QUA.

37 Crerar reported this sentiment following a trip to Saskatchewan in November: "During the four days I spent in Saskatchewan I found frequent expression of opinion against members of the provincial government because of the active part they are taking in pushing the interests of some Liberal candidates as against the Progressives. This invariably came to me from men who had supported the provincial government in the last election and some of whom had voted against independent candidates at that time. They had felt that Premier Martin's declaration that the provincial government was disassociated entirely from the federal Liberal party entitled it to their support." Crerar to Dunning, 27 November 1921, file "Dunning, Hon. Charles A., January 1914–August 1915, April 1920, September 1921–December 1922," box 5, Crerar Papers, QUA.

38 J.W. Dafoe to Clifford Sifton, 31 December 1921, quoted in Smith, *Prairie Liberalism*, 92.

39 Ward and Smith, *Jimmy Gardiner*, 41.

40 Grant Dexter quoted in Ward and Smith, *Jimmy Gardiner*, 61.

41 Dunning to A.K. Cameron, 12 April 1922, vol. 6, A. Kirk Cameron Papers, MG 27 III F2, Library and Archives Canada [LAC].

42 Dunning to King, 27 July 1923, file 16, box 2, Dunning Papers, QUA. King responded to Dunning by claiming that Fielding had been misinterpreted in the press. See King to Dunning, 1 August 1923, 72537, vol. 91, William Lyon Mackenzie King Papers, MG 26 J1, LAC.

43 Reginald Whitaker, *The Government Party: Organizing and Financing the Liberal Party of Canada, 1930–58* (Toronto: University of Toronto Press, 1977), 6.

44 H. Blair Neatby, *William Lyon Mackenzie King: The Lonely Heights, 1924–1932* (Toronto: University of Toronto Press, 1963), 14.

45 Monte Black to Dunning, 5 March 1924, file 21, box 2, Dunning Papers, QUA.

46 T.R. Deacon to Dunning, 24 September 1924, file 27, box 3, Dunning
    Papers, QUA.

47 H.M. Peacock to Dunning, 17 May 1925, file 35, box 4, Dunning Papers,
    QUA.

48 Erastus S. Miller to Dunning, 19 February 1925, file 32, box 4, Dunning
    Papers, QUA.

49 It is interesting that both Dunning and Bracken were promoted as na-
    tional leaders at various times by the right wing of the nation's business
    class, suggestive of the increasingly conservative implications of the
    ideas originally embraced by moderate western progressives. Bracken,
    too, had forged a reputation for economical government. Bracken's Pro-
    gressive government in Manitoba, which maintained independence in
    federal affairs and depended considerably upon Conservative votes, pre-
    vented a near complete merging between Liberal and Progressive forces
    as would take place in Saskatchewan. See Morton, *Progressive Party*,
    264. For Bracken's record as Manitoba premier, see John Kendle, *John
    Bracken: A Political Biography* (Toronto: University of Toronto Press,
    1979), 24–182.

50 Brennan, "Public Career of Charles Avery Dunning," 109.

51 Ibid., 214.

52 Brennan, "C.A. Dunning and the Challenge of The Progressives," 12.

53 J. William Brennan, "A Political History of Saskatchewan, 1905–1929"
    (PhD thesis, University of Alberta, 1976), 568.

54 Smith, *Prairie Liberalism*, 92–9; Morton, *Progressive Party*, 276–7.

55 Sifton to Dafoe, 28 January 1925, J.W. Dafoe Papers, MG 30 D 45,
    LAC. A year earlier, Dunning had said in private conversation that Cre-
    rar was too much influenced by the *Free Press*. He claimed to welcome
    an open breach with the paper. Alex Smith to King, 12 January 1924,
    93066-9, vol. 123, King Papers, LAC.

56 In 1920 William Irvine, a year later to become a Labour MP with UFA
    backing, theorized "group government" in *The Farmers in Politics*.
    Wood's embrace of the concept would prove limited once in power. See
    William Irvine, *The Farmers in Politics*, intro. Reginald Whitaker (To-
    ronto: McClelland & Stewart, 1976 [1920]).

57 Wood and the governing UFA members became increasingly conser-
    vative during the 1920s and 1930s as the party base moved to the left.
    Alvin Finkel's important study on the rise of Social Credit in Alberta

demonstrates the formidable presence of socialist politics within the agrarian protest movement that underpinned the rise of Social Credit. See Alvin Finkel, *The Social Credit Phenomenon in Alberta* (Toronto: University of Toronto Press, 1989), especially 18–28. Finkel's findings are a significant corrective to C.B. Macpherson's argument that agrarian protest in Alberta was unable to overcome the ideological limitations of its petit-bourgeois outlook. See C.B. Macpherson, *Democracy in Alberta: Social Credit and the Party System* (Toronto: University of Toronto Press, 1953). Also, Laycock's study, *Populism and Democratic Thought in the Prairie West,* examines the heterogeneous strains of populism in the Prairie West and underlines the problematic reductionism involved in characterizing western populism as the manifestation of petit-bourgeois protest.

58 John Evans to Dunning, 30 March 1925, file 33, box 4, Dunning Papers, QUA.

59 For an overview, focusing on the experience of the labour movement, see Bryan D. Palmer, *Working-Class Experience: Rethinking the History of Canadian Labour, 1800–1991* (Toronto: McClelland & Stewart, 1992), 214–67. See also Gregory S. Kealey, "State Repression of Labour and the Left in Canada, 1914–1920: The Impact of the First World War," *Canadian Historical Review* 73, no. 3 (September 1992): 281–314.

60 Dunning to Evans, 3 April 1925, file 34, box 4, Dunning Papers, QUA.

61 Dunning explained in private conversation with J.W. Dafoe that the Liberal Party in the West needed to pursue some type of merger with the Progressives. Though Dafoe felt that Dunning's view was "realistic" and "almost identical" with his own, he did not think Dunning's plan for initiating a broader merger – to have Dafoe press for a merger in Manitoba between the Progressives and Liberals – desirable. See Dafoe to Sifton, 30 June 1925, Dafoe Papers, LAC.

62 Dunning's refusal to enter the King administration signalled a lack of confidence to observers. See J.P.B. Casgrain to King, 14 September 1925, 96305 (and King to Casgrain, 16 September 1925, 96306), vol. 128, King Papers, LAC.

63 H.J. Symington to A.B. Hudson, n.d., quoted in S. Peter Regenstreif, "A Threat to Leadership: C.A. Dunning and Mackenzie King," *Dalhousie Review* 3, no. 44 (Autumn 1964): 279.

64 Regenstreif, "A Threat to Leadership," 277–9.

65 Robert A. Wardhaugh, *Mackenzie King and the Prairie West* (Toronto: University of Toronto Press, 2000), 94.

66 "Dominion-Wide Appeal Is Voiced by Speakers at Massey Hall Meeting," *Globe* (Toronto), 24 October 1925, 1 and 6; L.T. McDonald to Dunning, 26 October 1925, file 40, box 5, Dunning Papers, QUA.

67 Lears, "Managerial Revitalization," 189–90 and passim.

68 A.H. Williamson to Dunning, 23 February 1926, file 46, box 6, Dunning Papers, QUA.

69 W. Rupert Davies to Dunning, 23 November 1925, file 41, box 5, Dunning Papers, QUA.

70 J. Vernon McKenzie to Dunning, 24 February 1926, file 47, box 6, Dunning Papers, QUA.

71 George W. Allan to Dunning, 26 February 1926, file 47, box 6, Dunning Papers, QUA.

72 W.A. Matheson to Dunning, 25 February 1926, file 47, box 6, Dunning Papers, QUA.

73 Dafoe to Harry Sifton, 26 May 1926, Dafoe Papers, LAC; Brennan, "C.A. Dunning, 1916–30," 261.

74 Dunning to W.R. Motherwell, 16 November 1925, file 41, box 5, Dunning Papers, QUA.

75 For more on the negotiations that led to Dunning's entry into the King government, see Don Nerbas, "The Politics of Capital: The Crisis and Transformation of Canada's Big Bourgeoisie, 1917–1947" (PhD thesis, University of New Brunswick, 2010), 138.

76 Wardhaugh, *Mackenzie King*, 112.

77 King to J.A. Robb, 28 September 1925, 104235, vol. 141, King Papers, LAC; Morton, *Progressive Party*, 242.

78 King to Dunning, 26 November 1925, and Dunning to King, 30 November 1925, file 41, box 5, Dunning Papers, QUA.

79 King to Dunning, 5 February 1925, file 44, box 6, Dunning Papers, QUA.

80 Dunning was warned by his crony George M. Bell on 24 January that some Progressives would withdraw their support, and Bell thought Dunning's move to Ottawa a mistake – but with Jimmy Gardiner, who was far less sympathetic to Bell's interests, as the heir apparent in Saskatchewan, Bell was not a disinterested observer. See George M. Bell to Dunning, 23 and 24 January 1926, file 43, box 6, Dunning Papers, QUA.

Indeed, the support of Saskatchewan Progressives was not solid; in fact, they threatened to withdraw it specifically if Dunning were taken into the government. See King Diaries, 28 January 1926, LAC, and letter signed "SASKATCHEWAN PROGRESSIVES" [on House of Commons letterhead] to King, 15 February 1926, 117183, vol. 162, King Papers, LAC.

81 See Neatby, *Lonely Heights*, 145–75.

82 The Conservatives reportedly spent $50,000 in Regina and a rumour was spread that Dunning had made $150,000 in a grain deal. See Dunning to Edward Brown, 28 September 1926, file 49, box 6, Dunning Papers, QUA.

83 G.R. Stevens, *History of the Canadian National Railways* (New York: Macmillan, 1973), 272–300.

84 Dunning to W.J. Jeffers, Editor, *Financial Post*, 21 December 1928, file 200, box 21, Dunning Papers, QUA.

85 E.W. Beatty to Dunning, 20 September 1926, file 49, box 6, Dunning Papers, QUA.

86 H.W. Thornton to Dunning, 23 February 1926, file 46, box 6, Dunning Papers, QUA.

87 Dafoe to Harry Sifton, 10 January 1929, Dafoe Papers, LAC.

88 Dafoe to Clifford Sifton, 15 July 1927, Dafoe Papers, LAC. Dafoe, apparently, was in contact with CNR officials who passed along inside information.

89 George W. Allan to Dunning, 30 November 1929, file 69, box 8, Dunning Papers, QUA.

90 Morton, *Progressive Party*, 252; Dunning, Address to the Ottawa Kiwanis Club, 9 December 1927, file 289, box 34, Dunning Papers, QUA. As the regional elite in the West grew suspicious of Dunning for harbouring pro-CPR sympathies, he also drew criticism in the Maritimes for the apparent opposite: his connection with the CNR. In the West, the CNR was appreciated as a competitor to what was widely perceived as the rapacious CPR; however, in the Maritimes, the situation was different. Indeed, the Maritimes already had a competitor to the CPR in the Intercolonial. But, with the Intercolonial's absorption into the CNR, the government-owned line became, in the minds of many regional political and business leaders, an emblem of unjust federal policies and a cooption of regional control. Dunning described a letter received from J.D. McKenna, editor of the Saint John *Telegraph-Journal* and an important figure in the Maritime Rights movement, as "an amazing compound

of error and abuse," and explained to McKenna: "I should not think of replying to it save for your statement that you are a Liberal." Dunning viewed, somewhat incorrectly, the attacks upon the CNR emanating from the Maritimes as a Tory ploy. He also believed such attacks would discredit Maritime claims in other parts of Canada. See Dunning to J.D. McKenna, 2 December 1927, 121245-6, vol. 168, King Papers, LAC; also see Ernest R. Forbes, "Misguided Symmetry: The Destruction of Regional Transportation Policy for the Maritimes," in *Canada and the Burden of Unity*, ed. David Jay Bercuson (Toronto: Macmillan of Canada, 1977), 60–86. McKenna also criticized Dunning for his attitude towards implementing the recommendations of the Royal Commission on Maritime Claims, popularly known as the Duncan Commission. See McKenna to Dunning, 19 December 1927, 123652, vol. 171, King Papers, LAC.

91   This point is made in Regenstreif, "A Threat to Leadership," 286.

92   Ward and Smith, *Jimmy Gardiner*, 69; Dunning to Gardiner, 19 February 1927, and Gardiner to Dunning, 21 February 1927, file 52, box 7, Dunning Papers, QUA.

93   The discussion at the convention apparently centred upon an article that appeared in an issue of the *Grain Growers' Guide*, which was distributed to delegates at the convention. Written by Grattan O'Leary, Tory partisan and parliamentary correspondent for the *Ottawa Journal*, the article furthered rumours of a Dunning-Gardiner split. See J.B. Parker to Dunning, 17 December 1927, file 55, box 7, Dunning Papers, QUA.

94   Dunning to J.B. Parker, 28 December 1927, file 55, box 7, Dunning Papers, QUA.

95   King Diaries, 26 May 1927, LAC.

96   "Speech in Part of Honourable Chas. A. Dunning at Regina Banquet, February 6th, 1930," file 293, box 34, Dunning Papers, QUA.

97   For Dunning, negotiation was necessary for the well-being of the body politic. In the Dominion government, he had continued to rail against the perils of "group government," or any class-based political strategies. The task of governance required conciliating competing interests, not supporting the triumph of one over the other. This view assumed a nation's economic and political leadership to be determined by merit, where only the "best" rose to the top. As such, political negotiation, as put into practice by Dunning, meant negotiation pretty much exclusively at the upper

echelons of politics and business. See *Vancouver Daily Province*, clipping, 8 March 1928, file 57, box 7, Dunning Papers, QUA.

98 Raoul Dandurand to Dunning, 28 November 1929, and L.A. Taschereau to Dunning, 27 November 1929, file 69, box 8, Dunning Papers, QUA.

99 Smeaton White to Dunning, 28 November 1929, file 69, box 8, Dunning Papers, QUA.

100 Dunning to Smeaton White, 30 November 1929, file 69, box 8, Dunning Papers, QUA.

101 J. Fred Johnson to Dunning, 8 November 1929, file 69, box 8, Dunning Papers, QUA; Wardhaugh, *Mackenzie King*, 156 and 160.

102 *Debates, House of Commons*, vol. 2, 1930, 1 May 1930, 1678. Dunning was worried about losing his seat while crafting the budget and "almost broke down" because of attacks on him from protectionist elements in cabinet. See Robert B. Bryce, *Maturing in Hard Times: Canada's Department of Finance through the Great Depression* (Kingston and Montreal: McGill-Queen's University Press, 1986), 67–71.

103 H. Blair Neatby, *The Politics of Chaos: Canada in the Thirties* (Toronto: Macmillan of Canada, 1972), 55–6.

104 Gardiner, a brokerage politician, had taken a principled stance against the anti-Catholic and anti-immigrant sentiment of the Conservatives; he, indeed, did not believe "the solid citizens of Saskatchewan would vote for candidates espousing lunatic issues." See Ward and Smith, *Jimmy Gardiner*, 104.

105 Dunning to W.A. Fraser, 4 August 1930, file 79, box 9, Dunning Papers, QUA.

106 Dunning to W.A. MacLeod, 4 August 1930, file 79, box 9, Dunning Papers, QUA.

107 One admiring businessman claimed the Dunning Budget commanded much support within the business community of "Tory Toronto": "I happen to be a member of the National Club, Toronto. The members of the Club are the leading manufacturers and business men of Toronto. I should think about ninety per cent of them are Conservatives. Of course, the budget has been discussed at great length in the Club, and you will be gratified to learn that they are almost unanimously in favour of it. In fact several very strong Conservatives have told me that they are going to vote Liberal this time and hope we will get out some strong candidates in Toronto. Practically all of them think that Bennett's criticisms are

quite futile." John M. Godfrey to Dunning, 13 May 1930, file 76, box 9, Dunning Papers, QUA.

108 Dunning to J.A. Cross, 22 August 1930, file 79, box 9, Dunning Papers, QUA.

109 King Diaries, 31 October 1932, LAC.

110 The party had to return campaign funds "collected expressly for Dunning under the auspices of Vincent Massey and W.E. Rundle, general manager of National Trust." Whitaker, *Government Party*, 14. King asked Rundle if it was possible for the party to retain a portion or the whole sum collected for the "Dunning fund" for general purposes. The subscribers refused. King to W.E. Rundle, 6 November 1930, 154089-93 (and Rundle to King, 12 December 1930, 154095-6), vol. 220, King Papers, LAC.

111 Neatby, *Lonely Heights*, 385.

112 H.A. Robson to Dunning, 24 August 1930, file 79, box 9, Dunning Papers, QUA.

113 Dunning to E.W. Stapleford, 10 October 1930, file 80, box, 9, Dunning Papers, QUA.

114 Harry Sifton to Dafoe, 20 November 1930, Dafoe Papers, LAC.

115 Dunning to J.R. Bird, 27 October 1930, file 80, box 8, Dunning Papers, QUA.

116 Wardhaugh, *Mackenzie King*, 160.

117 Dexter to Dafoe, 25 October 1930, Dafoe Papers, LAC.

118 Dunning was included in a book entitled *Bigwigs*, published in 1935, that consisted of a series of character portraits of leading businessmen and politicians. See Charles Vining, *Bigwigs: Canadians Wise and Otherwise*, illustrated by Ivan Glassco (Freeport, NY: Libraries Press, 1935), 42–5.

119 John Murray Gibbon, *Steel of Empire: The Romantic History of the Canadian Pacific, the Northwest Passage of Today* (New York: Bobbs-Merrill, 1935), 395; *Lucerne-in-Quebec* (Lucerne-in-Quebec Community Association Limited, 1930).

120 Beatty to Dunning, 30 May 1932, 295, vol. 143, box 23-006, President's Letter-Books, RG 23, Canadian Pacific Railway Archives [CPRA]. Bennett believed Lucerne too far outside Ottawa for conference delegates. He told Beatty the government would send delegates to Lucerne only for the weekend. See Beatty to Dunning, 4 June 1932, vol. 143, box 23-006, President's Letter-Books, CPRA.

121 Duncan McDowall, *Steel at the Sault: Francis H. Clergue, Sir James Dunn, and the Algoma Steel Corporation* (Toronto: University of Toronto Press, 1984), 190.
122 "Parks Canada – The Occupants of the Seigneury," <http://www.pc.gc.ca/eng/lhn-nhs/qc/manoirpapineau/natcul/natcul1/d.aspx> [consulted 10 July 2009]; *Lucerne-in-Quebec*. On the intellectual appropriation of landscape in Quebec during an earlier period, see Colin M. Coates, *The Metamorphoses of Landscape and Community in Early Quebec* (Montreal: McGill-Queen's University Press, 2000).
123 Beatty to Ross H. McMaster, 30 January 1931, 247, vol. 136, box 23-005, President's Letter-Books, CPRA.
124 Beatty claimed no responsibility for the policy, arguing that the charter had been originally written by Americans who started the project, in which the CPR was but a minority partner, and could not be changed without breach of contract. See Beatty to James D. Stein, 30 June 1931, 263–4, vol. 139, box 23-006, President's Letter-Books, CPRA.
125 See *Lucerne-in-Quebec*, which also states that "no application for membership will be considered until the prospective member has been personally interviewed by a representative of the Seigniory Club and his application has been approved by the Club membership Committee."
126 Beatty to Dunning, 15 July 1931, 365, vol. 139, box 23-006, President's Letter-Books, CPRA.
127 Beatty to Dunning, 30 April 1932, 242, vol. 138, box 23-006, President's Letter-Books, CPRA.
128 *Our History: Le Château Montebello* (CP Hotels, n.d.); *Lucerne-in-Quebec*.
129 In 1929 the value of its gross products was $243,970,761. It was listed as the industry with the second largest capitalization, behind "central electric stations," but the two sectors were closely aligned since power generation and pulp and paper production were often pursued by the same or associated companies. See *Canada Year Book, 1932* (Ottawa: Dominion Bureau of Statistics, 1932), 340–1.
130 William L. Marr and Donald G. Paterson, *Canada: An Economic History* (Toronto: Macmillan of Canada, 1980), 365.
131 John A. Guthrie, *The Newsprint Paper Industry: An Economic Analysis* (Cambridge, MA: Harvard University Press, 1941), 55–66; and Gilles Piédalue, "Les groupes financiers et la guerre du papier au Canada,

1920–1930," *Revue d'histoire de l'Amérique française* 30, no. 2 (September 1976): 229.

132 "Canada Power & Paper Bondholders in Dark Position," *Financial Post* (Toronto), 9 April 1931, 18.

133 The companies were: the Laurentide Company; the Belgo-Canadian Paper Company; the St Maurice Paper Company; the Port Alfred Pulp and Paper Company; and the Wayagamack Pulp and Paper Company.

134 The following companies held securities in Canada Power and Paper: "Canadian Pacific Railway, Sun Life Assurance of Canada, Great West Life Assurance Company, Canada Life Assurance, Mutual Life Assurance Company of Canada, Dominion Life and Manufacturers' Life Assurance Company." See "Big Security Deposits in Canada Power Plan," *New York Times*, 14 July 1931, 36.

135 "Can. Power, Paper Shows Present Status to Stock Exchange," *Financial Post*, 12 February 1931, 1; "Defer for Time All Dividends C.P.P. Companies," *Financial Post*, 26 February 1931, 15; "Canada Power to Reorganize States Gundy," *Financial Post*, 2 April 1931, 24. This signalled a departure from the recent history of the Laurentide Company, which had been the country's largest newsprint producer from 1898 and 1919 before it came under the control of Canada Power and Paper in 1928. In his examination of Laurentide, Jorge Niosi concludes that, even though Laurentide's board of directors included figures from the Bank of Montreal, the CPR, and Royal Trust, effective control of the company remained in the hands of executives who operated autonomous of bank control. See Jorge Niosi, "La Laurentide (1887–1928): Pionnière du papier journal au Canada," *Revue d'histoire de l'Amerique française* 29, no. 3 (December 1975): 408, 414, and passim.

136 Dunning to A. MacGillivray Young, 4 May 1931, file 81, box 10, Dunning Papers, QUA.

137 "Paper Merger Plans Still in Abeyance," *Financial Post*, 16 April 1931, 1.

138 "Can. Power New Scheme Ready Soon," *Financial Post*, 28 May 1931, 3.

139 Ibid., 1.

140 The *Financial Post* listed the members of the committee after its reorganization scheme was released: "Charles A. Dunning, chairman; R.H. Collins, of the financial firm of Kitcat and Aitken, London, Eng.; Norman J. Dawes, president of the Montreal board of trade; Strachan Johnson, K.C., of Tilley, Johnson, Thompson and Parmenter, Toronto;

H.D. Lockhart Gordon, C.A., of Messrs. Clarkson, Gordon, Dilworth, Guilfoyle and Nash, Toronto; Stewart Kilpatrick, of Govett, Sons and Co., London, Eng.; E.A. Macnutt, treasurer of Sun Life Assurance Co. of Canada; John J. Rudolf, of A. Iselin and Co., New York; Gordon W. Scott, secretary, of Messrs. P.S. Ross and Soris, Montreal; and J.L. Ralston, K.C., counsel, of Mitchell, Ralston, Kearney & Duquest, Montreal." See "Canada Power and Paper Reorganization Is Sweeping; Old Capital Reduced by Half," *Financial Post*, 4 June 1931, 2.

141 "Reorganizing Plan for Canada Power Is Made Public," *Globe*, 4 June 1931, 1 and 6. Later figures revealed an even more drastic reduction. Guthrie has written: "Approximately 95 million dollars of bonded indebtedness, 32 million dollars of preferred stock and a large block of common stock was replaced by a little over 51 million dollars of 5 ½ per cent bonds and roughly 1 ½ million shares of common stock." Guthrie, *Newsprint Paper Industry*, 68.

142 "Canada Power and Paper Plan Depends for Success on Confidence in Committee," *Financial Post*, 11 June 1931, 1 and 8.

143 "Belgo Holders Seeking More Preferred Stock," *Financial Post*, 18 June 1931, 28.

144 "Canada Power Plan Meeting Fair Response," *Financial Post*, 25 June 1931, 2.

145 "Paper Deal Is Assailed," *New York Times*, 4 July 1931, 13.

146 "Canada Power Meetings Approve Dunning Plan," *Financial Post*, 14 November 1931, 13.

147 "Dunning's Group To Name Its Board as Fight Goes On," *Financial Post*, 18 July 1931, 1; "Can. Power Plan Near Completion," *Financial Post*, 25 July 1931, 2.

148 [First name illegible] Jones to R.B. Bennett, 28 July 1931, 417587, and C.H. Cahan to R.B. Bennett, 26 September 1931, 417588, D-440-C, R.B. Bennett Papers, MG 26 K, LAC.

149 "Dunning's Group To Name Its Board," 3; "L.J. Belnap Will Be Head Can. Power," *Financial Post*, 1 August 1931, 1. Anglo-Canadian Paper Mills Ltd. had been allied with Canada Power and Paper, but, since the conditions of its agreement with Canada Power and Paper were unfavourable for the latter, the relationship was severed in the reorganization. "Anglo-Canadian Resumes Status Prior to Merger," *Financial Post*, 19 August 1931, 10.

150 Edward Beatty reported to R.J. Manion in 1933: "When Mr. Mackenzie
     King was Prime Minister, his standing among the substantial people of
     Montreal was seriously jeopardized by ex-Senator McDougald, and this
     a long while before any of them ever heard of Beauharnois." Beatty to
     R.J. Manion, 30 November 1933, file 3-9, vol. 3, R.J. Manion Papers,
     MG 27 III B7, LAC. In 1924 Beatty told King that McDougald "had no
     friends among his contemporaries, his ambition was to be a member of
     the Mount Royal Club, of the Bank of Montreal & to have a high posi-
     tion." King Diaries, 2 December 1924, LAC. See also T.D. Regehr, *The
     Beauharnois Scandal: A Story of Canadian Entrepreneurship and Poli-
     tics* (Toronto: University of Toronto Press, 1990), 16 and passim.
151 Duncan McDowall, *Quick to the Frontier: Canada's Royal Bank* (To-
     ronto: McClelland & Stewart, 1993), 256; William Fong, *J.W. Mc-
     Connell: Financier, Philanthropist, Patriot* (Montreal and Kingston:
     McGill-Queen's University Press, 2008), 192; Peter C. Newman, *Flame
     of Power* (Toronto: Longmans, Green, 1959), 43–4; "Montreal Broker
     Dies," *New York Times*, 31 May 1932, 11; "Brokers Held Bankrupt,"
     New York Times, 2 June 1932, 38; "Broker Succumbs to Heart Attack,"
     Globe and Mail, 31 May 1932, 3. Duncan McDowall has observed that
     Holt's shooting and Luther's suicide went unreported, save for in the
     Toronto tabloid *Hush*, which claimed that Holt's bodyguard shot Luther
     and staged his suicide at his Oka home. Both the *New York Times* and the
     Toronto *Globe and Mail* reported that a coroner's jury deemed Luther's
     death to be from natural causes, a heart attack.
152 King Diaries, 20 January 1933, LAC.
153 Dunning to A. MacGillivray Young, 28 March 1934, file 88, box 10,
     Dunning Papers, QUA.
154 A.K. Cameron to Dunning, 7 December 1934, file "C.A. Dunning,
     1935," vol. 20, Cameron Papers, LAC.
155 King Diaries, 25 August 1932, LAC.
156 Dunning to E.M. Macdonald, 25 January 1932, file 83, box 10, Dunning
     Papers, QUA.
157 *Globe*, 21 December 1931, clipping, in file 83, box 10, Dunning Pa-
     pers, QUA. A Saskatchewan Liberal colleague expressed concern to
     Dunning regarding his position on the railway question and speculation
     that Dunning was slated to enter the Bennett administration as minister
     of finance. Dunning denied speculation about his becoming minister of

finance under Bennett. On the railway question, interestingly, he wrote: "I may say to you privately ... that it is becoming increasingly difficult for me to see how Canada can possibly carry its present transportation load having regard to the fact that even when times do improve other forms of transportation will [be] continuously making further inroads upon those forms of traffic most profitable to the railway." See Dunning to A. MacGillivray Young, 5 January 1932 (and A. MacGillivray Young to Dunning, 28 December 1931), file 83, box 10, Dunning Papers, QUA.

158 King Diaries, 25 August 1932, LAC.

159 Floyd S. Chalmers to John B. Maclean, 27 January 1933, file 2, "Conversations, 1933," box 6, series 3, Floyd S. Chalmers Papers, F 4153, Archives of Ontario [AO]. In 1931 Dunning and Meighen discussed the possibility of heading up a National Government together. The discussion was never serious, though both liked the idea and articles were later published in *Saturday Night* and *Maclean's* speculating that Dunning and Meighen would enter a reorganized Dominion cabinet. See Meighen to Dunning, 27 November 1931, and Dunning to Meighen, 30 November 1931, file 82, box 10, Dunning Papers, QUA. Ontario Liberal MP Fraser reported to Dunning, following a trip to Ottawa, the "idea of a Coalition Government seemed to be in the air." Should "there be any change forced by necessity or otherwise" to require a National Government, Fraser felt Dunning should be at its head, King and Bennett left out, and that it should be elected. Dunning claimed he had heard no such discussions, not mentioning his correspondence with Meighen. See W.A. Fraser to Dunning, 22 December 1931, and Dunning to Fraser, 28 December 1931, file 82, box 10, Dunning Papers, QUA.

160 Norman Lambert Diaries, 12 March 1933, box 9, Lambert Papers, QUA.

161 Dunning to Meighen, 15 May 1931, file 81, box 10, Dunning Papers, QUA.

162 Dunning's superior at the CPR, president Edward Beatty, expressed the view to Mackenzie King in 1922 that he felt it was a "great mistake Jews had come in such numbers," and "did not think they made very good citizens." King Diaries, 8 February 1932, LAC. This should not be viewed as an isolated belief within the Canadian bourgeoisie. For example, Winnipeg's powerful grain dealer, financier, and pioneer in aviation, James Richardson, expressed similarly anti-Semitic views in suggesting that allowing a Jewish grain-dealing firm based in Europe to do business

in Canada would negatively affect the country's business morals. See James A. Richardson to Norman Lambert, 18 June 1938, "General Correspondence, 1938," box 2, Lambert Papers, QUA.

163 Dunning to J.A. Cross, 27 December 1932, file 85, box 10, Dunning Papers, QUA. See also Dunning to J.R. Bird, 10 May 1932, file 84, box 10, Dunning Papers, QUA: "economic law is working in its usual inexorable fashion, and there is no doubt that what is now going on in an economic sense is a severe dose of medicine for humanity, but if the patient survives the severity of the medicine, his after condition will be very much better."

164 See Ian McKay, "Canada as a Long Liberal Revolution: On Writing the History of Actually Existing Canadian Liberalism, 1840s–1940s," in *Liberalism and Hegemony: Debating the Canadian Liberal Revolution*, eds Jean-François Constant and Michel Ducharme (Toronto: University of Toronto Press, 2009), 347–452.

165 The significant fact was not that Dunning's worldview had changed, but that it had not changed, and had even become more doctrinaire; these ideological formulations assumed a different significance because of the changing historical context as well as his changed personal circumstances. CCF founder J.S. Woodsworth had, for example, given up the rugged individualism of his earlier life, coming to the conclusion that the ills of modern industrial society could be adequately confronted only through collective action and an interventionist state; Dunning, by contrast, clung to his earlier liberal individualist philosophy. For the evolution of J.S. Woodsworth's political thought, see Allen Mills, *Fool for Christ: The Political Thought of J.S. Woodsworth* (Toronto: University of Toronto Press, 1991).

166 Dunning to D.C. Coleman, 16 November 1932, file 85, box, 10, Dunning Papers, QUA. See Lord Hewart of Bury, *The New Despotism* (London: Ernest Benn, 1929); and James M. Beck, *Our Wonderland of Bureaucracy: A Study of the Growth of Bureaucracy in the Federal Government, and Its Destructive Effect Upon the Constitution* (New York: Macmillan, 1932).

167 Lambert Diaries, 16 October 1933, QUA.

168 King Diaries, 3 November 1933, LAC.

169 King Diaries, 20 December 1933, LAC.

170 Lambert Diaries, 8 April 1934, QUA. Dunning had claimed in 1932 that he would never join the Liberals while King was leader. "He hates King

intensely," reported Grant Dexter. But he also believed at the time that
Bennett "would probably trim King next election." Dexter to Dafoe,
"Monday 1932," Dafoe Papers, LAC.

171 King Diaries, 12 June 1934, LAC.

172 Beatty to Dunning, 4 April 1934, 410–11, vol. 148, box 23-007, President's Letter-Books, CPRA. See also Beatty to McLaughlin, 26 March
1934, 361–2, and Beatty to McLaughlin, 6 April 1934, 423–4, vol. 148,
box 23-007, President's Letter-Books, CPRA.

173 Frank Common to Dunning, 14 November 1934, file 90, box 10, Dunning Papers, QUA.

174 F.S. Chalmers, "Memorandum of Conversation with Hon. Charles A.
Dunning," 5 August 1937, file 36, series 2, box 3, Chalmers Papers, AO.

175 King Diaries, 18 January 1935, LAC. W.M. Martin, whom Dunning had
succeeded as Saskatchewan premier in the 1920s, told King in late 1934
that Dunning would only return to politics if made leader. See King Diaries, 29 December 1934, LAC.

176 This suggestion was made by G.F. Millar, president of Canadian Vegeta-
ble Oils, Limited. Unlike most of the National Government suggestions
coming from the business community, Millar wanted a National Government that would not amalgamate the two railway systems. See G.F. Millar to Dunning, 8 January 1935; H.H. Stevens to G.F. Millar, 17 January
1935; Dunning to G.F. Millar, 18 January 1935, file 91, box 10, Dunning
Papers, QUA.

177 "Merger Group Thinks Bennett Ready to Quit," *Globe*, 12 March 1935,
1; Lambert Diaries, 12 March 1935, QUA; "No Time Is Lost in Re-
pudiating Union Cabinet," *Globe*, 13 March 1935, 1. Jimmy Gardiner
claimed that Dunning asked to see "Beatty, [J.W.] McConnell, + one
other in Montreal" before responding in writing to the *Globe*'s story, but
they were "in the South" and could not be reached. As a result, Dunning
decided to respond by telephone. If Gardiner, perhaps not the most reliable source on matters to do with Dunning, was correct in reporting that
Dunning had sought to discuss the matter with Beatty and McConnell,
one is inclined to wonder whether, in fact, Dunning had been seriously
discussing the matter with Beatty and others, though his response in
the *Globe* suggests not. In either case, Beatty had been trying to secure
support for National Government in Saskatchewan. Norman Lambert received information from Gardiner that "Beatty had seen Judge Peter [?]

McKenzie of Saskatoon re Nat'l Govt." See Lambert Diaries, 17 March 1935, QUA.

178 Lambert Diaries, 21 March 1935, QUA.

179 Lambert Diaries, 14 April 1935, QUA.

180 Lambert Diaries, 5 May 1935, QUA.

181 Lambert Diaries, 12 June 1935, QUA.

182 R.L. Borden to L.A. Taschereau, 17 October 1935, file 92, box 10, Dunning Papers, QUA.

183 Robert Craig Brown, *Robert Laird Borden: A Biography*, vol. 2 (Toronto: Macmillan of Canada, 1980), 196.

184 Neatby, *William Lyon Mackenzie King: The Prism of Unity* (Toronto: University of Toronto Press, 1976), 129.

185 Neatby, *Prism of Unity*, 129–30.

186 King Diaries, 22 October 1935 and 23 October 1935, LAC.

187 Lambert Diaries, 17 December 1935, QUA.

188 W. Chester S. McClure to R.B. Bennett, 20 December 1935, 52226, Bennett Papers, LAC.

189 Lambert Diaries, 25 December 1925, QUA.

190 W. Chester S. McClure to R.B. Bennett, 20 December 1935, 52227-8, Bennett Papers, LAC.

191 W. Chester S. McClure to R.B. Bennett, 9 January 1936, 52250, Bennett Papers, LAC. Merlyn Brown was the emissary who advised McClure of the Ottawa view and encouraged him not to contest the seat. There is some uncertainty in the sources regarding Brown's role. Lambert reported on 25 December, "I phoned Dunning + found that Brown was not CAD's man + hoped he c'd be got rid of." See Lambert Diaries, 25 December 1935, QUA. In either case, Brown was still pressuring McClure to relent in his resolve to contest the seat.

192 King Diaries, 21 October 1935, LAC.

193 Dunning to E.M. Macdonald, 15 February 1935, file 91, box 10, Dunning Papers, QUA.

194 *Radio Address: CFRB Studio, 37 Bloor Street, West, Toronto, 9.30 to 10.00 p.m., Wednesday, 25 September 1935*, 1, file 294, box 34, Dunning Papers, QUA.

195 Ibid., 2.

196 *Budget Speech Delivered by Hon. Chas. A. Dunning, Minister of Finance, Member for Queens, Prince Edward Island, in the House*

of Commons, May 1, 1936 (Ottawa, 1936), 92433, vol. 152, Arthur Meighen Papers, MG 26 I, LAC.

197 Dunning to Mackenzie King, 12 January 1938, 212728, vol. 249, King Papers, LAC.

198 "Dunning, Heat Victim, Collapses in House," *Globe and Mail*, 23 June 1938, 1 and 9.

199 Neatby, *Politics of Chaos*, 85.

200 Dunning "had had a minor stroke," reported Norman Lambert in August. See Lambert Diaries, 26 August 1938, QUA.

201 *Budget Speech Delivered by Hon. Chas. A. Dunning, April 25, 1939*, 92662, vol. 152, Meighen Papers, LAC.

202 Bryce, *Maturing in Hard Times*, 119–21.

203 *Budget Speech Delivered by Hon. Chas. A. Dunning, April 25, 1939*, 92661, vol. 152, Meighen Papers, LAC.

204 For an overview of Dunning's record as minister of finance, see Neatby, *Prism of Unity*, 129–31, 157–60, 250–8 and passim. Canadian chartered banks had become more heavily invested in provincial and federal government securities with First World War financing; moreover, the banks moved away, in relative terms, from corporate securities after the financial fragility of the railways was revealed during the war. See E.P. Neufeld, *The Financial System of Canada* (Toronto: Macmillan of Canada, 1972), 113.

205 Alvin Finkel examines the establishment of the Wheat Board and the Bank of Canada in *Business and Social Reform in the Thirties* (Toronto: James Lorimer, 1979), 58–80 and 117–35.

206 This, of course, is not to imply that the tariff was solely a tool of big business. For more on the complex political dimensions of the protective tariff, see Paul Craven and Tom Traves, "The Class Politics of the National Policy, 1872–1933," *Journal of Canadian Studies* 14, no. 3 (Fall 1979): 14–38.

207 Lambert reported that McConnell was trying to get Dunning to head Ogilvie as early as 1937. See F.S. Chalmers, "Memorandum of Conversation with Hon. Charles A. Dunning," 5 August 1937, file 36, box 3, series 2, Chalmers Papers, AO. In 1939 Dunning was appointed vice-president of the Ogilvie company, and in 1940 he succeeded McConnell as president. See Fong, *J.W. McConnell*, 227.

208 The activities of the Allied War Supplies Corporation are outlined in J. de N. Kennedy, *History of the Department of Munitions and Supply:*

Canada in the Second World War. Vol. 1: *Production Branches and Crown Companies* (Ottawa, 1950), 290–317.

209 Don Nerbas, "Managing Democracy, Defending Capitalism: Gilbert E. Jackson, the Canadian Committee on Industrial Reconstruction, and the Changing Form of Elite Politics in Canada," *Histoire sociale/Social History* 46, no. 91 (forthcoming, May 2013).

210 R.J. Manion to Sir Thomas White, 15 January 1936, file 17, "Personal Correspondence, White, Sir Thomas 1935-1936," vol. 14, Manion Papers, LAC.

3 The Dilemma of Democracy

1 Report of the Royal Commission to Inquire into Railways and Transportation in Canada, 1931–2 (Ottawa, 1932), 5.

2 Ibid., 63.

3 Beatty to Gilbert E. Jackson, Department of Political Science, University of Toronto, 19 November 1932, 470, vol. 142, box 23-006, President's Letter-Books, RG 23, Canadian Pacific Railway Archives [CPRA].

4 The nation-building aspect of the CPR has been most famously written about in Pierre Berton's two-volume popular history, *The National Dream: The Great Railway, 1871–1881* (Toronto: McClelland & Stewart, 1970) and *The Last Spike: The Great Railway, 1881–1885* (Toronto: McClelland & Stewart, 1971). A counterpoint to Berton's celebratory history is Robert Chodos, *The CPR: A Century of Corporate Welfare* (Toronto: James, Lewis & Samuel, 1973). For an overview of the economic activities of the CPR in the West during the boom years of the National Policy period, see John A. Eagle, *The Canadian Pacific Railway and the Development of Western Canada, 1896–1914* (Montreal: McGill-Queen's University Press, 1989). Andy A. den Otter's *Civilizing the West: The Galts and the Development of Western Canada* (Edmonton: University of Alberta Press, 1982) is an important study of the political economy of early development in the West through the prism of one influential family, which throws light upon the ubiquity of the CPR role.

5 Richard White, *Railroaded: The Transcontinentals and the Making of Modern America* (New York: W.W. Norton, 2011), 511.

6 T.D. Regehr, *The Canadian Northern Railway: Pioneer Road of the Northern Prairies, 1895–1918* (Toronto: Macmillan of Canada, 1976), 462–3.

7 For an institutional history of the Grand Trunk, see A.W. Currie, *The Grand Trunk Railway of Canada* (Toronto: University of Toronto Press, 1957).

8 Leslie Roberts, *These Be Your Gods* (Toronto: Musson Book Company, 1929), 159–70.

9 John Murray Gibbon, *Steel of Empire: The Romantic History of the Canadian Pacific, the Northwest Passage of Today* (New York: Bobbs-Merrill, 1935), 104 and 246; D.H. Miller-Barstow, *Beatty of the C.P.R.: A Biography* (Toronto: McClelland & Stewart, 1951), 5–6 and 14–16; David Cruise and Allison Griffiths, *Lords of the Line* (Markham, ON: Viking, 1988), 296–8. Cruise and Griffiths entitled one of their chapters on Beatty "The Man Who Wed the CPR."

10 Miller-Barstow, *Beatty of the C.P.R.*, 17.

11 Ibid., 18.

12 "Address delivered by Sir Edward Beatty at Hart House on Thursday, March 30, 1939 on the occasion of the Annual Banquet of the University of Toronto Athletic Association," *University of Toronto Monthly*, file R-104-B, vol. 66, R.J. Manion Papers, MG 27 III B 27, Library and Archives Canada [LAC].

13 Donald MacKay, *The Square Mile: Merchant Princes of Montreal* (Vancouver: Douglas & McIntyre, 1987), 194; Jackson Lears, "The Managerial Revitalization of the Rich," in *Ruling America: A History of Wealth and Power in a Democracy*, eds Steve Fraser and Gary Gerstle (Cambridge, MA: Harvard University Press, 2005), 183–4.

14 Gibbon, *Steel of Empire*, 384.

15 Biographical information for the paragraph was gleaned from Cruise and Griffiths, *Lords of the Line*, 293–309; Miller-Barstow, *Beatty of the C.P.R.*, 16–30; Gibbon, *Steel of Empire*, 384–5; "Sir E.W. Beatty – Biographical Note n.d.," Edward Wentworth Beatty Fonds, MG 30 A 57, LAC; and Charles Vining, "They All Said 'Poor Beatty!'" *Toronto Star Weekly*, 23 July 1927, file "Press Clipping," Beatty Fonds, LAC.

16 Quoted in Miller-Barstow, *Beatty of the C.P.R.*, 23.

17 Cruise and Griffiths, *Lords of the Line*, 295.

18   Kathryn J. Banham, "The Architecture and Painting Collection of the
     Mount Royal Club, Montreal, 1899–1920" (MA thesis, Concordia Uni-
     versity, 2006), 14.
19   Stanley Brice Frost, *McGill University: For the Advancement of Learn-
     ing*. Vol. 2: *1895–1971* (Kingston and Montreal: McGill-Queen's Uni-
     versity Press, 1984), 187–209; Marlene Shore, *The Science of Social
     Redemption: McGill, the Chicago School, and the Origins of Social Re-
     search in Canada* (Toronto: University of Toronto Press, 1987), 20–1 and
     passim; Cruise and Griffiths, *Lords of the Line*, 336–44.
20   Vining, "They All Said 'Poor Beatty!'"
21   Scott A. Sandage, *Born Losers: A History of Failure in America* (Cam-
     bridge, MA: Harvard University Press, 2005), 114.
22   Vining, "They All Said 'Poor Beatty!'"
23   Ibid.
24   See Lears, "Managerial Revitalization."
25   G.R. Stevens, *History of the Canadian National Railways* (New York:
     Macmillan, 1973), 238–300; Donald MacKay, *The People's Railway: A
     History of Canadian National* (Vancouver: Douglas & McIntyre, 1992),
     5–32; Regehr, *Canadian Northern Railway*, 385–409; Currie, *Grand
     Trunk*, 432–60.
26   Ken Cruikshank, *Close Ties: Railways, Government, and the Board
     of Railway Commissioners, 1851–1933* (Montreal and Kingston:
     McGill-Queen's University Press, 1991), 130–1.
27   John English, *The Decline of Politics: The Conservatives and the Party
     System, 1901–20* (Toronto: University of Toronto Press, 1977), 64–5 and
     68.
28   Ibid., 148 and 176 (n. 45).
29   John A. Eagle, "Sir Robert Borden, Union Government and Railway Na-
     tionalization," *Journal of Canadian Studies* 10 (November 1975): 59–66.
30   See Roger Graham, *Arthur Meighen: The Door of Opportunity*, Vol. 1
     (Toronto: Clarke, Irwin, 1960), 253–5 and 260–72.
31   Roger Graham, *Arthur Meighen: And Fortune Fled*, Vol. 2 (Toronto:
     Clarke, Irwin, 1963), 292; J.W. Dafoe to Joseph Flavelle, 9 December
     1921, J.W. Dafoe Papers, MG 30 D 45, LAC.
32   Arthur Meighen to Roger Graham, 2 April 1952, 148520, vol. 226, Ar-
     thur Meighen Papers, MG 26 I, LAC.

33 S.F. Tolmie to Arthur Meighen, 20 September 1921, 26156, vol. 45, Meighen Papers, LAC. On Beatty's attitude toward King, see John Willison to Mackenzie King, 31 October 1922, 39954, vol. 87, William Lyon Mackenzie King Papers, MG 26 J1, LAC.
34 Lord Shaughnessy, Pamphlet, The Railway Transportation Problem in Canada, 6 April 1921; Memorandum for Minister of Railways and Canals, R.J. Manion, 4 May 1931, 3–4, file 41, vol. 27, Manion Papers, LAC.
35 Michael Bliss, *A Canadian Millionaire: The Life and Business Times of Sir Joseph Flavelle, Bart., 1858–1939* (Toronto: Macmillan of Canada, 1978), 405.
36 While presenting this view to Dafoe, Flavelle reiterated his general suspicion of public enterprise: "Do not misunderstand me. I personally have less, rather than more confidence in public ownership." Flavelle to Dafoe, 15 January 1924, Dafoe Papers, LAC.
37 Bliss, *Canadian Millionaire*, 409–11.
38 Regehr, *Canadian Northern Railway*, 411 and 438–51.
39 Beatty to Meighen, 4 October 1920, 26390, vol. 45, Meighen Papers, LAC.
40 English, *Decline of Politics*, 68.
41 H.V. Nelles, *The Politics of Development: Forests, Mines and Hydro Electric Power in Ontario, 1849–1941*, 2nd ed., intro. R.A. Young (Montreal and Kingston: McGill-Queen's University Press, 2005 [1974]), 256–306.
42 William Lyon Mackenzie King Diaries, 28 July 1925, LAC.
43 D'Arcy Marsh, *The Tragedy of Sir Henry Thornton* (Toronto: Macmillan of Canada, 1935), 6.
44 Stevens, *History of the Canadian National Railways*, 306–10. One of Thornton's first acts was to restore the 1910 pension rights of former Grand Trunk employees, a measure that had been strenuously resisted by Flavelle. Bliss, *Canadian Millionaire*, 412–13.
45 Flavelle to Dafoe, 12 December 1922, Dafoe Papers, LAC.
46 Flavelle to Dafoe, 13 December 1922; Dafoe to Flavelle, 20 December 1922; Dafoe to Henry Thornton, 11 June 1924, Dafoe Papers, LAC.
47 "Beatty Thinks Biggest Job Is Public Relations," *Financial Post* (Toronto), 31 July 1925, 10.

48 Stevens, *History of the Canadian National Railways*, 315–6.
49 Edward Beatty to J.A. Macdonell, Alexandria, Ont., 22 October 1925, 737–8, vol. 121, box 23-003, President's Letter-Books, CPRA; Cruise and Griffiths, *Lords of the Line*, 327.
50 King Diaries, 24 August 1925, LAC.
51 Dafoe to Clifford Sifton, 29 April 1925, Dafoe Papers, LAC.
52 Sifton worried that the CPR was trying to unload its railway upon the government with proposals for continuance of CPR management and guaranteed dividends for its shareholders. See Clifford Sifton to Dafoe, 24 April 1925, Dafoe Papers, LAC. Nonetheless, St James Street remained ideologically opposed to government ownership, and Beatty never thought it an acceptable solution.
53 Senator W.A. Griesbach to Arthur Meighen, 16 June 1925, 74908, vol. 126, Meighen Papers, LAC.
54 Leslie T. Fournier, *Railway Nationalization in Canada: The Problem of the Canadian National Railways* (Toronto: Macmillan of Canada, 1935), 299; Beatty to Watson Griffin, 16 December 1932, 592, vol. 143, box 23-006, President's Letter-Books, CPRA.
55 Beatty to King, 2 September 1925, 94872-3, vol. 126, King Papers, LAC; King Diaries, 8 July 1926, LAC.
56 Beatty, in fact, voiced public approval of the principle of competition between the two railways in 1926, though amalgamation remained his ideal solution. "For Bad Times Only," *Globe* (Toronto), 9 November 1934, 6.
57 Beatty to J. Buchanan, 15 June 1931, 113, vol. 139, box 23-006, President's Letter-Books, CPRA.
58 Allen Seager, "'A New Labour Era?' Canadian National Railways and the Railway Worker, 1919-1929," *Journal of the Canadian Historical Association* 3 (1992): 172–3.
59 Graham, *Meighen*, Vol. 2, 380.
60 King Diaries, 23 October 1930, LAC.
61 Larry A. Glassford, *Reaction and Reform: The Politics of the Conservative Party Under R.B. Bennett, 1927–1938* (Toronto: University of Toronto Press, 1992), 88.
62 Marsh, *Tragedy of Henry Thornton*, 150–1.
63 Beatty would in 1934 write Bennett to lament the promises of 1930: "by reason of your pre-election commitments ... the future of the Canadian

Pacific has been prejudiced and the transportation burdens on the country itself increased rather than lessened." Beatty to Bennett, 20 December 1934, 596496-7, vol. 944, R.B. Bennett Papers, MG 26 K, LAC.
64 Report of the Royal Commission, 39.
65 "Dividend Is Reduced for Time at Least by C.P.R. Directors," *Globe*, 7 May 1931, 1.
66 Stevens, *History of the Canadian National Railways*, 348–9.
67 Bennett (from London, England) to R.J. Manion, 16 October 1930, file 37, vol. 73, Manion Papers, LAC.
68 Mrs Henry James (formerly Lady Thornton) to G.R. Stevens, n.d., quoted in Stevens, *History of the Canadian National Railways*, 347–8.
69 Manion to Bennett, 30 December 1930, file 4-1, vol. 4, Manion Papers, LAC.
70 Marsh, *Tragedy of Henry Thornton*, 166–84.
71 Stevens, *History of the Canadian National Railways*, 352.
72 D'Arcy Marsh to Dafoe, 12 December 1934, Dafoe Papers, LAC.
73 Floyd Chalmers, memo, 30 October 1931, file 1, box 6, series 3, Floyd S. Chalmers Papers, F 4153, Archives of Ontario [AO].
74 Beatty to George Bell, 28 December 1931, 484; Beatty to Howard P. Robinson, 25 November 1931, 338, vol. 141, box 23-006, President's Letter-Books, CPRA.
75 Dafoe to John A. Stevenson, 9 December 1931, Dafoe Papers, LAC.
76 Dexter to Dafoe, 15 November 1931, Dafoe Papers, LAC; Chalmers, memo, 30 October 1931, file 1, box 6, series 3, Chalmers Papers, AO.
77 Dafoe to Marsh, 16 July 1934; Marsh to Dafoe, 5 September 1934, Dafoe Papers, LAC.
78 Marsh to Dafoe, 6 July 1934; Dexter to Dafoe, 15 November 1931, Dafoe Papers, LAC.
79 Report of Proceedings, vol. 2, 670, 683–4, 4 January 1932, Royal Commission on Transportation Fonds, RG 33, LAC.
80 Marsh described it as one of several "buffets" in Thornton's heroic image that emerged as he fell from prominence. See Marsh to Dafoe, 6 July 1934, Dafoe Papers, LAC.
81 Report of Proceedings, vol. 2, 801, 5 January 1931.
82 Report of Proceedings, vol. 1, 108, 4 December 1931, Royal Commission on Transportation Fonds, LAC.

83   Report of Proceedings, vol. 1, 127, 5 December 1931, LAC.

84   Beatty to Manion, 17 May 1934, file 3-9, vol. 3, Manion Papers, LAC; Seager, "A New Era of Labour?"181.

85   Report of Proceedings, vol. 2, 668, 4 January 1932, LAC.

86   Report of Proceedings, vol. 2, 963 and 968, 5 January 1931, LAC.

87   Floyd Chalmers to John B. Maclean, 30 March 1933, file 31, box 2, series 2, Chalmers Papers, AO.

88   J.C. Webster to Meighen, 20 November 1932, 93243, vol. 153, Meighen Papers, LAC.

89   Report of Proceedings, vol. 2, 942, 5 January 1932.

90   Report of Proceedings, vol. 2, 960, 5 January 1932.

91   Report of Proceedings, vol. 4, 2459–60, 19 February 1932, Royal Commission on Transportation Fonds, LAC.

92   Report of Proceedings, vol. 4, 2460, 19 February 1932, LAC.

93   Marsh, *Tragedy of Henry Thornton*, 241–73.

94   King Diaries, 2 August 1932, LAC.

95   Thornton to King, 11 October 1932, 164824-5, vol. 237, King Papers, LAC.

96   Thornton to King, 12 October 1932, 164827, vol. 237, King Papers, LAC.

97   Thornton to Dafoe, 5 November 1932, Dafoe Papers, LAC.

98   "Sir Henry Resigns," *Canadian Forum* 12, no. 144 (September 1932): 444.

99   Beatty to Bennett, 31 October 1932, 596415, vol. 944, Bennett Papers, LAC.

100 "Rights of Railway Endangered by Bill Beatty Considers," *Globe*, 18 November 1932, 3.

101 Beatty to Ernest Iselin, Wall Street, New York, 9 December 1932, 558, vol. 144, box 23-006, President's Letter-Books, CPRA.

102 "Beatty Asks Compensation," *Globe*, 18 November 1932, 3; F.C. Goodenough, Barclays Bank, to Edward Beatty, 1 March 1933, 375143, vol. 606, Bennett Papers, LAC.

103 David Ricardo Williams, *Duff: A Life in the Law* (Vancouver: University of British Columbia Press, 1984), 155; Dexter to Dafoe, 25 January 1932, Dafoe Papers, LAC.

104 Edward Beatty, *Canada's Railway Problem and Its Solution*, Toronto, 16 January 1933, 4, 15, 17.

105 King Diaries, 14 January 1933, LAC.

106 "The Merger Danger," *Globe*, 20 January 1933, 4.

107 "Still After the Merger," *Globe*, 17 January 1933, 4.

108 Norman Rogers to King, 23 January 1933, 167578, vol. 197, King Papers, LAC.

109 John F. MacMillan to Senator Meighen, 27 February 1933, 367750, vol. 593, Bennett Papers, LAC.

110 Floyd Chalmers to J.B. Maclean, 27 January 1933, file 2, box 6, series 3, Chalmers Papers, AO.

111 Chalmers to J.B. Maclean, 27 January 1933, file 2, box 6, series 3, Chalmers Papers, AO.

112 Beatty to Bennett, 20 January 1933, 596422, vol. 944, Bennett Papers, LAC.

113 Chalmers to J.B. Maclean, 9 March 1933, file 2, box 6, series 3, Chalmers Papers, AO.

114 Dexter to Dafoe, 18 January [dated 1930 but more likely from 1935], Dafoe Papers, LAC.

115 Dafoe to Harry Sifton, 31 December 1931, Dafoe Papers, LAC. Grant Dexter wrote in early 1932: "As to a national government, I gather from more than one source – Dunning for example – that our captains of industry are strongly in favour of one, but that R.B., [sic] has given no encouragement whatever." Dexter to Dafoe, 25 January 1932, Dafoe Papers, LAC.

116 H.J. Symington to J.W. Dafoe, 1[?] March 1933; Dafoe to Symington, 11 March 1933, Dafoe Papers, LAC.

117 Symington noted, from information gathered at the dinner he attended, that "Sir Arthur is going to Ottawa to work for and to make a speech on 'Unity in government the same as in England' which I think was his exact language." See Symington to Dafoe, 1[?] March 1933, Dafoe Papers, LAC. It appears, then, that the dinner occurred before Currie gave his speech.

118 King Diaries, 2 March 1933, LAC.

119 Bennett to C.C. Ballantyne, 6 March 1933, 418824, vol. 681, Bennett Papers, LAC.

120 King Diaries, 17 March 1933, LAC. Beatty described the interview with King to Chalmers. Chalmers reported: "Beatty went to see King and tried to argue him into a national government. King said that he would make an offer to the government of complete co-operation in matters of

national interest in order to avoid petty political bickering at a time of crisis but that he would not go as far as national government. King said he was afraid that national government would unite the forces of socialism. Beatty and others, of course, feel that a national government is our best guarantee against disruption in Canada but King thinks that to make them the sole opposition would give them a dignity and importance and influence that they could not possibly get in any other way." See Floyd Chalmers to J.B. Maclean, 30 March 1933, file 31, box 2, series 2, Chalmers Papers, AO.

121 Dafoe to Henry Thornton, 3 October 1932, Dafoe Papers, LAC.
122 In September 1933, Bennett provided a government guarantee for a $60,000,000 loan to the CPR from the five major Canadian banks to finance the cash-strapped railway, and a great deal of public criticism ensued. It confirmed to many the close relationship between Bennett and the CPR, and even the *Financial Post* criticized the arrangement. See *Financial Post*, clipping, 4 November 1933, 375523, vol. 606, Bennett Papers, LAC.
123 Beatty to Bennett, 29 December 1933, 555839, vol. 891, Bennett Papers, LAC.
124 Edward Beatty, *The Case for Railway Unification*, 22 May 1934, 2.
125 Take, for example, the advice wealthy Montreal jeweler and St James Street mogul, W.M. Birks, gave R.J. Manion when Manion was federal Conservative Party leader in August 1939. Looking forward to a general election, Birks referred to a recent book published in England on propaganda techniques, although he noted that it may be "thrashing old straw" for Manion. Birks laid out the propaganda principles as contained in the book. He wrote:

The rules laid down are –
1. – Repetition – as the public quickly forgets.
2. – Colour – the mass are not interested in abstractions, but intensely interested in personalities and facts
3. – At least a kernel of truth.
4. Build around a slogan! The slogan is the supreme illustration of the power of brevity in propaganda – a rallying cry – a focusing on the emotions in one vivid phrase. It must be simple, fluid and dramatic!
5. – Directed towards a specific objective.

6. Concealment of motive.

7. Timing – space out the appeals.

    See W.M. Birks to R.J. Manion, 21 August 1939, file 7, vol. 4, Manion Papers, LAC. Walter Lippmann famously argued that public opinion was irrational in *Public Opinion* (New York: Macmillan, 1922).

126 In February 1930 Beatty had announced a stock split of four for one in an attempt to attract more Canadians to invest and identify with the CPR. See "Canadian Pacific Common Split-Up," *Globe*, 8 February 1930, 8.

127 Chalmers reported: "Beatty is strongly favorable to the appointment of a May Committee for Canada to go into the entire question of public expenses and make recommendations for a ruthless cutting down of expenditures." See Floyd Chalmers to J.B. Maclean, 30 March 1933, file 31, box 2, series 2, Chalmers Papers, AO.

128 Quoted in H. Blair Neatby, *William Lyon Mackenzie King: The Lonely Heights, 1924–1932* (Toronto: University of Toronto Press, 1963), 278.

129 "National Government Regarded as Unlikely," *Globe*, 5 September 1934, 2.

130 C.C. Ballantyne to R.B. Bennett, 7 November 1934, 336749-50, vol. 543, Bennett Papers, LAC.

131 Beatty to Bennett, 29 November 1934, 596494-5, vol. 944, Bennett Papers, LAC.

132 Chalmers, memo, 13 May 1938, file 7, box 6, series 3, Chalmers Papers, AO.

133 See Brian J. Young, "C. George McCullagh and the Leadership League" (MA thesis, Queen's University, 1964). Beatty applauded McCullagh's Leadership League radio broadcasts. See Beatty to C. George McCullagh, 16 January 1939, 181; 30 January 1939, 335, vol. 179, and Beatty to McCullagh, 22 February 1939, 229–31, vol. 180, box 23-011, President's Letter-Books, CPRA.

134 Chalmers, memo, 13 May 1938, file 7, box 6, series 3, Chalmers Papers, AO. Massey claimed years later to have had no recollection of the incident, although Bruce repeated the story on at least two separate occasions. See Young, "Leadership League," 149.

135 R.B. Bennett to Harvey H. Black, 21 December 1934, 336756, vol. 543, Bennett Papers, LAC.

136 See Beatty to Bennett, 27 August 1934, 596490-1, vol. 944, Bennett Papers, LAC.

137 King Diaries, 29 September 1934, LAC.

138 Beatty to Borden, 3 January 1935, 146650, vol. 261, Robert Laird Borden Papers, MG 26 H, LAC.

139 Dexter to George V. Ferguson, 7 December 1934, Dafoe Papers, LAC.

140 T.A. Thompson to Bennett, 22 February 1935, 369080, vol. 593, Bennett Papers, LAC.

141 Beatty to Bennett, 20 December 1934, 596501, vol. 944, Bennett Papers, LAC.

142 J.L. Granatstein, *The Politics of Survival: The Conservative Party of Canada, 1939–1945* (Toronto: University of Toronto Press, 1967), 85.

143 Borden to Beatty, 30 April 1935, 157609, vol. 281, Borden Papers, LAC.

144 See the classic study by Alvin Finkel, *Business and Social Reform in the Thirties* (Toronto: James Lorimer, 1979), which emphasizes the reformist tendencies within the business elite.

145 Beatty believed "that National Government is never obtained by a deliberate campaign to bring it about," but that it emerges organically from a nation's high-minded citizens in a period of crisis: "It comes automatically when men in public life decide that a crisis exists so grave that to exercise the normal type of party rivalry would be treasonous to the nation. All that it means is that leaders decide to place country before party, and to sacrifice personal ambition to a patriotic desire to serve the nation." See Beatty to John Danner, Esq., Sarnia, 26 September 1935, 225, vol. 154, box 23-008, President's Letter-Books, CPRA.

146 "Favors Honors in Recipient Worthy," *Montreal Gazette*, 22 February 1935.

147 Young, "Leadership League," 150–2. See also Granatstein, *Politics of Survival*, 43.

148 J.R.H. Wilbur, "H.H. Stevens and the Reconstruction Party," *Canadian Historical Review* 45, no. 1 (March 1964): 18. Grant Dexter reported that Pitfield and Canadian Cottons president A.O. Dawson interviewed Bennett regarding the formation of a National Government in June. Dawson denied that such a meeting ever took place but admitted that a coalition government – composed of "the best men of both our great Parties to work for the general good of Canada" – would be a "wise" step. He believed such an outcome unlikely, however: "I am afraid ... that those who are trying to establish a National Government in Canada are facing a

very formidable, if not impossible, task." See A.O. Dawson to Dafoe, 25 June 1934, Dafoe Papers, LAC.

149 "Merger Group Thinks Bennett Ready to Quit," *Globe*, 12 March 1935, 1.

150 King Diaries, 13 March 1935, LAC.

151 King Diaries, 13 June 1935, LAC.

152 "Whither Are We Tending To-day?" *Maritime Advocate and Busy East* (August 1935): 7.

153 E.G. Jones to Arthur Meighen, 4 March 1935, 93777, vol. 153, Meighen Papers, LAC.

154 A digest of the Duff Commission's proceedings observed: "The views of Organized Labour wherever ascertained in the course of the inquiry were uniformly to the effect that, if there was to be amalgamation or consolidation of services, it should be on the basis of public ownership and what was termed democratic control of transportation facilities." See Digest of Transcripts of Proceedings, 31, vol. 5, Royal Commission on Transportation Fonds, LAC.

155 Beatty to Smeaton White, 9 September 1935, 154, vol. 154, box 23-008, President's Letter-Books, CPRA.

156 Beatty to Donald S. Drennan, 26 September 1935, 215, vol. 154, box 23-008, President's Letter-Books, CPRA.

157 Beatty to Alex McA. Murphy, 10 October 1935, 284, vol. 154, box 23-008, President's Letter-Books, CPRA.

158 Edward Beatty, *Obligations of Business* (an address delivered before a joint meeting of the Canadian Chamber of Commerce and the Kiwanis Club of Toronto), 5 February 1936, 3, 9, and 11.

159 Edward Beatty, *Citizen Obligation in Democratic Government*, Calgary, 2 September 1936.

160 "To those who hold that some mechanism exists in this country known as the present system of society, and that all that is necessary to move us forward on a path of greater wealth and greater happiness is some tinkering with this machine," Beatty said in a convocation address at Queen's University in 1937, "I venture to offer the thought that human society is not a machine but an organism [and] that it[s] improvement is by slow process – not rash remodeling of the system." This language, reminiscent of Herbert Spencer, was conveyed on another occasion that same year as follows: "Human society is a human entity – as truly organic as is a plant or an animal. As with plants and animals, we can stimulate, and, to a very limited extent, control the amount of direction of the growth

of society. We cannot alter its rate or type by substituting a larger gear for a smaller one, or by any other simple mechanical device. Organisms are not machines." See Edward Beatty, "Freedom and the Universities," *Queen's Quarterly* 44 (Winter 1937): 471; Beatty, *The Ideals of a Business Man* (delivered before the United States Chamber of Commerce, Washington), 20 April 1937, 9–10.

161 Chalmers, memo, Montreal, 6 January 1938, file 7, box 6, series 3, Chalmers Papers, AO.

162 Beatty, "Freedom and the Universities," 468.

163 Shore, *Science of Social Redemption*, xviii.

164 Ibid., 233–43.

165 Frost, *McGill University*, 190.

166 Ibid., 190–7. Carleton Stanley had been assistant to the principal at McGill and would have been slated to take over as principal at McGill following Currie's death had he, Stanley, not left in 1931 to become president of Dalhousie University. But, as Barry Cahill writes, "Stanley's left-liberalism and his contemptuous attitude towards the vested interests inevitably made him enemies," most notably the influential Halifax businessman James McGregor Stewart, a member of Dalhousie's board of governors since 1929. Stewart worked within Dalhousie's board to orchestrate Stanley's removal as president – and succeeded in 1945. Cahill observes, "The Morgan affair at McGill was eerily anticipatory of the Stanley affair at Dalhousie some eight years later." See Barry Cahill, "Dismissal of a President: The Ordeal of Carleton Stanley at Dalhousie University, 1943–1944," *Acadiensis* 31, no. 1 (Autumn 2001): 76–102.

167 Frost, *McGill University*, 200–3. In 1941 Conservative Party stalwart and Montreal corporation lawyer C.H. Cahan asked Beatty to use his influence at McGill to effect reconsideration of Eugene Forsey's impending dismissal. Cahan had known Forsey since he was a child. His father had worked under Cahan as a translator and manager of the operating staff of the Mexican Light & Power Company in Mexico City in the early twentieth century, but, suffering from ill health, the elder Forsey died of a hemorrhage on the train in Mexico City. Cahan explained: "I arranged to send the mother and child home to Ottawa, where she secured employment as librarian in one of the government departments; and ever since, because of my warm friendship for his father, and the circumstances of his sudden death, I have taken an interest in the lad's

welfare and advancement." Pleading Forsey's professional competence, Cahan asked Beatty to exercise his influence on Forsey's behalf. Beatty, whose active involvement in university affairs had halted since having fallen ill in 1939, was unmoved and delivered what can only be described as a lie: "I can assure you that Mr. Forsey's personal opinions on political and social questions have no influence on the action which the University authorities contemplate taking." C.H. Cahan to E.W. Beatty, 11 March 1941, and E.W. Beatty to C.H. Cahan, 14 March 1941, 517–20, vol. 2, Charles Hazlitt Cahan Papers, MG 27 B1, LAC.

168 Beatty to A.J. Nesbitt, 25 November 1932, 490, vol. 43, box 23-006, President's Letter-Books, CPRA.

169 Beatty, "Freedom and the Universities," 470–1; Edward Beatty, *University Education and Economics* (on the occasion of receiving honorary degree at the University of Western Ontario, London, Ontario), 25 October 1935.

170 Beatty to George Drew, 25 February 1938, file 88, vol. 12, George Drew Papers, MG 32 C 3, LAC.

171 Sean Mills, "When Democratic Socialists Discovered Democracy: The League for Social Reconstruction Confronts the 'Quebec Problem,'" *Canadian Historical Review* 86, no. 1 (March 2005): 53–81.

172 Beatty, *Ideals of a Business Man*, 14–15. See also Edward Beatty, *The Average Citizen*, Ottawa, 27 November 1937, an address that touches upon what Beatty perceived as the obstacles hindering the "Forgotten Man's" or "average citizen's" ability to embrace a truly national outlook. Made afraid by demagogues who scare him and politicians who appeal to his sectional interest, the potential of the "average citizen" is, Beatty maintains, limited. Beatty claimed to have faith in the future: "It is precisely because I believe in democracy, and in ability of the average citizen to see the fallacies and weaknesses of our present public policies that I assert the coming of a change. I believe in all sincerity that the time is near at hand when the average citizen will demand the adoption of those policies which will give him a chance to reap fuller rewards from his industry and thrift than now are possible." See Beatty, *Average Citizen*, 11. Taken with his other addresses, one must conclude that the ability of the "average citizen" to find such a path depended upon the guidance of individuals such as Beatty.

173 Beatty, *Ideals of a Business Man*, 11. American big business was well aware of the importance of public relations by this time, and major

corporations had invested considerable resources in public relations in an effort to counter the New Deal and reinstate confidence in capitalist enterprise. See Roland Marchand, *Creating the Corporate Soul: The Rise of Public Relations and Corporate Imagery in American Business* (Berkeley: University of California Press, 1998), 202–48.

174 See Beatty, *After Unification* (delivered before the Woodstock Board of Trade, Woodstock, Ontario), 6 April 1938.

175 Chalmers, memo, Montreal, 6 January 1938, file 7, box 6, series 3, Chalmers Papers, AO.

176 This quotation comes from a memo written by Floyd Chalmers that reported a conversation with Beatty, where Beatty expressed concern regarding Franklin Roosevelt's decision to publicly broadcast his message to Congress. Beatty, as Chalmers reported, believed the decision "meant inevitably that the message would be written for its effect upon the larger audience outside and this meant that the White House executive message to Congress would inevitably stoop lower and lower to get down to the democratic [intellectual – written in pencil] level of the masses." Chalmers, memo, Montreal, 6 January 1938, file 7, box 6, series 3, Chalmers Papers, AO.

Beatty argued that those who believed railway unification impossible were, in fact, admitting the failure of democracy, which reveals Beatty's fragile – perhaps opportunist – commitment to democracy. See Beatty, *The Inevitable Way to Lower Transportation Costs*, Windsor, Ontario, 8 December 1937, 15. On another occasion Beatty claimed: "The time is past to play political tricks with railways. Rationalization of an intolerable situation is inevitable. I, for one, deny that it cannot be brought about safely under democratic Government." Beatty, *After Unification*, 16.

177 Dafoe to Dexter, 30 October 1936, Dafoe Papers, LAC.

178 King Diaries, 27 October 1936, LAC.

179 James Overton, "Economic Crisis and the End of Democracy: Politics in Newfoundland during the Great Depression," *Labour/Le Travail* 26 (Fall 1990): 85–124.

4 Stewardship and Dependency

1 Mitch Hepburn to Ernest Lapointe, 8 April 1937, file "Strike at Oshawa: General (Folder 1)," box 282, Mitchell F. Hepburn Papers, RG 3-10, Archives of Ontario [AO].

2 *Handbook of Oshawa* (Oshawa Chamber of Commerce, 1928), 17.

3 Dimitry Anastakis, *Car Nation: An Illustrated History of Canada's Transformation Behind the Wheel* (Toronto: James Lorimer, 2008), 24.

4 Christine McLaughlin, "The McLaughlin Legacy and the Struggle for Labour Organization: Community, Class, and Oshawa's UAW Local 222, 1944–49" (MA thesis, Trent University, 2007), 43–4; Heather Robertson, *Driving Force: The McLaughlin Family and the Age of the Car* (Toronto: McClelland & Stewart, 1995), 250.

5 This runs contrary to Irving Abella's suggestion, in his classic account of the 1937 strike, that GM had been conciliatory before Mitch Hepburn stiffened its resolve to fight the union. See Irving Abella, "Oshawa 1937," in *On Strike: Six Key Labour Struggles in Canada, 1919–1949*, ed. Irving Abella (Toronto: James Lewis & Samuel, 1974), 93–128, and discussion below.

6 This view is presented in Robertson, *Driving Force*, 209.

7 Milton Bergey, "A Great Canadian Industry and Its Founder," *Motor Sparks* (Oshawa), 23 November 1921.

8 M. McIntyre Hood, *Oshawa: "The Crossing between the Waters"* (Oshawa: McLaughlin Public Library, 1968), 116–18; "Fine Romance in the Career of Auto Maker," *Globe* (Toronto), 25 November 1919, 13.

9 R.S. McLaughlin, as told to Eric Hutton, "My Eighty Years on Wheels, Part I," *Maclean's* (15 September 1954): 90; *The Manchester of Canada* (Toronto: Canadian Souvenir Publishing, 1898), 13.

10 Chris Kloepfer, a Guelph merchant, heard about the device from one of his travelling salesmen and made the trip to Oshawa to inspect it, eventually offering $10,000 for the patent. Robert refused the deal and instead offered Kloepfer exclusive rights to sell the gear in Canada. Kloepfer agreed to purchase a minimum of 1,000 gears over a two-year period.

11 McLaughlin, "My Eighty Years on Wheels, Part I," 90 and 92; Dorothy McLaughlin Henderson, *Robert McLaughlin – Carriage Builder* (Oshawa: Alger Press Limited, 1968), 14–16; Robert McLaughlin, "Established in Enniskillen" (1881), file 2, box 2, George McLaughlin Papers, 5127, Queen's University Archives [QUA].

12 John James "Jack" McLaughlin became a successful businessman himself. He attended the Ontario College of Pharmacy and engaged in the manufacture of soda water in Toronto, developing the formula for Canada Dry Ginger Ale. When he died of a heart attack in 1914 at the age

of forty-eight, he was described as "one of Toronto's leading business men." In the late 1880s, Jack lived in Brooklyn, New York, where he managed one of its largest pharmacies and took a postgraduate course. See "Death Summons Leading Citizen," n.d., Family Scrapbook, 1908–1971, reel 1 MS 674, C. Ewart McLaughlin Collection, C 88-3, AO; M. Patricia Bishop, "John James McLaughlin," *Dictionary of Canadian Biography*, vol. 14 (Toronto: University of Toronto Press, 1998), 720–1.

13 He swept the floors and performed other menial tasks for three dollars a week, all but fifty cents of which went towards his room and board. McLaughlin, "My Eighty Years on Wheels, Part I," 92–3.

14 McLaughlin, "My Eighty Years on Wheels, Part I," 93; Robertson, *Driving Force*, 81.

15 McLaughlin, "My Eighty Years on Wheels: How the Auto Beat the Horse, Part II," *Maclean's* (1 October 1954): 38.

16 Robert secured credit from Oshawa's leading bank, the Dominion Bank, which made possible the expansion of the carriage business. And before long, Robert accepted expanded credit from the Western Bank, a local bank established in 1882. In 1899 his daughter would marry J.P. Owens, a clerk and later manager at the bank, and Robert later joined the bank's board of directors, in 1907. McLaughlin, "My Eighty Years on Wheels, Part II," 22–3; David Roberts, "Robert McLaughlin," *Dictionary of Canadian Biography*, vol. 15 (Toronto: University of Toronto Press, 2005), 672 and 674. The Western Bank was taken over by the Standard Bank of Toronto in 1908. Tom Naylor has claimed: "not only did local control vanish, but all activities towards promoting local industrialization reputedly stopped." See Tom Naylor, *The History of Canadian Business, 1867-1914*, Vol. 1 (Toronto: James Lorimer, 1975), 102. It was true that Robert McLaughlin remained a director of the bank only "up to the date that it was merged into the Standard." See "Oshawa's Grand Old Man Passes to His Reward," *Oshawa Telegram*, 29 November 1921, file 4, C. Ewart McLaughlin Collection, AO. McLaughlin reported that after the merger the family resumed connections with the Dominion Bank, dividing their business between the Dominion and the Standard. See McLaughlin, "My Eighty Years on Wheels, Part II," 22–3. Naylor's conclusion is too categorical, since the McLaughlins were about to spearhead a new phase of industrialization.

17 The town raised the money for the loan by issuing bonds at 4 per cent
    interest. See By-Law No. 480, of the Corporation of the Town of Oshawa
    to grant $50,000.00 by way of Loan to The McLaughlin Carriage Com-
    pany, file 14 "McLaughlin Carriage Co. documents," reel 1, MS 674, C.
    Ewart McLaughlin Collection, AO. For the agreement with the Grand
    Trunk, see Memo. of Agreement Between Messrs McLaughlin Carriage
    Co., Oshawa, White and Loud, in Reference to Mr. McLaughlin Rebuild-
    ing Works at Oshawa, file 14 "McLaughlin Carriage Co. documents,"
    reel 1, MS 674, C. Ewart McLaughlin Collection, AO. The agreement
    gave the McLaughlin company some of the freight rate advantages ac-
    corded to Toronto manufacturers and promised "that the Grand Trunk
    System will at all times see that Oshawa is kept on an equitable basis
    with the other points manufacturing the same product."
18 McLaughlin, "My Eighty Years on Wheels, Part II," 39–40; Roberts,
    "Robert McLaughlin," 673.
19 *The Manchester of Canada: Oshawa* (Oshawa: Reformer Printing and
    Publishing Company, 1911), 21; *Canada Year Book, 1911* (Ottawa: Cen-
    sus and Statistics Office, 1912), 8.
20 Mira Wilkins and Frank Ernest Hill, *American Business Abroad: Ford on Six
    Continents* (Detroit: Wayne State University, 1964), 14–19. For a biographi-
    cal treatment of McGregor and the early history of Ford in Canada, see David
    Roberts, *In the Shadow of Detroit: Gordon M. McGregor, Ford of Canada,
    and Motoropolis* (Detroit: Wayne State University Press, 2006).
21 This aspect of the tariff is emphasized by Michael Bliss in "Canadian-
    izing American Business: The Roots of the Branch Plant," in *Close the
    49th Parallel Etc: The Americanization of Canada*, ed. Ian Lumsden
    (Toronto: University of Toronto Press, 1970), 27–42.
22 McLaughlin, "My Eighty Years on Wheels, Part II," 41.
23 Bernhard A. Weisberger, *The Dream Màker: William C. Durant,
    Founder of General Motors* (Boston: Little, Brown, 1979), 83–116.
24 C.W. Stollery, "Robert McLaughlin's 'Go Ahead' Started General Mo-
    tors," *Financial Post*, 23 September 1933, General Motors of Canada
    clippings, 1922–1949, vol. 21, Financial Post Fonds, MG 28 III 21,
    Library and Archives Canada [LAC]. Years after, McLaughlin claimed
    that they abandoned the idea of trying to market their own car, the
    McLaughlin Model A, because their engineer, a man from Milwaukee

named Arthur Milbraith, came down with pleurisy. McLaughlin, so the story goes, was in a bind and asked Durant if he could spare an engineer; however, Durant instead travelled to Oshawa and convinced McLaughlin to produce Buicks – even though the factory was tooled and near ready to begin production. For this version, see McLaughlin, "My Eighty Years on Wheels, Part II," 42 and "My Eighty Years on Wheels – Conclusion: The Men Cars Made Famous," *Maclean's* (15 October 1954): 28–9. Writers familiar with the episode such as Robertson and Richard White have been sceptical of McLaughlin's story. Rather than an engineer's illness causing the end of the project, Robertson and White have suggested that the Model A endeavour was a disaster and made the alliance with Durant an attractive alternative. Certainly, Robertson and White present the more persuasive case, especially since McLaughlin's earlier account does not mention anything about an engineer falling ill. See Robertson, *Driving Force*, 109–12; Richard White, *Making Cars in Canada, A Brief History of the Canadian Automobile Industry, 1900–1980* (Ottawa: Canada Science and Technology Museum, 2007), 14.

25 George W. McLaughlin to Clarence E. Bogart, 31 December 1936, and Bogart to George McLaughlin, 4 January 1937, file 2, box 1, George McLaughlin Papers, QUA.

26 Robertson, *Driving Force*, 111.

27 Ibid., 112–14.

28 Donald F. Davis, "Dependent Motorization: Canada and the Automobile to the 1930s," *Journal of Canadian Studies* 21, no. 3 (Fall 1986): 114. Davis notes that Robert Ankli and Fred Fredericksen attributed the technological dependence of the Canadian auto industry to its connection to carriage makers who "refused to give motor cars their undivided attention as long as carriage sales held up"; more importantly, the manufacture of carriages did not demand the precision required in making of automobiles. Ankli and Frederickson observe: "Metal-working in the carriage-building industry was at a rudimentary level and tolerances were more likely to be in sixteenths of an inch rather than thousandths." Robert E. Ankli and Fred Frederiksen, "The Influence of American Manufacturers on the Canadian Automotive Industry," *Business and Economic History*, 2nd series, 9 (1981): 101, quoted in Davis, "Dependent Motorization," 114.

29 White, *Making Cars in Canada*, 7 and 12.

30 Historian of the automobile industry Donald Davis has suggested that Canadian automobile entrepreneurs did not embrace the mass-production ethos and thus failed to develop the technological know-how that gave rise to the automobile industry in the United States. Emphasizing the role of mechanic-entrepreneurs in leading the way towards the production of inexpensive, mass-produced cars in the United States that came to dominate the industry's production, Davis claims that Canada's more rigid class structure stifled the rise of this sort of entrepreneurial initiative. This seems an overstated – and perhaps even unlikely – argument. See Davis, "Dependent Motorization," 109–16.

31 Stephanie Beatty and Susan Gale Hall, *Parkwood* (Erin, ON: Boston Mills Press, 1999), 14; Roberston, *Driving Force*, 165 and 191–6; Robert Hunter, "The Design Work of H.B. and L.A. Dunnington-Grubb at Parkwood, Oshawa," *Canadian Horticultural History* 2, no. 3 (1990): 135–6; Marilyn Litvak, "A Tour Through 'Parkwood' Oshawa," *City & Country Home* (Fall 1982): 66 and 68; *Colonel R.S. McLaughlin*, 2nd ed. (Oshawa: McLaughlin-Parkwood Research Project, 1980), 11.

32 "[W]e didn't have much chance to do very much in the First War," explained McLaughlin in laconic fashion years later. See "Arts and Science ... McLaughlin Special," n.d., file "McLaughlin, R.S. – Correspondence – General," box LH S 100 BIO, McLaughlin Library. See also Robertson, *Driving Force*, 163–4; Hugh Durnford and Glenn Baechler, *Cars in Canada* (Toronto: McClelland & Stewart, 1973), 22 and 314.

33 "New Senator Motor Magnate," 15 September 1917, newspaper clipping, file "Scrapbooks/Album, 1920–1941," reel 1, MS 674, C. Ewart McLaughlin Collection, AO.

34 He was, however, interested in political rewards and appears to have been willing to support Laurier during the conscription crisis in exchange for a place in the Senate. McLaughlin must have miscalculated, since Laurier lost the election. See Robertson, *Driving Force*, 164. Robertson incorrectly attributed the story entitled "New Senator Motor Magnate," cited above, to the Toronto *Globe*. A search of the 15 September 1917 issue of the *Globe* revealed no story by that title.

35 "New Senator Motor Magnate."

36 See Thorstein Veblen, *The Theory of the Leisure Class*, intro. John Kenneth Galbraith (Boston: Houghton Mifflin, 1973 [1899]); Stephen

Leacock, *Arcadian Adventures with the Idle Rich* (Toronto: Bell and Cockburn, 1914).

37 Sam McLaughlin to Isabel McLaughlin, 26 March 1924, file 8, box 12, Isabel McLaughlin Papers, 2303.37, QUA.

38 Jackson Lears, "The Managerial Revitalization of the Rich," in *Ruling America: A History of Wealth and Power in a Democracy*, eds Steve Fraser and Gary Gerstle (Cambridge, MA: Harvard University Press, 2005), especially 181–93. Indeed, as Lears observes, Veblen's rhetoric against the stodgy plutocrats of the nineteenth-century mould helped to legitimize a revitalized ruling class in the United States that was sleeker, healthier, and more aggressive than the older version. The present analysis places McLaughlin within the framework of these broader cultural tendencies.

39 The creed of paternalistic responsibility was, according to Lears, another aspect of elite revitalization. See Lears, "Managerial Revitalization," 182.

40 Though Sam McLaughlin years later claimed that his father wanted nothing to do with the manufacture of automobiles, Heather Robertson has shown that Robert McLaughlin played a role in drafting the original agreement with Durant and felt the automobile business a good "sideline" to carriages. See Robertson, *Driving Force*, 107. O.J. McDiarmid, "Some Aspects of the Canadian Automobile Industry," *Canadian Journal of Economics and Political Science* 6, no. 2 (May 1940): 259.

41 McLaughlin, "My Eighty Years on Wheels – Conclusion," 65.

42 Weisberger, *Dream Maker*, 151.

43 Ibid., 167–8.

44 McLaughlin, "My Eighty Years on Wheels – Conclusion," 65–6; Axel Madsen's *The Deal Maker: How William C. Durant Made General Motors* (New York: John Wiley, 1999), 155, indicates the restaurant in which McLaughlin and Durant met. Madsen's account claims that Sam explained during the meeting that lack of factory space and his father's reticence to admit the passing of the horse-and-buggy era might stop the deal from being made. Durant, so this account claims, phoned the "Governor" and convinced him to end the carriage business. The account seems less likely than the one provided by McLaughlin himself, and, indeed, it refers to Sam's father as "'Governor' George McLaughlin," thus combining elder brother and father in one personage. The older Durant

biography by Weisberger, *Dream Maker*, 172–3, provides an account that squares up with McLaughlin's telling.

45 Roberts, "Robert McLaughlin," 675.

46 Sam's portrayal of his father's attitude changed over time somewhat. In a speech delivered in Oshawa on 18 September 1944, which later served as the basis of the 1954 article in *Maclean's*, Sam emphasized his father's resignation: "Sam, I am about through ... Do what you please." In an earlier rendition Sam simply stated: "Father, who was a very elderly man, was quite agreeable." See "Hobbies and Health," *News and Views* (July 1929): 12. *News and Views* was a company publication; this specific issue can be consulted at the Oshawa Community Museum and Archives [OCM]: file 3: "General Motors, 'News and Views,'" box 18, S 3.

47 J. Herbert Hodgins, "Making Motor Dreams Come True," *Maclean's Magazine* 37, no. 17 (1 September 1924): 18.

48 Hodgins, "Making Motor Dreams Come True," 45–6; Weisberger, *Dream Maker*, 173.

49 Weisberger, *Dream Maker*, 193–201.

50 Memorandum, George W. McLaughlin to Sam McLaughlin, 4 July 1918, file 28, box 1, George McLaughlin Papers, QUA; Alfred D. Chandler Jr and Stephen Salsbury, *Pierre S. Du Pont and the Making of the Modern Corporation* (New York: Harper & Row, 1971), 462–4; A.B.C. Hardy to W.C. Durant, 27 November 1918, file 8, box 1, George McLaughlin Papers, QUA.

51 R.S. McLaughlin, *75 Years of Progress* (Oshawa, 1944), 32.

52 An expansionary project in the amount of $52.8 million was proposed; GM would offer $6.5 million in stock for the McLaughlin-Buick properties. J.J. Raskob to General Motors Finance Committee, 12 December 1918, Du Pont-General Motors Anti-trust Case, Government Trial Exhibit, no. 134, reproduced in Alfred D. Chandler Jr, ed., *Giant Enterprise: Ford, General Motors and the Automobile Industry: Sources and Readings* (New York: Harcourt, Brace & World, 1964), 68–9.

53 McLaughlin, "My Eighty Years on Wheels – Conclusion," 66.

54 Weisberger, *Dream Maker*, 237 and 243–74; Chandler and Salsbury, *Pierre S. Dupont*, 482–91.

55 "When you permitted your controlling interest to pass from your hands," wrote C.W. Nash of the Nash Motors Company in 1924 to George

McLaughlin, "I said then that I was sure the McLaughlin boys would never be happy again." Nash had served as president of GM during the interlude between the years of Durant – and Durant–du Pont – control and counted himself among the McLaughlins' friends. George appeared unhappy with GM when he retired in 1924. Nash described George's decision to retire from GM as "wise." He explained: "My reason for saying this is that I was positive, when I visited you a year or so ago, and we had a little chat, that you were not at all happy in your position. As a matter of fact it has been a quandary in my mind for some time how you and Sam could stand the proposition at all." See C.W. Nash to George McLaughlin, 10 July 1924, file 28, box 1, George McLaughlin Papers, QUA.

56 Roberts, "Robert McLaughlin," 675.

57 "Fine Romance in the Career of Auto Maker," 13.

58 "Long Service Employees of General Motors Are Honored by Company," *Oshawa Daily Times*, 19 June 1928, 8, file 1 "General Motors, General Information," box 11, S 3, OCM.

59 Craig Heron, "The Second Industrial Revolution in Canada, 1890–1930," in *Class, Community and the Labour Movement: Wales and Canada, 1850–1930*, eds Deian R. Hopkin and Gregory S. Kealey (St John's: Llafur/Canadian Committee on Labour History, 1989), 48–66.

60 William L. Marr and Donald G. Paterson, *Canada: An Economic History* (Toronto: Macmillan of Canada, 1980), 390.

61 White, *Making Cars in Canada*, 35; C. Howard Aikman, *The Automobile Industry of Canada* (Toronto: Macmillan of Canada, 1926), 8, 31, and 36.

62 Tom Traves, *The State and Enterprise: Canadian Manufacturers and the Federal Government, 1917–1931* (Toronto: University of Toronto Press, 1979), 101.

63 *GM in Canada: The Early Years, Story and Photos Courtesy of the Public Relations Department, General Motors of Canada Limited, Oshawa, Ontario*, n.d., 10, see table entitled "General Motors of Canada Limited, Domestic and Export Production 1908–December 31, 1973 (Calendar Years)."

64 R.S. McLaughlin to J.A. Robb, 30 December 1925, 101189, vol. 136, William Lyon Mackenzie King Papers, MG 26 J1, LAC.

65 "Mr. G.W. McLaughlin Retires from Active Local Business Life," *Oshawa Daily Telegram*, 3 June 1924, 1.

66 McLaughlin, *75 Years of Progress*, 35–6; Sam McLaughlin to Isabel McLaughlin, 17 April 1924, file 8, box 12, Isabel McLaughlin Papers, QUA. An archetypical corporate administrator, Sloan played an important role in forging the company's administrative apparatus before Pierre S. du Pont retired to hand him the reins of the presidency in May 1923. For General Motors during du Pont's time as president, see Chandler and Salsbury, *Pierre S. du Pont*, 492–536. Though Sloan introduced innovative marketing strategies, George believed he was paying insufficient attention to quality – contrary, of course, to the stated business philosophy of the McLaughlin family. George wrote to C.W. Nash: "The fancy systems of intensive advertising, schools of instruction, and the hundred and one intensive methods that are now being employed through Sales Departments are in the main alright, but, during the last few years of my association with General Motors Corporation I became more thoroughly grounded in the belief, and upon every occasion where I felt I had influence, I did not hesitate to take the stand that all these things were as 'The Mist on the Mountain' unless the man at the head of the institution gave first and principal heed to the fact that no matter what class of product they were offering to the public that it had to be built just as well and just as conscientiously, or even a little better [*sic*] than that of any competitor." See George McLaughlin to C.W. Nash, 15 January 1924, file 28, box 1, George McLaughlin Papers, QUA.

67 McLaughlin explained that the work "will give me added responsibilities – not that I want them or like them, but one has to do his duty." See Sam McLaughlin to Isabel McLaughlin, 7 October 1921, file 5, box 12, Isabel McLaughlin Papers, QUA. McLaughlin admitted, nonetheless, that the work "will be very interesting. We have already shipped quite a few cars, and a recent shipment comprised two beautiful Oldsmobile Sedans which went to one of those wealthy Princes in India." Donald Davis has suggested that this elitist mentality – focusing on making cars for one's social peers – held back indigenous car manufacturing in Canada. Davis, "Dependent Motorization," 116–17. McLaughlin made a car for the Prince of Wales in 1927 and a limousine in 1936, just before the prince was to become King Edward VIII.

68 "Hobbies and Health," 12.

324   NOTES TO PAGES 171–4

69 Lex Schragg, *History of the Ontario Regiment, 1866–1951* (Oshawa: Ontario Regimental Association, 1951), 31.

70 John Manley, "Communists and Autoworkers: The Struggle for Industrial Unionism in the Canadian Automobile Industry, 1925–36," *Labour/ Le Travail* 17 (Spring 1986): 113; Robertson, *Driving Force*, 261–2.

71 "Mr. Sam," *News and Views* (New York) 7, no. 3 (September 1928): 3–4.

72 Sam McLaughlin to Isabel McLaughlin, 7 January 1922, file 5, box 12, Isabel McLaughlin Papers, QUA.

73 The 1921 census categorizes 10,673 of 11,940 Oshawa residents as belonging to the "British races." The figures for the 1931 census are 19,219 of 23,439. Thus, as a percentage of the local population, the relative decline of the British population was only 7 per cent during the period from 1921 to 1931, moving from 89 per cent to 82 per cent of the total population. See *Sixth Census of Canada, 1921*, Vol. 1 (Ottawa, 1924), 472–3; *Seventh Census of Canada, 1931*, Vol. 2 (Ottawa, 1933), 416–17.

74 "Tariff Reduction Would Be Ruinous to Oshawa, States Dr. T.E. Kaiser M.P.," *Oshawa Daily Reformer*, 3 April 1926, 1 and 6.

75 "Tariff Low Priced Cars Reduced to 20 Percent; Over $1,200 Value, 27 ½," *Oshawa Daily Reformer*, 15 April 1926, 1.

76 See *Oshawa Daily Reformer*, 17 April 1926, 1.

77 "Official Statement Is Issued," *Oshawa Daily Reformer*, 16 April 1926, 1.

78 "Budget Is Disastrous to Motor Car Industry Domestic and Export," *Oshawa Daily Reformer*, 16 April 1916, 1; Roberts, *In the Shadow of Detroit*, 200.

79 Traves, *State and Enterprise*, 107.

80 Hon. William H. Price, Ontario Provincial Treasurer, memo, "Increased Duty on Automobile and Parts Levy Luxury," 14 May 1926, file "Automobile Industry," reel MS 1700, Province of Ontario, Office of the Premier, Howard Ferguson Papers, RG 3-6-0-360, AO. Automobiles began to seriously compete with the country's major department stores for consumer spending in the 1920s. This seems very likely to explain some of the opposition to the expansion of automobile sales in Ontario, which was home to retailing giants Eaton's and Simpson's. See Donica Belisle, *Retail Nation: Department Stores and the Making of Modern Canada* (Vancouver: UBC Press, 2011), 37.

81 W.R. Morson, President, the Prosperity League of Canada, to Howard Ferguson, 18 August 1926, as well as Morson to Ferguson, 20 August 1926, file "Automobile Industry," Office of the Premier, Howard Ferguson, AO.

82 "All Classes View with Alarm Government Action in Tariff Changes," *Oshawa Daily Reformer*, 19 April 1926, 5.

83 "Two Thousand Veterans Endorse Pilgrimage to Ottawa to Lodge Protest," *Oshawa Daily Reformer*, 20 April 1926, 1 and 4.

84 "G.M.C. Head Convinces Monster Mass Meeting Situation Is Serious," *Oshawa Daily Reformer*, 21 April 1926, 1 and 3.

85 "Name Committees for Delegation," *Oshawa Daily Reformer*, 22 April 1926, 1.

86 William Lyon Mackenzie King Diaries, 16 April 1926, LAC.

87 King Diaries, 13 April 1923, LAC, quoted in Traves, *State and Enterprise*, 108.

88 J.A. McGibbon to Arthur Meighen, 28 April 1926, 80762-3, vol. 134, Arthur Meighen Papers, MG 26 I, LAC.

89 "'I Intend to Stand by My Guns' Hon. J.A. Robb Tells Deputation in No Unmistakable Language," *Oshawa Daily Reformer*, 23 April 1926, 3; King Diaries, 23 April 1926, LAC.

90 "General Motors Not Active in Protest to Ottawa," *Globe*, 22 April 1926, 9.

91 "Council Votes $3,000 to Send Deputation to Protest Tariff," *Globe*, 22 April 1926, 9.

92 "Three Thousand in Delegation to Wait on Cabinet," *Oshawa Daily Reformer*, 22 April 1926, 1; "Many Veterans Ready for Oshawa," *Oshawa Daily Reformer*, 22 April 1926, section 2, 1.

93 "'I Intend to Stand by My Guns,'" 1; "Cabinet Ministers Attitude Scored," *Oshawa Daily Reformer*, 30 April 1926, 2 and 8.

94 "Three Thousand in Delegation to Wait on Cabinet," 1.

95 "'I Intend to Stand By My Guns,'" 1.

96 "Government Did Not Keep Promises, Dr. Kaiser Tells House," *Oshawa Daily Reformer*, 24 April 1923, 1.

97 King viewed the demonstration in partisan terms, as a Tory exercise, and congratulated himself with the way he handled the crowd, preempting the gathering at Parliament Hill by unexpectedly meeting the delegation beforehand at Keith's Theatre, where he and Robb addressed the crowd. See King Diaries, 23 April 1923, LAC.

98 Memorandum, T.H. Blalock to Arthur Meighen, 12 September 1925, 40349, vol. 72, Meighen Papers, LAC; Robertson, *Driving Force*, 229.

99 McDiarmid, "Aspects of the Canadian Automobile Industry," 262; Traves, *State and Enterprise*, 111.

100 Aikman, *Automobile Industry of Canada*, 16–17.

101 Traves, *State and Enterprise*, 111–12.

102 *GM in Canada*, 10; Traves, *State and Enterprise*, 114.

103 Stephen Meyer, III, *The Five Dollar Day: Labor Management and Social Control in the Ford Motor Company, 1908–1921* (Albany: State University of New York Press, 1981), 2, 10, and 169–94.

104 Walter A. Friedman, *Birth of a Salesman: The Transformation of Selling in America* (Cambridge, MA: Harvard University Press, 2004), 218–24; Durnford and Bachler, *Cars in Canada*, 262.

105 John J. Raskob, "Management Is Major Factor in Industry," *Financial Post*, 16 September 1927, file "General Motors of Canada clippings (part 1), 1922–1949," vol. 21, Financial Post Fonds, LAC.

106 "Company and Staff Closely Co-operate," *Oshawa Daily Reformer*, 30 June 1927, 66, file 1 "General Motors, General Information," box 11, S 3, OCM.

107 "Mr. Sam," 3. A booklet was produced to commemorate the event. See *A Tribute to Those Who Have Been in the Service of General Motors of Canada, Limited for Ten Years Upward* (1928).

108 "More Than 12,000 People Enjoy Greatest Picnic in the History of This City," *Oshawa Daily Reformer*, 16 August 1926, file 4 "General Motors, Picnics," box 11, S 3, OCM; "G.M. Picnic Largest Ever Held in Canada," *Oshawa Daily Times*, 13 August 1928, 1.

109 "More Than 12,000 People Enjoy Greatest Picnic"; "Diving Display Proved Fine Picnic Attraction," *Oshawa Daily Times*, 13 August 1928, file 1 "General Motors, General Information," box 11, S 3, OCM.

110 "Long Service Employees of General Motors Are Honored by Company," *Oshawa Daily Times*, 19 June 1928, file 1 "General Motors, General Information," box 11, S 3, OCM.

111 Tom Traves has observed, for example: "in contrast to Ford's glorification of the assembly line, GM stressed the traditional artisanship and craft skills that its employees brought to the job – although the progressive degradation of job skills was just as obvious in Oshawa as it was in

Windsor." See Tom Traves, "The Development of the Ontario Automobile Industry to 1939," in Ian Drummond, *Progress Without Planning: The Economic History of Ontario from Confederation to the Second World War* (Toronto: University of Toronto Press, 1987), 222.

112 R.S. McLaughlin to W.H. Perryman, 26 February 1959, file 11, box 13, S 13, OCM.

113 James Alexander Pendergest, "Labour and Politics in Oshawa and Its District, 1928–1943" (MA thesis, Queen's University, 1973), 18–19; "Walkout Is Protest Against Cut in Chev. and Pontiac Depts.," *Oshawa Daily Times*, 26 March 1928, 1.

114 "Walkout Is Protest," 1; "Refuse to Accept Men's Proposals at Meeting This Afternoon," *Oshawa Daily Times*, 27 March 1928, 1; "Men Engaged to Replace Strikers Will Be Kept on Is Announcement Today," *Oshawa Daily Times*, 28 March 1928, 1; "General Manager Also Gives 1927 Statistics for Trimming Depts.," *Oshawa Daily Times*, 28 March 1928, 3; "Strikers Repudiate All Connection with Communist Principles," *Oshawa Daily Times*, 30 March 1928, 3; Pendergest, "Labour and Politics in Oshawa," 15; Roberts, "Robert McLaughlin," 673. John Manley has observed that the plant committee – the company union – was exposed as fraudulent during the course of the strike. See Manley, "Communists and Auto Workers," 114.

115 Robertson, *Driving Force*, 127.

116 "Company's Offer to Hon. Peter Heenan Accepted by Men," *Oshawa Daily Times*, 30 March 1928, 1; "City Quiet After Settlement," *Oshawa Daily Times*, 31 March 1928, 1.

117 "Strikers Decide to Form Union Passing a Strong Resolution," *Oshawa Daily Times*, 30 March 1928, 1 and 3; Pendergest, "Labour and Politics in Oshawa," 24 and 30. Communist leader Jack MacDonald and organizer L.R. Menzies also travelled to Oshawa during the strike but failed to gain many followers, causing the *Daily Times* to editorialize: "The heart of Oshawa is too loyal to British traditions to be carried away by the red element." See "A Wise Decision," *Oshawa Daily Times*, 31 March 1928, 4.

118 "Amicable and Fair Settlement Made Between General Motors Employees and the Company," *Oshawa Daily Times*, 7 May 1928, 1.

119 "R.S. McLaughlin Pleased Settlement Is Reached," *Oshawa Daily Times*, 7 May 1928, 1.

120 John Manley's research has shown that at least three members of the union's local executive by the end of 1928 were working as spies, having been planted by the Corporations' Auxiliary. See Manley, "Communists and Auto Workers," 119.

121 Pendergest, "Labour and Politics in Oshawa," 32. For more on the unions, see also John Manley, "Communism and the Canadian Working-Class During the Great Depression: The Workers' Unity League, 1930–1936" (PhD thesis, Dalhousie University, 1984), 414–24.

122 Pendergest, "Labour and Politics in Oshawa," 33–42.

123 "Refuse to Accept Men's Proposals," 1 and 3.

124 Pendergest, "Labour and Politics in Oshawa," 12; Pamela Sugiman, *Labour's Dilemma: The Gender Politics of Auto Workers in Canada, 1937–1979* (Toronto: University of Toronto Press, 1994), 12.

125 Sugiman, *Labour's Dilemma*, 12 and 14.

126 Sun Life Assurance Company of Canada, *The Canadian Automobile Industry* (Royal Commission on Economic Prospects, September 1956), 7–8; *GM in Canada*, 10.

127 McLaughlin, "The McLaughlin Legacy," 58–62.

128 *Colonel R.S. McLaughlin*, 8–9; McLaughlin, "The McLaughlin Legacy," 62–3.

129 See, for example, "Workers Start Fund at Dinner by Making Their Own Donations," *Oshawa Daily Times*, 17 November 1931, 1.

130 Pendergest, "Labour and Politics in Oshawa," 90–3; "Motor Trade Leader Dies in Oshawa," n.d., file 2, box 2, George McLaughlin Papers, QUA.

131 Hood, *Oshawa*, 284.

132 "Ald. McLaughlin Denies Election Criticisms," n.d., file "Scrapbooks/Album, 1920–1942," reel 2, MS 674, C. Ewart McLaughlin Collection, AO; Hood, *Oshawa*, 283.

133 Pendergest, "Labour and Politics in Oshawa," 110–11.

134 George McLaughlin to R.B. Bennett, 23 July 1935, file 2, box 1, George McLaughlin Papers, QUA.

135 For an analysis of the ongoing activism of Communists in the auto industry during this period, see Manley, "Communists and Auto Workers."

136 *Colonel R.S. McLaughlin*, 12–13.

137 Floyd S. Chalmers to McLaughlin-Parkwood Research Project, 18 June 1979, quoted in *Colonel R.S. McLaughlin*, 12–13.

138 "Parkwood's Brilliant Wedding," *Mayfair* (October 1930): 28–9; "Hundreds Attend Fashionable Wedding at Parkwood, Oshawa, the Home of R.S. McLaughlin," *Globe*, City News Section, 1 September 1930, 1.

139 In March 1924, McLaughlin wrote to Isabel of his plans to take riding lessons in Toronto. He explained: "I am quite serious about making up my mind to do considerable riding and believe it will be the best kind of exercise I can take." See Sam McLaughlin to Isabel McLaughlin, 26 March 1924, file 8, box 12, Isabel McLaughlin Papers, QUA.

140 Virginia Brass, "The Squire of Oshawa," *Mayfair* (August 1948): 94; McLaughlin, "The McLaughlin Legacy," 58.

141 "Canada Captures Lake Yacht Prize," *New York Times*, 11 September 1926, 11; Robertson, *Driving Force*, 212.

142 Sam McLaughlin to Isabel McLaughlin, 30 April 1924, file 8, box 12, Isabel McLaughlin Papers, QUA; Beatty and Hall, *Parkwood*, passim; Litvak, "A Tour Through 'Parkwood' Canada," 68, 71, and 75. For the concept of cultural capital, see Pierre Bourdieu, *Distinction: A Social Critique of the Judgement of Taste*, trans. Richard Nice (Cambridge, MA: Harvard University Press, 1984).

143 *Colonel R.S. McLaughlin*, 12–13; J. Herbert Hodgins, "Cedar Lodge: The Bermuda Estate of Col. R.S. McLaughlin," *Canadian Homes and Gardens* (July 1938): 18 and 39.

144 *Colonel R.S. McLaughlin*, 47–8; Brass, "The Squire of Oshawa," 95.

145 Duncan McLeod, "They Shoot Canada's Most Expensive Ducks," *Star Weekly* (Toronto), 18 September 1965, 37–39; *Colonel R.S. McLaughlin*, 48–9.

146 Sam McLaughlin to Isabel McLaughlin, 30 October 1934, file 5, box 12; Sam McLaughlin to Isabel McLaughlin, 23 October 1944, file 4, box 11, Isabel McLaughlin Papers, QUA. The 1934 correspondence lists a "Mr. Howe" among the group that went to Long Point. It is unclear whether McLaughlin was referring to C.D. Howe, the future "minister of everything," who at that time remained a relatively unknown. In later years, Howe would become a regular visitor at McLaughlin's camp at Cap Chat (see chapter 5).

    McLaughlin built a car for the Duke, when the Duke was the Prince of Wales, in 1927, and in 1936, when he was about to assume the throne early in 1936 as Edward VIII, McLaughlin completed a custom-made limousine for the soon-to-be king. See Robertson, *Driving Force*, 257–8.

McLaughlin had Junius and Harry Morgan at his camp in Cap Chat in
1934. It should be noted that the 1944 correspondence above does not
name the Duke of Windsor specifically, but other evidence almost defin-
itively indicates that McLaughlin was referring to the Duke of Windsor.
The Duke and Duchess were visiting the United States during that period
so that the Duchess could undergo an appendectomy in New York; they
arrived in July and departed in early November. The lieutenant governor
of Ontario, meanwhile, was visiting the Dunlap Observatory in Rich-
mond Hill on 23 October 1944. "Windsors Leave City," *New York Times*,
6 November 1944, 21; "Personal Notes," *Globe and Mail*, 24 October
1944, 12.

147 Indicative of the pace and travel characteristic of McLaughlin's social
world, he wrote Isabel in 1938: "I have been skidding around to New
York, Montreal and Toronto to the Horse Show, and all that sort of
thing, so have not had time to settle down to write." Sam McLaughlin to
Isabel McLaughlin, 24 November 1938, file 5, box 11, Isabel McLaughlin Papers, QUA.

148 "Canadian Famous Players Elects," *New York Times*, 30 April 1931, 35;
Colonel R.S. McLaughlin, Appendix 1; *New York Times*, 18 December
1934, 36; "Increase in Gold Mined in Ontario," *New York Times*, 17 September 1933, N9.

149 See Accounts Books, file 19, box 4, George McLaughlin Papers, QUA;
B.M. Greene, ed., *Who's Who in Canada, 1934–35* (Toronto: International Press, 1935), 169; Edward Beatty to Ross H. McMaster, 30 January 1931, 247, vol. 136, box 23-005, President's Letter-Books, Canadian
Pacific Railway Archives [CPRA]. Another example of the deepening integration of General Motors in Canada's business world, in 1933 the *Financial Post* reported that Canadian Industries Limited was "understood
to hold a substantial block" of General Motors stock, although Canadian
Industries announced that it had sold some of its GM holdings in its
1929 annual report. See "General Motors Cut Affects Income of C.I.L.,"
Financial Post, 14 May 1932, 2.

150 Edward Beatty to S.C. Mewburn, 15 August 1934, 518, vol. 149, box
23-007; Edward Beatty to James A. Richardson, 30 July 1935, 280, vol.
153, box 23-008, President's Letter-Books, CPRA.

151 *Colonel R.S. McLaughlin*, Appendix 1.

152 William Fong, *J.W. McConnell: Financier, Philanthropist, Patriot* (Montreal and Kingston: McGill-Queen's University Press, 2008), 181–240.

153 Financial Statement, 31 December 1932, file 9, box 1, George McLaughlin Papers, QUA.

154 "Big Share Holdings Summarized by SEC," *New York Times*, 17 September 1936, 23. See also "More Holdings Detailed," *New York Times*, 1 February 1935, 29.

155 Sam McLaughlin to C.S. Mott, 13 April 1944, and see also Sam McLaughlin to C.S. Mott, 24 September 1943, file "R.S. McLaughlin – Correspondence – General," box LH S 100 BIO, "McLaughlin Family, Murphy Family," McLaughlin Library.

156 Martin J. Sklar, *The Corporate Reconstruction of American Capitalism, 1890–1916* (Cambridge: Cambridge University Press, 1988), 27–8.

157 White, *Making Cars in Canada*, 47.

158 "General Motors of Canada – 'A Good Neighbor,'" *Financial Post*, 9 July 1938, file "General Motors of Canada Clippings (Part 1), 1922–1949," Financial Post Fonds, LAC.

159 *GM in Canada*, 10. The auto industry experienced a greater decline than manufacturing as a whole between 1929 and 1933: employment declined 54 per cent and value of production declined 76 per cent in the auto industry, whereas manufacturing as a whole experienced declines of 31 per cent and 50 per cent, respectively. By contrast, between 1933 and 1937, the value of automobile production rose 220 per cent, compared to 85 per cent for manufacturing as a whole. See *Canadian Automotive Industry*, 8.

160 "R.S. McLaughlin, Back in Oshawa, Happy at Result," *Ottawa Morning Citizen*, 24 April 1937, file 68, vol. 383, Strikes and Lockouts files, RG 27, LAC.

161 See Melvyn Dubofsky and Warren Van Tine, *John L. Lewis: A Biography* (New York: Quandrangle, 1977), 222–47.

162 For more background, see Sidney Fine, *Sit-Down: The General Motors Strike of 1936–1937* (Ann Arbor: University of Michigan Press, 1969), 63–99 and 121–55.

163 Advocating collaboration with communists, Lewis asked rhetorically: "Who gets the bird, the hunter or the dog?" Quoted in John T. Saywell, *"Just Call Me Mitch": The Life of Mitchell F. Hepburn* (Toronto: University of Toronto Press, 1991), 303.

164 Fine, *Sit-Down*, 309. The strikers had acted independently of John L. Lewis, who had expected to organize steel before the auto industry. See Dubofsky and Van Tine, *John L. Lewis*, 255 and 272–3.

165 Pendergest, "Labour and Politics in Oshawa," 136. Communist leader Tim Buck claimed that Joe Salsberg, the party's union strategist, made the call to Thompson. See Saywell, *"Just Call Me Mitch,"* 580–1 (n. 5).

166 Abella, "Oshawa 1937," 95–6.

167 McLaughlin, "The McLaughlin Legacy," 77; David Croll to Mitch Hepburn, 14 April 1937, file 1, box 267, Hepburn Papers, AO.

168 Quoted in Abella, "Oshawa 1937," 99.

169 Abella, "Oshawa 1937," 102.

170 See Abella, "Oshawa 1937," 102; Saywell, *"Just Call Me Mitch,"* 582–3 (ns. 16 and 18); Robertson, *Driving Force*, 276–9.

171 J.H. MacBrien to Ernest Lapointe, 8 April 1937, file 115, vol. 28, Ernest Lapointe Papers, MG 27 III B 10, LAC.

172 MacBrien to Lapointe, 9 April 1937, MacBrien to Officer Commanding, Toronto, 9 April 1937, file 115, vol. 28, Lapointe Papers, LAC.

173 MacBrien to Lapointe, 8 April 1937, file 115, vol. 28, Lapointe Papers, LAC.

174 Hepburn's refusal to grant striking GM employees relief pay was thus explained by his secretary: "The Prime Minister feels that these employees are rejecting the opportunity of work at fair wages and fair hours and that, as a result, they need not look to the Government for relief assistance." See Roger Elmhirst to Miss N.H. Wark, Assistant Deputy Minister, Department of Public Welfare, Unemployment Relief Branch, 8 April 1937, file 1, "Oshawa Strike: General," box 282, Hepburn Papers, AO.

175 Quoted in Abella, "Oshawa 1937," 103.

176 McCullagh claimed in 1943: "I alone fought the C.I.O. in this province in 1937. Whatever Mr. Hepburn did as a government leader, was only as a result of information I placed before him in regard to government and trade unionism, a subject on which I have some knowledge." McCullagh to R.H. McMaster, 18 January 1943, quoted in Brian J. Young, "C. George McCullagh and the Leadership League" (MA thesis, Queen's University, 1964), 47.

177 "Mr. Hepburn Helping Labour," *Globe and Mail*, 13 April 1937, file 68, vol. 383, Strikes and Lockouts files, LAC.

178 Abella, "Oshawa 1937," 105–7; J.L. Cohen's statement to the press, which gives his account of the 16 April meeting with Hepburn, can be

found in file 2609, vol. 8, J.L. Cohen Papers, MG 30 A 94, LAC; "Strikers Ask Dominion Help in Mediation," *Ottawa Morning Journal*, 13 April 1937, "Oshawa Citizens to Assist Auto Strikers," *Toronto Clarion*, 13 April 1937, file 68, vol. 383, Strikes and Lockouts files, LAC; Alex Hall to Mitch Hepburn, 13 April 1937, file 1, "Strike at Oshawa: General," box 282, Hepburn Papers, AO.

179 "Queen's Park Enrolls 200 Special Officers for Emergency Duty," *Toronto Star*, 13 April 1937, file 68, vol. 383, Strikes and Lockouts files, LAC; Hepburn to Lapointe, 13 April 1937, and Lapointe to Hepburn, 14 April 1937, file "Strike at Oshawa: General (Folder #1)," box 282, Hepburn Papers, AO; "Strikers Ask Dominion Help in Mediation," *Ottawa Morning Journal*, 13 April 1937, "Ottawa Fears to Take Hand in G.M. Strike," *Toronto Telegram*, 14 April 1937, file 68, vol. 383, Strikes and Lockouts files, LAC; Mackenzie King to Hepburn, 13 April 1937, file "Strike at Oshawa: General (Folder #1)," box 282, Hepburn Papers, AO; "Determined Labor Won't Be Hoodwinked – Premier,' *Toronto Star*, 13 April 1937, "Hepburn Will Ask for Resignations of Croll, Roebuck," *Montreal Gazette*, 14 April 1937, file 68, vol. 383, Strikes and Lockouts files, LAC; James Y. Murdoch to Hepburn, 9 April 1937, Robert H. Bryce to Hepburn, 14 April 1937, file "(Oshawa Strike) Favourable Comments on Government Action," box 283, Hepburn Papers, AO; "Hepburn Given Fullest Support of War Veterans," *Hamilton Spectator*, 14 April 1937, file 68, vol. 383, Strikes and Lockouts files, LAC.

180 "Veterans Protest Premier's Actions – Pass Resolution," *Oshawa Daily Times*, 14 April 1937, file 68, vol. 383, Strikes and Lockouts files, LAC. Colonel Fraser Hunter, Liberal member of Toronto–St Patrick, was appointed by Hepburn to recruit for the special force. See "Queen's Park Enrolls 200 Special Officers for Emergency Duty," *Toronto Star*, 13 April 1937, file 68, vol. 383, Strikes and Lockouts files, LAC.

181 See Laurel Sefton MacDowell, "The Career of a Canadian Trade Union Leader," *Relations Industrielles* 43, no. 3 (1988): 610–11.

182 Memo, OPP Staff Inspector, 12 April 1937, file "Strike at Oshawa: General (Folder #1)," box 282, Hepburn Papers, AO.

183 "Charges Company Tried to Incite Plant Disorders," *Ottawa Morning Citizen*, 19 April 1937, file 68, vol. 383, Strikes and Lockouts files, LAC.

184 Eric Havelock, "Forty-Five Years Ago: The Oshawa Strike: Part One," *Labour/Le Travail* 11 (Spring 1983): 120.

185 A memo in the Hepburn papers dated 22 April indicates that some workers felt "Thompson and Martin had not kept faith with the men." Certainly, the morale of the workers had been strained. On 17 April, Hepburn received the following report, based on information from OPP constable Alex Wilson: "The pickets are half-hearted. Many members left last night's meeting long before the meeting was finished." On 20 April, GM workers having voted against terms of settlement offered by GM the day before, Mitch Hepburn met with a dozen strikers, "many of whom were unionists," who "claimed to represent from 1,000 to 1,500 of the strikers who were ready to accept General Motors' terms of settlement." Hepburn appears to have tried to exploit this discord. He wired Sam McLaughlin the same day: "Would urgently request that you advise Carmichael to suspend any negotiations with strikers until your return Thursday morning. Would also ask you to give no statements regarding situation until I have had chance to confer with you. Confidential reports indicate total collapse of strike imminent." Memo on Oshawa Strike Situation, 22 April 1937, file 1, "Strike at Oshawa: General," box 282, Hepburn Papers, AO; "Strikers See Hepburn," *Ottawa Morning Citizen*, 21 April 1937, file 68, vol. 383, Strikes and Lockouts files, LAC; R.H. Elmhirst to Hepburn, 17 April 1937, and Hepburn to R.S. McLaughlin, 20 April 1937, file 1, "Strike at Oshawa: General," box 282, Hepburn Papers, AO.

186 Laurel Sefton MacDowell, *Renegade Lawyer: The Life of J.L. Cohen* (Toronto: University of Toronto Press, 2002), 89. Pressure from the United States may have also helped encourage a settlement, at least if one is to accept George McCullagh's later lament that the CIO would have been defeated more decisively "had it not been for prominent industrial leaders in the United States." See Young, "Leadership League," 44.

187 "McLaughlin in Bermuda Silent About Strike," *Toronto Telegram*, 12 April 1937, file 68, vol. 383, Strikes and Lockouts files, LAC.

188 "Oshawa Celebrates End of Automobile Strike," *Ottawa Evening Citizen*, 24 April 1937, file 68, vol. 383, Strikes and Lockouts files, LAC; "R.S. McLaughlin, Back in Oshawa, Happy at Result."

189 This statement was made in a response to a solicitation for a Victoria College fundraising drive. Professor Eric Havelock of Victoria College had, to George's mind, delivered a particularly "bitter" and "biased" speech during the strike. See George McLaughlin to John A. Rowland,

17 April 1937, file 29, box 1, George McLaughlin Papers, QUA. George
McLaughlin was also upset with Mayor Hall. He demanded that Hall
clear up a bank loan, which George had guaranteed. For more detail, see
Don Nerbas, "The Politics of Capital: The Crisis and Transformation of
Canada's Big Bourgeoisie, 1917–1947" (PhD thesis, University of New
Brunswick, 2010), 338–40.

190 Nelson Lichtenstein, *Walter Reuther: The Most Dangerous Man in Detroit* (Urbana and Chicago: University of Illinois Press, 1995), 75.

191 Sam McLaughlin to Isabel McLaughlin, 9 June 1937, file 5, box 12,
Isabel McLaughlin Papers, QUA. McLaughlin again mentioned the
possibility of leaving Canada, should the political climate worsen.
"If conditions get much worse here," he worried, "I will probably get
through my work and retire to Bermuda or something like that."

192 McCullagh to McLaughlin, 26 January 1945, quoted in Young, "Leadership League," 47.

193 George Drew to Earl Rowe, 26 April 1937 and 30 April 1937, file 1256,
vol. 123, George Drew Papers, MG 32 C 3, LAC; Saywell, *"Just Call
Me Mitch,"* 329; "Memorandum C.I.O. Issue," [This memo is dated 23
April at the top, but 9 May at the bottom. It was obviously not completed
until 9 May. Though no author is indicated, internal evidence indicates
that the memo was written by George Drew's wife, Fiorenza Johnson
Drew. She apparently sent a copy of the memo along with a letter to her
father, Edward Johnson, famed Canadian operatic tenor.], file 33, vol.
303, Drew Papers, LAC; Rowe to Drew, 2 May 1937, file 1256, vol.
123, Drew Papers, LAC.

194 *Saturday Night*, 13 May 1937, clipping, in file "CIO #4," box 267, Hepburn Papers, AO.

195 See Ibid.

196 King Diaries, 27 February 1939 and 10 September 1939, LAC.

197 C.H. Millard to J.L. Cohen, 11 June 1937, file 2611, vol. 8, Cohen Papers, LAC.

198 Gordon Sinclair, "Mr. R.S. ... ," in *Achievement* (Oshawa: General Motors of Canada, 1943), 35.

199 Beatty to J.W. McConnell, 17 November 1938, 224, vol. 165, box 23-
008, President's Letter-Books, CPRA.

200 C.H. Millard to J.L. Cohen, 26 July 1937, file 2611, vol. 8, Cohen Papers, LAC.

5 Engineering Canada

1 C.D. Howe to E.P. Murphy, 10 December 1946; C.F. Sise to Howe, 6
December 1946; Howe to C.F. Sise, 28 November 1946; Howe to E.K.
Davis, 30 January 1945; vol. 189, C.D. Howe Papers, MG 27 III B 20,
Library and Archives Canada [LAC]; Eric Hutton, "What You Don't
Know About Howe," *Maclean's* (21 July 1942): 57; Duncan McDowall,
*Steel at the Sault: Francis Clergue, Sir James Dunn, and the Algoma
Steel Corporation 1901–1956* (Toronto: University of Toronto Press,
1984), 234.

2 Depictions of Howe tend to focus upon his postwar performance. As
such, Howe has often been presented as a straightforward representative
of business and its Americanizing tendencies after the Second World
War. For this perspective, see, for example, Donald Creighton, *The
Forked Road: Canada, 1939–1957* (Toronto: McClelland & Stewart,
1976), 263–73, 284 and passim.

3 In their substantial 1979 biography of Howe, Robert Bothwell and William Kilbourn concluded that "Howe's essence was power; his spirit was
action; his style was rough and ready, but effective." Uncommitted to
any particular ideology, they suggest, Howe was primarily interested in
making things work. See Robert Bothwell and William Kilbourn, *C.D.
Howe: A Biography* (Toronto: McClelland & Stewart, 1979), 349. That
conclusion echoed one made two years earlier in a PhD thesis by Stanley
Howe, who considered Howe – in line with Howe's estimation of himself – to be a "builder" above all else. See Stanley Russell Howe, "C.D.
Howe and the Americans: 1940–1957" (PhD thesis, University of Maine,
1977), 26. Differing somewhat from the standard scholarly accounts, Michael Bliss has emphasized Howe's departure from the traditional outlook of the Canadian business community. See Michael Bliss, *Northern
Enterprise: Five Centuries of Canadian Business* (Toronto: McClelland
& Stewart, 1987), 445–477.

4 David F. Noble, *America by Design: Science, Technology, and the Rise
of Corporate Capitalism* (Oxford: Oxford University Press, 1977).

5 See J. Rodney Millard, *The Master Spirit of the Age: Canadian Engineers and the Politics of Professionalism, 1887–1922* (Toronto: University of Toronto Press, 1988).

6 Howe evinced a masculine ideal that approximated closely what Christopher Dummitt has described as the "manly modern." See Christopher Dummitt, *The Manly Modern: Masculinity in Postwar Canada* (Vancouver: UBC Press, 2007), passim.

7 This process can be viewed in terms of a transition towards "managerial capitalism," but it was part of a broader transition – involving the creation of a new managerial role for the state – than has been examined in Alfred D. Chandler's classic account, *The Visible Hand: The Managerial Revolution in American Business* (Cambridge, MA: Belknap Press, 1977), 9–10, 490–3, and passim, which focuses upon the internal transformation of business enterprise and essentially leaves out politics.

8 Bothwell and Kilbourn, *C.D. Howe*, 15–19; Howe, "C.D. Howe and the Americans," 12–14; Grant Dexter, "Minister of Supply," *Maclean's* (15 May 1942): 57–8.

9 Howe, "C.D. Howe and the Americans," 15–16.

10 See E.R. Forbes, "Consolidating Disparity: The Maritimes and the Industrialization of Canada during the Second World War," *Acadiensis* 15, no. 2 (Spring 1986): 3–27.

11 Dunning claimed that he had given Howe an "early start on some things," while Howe "had shown Dunning where much money could be saved on public works." William Lyon Mackenzie King Diaries, 21 October 1935, LAC.

12 Charles F. Wilson, "C.D. Howe: An Optimist's Response to a Surfeit of Grain" (Ottawa: Grains Group, October 1980), 11; Anthony W. Rasporich, "A Boston Yankee in Prince Arthur's Landing: C.D. Howe and His Constituency," *Canada* 1, no. 2 (Winter 1973): 23–4.

13 William Stephenson, "A Yankee Alger in Canada," *Coronet Magazine* (February 1949): 125; "Canada: The Indispensable Ally," *Time*, 4 February 1952, 27, 30; "Beta Gamma Alumnus Is a King's Minister," *The Palm (of Alpha Tau Omega)* (February 1938): 7; Bothwell and Kilbourn, *C.D. Howe*, 29–51.

14 "An Engineer in the Cabinet," *The Canadian Engineer*, 17 December 1935.

15 Bothwell and Kilbourn, *C.D. Howe*, 42.

16 Rasporich, "A Boston Yankee," 27.

17 Norman Lambert Diaries, 30 April 1933, box 9, Norman Lambert Papers, 2130, Queen's University Archives [QUA].

18 Bothwell and Kilbourn, *C.D. Howe*, 55.

19 See, for example, Hutton, "What You Don't Know About Howe," 60.

20 Howe, Memo, "Federal Situation in Fort William Riding," n.d., 177884-8, vol. 207, William Lyon Mackenzie King Papers, MG 26 J1, LAC; Bothwell and Kilbourn, *C.D. Howe*, 58–9; King Diaries, 19 October 1935, LAC; J.W. Pickersgill, *The Mackenzie King Record, 1939–1944*, Vol. 1 (Toronto: University of Toronto Press, 1960), 34.

21 Eric Hutton, "What You Don't Know About Howe," *Maclean's* (21 July 1956): 57.

22 "Mr. Howe's Fine Record," *Globe and Mail*, 5 December 1936.

23 Norman M. MacLeod, "Ottawa Day By Day," *Mail and Empire*, 3 November 1936.

24 This quotation comes from the subtitle of Chandler's *The Visible Hand: The Managerial Revolution in American Business*.

25 C.D. Howe to Mackenzie King, 13 December 1935, 177269-70, vol. 206, King Papers, LAC.

26 "Mr. Howe's Fine Record," *Globe and Mail*, 5 December 1936.

27 Interview with Chubby Power, n.d., 4, file "IV Memoirs, Queen's Professor F.W. Gibson (2)," box 86, Charles Gavin Power Papers, 2150, QUA.

28 King Diaries, 28 October 1935, LAC.

29 C.D. Howe, Memo, "Harbours Commission," 29 October 1935, 177267-8, vol. 206, King Papers, LAC; "To Do Away with Cut-Throat Rates Between Harbors," *Financial Times*, 31 January 1936.

30 Leslie Roberts, *C.D.: The Life and Times of Clarence Decatur Howe* (Toronto: Clarke, Irwin, 1957), 29; "Howe Sees End of C.N. Deficits," *Montreal Gazette*, 3 November 1936.

31 "Central Staff to Handle All New Port Projects at Canadian Ports," *Shipping Register and World Ports*, 7 December 1935.

32 Roberts, *C.D.*, 181, 240–3, and passim.

33 Edward Beatty to C.D. Howe, 1 November 1935, 3, vol. 155, President's Letter-Books, RG 23, Canadian Pacific Railway Archives [CPRA].

34 For the relationship between Beatty and Dunning, as minister of railways and canals, see chapter 2. Beatty also had an amicable relationship with Bennett's minister of railways and canals, R.J. Manion. After Manion took up the portfolio, Beatty wrote him: "I have known you for

so long and so well that I am going to presume upon my acquaintance to the extent of saying that I hope you will always permit me to discuss railway matters with you with the utmost frankness. The interests of the [CPR] in Canada are so varied and so extensive that I feel the Minister of Railways is entitled to know our point of view so that he may give it such consideration as he thinks it merits." See Edward Beatty to R.J. Manion, 14 August 1930, file 9, vol. 3, R.J. Manion Papers, MG 27 III B 27, LAC. Though Beatty was encouraged by Manion's criticism of Sir Henry Thornton's management of the CNR around the time of the Duff Commission, by 1934 Beatty was exasperated by Manion's refusal to consider the policy of railway amalgamation under CPR ownership. See chapter 3. As we shall see, this conflict became even more heated after Manion became leader of the Conservative Party in 1938.

35 King Diaries, 12 August 1936, LAC.
36 C.D. Howe, Memo, "Canadian National Management," 31 January 1936, 187788, vol. 218, King Papers, LAC.
37 "Minister of Transport Speaks," *Canadian Railway and Marine World* (January 1936).
38 C.D. Howe, Memo, "Canadian National Management," 31 January 1936, 187784, vol. 218, King Papers, LAC.
39 "Minister of Transport Speaks."
40 Howe to King, 20 June 1936, 187862, vol. 218, King Papers, LAC.
41 Sir Henry Thornton, memo, n.d., file 1, vol. 22, Manion Papers, LAC.
42 Report by George A. Touche & Company, "Canadian National Railways System: Tentative Outline Covering Dominion of Canada – As Controlling Shareholder," n.d., 2, file 12, vol. 22, Manion Papers, LAC.
43 Bennett to C.P. Fullerton, 15 May 1934, file 12, vol. 22, Manion Papers, LAC.
44 Beatty to Howe, 30 November 1936, 453, vol. 160, President's Letter-Books, CPRA.
45 Beatty to Dunning, 20 January 1937, 387, vol. 161, President's Letter-Books, CPRA.
46 Howe to King, 31 March 1937, 202313, vol. 235, King Papers, LAC.
47 G.R. Stevens, *History of the Canadian National Railways* (New York: Macmillan, 1973), 368.
48 C.A. Ashley, *A Study of Trans-Canada Airlines: The First Twenty-Five Years* (Toronto: Macmillan of Canada, 1963), 1–2; Peter Pigott, *National*

Treasure: The History of Trans Canada Airlines (Madeira Park, BC: Harbour Publishing, 2001), 3–5; Bothwell and Kilbourn, *C.D. Howe*, 104; James A. Richardson, "Canadian Airways Limited: Memorandum," 7 April 1934, 1-6, file 21, vol. 17, Financial Post Fonds, MG 28 III 121, LAC.

49 Pigott, *National Treasure*, 4–6; Richardson, "Canadian Airways Limited," 7.

50 King Diaries, 19 November 1936, LAC. The intensity of the lobbying was later made clear by Howe in the House of Commons: "The question now arises: Have we invited the private interests to participate? That question was asked. May I say we did not need to invite them. They came from every part of Canada and the United States, and put on the most persistent lobby in Ottawa that I have ever seen. The only way we could make progress was to absolutely refuse to talk to them. We said, 'Go back home. We will write our bill, and when we get it written and bring it down you will see it. If you then want any part in it we will give you the chance to discuss the matter.' How could we make a deal on the one hand with perhaps a dozen clamouring aviation companies, or with one of two of them, and on the other hand bring down a bill which the government or parliament would approve? The thing was absolutely impossible. Someone had to make up his mind as to the proper set-up, pick out the responsible people to take care of the initial financing, and after that sit down and see what these services had to offer in the way of experienced personnel, trained operators, and so on; and then decide whether one, two, four or some other number of private companies should be associated in the new organization, whether each would give it strength or otherwise, and then determine the final set-up accordingly. I do not see how any other method could have been used, and I may say I have been living with this problem for several months." *Debates, House of Commons*, vol. 3, 1937, 2216.

51 Lambert Diaries, 17 November 1936, 4 January 1937; 16 January 1937; 1 February 1937, QUA.

52 Beatty to Howe, 12 March 1937, 391, vol. 162, President's Letter-Books, CPRA.

53 Beatty to Richardson, 10 March 1937, 369, and Beatty to Howe, 16 March 1937, 423, vol. 162, President's Letter-Books, CPRA.

54 *Debates, House of Commons*, vol. 2, 1937, 2042.

55 *Debates, House of Commons*, vol. 3, 1937, 2205–7.

56 Ibid., 2208–12.

57 Ibid., 2217.

58 "Aviation Stock Warning Given," *Montreal Gazette*, 5 December 1936, file 18, vol. 206, Howe Papers, LAC.

59 J.W. Dafoe to Grant Dexter, 23 January 1937, file 2, box 1, Grant Dexter Papers, 2142, QUA.

60 Brian J. Young, "C. George McCullagh and the Leadership League" (MA thesis, Queen's University, 1964), 66; Harold A. Naugler, "R.J. Manion and the Conservative Party, 1938–1940" (MA thesis, Queen's University, 1966), 82 and 97.

61 For more on the CPR's activities at the 1938 Conservative convention as well as Beatty's correspondence with McCullagh on the Leadership League, see Don Nerbas, "The Politics of Capital: The Crisis and Transformation of Canada's Big Bourgeoisie, 1917–1947" (PhD thesis, University of New Brunswick, 2010), 379–83.

62 Young, "Leadership League," 153, 157, 186–7; Michael Bliss, *Banting: A Biography* (Toronto: McClelland & Stewart, 1984), 251–2.

63 Howe to Mackenzie King, 20 June 1936, 187862, vol. 218, King Papers, LAC.

64 Howe to Murdoch, 6 February 1939, 232989-9, and 14 February 1939, 232995; Murdoch to Howe, 14 February 1939, 232995, and 15 February 1939, 232997; vol. 275, King Papers, LAC; Young, "Leadership League," 153.

65 Beatty to George McCullagh, 22 February 1939, vol. 180, President's Letter-Books, CPRA.

66 Quoted in Young, "Leadership League," 153.

67 See *Debates, House of Commons, 1939*, vol. 1, 12–14, 186 and 189.

68 George McCullagh, *The Leadership League: Fifth in Series of Five Radio Addresses*, 12 February 1939, 3.

69 Grant Dexter to Victor Sifton, 9 October 1939, file 16, box 2, Dexter Papers, QUA. Dexter was rendered apoplectic by one of McCullagh's addresses, claiming that "McCullagh, himself, has done more damage to the cause than any other damn man I know of. His speeches assuredly will be reproduced in Germany and this kind of thing, if anything, constitutes sabotage. He is a God damned bull head and he absolutely

infuriates me." Dexter to George Ferguson, 22 November 1939, file 16, box 2, Dexter Papers, QUA.

70 Indicative of his willingness to embrace unorthodox economic doctrine "to capture the imagination of the people" and hasten economic recovery, in 1933 Manion proposed to Bennett the initiation of a public works program akin to those devised by Franklin Roosevelt. See Manion to Bennett, 24 August 1933, file 2, vol. 4, Manion Papers, LAC. H. Napier Moore of the *Financial Post* reported that during a trip to Western Canada he "encountered a very strong feeling against Mackenzie King," but neither did he meet "a single person having much faith in Manion." He further explained: "The reasoning of most business men with whom I talked was something like this – 'We certainly haven't any use for Mackenzie King. On the other hand, Manion has given no indications whatever that he is a capable leader. It's a choice between one of the other as against the leader of some newer and untried party. Of the two, perhaps we would be safer in voting for King again, though we certainly don't think he has done much for this country.'" See Moore to Colonel J.B. Maclean, 12 June 1939, file 8, box 6, series 3, Floyd S. Chalmers Papers, F 4153, Archives of Ontario [AO].

71 Cahan to Manion, 25 October 1938, and Manion to Cahan, 27 October 1938, file 12, vol. 65, Manion Papers, LAC; J.M. Macdonnell to Manion, 3 August 1939, and Manion to Macdonnell, 10 August 1939, file 13, vol. 17, Manion Papers, LAC.

72 Beatty to Meighen, 29 May 1939, 119786-8, vol. 188, Arthur Meighen Papers, MG 26 I, LAC; Naugler, "Manion and the Conservative Party," 212.

73 Manion to Errick F. Willis, 23 January 1939, file 12, vol. 65, Manion Papers, LAC.

74 William H. Price to Manion, 14 June 1939, file 13, vol. 17, Manion Papers, LAC.

75 See, for example, "Liberals Want Two Railways Kept Separate," *Ottawa Journal*, 24 July 1939, file 20, vol. 207, Howe Papers, LAC. Manion's past was also coming back to haunt him politically. He had, as Bennett's minister of railways and canals, wielded a hatchet against the beleaguered but still popular CNR president, Sir Henry Thornton. This was great fodder for Liberal propagandists intent on raising concerns about Manion's character and commitment to the CNR. See,

for example, George R. Gardiner to Manion, 14 February 1939, with clipping enclosed from the *Windsor Daily Star*, 13 February 1939, file 3, vol. 66, Manion Papers, LAC. Manion also complained in August 1939 of a Liberal "whispering campaign" being carried out against him among railway workers: "My railway policy is the only one that is before the people outside of unification and if the railway men were wise they would back someone who has been friendly to them but, quite frankly, I do not think the C.N. men as a whole are too friendly, largely because of this type of whispering campaign that is being carried on." See Manion to C.D.H. MacAlpine, August 1939, file 6, vol. 16, Manion Papers, LAC.

76 Manion to Hanson, 3 August 1939, 46377, vol. 62, R.B. Hanson Papers, MG 27 III B 22, LAC. For more on Manion's persisting effort to reach an accommodation with Montreal in this period, see Nerbas, "Politics of Capital," 388–9.

77 Clement Leibovitz and Alvin Finkel argue in their monograph *In Our Time: The Chamberlain–Hitler Collusion* (New York: Monthly Review Press, 1997) that Chamberlain's policy represented an attempt to collaborate with Hitler in a broader strategy designed to crush communism. They argue that appeasement is a myth.

78 Young, "Leadership League," 25. See also, for example, the editorial "Duff Cooper's Resignation," *Montreal Star*, 3 October 1938, 10. Preference for accommodation with Hitler and Mussolini was assumed in Sir James Dunn's correspondence with R.B. Bennett in 1938. Dunn, the president of Algoma Steel, wrote to Bennett: "I find myself very pessimistic on the European outlook but I am glad to say that Max [Lord Beaverbrook] with much better information and finer judgement on these matters does not agree with me. He thinks Chamberlain will find a way to friendship with both Germany and Italy." See Sir James Dunn to R.B. Bennett, 11 March 1938, file "A-C, January 1, 1937 to May 1938," vol. 179, James Hamet Dunn Papers, MG 30 A 51, LAC.

79 Arthur Bartlett, "A Yank Bosses Canada's War Effort," *Boston Herald*, Magazine Section, 23 November 1941, 18.

80 For an overview of the crown corporations established during the war, see J. de N. Kennedy, *History of the Department of Munitions and Supply: Canada in the Second World War. Vol. 1: Production Branches and Crown Companies* (Ottawa, 1950), 287–520.

81 The *Globe and Mail* called for the establishment of a National Government almost immediately after the outbreak of war. See "Canada's
Paramount Duty," *Globe and Mail*, 5 September 1939, file 294, vol. 32,
George A. Drew Papers, MG 32 C 3, LAC. Manion wrote to Hanson on
20 September 1939: "There is a good deal of talk of a National Government and quite a few people are insisting that King should immediately
propose such." But Manion and Hanson were reticent about the idea,
feeling that it might destroy the party. See Manion to Hanson, 20 September 1939, 46411, and Hanson to Manion, 24 September 1939, 46412,
vol. 62, Hanson Papers, LAC.

82 Hanson to Manion, 30 October 1939, 46420, vol. 62, Hanson Papers,
LAC.

83 Days before King announced the election, Manion stated that he did not
expect King to call an election until July. See Manion to D.M. Hogarth,
20 January 1940, file 9, vol. 17, Manion Papers, LAC. Manion had been
contemplating adopting a National Government platform since the fall.
See Naugler, "R.J. Manion and the Conservative Party," 244–8.

84 Manion to Harry Price, 2 February 1940, file 10, vol. 16, Manion Papers,
LAC. Manion wrote: "I may say that Wes Gordon mentioned it to me
first and I was so emphatic and rough in my refusal that he didn't push it
very far." See Manion to D.M. Hogarth, 2 February 1940, file 9, vol. 17,
Manion Papers, LAC.

85 For accounts of this episode, see clipping, Politicus [Lou Golden],
"Now It Can Be Told," *Saturday Night*, 4 May 1940, and R.A. Bell to
Lou Golden, 7 May 1940, file 9, vol. 16, Manion Papers, LAC. Bell
served as secretary of the Conservative Party under Manion, and his
7 May letter to Lou Golden generally confirms the truth of Golden's
piece published in *Saturday Night*. Bell wrote Golden: "I am at liberty
to tell you with a few exceptions of minor nature – such as time and
place – the latter part of your article is substantially correct. A proposal
was made to the effect that Dr. Manion should announce that he was
ready, after the election, to retire in favour of someone else to lead a
National Government – by whom such person would be chosen was
not mentioned. The proposal amounted to this – Dr. Manion was to run
the election and then step aside in favour of someone else." Manion's
response to the proposal can be found in the same file in "Memoran-

dum," n.d.; though the name of the author is not on the document, internal evidence reveals that it was Manion. This same file also contains a statement that was obviously intended for Manion to sign, which would have committed Manion to the Hogarth-Meighen plan. The statement declared: "when the coming election brings into being a National Government Party with a majority from which the Cabinet is to be chosen, the leadership of that majority will be as open as the Conventions of my own party now are; my leadership will be confirmed or another will be chosen by the caucus of the National Government Party members elected to the House of Commons." The statement may have been enclosed with the memo Manion received from Hogarth, but it also may have derived from another source, since numerous individuals approached Manion with the proposal in the first half of February. In particular, Manion identifies Colonel C.E. Reynolds, president of the Canadian Corps Association, as being at the centre of an effort to have Manion step down after winning the election. Manion wrote Mitch Hepburn on 7 February to alert him to Reynolds' activities:

I have just had a long visit from our mutual friend, Colonel Reynolds. He is a decent chap, and I have no doubt he means well, but he has had about as much political experience as one of those little children of yours.

Probably you know his proposal ["I doubt it – Bob" is written in pencil above this section of the text] because he states that you agree with him, namely, the proposal to the effect that I should on some platform in the near future make a statement to the effect that if I win the election I will immediately offer my resignation in order that the elected representatives may choose someone else if they desire.

In the following paragraph Manion describes his earlier interactions with Hogarth, but without using names, and provides more evidence to suggest that Meighen was behind the memo attached with Hogarth's correspondence. Manion describes the author of the memo as "someone whom you know but for whose political opinion none of us has much regard." See Manion to Hepburn, 7 February 1940, file 9, vol. 17, Manion Papers, LAC. On 12 February, Manion again referred to the activities of Reynolds and the earlier proposal received through Hogarth. He wrote C.O. Knowles, editor of the *Toronto Telegram*: "there is a very stupid play being attempted – inspired, I think, by that chap, Colonel Reynolds of the Corps, but supported by a few." Manion considered the movement to be ill conceived but worried that some of its supporters harboured "ulterior motives." "The thing is so silly, to my mind," continued Manion, "that it is more than stupid. One man sent me a memo about it which he said was made up by A.M." Manion to Knowles, 12 February 1940, file 9, vol. 17, Manion Papers, LAC. This episode has also been examined in Naugler, "R.J. Manion and the Conservative Party," 269–74.

86 Memo, "Post Policy," 1 March 1940, file 8, box 6, series 3, Chalmers Papers, AO.

87 Allan Ross of Toronto wrote to Manion: "[Harry Price] told me in great confidence about how you handled Jack McConnell yesterday in Montreal. Jack is an old friend of mine. We were on the War Trading Board in the Great War together. I completely endorse your firm stand against him. We don't need the Montreal Star or anyone else unless Jack wants to completely co-operate. Next time I see you I will tell you a lot about the sugar industry and which I have not felt was pertinent just yet. I cannot prove that there is an understanding with the present government, but every sign points to it." Allan Ross to Manion, 12 March 1940, file 9, vol. 16, Manion Papers, LAC.

88 William Fong, *J.W. McConnell: Financier, Philanthropist, Patriot* (Montreal and Kingston: McGill-Queen's University Press, 2008), 398.

89 Reginald Whitaker speculates that the Liberals succeeded in raising more money from St James Street because of Manion's unpopularity in those circles. "Certain big interests which had deserted the Tories over R.J. Manion's alleged 'radicalism' on the railway unification issue – the CPR, the Bank of Montreal, and the McConnell Montreal Star interests – appear to have positively supported the Liberal cause this time out, although in what amounts one can speculate." Reginald Whitaker, *The Government Party: Organizing and Financing the Liberal Party of Canada, 1930–58* (Toronto: University of Toronto Press, 1977), 126 and 197.

90 Dexter, memo, 11 and 27 January 1940, in *Ottawa at War: The Grant Dexter Memoranda, 1939–1945*, eds Frederick W. Gibson and Barbara Robertson (Winnipeg: Manitoba Record Society, 1994), 36 and 41–2.

91 "Says Manion Threatens National Radio," *Ottawa Journal*, 11 March 1940, file 21, vol. 207, Howe Papers, LAC.

92 Kennedy, *History of the Department of Munitions and Supply*, 5.

93 W.C. Clark, memo, 30 November 1939, in *Ottawa at War*, 21. Camp-
    bell's personality is touched upon in Mira Wilkins and Frank Ernest Hill,
    American Business Abroad: Ford on Six Continents (Detroit: Wayne
    State University, 1964), 118.

94 F.S. Chalmers, memo, 2 June 1940, file 9, box 6, series 3, Chalmers Pa-
    pers, AO. Campbell aired his criticism of the government early on, in an
    October 1939 interview with Chalmers of the *Financial Post*, a consis-
    tent critic of the government's war planning. See F.S. Chalmers, memo,
    26 October 1939, file 8, box 6, series 3, Chalmers Papers, AO. Indeed,
    Campbell was known to have "gossiped freely with visitors about his
    experiences and unburdened himself in the Rideau Club and elsewhere."
    See Chalmers, memo, 2 June 1940.

95 Bothwell and Kilbourn, *C.D. Howe*, 129–30.

96 Chalmers, memos, 21 June 1940, 7 June 1940, and 15 August 1940, file
    9, box 6, series 3, Chalmers Papers, AO.

97 "One-man Co-ordinator Needed for Supply," *Financial Post*, 8 June
    1940; "Mr. Howe Is No Superman," *Financial Post*, file 38, vol. 214,
    Howe Papers, LAC.

98 Chalmers, memo, to H.T. Hunter, 3 March 1940 and Chalmers, memo, 27
    February 1940, file 9, box 6, series 3, Chalmers Papers, AO. H.D. Burns,
    assistant manager of the Bank of Nova Scotia, and James S. Duncan, gen-
    eral manager of Massey-Harris, among others, also told Chalmers that the
    Financial Post had become too political. Chalmers also reported that the
    Canadian Chamber of Commerce had been discussing the idea of estab-
    lishing another business journal, which would compete with the *Financial
    Post*. Chalmers argued that the *Post* needed to temper its tone so as to
    "make sure we are carrying the business community along with us and
    really getting our story over to the public." See Chalmers, memo, 21 Feb-
    ruary 1940, file 9, box 6, series 3, Chalmers Papers, AO.

99 Bothwell and Kilbourn, *C.D. Howe*, 135.

100 Ibid., 134–5.

101 "Work and Pay in Race to Win, Howe Exhorts," *Globe and Mail*, 5 Sep-
    tember 1940, file 21, vol. 207, Howe Papers, LAC.

102 Gibson and Robertson, *Ottawa at War*, 62–3.

103 Chalmers, memo, 15 October 1940, file 9, box 6, series 3, Chalmers
    Papers, AO. Howe's deputy minister, G.K. Sheils, had, of course, no
    actual power; thus, MacMillan believed someone with experience in

big industry could assume the position and be delegated real power. W.E. Scully, the steel controller, favoured the more drastic solution of the appointment of an industrial "boss." Scully, too, was troubled by the department's lack of organization. Howe, Scully complained, was too casual and operated by addressing problems through informal talks. Scully also complained about the department's "1929" mood in regard to spending. Scully quoted one dollar-a-year man as having said "What's half a million dollars?" Interestingly, Howe would be tarred for having uttered a similar phrase, which in fact he never said – "What's a million?" – during an exchange in the House of Commons in the 1950s.

104 See R.A. Farquharson, memo, 21 January 1941, 257254, vol. 304, King Papers, LAC. MacMillan also believed that E.P. Taylor; Frank Ross, director-general of naval armaments; and W.F. Drysdale, director-general of munitions production should be replaced. MacMillan also brought in General Motors of Canada vice-president Harry J. Carmichael to assist him at the War Requirements Board, and he believed Carmichael could be of use to Munitions and Supply; Howe held a similar view and appointed Carmichael to help with gun production.

105 Bothwell and Kilbourn, *C.D. Howe*, 142–8; "Tirade in Parliament Accomplishes Nothing," *Toronto Telegram*, 28 February 1941, file 22, vol. 207, Howe Papers, LAC.

106 Dexter, memo, 2 April 1941, file 19, box 2, Dexter Papers, LAC.

107 Bothwell and Kilbourn, *C.D. Howe*, 148.

108 See J.L. Granatstein, "The York South By-Election of February 9, 1942: A Turning Point in Canadian Politics," *Canadian Historical Review* 48, no. 7 (June 1967): 142–58.

109 Beatty to Meighen, 22 May 1940, 95086, vol. 156, Meighen Papers, LAC.

110 Newman, *The Canadian Establishment*, Vol. 1 (Toronto: McClelland & Stewart, 1975), 290–1. Max Meighen did not use the term *class war*, but it nonetheless captures his meaning: "I wrote my father in 1944 that in my normal life expectancy all western nations would be under dictatorship and the form in the United States would be military. My nephew accused me of advocating dictatorship. I said, 'I don't advocate it at all. I say it's just bound to occur. There are more have-nots than there are haves, and you're going to end up in a German post-first-war type of inflation.'"

111 "The Optimistic Mr. Howe," *Montreal Gazette*, 29 November 1943, file
     25, vol. 209, Howe Papers, LAC.
112 "War Against Japan Aids Conversion: Howe," *Globe and Mail*, 29 No-
     vember 1943, file 25, vol. 209, Howe Papers, LAC.
113 New Brunswick lumberman J. Leonard O'Brien approved of Bracken's
     straightforward style and derided the "flag waving, drum thumping, faint-
     ing politicians and what not" at the Winnipeg convention at which Bracken
     was nominated leader. He continued: "No wonder Howard keeled over.
     It was one of the most sensible things he could have done; others should
     have done likewise." O'Brien's reference to "Howard" was perhaps a ref-
     erence to Howard P. Robinson, the subject of chapter 1. O'Brien to R.A.
     Bell, 26 December 1942, file "Convention 1942 Correspondence," vol.
     242, Progressive Conservative Party Papers, MG 28 IV 2, LAC.
114 Grant Dexter, memo, 29 October 1942, 388; J.W. Dafoe to Grant Dex-
     ter, 28 November 1942, 391; J.W. Dafoe to Grant Dexter, 15 September
     1943, 441, in *Ottawa at War*.
115 "Postwar Unemployment Needn't Be Feared, View of Minister of Muni-
     tions," *Globe and Mail*, 14 December 1943, file 16, vol. 209, Howe Pa-
     pers, LAC.
116 R.A. Farquharson, "Howe Plans Three Steps in Industry," *Globe and
     Mail*, 27 January 1941, file 22, vol. 207, Howe Papers, LAC; "Send Mu-
     nitions Chief to Aid U.S.–Canada Economic Plan," *Windsor Daily Star*,
     24 April 1941, file 23, vol. 208, Howe Papers, LAC.
117 Howe, "C.D. Howe and the Americans," 65–6.
118 Neither did Howe hesitate to criticize British ineptitude, to the annoy-
     ance of some of his colleagues. Norman Lambert reported tension within
     the government over attitudes towards the British in 1941. Dexter sum-
     marized the information from Lambert as follows: "Growing tendency
     by some ministers – notably Howe – to belittle British, to harp on their
     stupidity, their blundering. Ralston, too, inclined to take a whack at them
     now and again and King not always flattering. This is very unpleasant to
     Ilsley and some others who are ardent Imperialists and anti U.S." Dexter,
     memo, 21 April 1941, in *Ottawa at War*, 158.
119 P.J. Cain, "Gentlemanly Imperialism at Work: the Bank of England,
     Canada, and the Sterling Area," *Economic History Review* 49, no. 2
     (1996): 336–57. For the Hyde Park Declaration, see J.L. Granatstein
     and R.D. Cuff, "The Hyde Park Declaration, 1941: Origins and Signifi-
     cance," *Canadian Historical Review* 55 (March 1974): 59–80.

120 R.P. Bell to C.D. Howe, n.d., file "Family + Personal, January to August, 1945," vol. 170, Howe Papers, LAC.

121 For an overview of Alcan's evolution, see Isaiah A. Litvak and Christopher J. Maule, *Alcan Aluminum Limited: A Case Study* (Royal Commission on Corporate Concentration, Study no. 13, February 1977).

122 Howe to King, 26 July 1941, 258930-2, vol. 306, King Papers, LAC.

123 Howe tendered his resignation during this episode and claimed he was not receiving the necessary cooperation from his colleagues.

124 Ernest Lapointe to Mackenzie King, n.d., "Thursday night," 259677-9, vol. 307, King Papers, LAC.

125 John Macfarlane, "Agents of Control or Chaos? Arvida Helps Clarify Canadian Policy on Using Troops Against Workers during the Second World War," *Canadian Historical Review* 86, no. 4 (December 2005): 619–40; David Massell, "'As Though There Was No Boundary': The Shipshaw Project and Continental Integration," *American Review of Canadian Studies* 34, no. 2 (Summer 2004): 187–222.

126 Howe to C.W. Sherman, president, Dominion Foundries, Hamilton, Ontario, 3 October 1944, and attached notes, file 91, vol. 189, Howe Papers, LAC. Cabinet colleagues regarded Howe's pronouncements in favour of full employment as "pure CCF." Dexter, memo, 23 December 1943 in *Ottawa at War*, 451.

127 McDowall, *Steel at the Sault*, 178–247.

128 William Mulock, Postmaster General, to Mackenzie King, 17 January 1941, 264337-8; 28 January 1941, 264347-9; and 29 January 1941, 264351-2, vol. 312, King Papers, LAC; Ronald A. Keith, "Transport Titans Lock Horns?" *Financial Post*, 17 January 1942, file 12, vol. 51, Financial Post Fonds, LAC.

129 Howe to A.D.P. Heeney, 20 April 1943, 293884-7, vol. 342, King Papers, LAC.

130 D.C. Coleman to Mackenzie King, 30 March 1944, 309655-68, vol. 357, King Papers, LAC.

131 Howe to A.D.P. Heeney, 20 April 1943, 293884, vol. 342, King Papers, LAC; *Standing Committee of Railways and Shipping, Minutes of Proceeding and Evidence, No. 1, Trans Canada Air Lines Annual Report (1943), 27 March 1944* (Ottawa, 1944), 9; Pigott, *National Treasure*, 160.

132 J.W. Pickersgill, *The Mackenzie King Record, 1939–1944*, Vol. 1 (Toronto: University of Toronto Press, 1960), 648–9.

133 Coleman to King, 30 March 1944, 309655-68, vol. 357, King Papers, LAC.

134 Pickersgill, *The Mackenzie King Record*, Vol. 1, 648–9.

135 "No Order to Break up CPA, Says Howe," *Financial Post*, 8 July 1944, file 13, vol. 51, Financial Post Fonds, LAC.

136 Chalmers, memo, 15 August 1940, file 9, box 6, series 3, Chalmers Papers, AO.

137 Howe to A.D.P. Heeney, 20 April 1943, 293884-7, vol. 342, King Papers, LAC.

138 *Standing Committee of Railways and Shipping*, 35.

139 Pigott, *National Treasure*, 280–1 and 297–8.

140 Ashley, *The First Twenty-Five Years*, see especially chapter 8.

141 Howe to Colin Gibson, Minister of National Revenue, 20 August 1942, file 10, vol. 47, Howe Papers, LAC.

142 See Matthew J. Bellamy, *Profiting the Crown: Canada's Polymer Corporation, 1942–2000* (Montreal and Kingston: McGill-Queen's University Press, 2005).

143 J.W. Pickersgill and D.F. Forster, *The Mackenzie King Record, 1947–48*, Vol. 3 (Toronto: University of Toronto Press, 1970), 273. After negotiations for a customs union with the United States broke down in 1948, Howe "suggested to American officials that the Liberals should 'put a plank in the party platform advocating not merely the reduction, but complete removal of import duties on trade with other countries, provided this could be accomplished on a reciprocal basis in each case.'" See Robert Cuff and J.L. Granatstein, "The Rise and Fall of Canadian–American Free Trade, 1947–8," *Canadian Historical Review* 58,no. 4 (December 1977): 479.

144 Hugh G.J. Aitken, "Defensive Expansionism: The State and Economic Growth in Canada," in *The State and Economic Growth: Papers Held on October 11–13, 1956, under the Auspices of the Committee on Economic Growth*, ed. Hugh G.J. Aitken (New York: Social Science Research Council, 1959), 79–114. Howe also operated effectively within the bureaucratic environment that came to characterize the modern corporation. See McDowall, *Steel at the Sault*, 189–90.

145 Forbes, "Consolidating Disparity."

146 Howe to Robert G. Holmes, 23 June 1944, vol. 170, Howe Papers, LAC.

147 Hansard, 12 September 1945, 117–8, 348536, vol. 387, King Papers, LAC.

352 NOTES TO PAGES 236–8

148 Robert Black, president, subdistrict office, Kingston, Ontario, United
Steelworkers of America, to C.D. Howe, 21 February 1946, 360863, vol.
399, King Papers, LAC; Pickersgill and Forster, *The Mackenzie King Record*, Vol. 3, 340–1.

149 Pat Conroy to C.D. Howe, 27 October 1944, 309736-7, vol. 357, King
Papers, LAC.

150 C.H. Millard to Mackenzie King, 6 September 1945, 348533-4, vol. 387,
King Papers, LAC.

151 Howe to J.M. Gilchrist, vice-president, Searle Grain Company, Limited,
10 September 1945, vol. 171, Howe Papers, LAC.

152 "Postwar Unemployment Needn't Be Feared, View of Munitions Minister," *Globe and Mail*, 14 December 1943, 1, file 16, vol. 209, Howe Papers, LAC.

153 Howe argued "growth itself depends on the efficiency of labor and management, on their willingness to work together for higher standards of
living, and on their mutual determination to give value for costs." He
thus presented a form of cooperation, but it implied a highly unequal
relationship, which appeared natural according to his worldview. See
"Economy Needs Vigorous Unity, Howe Stresses," *Globe and Mail*, 30
October 1946, file 25, vol. 209, Howe Papers, LAC. He also congratulated the Trades and Labour Congress of Canada for remaining aloof
from the postwar strike wave. See "Can Recover Lost Ground," *Ottawa
Journal*, 24 September 1946, file 25, vol. 209, Howe Papers, LAC. For
organized labour and its changing relationship to the state under the
industrial-relations regime of "industrial legality" during this period, see
Peter S. McInnis, *Harnessing Labour Confrontation: Shaping the Postwar Settlement in Canada, 1943–1950* (Toronto: University of Toronto
Press, 2002).

154 Jackson Lears, "The Managerial Revitalization of the Rich," in *Ruling
America: A History of Wealth and Power in a Democracy*, eds Steve Fraser and Gary Gerstle (Cambridge, MA: Harvard University Press, 2005),
181–214.

155 Howe to R.E. Powell, 7 July 1958, file 90-6, vol. 188, Howe Papers,
LAC; Hutton, "What You Don't Know About Howe," 57; Alexander
Barrie, "The 'Devil' You Think You Know," *New Liberty* (December
1953), file 35, vol. 213, Howe Papers, LAC; Dummitt, *The Manly Modern*, 1–27. As the following memo from Grant Dexter suggests, W.A.

Mackintosh's experience in the civil service suggested that Howe was not that dissimilar from his fellow cabinet ministers: "Bill Mackintosh ... fed up with being a civil servant. Has no bump for organization and no temperament for the rough and bruising career of a civil servant. Prefers educating young men with open minds to trying to split open the solid craniums of cabinet ministers in order to get ideas in. Is convinced that there is no such thing as an open-minded minister. All hopeless. Why waste life in trying to reason with them. So, he goes home to Kingston, stars in his eyes, the moment the big show is over. Meantime he essays daily an intellectual form of volleyball – bouncing ideas off Mr. Howe's battleship steel headpiece. Some of 'em bounce pretty far. But perhaps I am exaggerating. He finds that Howe agrees but does he know what he is agreeing with[?]" Dexter, memo, 1 March 1945, in *Ottawa at War*, 498.

156 Pickersgill and Forster, *The Mackenzie King Record*, Vol. 3, 116. In early 1945 Mackenzie King noted: "There is little doubt that Howe has evidently in mind being possibly considered as a successor to myself. There are groups around him who are grooming him for that post. They would be the business groups but he will never be chosen by the party nor would he be able to sit in the Prime Minister's saddle for any length of time. He is too impatient. Has very little political judgment or sense." See J.W. Pickersgill and D.F. Forster, *The Mackenzie King Record, 1944–1945*, Vol. 2 (Toronto: University of Toronto Press, 1968), 357, 364–5.

157 Noble, *America by Design*, xxiiii.

158 C.D. Howe, *The Engineer and Government: The Fifth Wallberg Lecture, Convocation Hall, January 22nd, 1952* (Toronto: University of Toronto Press, 1952), 8.

159 For a discussion of the left's embrace of planning, see Ian McKay, *Rebels, Reds, Radicals: Rethinking Canada's Left History* (Toronto: Between the Lines, 2005), 169–83.

160 Don Nerbas, "Managing Democracy, Defending Capitalism: Gilbert E. Jackson, the Canadian Committee on Industrial Reconstruction, and the Changing Form of Elite Politics in Canada," *Histoire sociale/Social History* 46, no. 91 (forthcoming, May 2013).

161 Chandler, *Visible Hand*.

162 Du Pont sponsored a free enterprise political front, the American Liberty League, which opposed the expanded uses of the state that were being attempted by the Roosevelt administration. See Kim Phillips-Fein,

Invisible Hands: The Making of the Conservative Movement from the New Deal to Reagan (New York: W.W. Norton, 2009), 10–13.

163 "Second Look at a Legend," *Saturday Night*, 1 October 1955, 17, file 35, vol. 213, Howe Papers, LAC.

164 See Alvin Finkel, *Business and Social Reform in the Thirties* (Toronto: James Lorimer, 1979); James Struthers, *No Fault of Their Own: Unemployment and the Canadian Welfare State, 1914–1941* (Toronto: University of Toronto Press, 1981). The general theme of elite political adaptation has also been well established in other works, including J.L. Granatstein, *The Ottawa Men: The Civil Service Mandarins, 1935–1957* (Toronto: University of Toronto Press 1998 [1982]); Douglas Owram, *The Government Generation: Canadian Intellectuals and the State, 1900–1945* (Toronto: University of Toronto Press, 1986); and Barry Ferguson, *Remaking Liberalism: The Intellectual Legacy of Adam Shortt, O.D. Skelton, W.C. Clark, and W.A. Mackintosh* (Montreal and Kingston: McGill-Queen's University Press, 1993).

Conclusion

1 Peter C. Newman, *Flame of Power* (Toronto: Longmans, Green, 1959), 25–6, 44.

2 Grant Dexter, memo, 2 April 1941, file 19, box 2, Grant Dexter Papers, 2142, Queen's University Archives [QUA].

3 T.D. Regehr, *The Beauharnois Scandal: A Story of Canadian Entrepreneurship and Politics* (Toronto: University of Toronto Press, 1990), 182–3.

4 But it should be noted that Taschereau had also sought to counterbalance Holt's influence. See Bernard L. Vigod, *Quebec Before Duplessis: The Political Career of Louis-Alexandre Taschereau* (Montreal and Kingston: McGill-Queen's University Press, 1986).

5 See V.C. Fowke, "The National Policy – Old and New," *Canadian Journal of Economics and Political Science* 18, no. 3 (August 1952): 271–86.

6 Michael Bliss, *Northern Enterprise: Five Centuries of Canadian Business* (Toronto: McClelland & Stewart, 1987), 445–77. See also Peter C. Newman, *The Canadian Establishment*, Vol. 1 (Toronto: McClelland & Stewart, 1975), 313–46.

7 Watt Hugh McCollum [Louis Rosenberg], *Who Owns Canada? An Examination of the Facts Concerning the Concentration of Ownership and Control of the Means of Production, Distribution and Exchange in Canada* (Ottawa: Woodsworth House, 1947), 10–11.

8 Ibid., 8.

9 On the basis of counting directorships, Robert Sweeny has suggested that Toronto was already a more important capital market than Montreal as early as the late 1940s. See Sweeny, "The Evolution of Financial Groups in Canada and the Capital Market, Since the Second World War" (MA thesis, Université du Québec à Montréal, 1980), 133 and 138. Indeed, the total volume of trading on the Toronto Stock Exchange surpassed that of the Montreal Stock Exchange in 1931. See Table A.1 and Table A.3 in Christopher Armstrong, *Blue Skies and Boiler Rooms: Buying and Selling Securities in Canada, 1870–1940* (Toronto: University of Toronto Press, 1997), 305–13.

10 C.B. Macpherson, *The Real World of Democracy* (Toronto: Anansi, 2006 [1965]), 1–16.

11 Howard Robinson to W.C. Milner, 4 March 1935, file 7, W.C. Milner Papers, S11, New Brunswick Museum [NBM].

12 Robinson to Milner, 29 January 1934 and 24 February 1934, file 7, Milner Papers, NBM.

13 C.D. Howe, "Industrial Development in Canada," *Public Affairs* 11, no. 4 (December 1948): 213.

14 See Robert Chodos, *The CPR: A Century of Corporate Welfare* (Toronto: James, Lewis & Samuel, 1973).

15 For an overview of economic policy during the Keynesian era, see David A. Wolfe, "The Rise and Demise of the Keynesian Era in Canada: Economic Policy, 1930–1982," in *Modern Canada, 1930–1980's: Readings in Social History*, Vol. 5, eds Michael S. Cross and Gregory S. Kealey (Toronto: McClelland & Stewart, 1984), 46–78.

16 McCollum, *Who Owns Canada?*, 9.

17 The quotation comes from Murray Ballantyne in Margaret W. Westley, *Remembrance of Grandeur: The Anglo-Protestant Elite of Montreal, 1900–1950* (Montreal: Libre Expression, 1990), 160.

Index

Abella, Irving, 190
Aberhart, William, 111
Abitibi Power and Paper
  Company, 96
Acadians, 36–7, 46
Acworth, W.M., 122
A.E. Ames & Company, 79
Agar, Miles E., 46
Ahearn, Tom, 145
Aiken, South Carolina, 185
Aitken, Hugh, 235
Aitken, Max. *See* Beaverbrook,
  Lord
Alberta, 71, 80, 111
Alger, Horatio, 70, 204, 206
Algoma Steel, 94, 208, 232
Algonquin Hotel, 66
Allan, George W., 84–5, 89
All-Canadian Congress of Labour
  (ACCL), 180–1
Allied War Supplies
  Corporation, 113
Alma, New Brunswick, 33
Aluminum Company of Canada
  (Alcan), 201, 231

American Federation of Labor
  (AFL), 127, 158, 180, 188
American Securities Exchange Act
  (1934), 186
Ames, A.E., 92
Anderson, J.T.M., 92
Anglo-French War Supply Board,
  225
anti-Semitism, 95, 103, 245
Argus Corporation, 244
Armstrong, Christopher, 51
Arvida, Quebec, 231
Ashfield, Lord, 130
Associated Press, 63
Atholstan, Lord, 15, 67, 123–4, 126
Atlantic Bond Company Limited, 34
Automotive Industries of Canada
  (AIC), 173
automobile industry, 153; Canadian
  economy, changing role in, 5,
  159, 169, 187–8, 198–9, 244;
  carriage manufacturers, connec-
  tion to, 163, 318n28; department
  stores, as competition to, 324n80;
  parts making, 177, expansion

of, 187; political economy of,
157–8, 170; political weakness of,
173–4, 187; St James Street support for, 174; seasonal nature of,
182; U.S. technology, dependence
upon, 163–4. *See also* Conservative Party; Great Depression;
McLaughlin, R.S.; protective
tariff; United States; workers:
autoworkers
Automobile Workers' Industrial
Union of Canada (AWIUC), 181
aviation, 214, 232–4. *See also*
Canadian Airways Limited;
Canadian National Railways;
Canadian Pacific Railway; Howe,
C.D.; Trans-Canada Air Lines

Bahamas. *See* Nassau, Bahamas
Ballantyne, C.C., 139, 141
Bank of Canada, 111
Bank of England, 141
Bank of Montreal, 20, 91, 98, 113,
125, 138, 142, 145, 185–6, 223–4.
See also St James Street
Banting, Dr Frederick, 219
Banque Canadienne Nationale, 130
Barclays Bank, 135
Baring Brothers, 206
Bassett, John, 91, 138, 197, 222
Bateman, George, 226
Bathurst Power and Paper, 44, 48
Baxter, J.B.M., 35, 40, 43, 45–6,
48–9, 53; ideology of, 43–4,
57, 59
Beaverbrook, Lord, 29, 51, 63, 66,
92, 230
Beaverdale, Saskatchewan, 73
Beatty, Edward, 5, 17–18, 63, 91–2,
94–6, 100, 113, 153, 160, 165,

183, 185, 198, 200, 219, 221, 223,
232–3, 243, 247–9; Bennett,
R.B., efforts to influence, 137,
139–41, 143, view of and relationship with, 128, 131, 137–8,
144, 304–5n63; businessmen as
citizens, view of, 147; business
philosophy of, 120, 133; CPR, rise
within, 118–19, stock holdings
of, 119; death of, 152; democracy,
view of, 147–8, 150, 313n172,
314n176; Dunning, Charles, view
of, 88, 105; early life of, 117–18;
elitism of, 134, 144; French
Canadians, perception of, 150;
Howe, C.D., conflict with and
views of, 202, 210, 213–18, 225,
244; ideology of, 117, 147–51;
laissez-faire views of, 148, 218,
235, 311–12n160; Meighen,
Arthur, attitude towards, 135, 228;
meritocratic style of, 118–21, 152;
National Government, campaign
for, 136, 138–9, 145, 297n177,
307–8n120, 310n146; nationalism
of, 140, 235; plutocrat, as, 146;
public opinion, efforts to shape,
136–7, 147, 150–1, 220, opposition to and suspicion of, 132, 134,
139–40, 147, 151; railway question, and, 101, 114–15, 125–7,
130, 132, 135–6, 151–2, 233–4;
railway unification plan of, 133;
Robinson, Howard, relationship
with, 58, 276–7n130; socialism
and communism, efforts to com-
bat, 119, 148–50; university chancellor, as, 119, 148–50
Beatty (née Powell), Harriet, 117
Beatty, Henry, 117

Beauharnois Company, 242
Beauharnois scandal, 99
Beckert, Sven, 260n25
Béique, Frédéric Ligori, 95
Belgo-Canadian Paper Company, 98
Bell, George M., 85
Bell, Ralph P., 227, 231
Bellamy, Matthew, 234
Bell Telephone of Canada, 20, 66,
    186, 201; New Brunswick Tele-
    phone Company, relationship with,
    33–4, 53–6
Belnap, LaMonte J., 99
Bennett, R.B., 98, 101–2, 108,
    129–31, 137, 140, 215, 217; big
    business, relationship with, 138–9;
    CNR, policy of retrenchment for,
    211–13, 220; CPR, relationship
    to, 128, 308n122; National Gov-
    ernment, attitude towards, 138–9,
    141–2, 152, 307n115; "New Deal"
    address, 60; protective tariff,
    support for, 92, 128; railway leg-
    islation of, 135. See also Beatty,
    Edward
Bermuda, 158, 185
Bickell, J.P., 186, 190
Biermans, Hubert, 98
Birks, William, 174, 308–9n125
Black, Conrad, 79
Black, George Montagu (Monte), 79
Black, W.A., 20
Blacks Harbour, New Brunswick,
    49–50
Bliss, Michael, 124, 336n3
Board of Grain Commissioners,
    205
Board of Railway Commissioners,
    121
Bogart, Clarence E., 163

Borden, Robert, 36, 99, 106–7,
    143–4, 219; party system, attempt
    to change, 122; railway policy of,
    87, 121–5
Boston, Massachusetts, 204; capital
    from, 35, 48
Bothwell, Robert, 226, 336n3
bourgeoisie (Canadian): capital
    accumulation strategies of, 235,
    (1920s) 4; class consciousness
    of, 59; conflict and competition
    within, 123–4, 215–16; decline
    of (and growing government
    autonomy from), 7, 25, 64, 72,
    116, 152–3, 200, 202, 242–4, 250;
    definition of, 10–11; democracy,
    suspicion of, 59, 65, 68, 115, 140,
    151–2, 245; ethnic composition
    and identity of, 12–14; geograph-
    ical concentration of (1917), 13,
    (post-1945), 244; historiography
    on, 9, 254–6n16; history of, 7–8;
    interlocking directorships of, 20;
    laissez-faire views of, 58, 63,
    66–8, 72, 144, 203; left-nationalist
    interpretation of, 249, 256–7n17;
    masculinity of, 11–12; merito-
    cratic style and ideology of, 4,
    11; newspapers, control over, 67;
    provincial (New Brunswick), 47,
    50; religious affiliations of (1917),
    13–14; right-wing political con-
    solidation of, 21, 63, 72, 142, 153,
    160, 197–8, 243–4; social life of,
    51, 66, 94–5, 119; sociological
    characteristics of (1917), 12–14,
    (post-1945), 244;. See also Mc-
    Laughlin, R.S.; Montreal; Toronto;
    passim
Boy Scouts of Canada, 119

Bracken, John: businessmen's support for, 60, 63, 80, 229, 233, 284n49, 349n133
Brennan, J. William, 75, 80
Bretton Woods, 231
British Empire, 61, 115–16, 119, 128, 142, 151, 165, 197, 200, 219, 250; Canadian political economy, role in, 6, 158, 170, 203, 235, 240–1, 243; decline of, 25, 230–1; imperialist sentiment, 229. *See also* Robinson, Howard
Britishness, 169, 172, 193, 327n117. *See also* Robinson, Howard
"British world," 12, 243
Broomfield, H.L., 178
Brown, H.A., 179–80
Brown, Robert Craig, 8, 107
Bruce, Herbert A., 141–2, 196, 199, 219–20
Bryce, Robert H., 192
Buck, Tim, 66
Buenos Aires, Argentina, 206
Buick Motor Car Company, 159, 163
Burchill, G. Percy, 33, 48, 50, 54
Bury, George, 118

Cahan, C.H., 99, 144, 210, 221, 312–13n167
Calder, J.A., 75, 77
California: Gold Rush, 117
Cameron, Kirk, 78, 100
Campbell, M.S., 180
Campbell, Wallace R., 224–5; wife of, 220
Canada Cycle and Motor Company (CCM), 164
Canada Power and Paper, 96–9, 186, 293n141

Canadian Airways Limited (CAL), 214–15. *See also* Canadian Pacific Railway
Canadian Bankers' Association, 130
Canadian Bank of Commerce, 84, 124, 165, 174, 225
Canadian bourgeoisie. *See* bourgeoisie
Canadian Broadcasting Corporation, 220–1
Canadian Brotherhood of Railway Employees, 146, 180
Canadian Chamber of Commerce, 147
Canadian Council of Agriculture, 73
Canadian Engineers' Institute, 210
Canadian Federation of Home and School Associations, 182
Canadian Forum, 134–5
Canadian General Electric, 185
Canadian Group of Painters, 184
Canadian Industries Limited, 330n149. *See also* Purvis, Arthur
Canadian International Paper. *See* International Paper
Canadian Manufacturers' Association, 225
Canadian National Railways (CNR), 101, 111, 125, 143, 151, 208, 216–17, 220; board of trustees of, 211–12; capital structure of, 128–9, changes to, 212–4; creation of, 5, 87, 122; employees of, 126; Liberal support for, 141; management of, 129. *See also* Bennett, R.B.; Canadian Pacific Railway; Howe, C.D.; railway question; Thornton, Henry; Trans-Canada Air Lines

Canadian National Railways Act
(1919), 125
Canadian Northern Acquisition Bill,
122
Canadian Northern Railway, 5, 115,
121–2, 124, 212
Canadian Pacific Railway (CPR):
5, 29, 44, 66–7, 71, 96, 98, 100,
113, 114, 118–20, 126, 128, 159,
185–7, 202, 211, 216, 218, 232;
business elite, place within, 124;
CAL, acquisition of, 217; CNR
competition to, 87, 127, 213; CPA,
233–4; Conservative Party, relationship to, 122–4, 135, 218–21,
223, 229, 233; decline of, 116–17,
153, 169, 219, 241; Dunning,
Charles, relationship with, 87–90,
employment of, 93; Liberal Party,
relationship to, 122–3, 233–4;
National Government, support of,
138–9; national economy, place
within, 158, 235, 244; nation-state,
relationship to, 115–16, 250;
non-Canadian investment in, 140,
151; Prairie West view of, 87–8;
profits of, 127; pubic attitude towards, 137; second syndicate, formation of, 117; Senate, influence
within, 127, 135, 221; "sinister influence" of, 134. *See also* Beatty,
Edward; Bennett, R.B.; Canadian
Airways Limited; Conservative
Party; Meighen, Arthur; Seigniory
Club; St James Street
Canadian Press, 63, 223
Canadian Radio Broadcasting
Commission, 56, 145
Canadian Red Cross, 183

Canadian Shield, 214
Cap Chat, Quebec, 185, 201
capitalism: changing shape of
Canadian, 18, 111, 169, 230–1;
corporate, 202; managerial, 25,
153, 239, 249; state management
of, 24; U.S. literature on the his-
tory of, 9; welfare, 170, 178. *See
also* automobile industry; British
Empire; economy; National
Policy; pulp and paper indus-
try; railways; Second Industrial
Revolution; Second World War:
wartime economy
Cariboo, British Columbia, 117
Carmichael, H.J., 197
Caton's Island, New Brunswick, 51
Central Telephone Company, 33–4
CFBO (radio), 56
Chalmers, Floyd S., 101, 130, 137,
151, 225–7
Chamberlain, Neville, 222
Chandler, Alfred, 208, 239, 337n7
Chevrolet, Louis, 167
Chevrolet Motor Company, 167
Chicago Tribune, 97
Chipman, George F., 75
Chrysler, Walter P., 168
Chrysler Corporation, 158, 181, 186
CHSJ (Saint John), 56
Cockshutt, Colonel Henry, 20, 95
Cockshutt Plow Company, 20
Cohen, J.L., 192, 194
Coleman, D.C., 232–3
Committee for Industrial Or-
ganization (CIO), 157, 160,
188–97, 220; sit-down strikes
(U.S.), 188–9, 195. *See also*
Drew, George; General Motors

of Canada; Hepburn, Mitchell;
McCullagh, C. George
Communist Party (and communists),
58, 66, 104, 183, 189
Conant, Gordon D., 174, 176
conscription, 36–7, 77, 122, 223
Conservative Party, 101, 108, 134,
139; big business within, 223;
CPR, changing relationship with,
122, 128, 219, 223; fracturing
of, 143–4, 221; New Brunswick,
43–7; Ontario, view of automo-
bile industry, 173–4; Progressive
Conservative Party, 229; railway
unification, position on, 143,
218–21; right-wing in decline of
within, 229. *See also* Canadian
Pacific Railway; Manion, Robert;
Meighen, Arthur; protective tariff;
Saint John, N.B.; working class
Consolidated Mining and Smelting
Company of Canada (Cominco),
185
Co-operative Commonwealth
Federation (CCF), 21–4, 57,
81, 104, 149, 228–9; opposition
to, 60, 64–5, 109, 139. *See also*
Howe, C.D.
Connors Brothers Ltd, 49–50
Consolidated Paper Corporation, 99,
113, 224. *See also* Canada Power
and Paper
continental integration, 6, 153,
230–1, 235, 240–1, 244, 250. *See
also* United States
Cook, Ramsay, 8
Cottrelle, George, 226
Cox, George Albertus, 124, 174, 186
Creelman, A.R., 118
Crerar, T.A., 71, 83, 87, 106, 215

Croll, David, 190, 192
Cross, J.A., 93
Cruikshank, Ken, 122
Currie, Sir Arthur, 91, 138–9, 149
Curry, Nathaniel, 185

Dafoe, J.W., 78, 83, 123, 126, 130–1,
139, 218, 229; Dunning, Charles,
view of, 85–6, 88
Dalhousie, New Brunswick, 49
Dalhousie University, 203. *See also*
Howe, C.D.
Dandurand, Raoul, 91
Darling and Pearson (architectural
firm), 164
Davies, W. Rupert, 84
Davis, Donald, 319n30, 323n67
Dawes, Norman J., 20, 186
Dawson, A.O., 174, 310–11n148
Deacon, T.R., 79
Delaware and Hudson Railway
Company, 130
democracy: contestation of, 245;
elite scepticism for, 59, 115, 144;
erosion of, 150; limitation of, 240.
See also bourgeoisie; Beatty,
Edward; liberalism; National
Government; public opinion
Dennis, William, 32–3
Detroit, Michigan, 186
Dexter, Grant, 78, 130–1, 143, 229
Diefenbaker, John: government of,
234
Direct Legislation League, 75
Dodds, Jackson, 91, 138
Dominion Bank, 163, 165
Douglas, Lewis Williams, 149
Drayton, Henry, 121
Drew, George: CIO, opposition to,
160, 196–7, 199, 220

Drummie, T.F., 39, 56
Duff, Lyman, 114, 130
Duff Commission. *See* Royal Commission to Inquire into Railways and Transportation in Canada
Dummitt, Christopher, 12, 237–8
Duncan, James S., 347n98
Dunn, James, 29, 51, 66, 94, 232, 343n78
Dunning (née Rowlett), Ada, 74, 101
Dunning, Charles, 16–17, 111–13, 140, 145, 147, 160, 170, 202, 205, 207, 214–15, 238, 243–4, 246–7; big business, involvement with, 93, 113, 224, public association with, 94, 108, 112; bipartisan support for, 107–8; businessmen's support for, 79–80, 91–3, 106–7, 289n107; Canada Power and Paper, reorganization of, 96–9; conservatism of, 81–3, 102–4, 109–10, 239, 296n163; democratic outlook of, 75–6; early life and career of, 73–4; fiscal conservatism of, 79–80, 84, 107–10; Great Depression, response to, 102–4; health problems of, 110; King, W.L.M., as prospective successor to, 83, 105, 112, criticism of, 100–1, 105; Liberal Party (federal), entry into, 86, support for, 109–10, 224; meritocratic depiction of, 72–3, 80, 83–5, 88; minister of finance, as, (1929–1930) 90–2, (1935–1939) 110–11; minister of railways and canals, as, 87–90; Ottawa, settlement in, 90; plutocrat, as, 99–100; Prairie West, estrangement from, 89, 92–4, 111–12; private life of, 74, 93, 101; Progressive Party, attitude towards, 78, 82, 285n61, 286–7n80; progressivism of, 70–1, 79–80, 86, 102, 111–12; protective tariff, attitude towards, 78, 90–2, 112; railway question, position on, 100–2, 294–5n157; Saskatchewan premier, becomes, 78; social mobility of, 69–70, 72; Toronto, departure for, 105. *See also* Beatty, Edward; Canadian Pacific Railway; King, W.L.M., National Government; Thornton, Henry; Union government
Dunning Committee: formation of, 96; members of, 292–3n140
Duplessis, Maurice, 150
du Pont, Pierre S., 167–8
Du Pont Company, 240
Durant, William C. (Billy), 163, 166–9
Dysart, A.A., 59

Eagle, John, 122
economy: Canadian, 158, 169, 235, 243. *See also* automobile industry; British Empire; capitalism; National Policy; pulp and paper industry; railways; Second Industrial Revolution; Second World War: wartime economy; passim
Edmonton, Alberta, 137
Edward VIII, King (Prince of Wales and Duke of Windsor), 151, 185, 201, 329–30n146
elections: federal, (1911) 122, (1917) 36, 37, 122, (1921) 78, 123, (1925) 83, 125, (1926) 127 (1930) 92–3, 223, (1935), 106, 146–7,

(1940), 223–4; New Brunswick
(1925), 43–7, 92; Saskatchewan,
(1921) 77–8, (1929), 92
Elgin, Albert County, New
Brunswick, 31
Emmerson, H.R., 34
Empire Free Trade campaign, 63,
230
England, 13, 74; investment from,
140
English, John, 122
Enniskillen, Ontario, 160–1
Enterprise Foundry, 43
Estabrooks, T.H., 33–4, 62
Evans, John, 82
Evening Times-Globe (Saint John),
56

fascism, 59, 64–5, 148
Family Compact, 64
Famous Players Canadian
Corporation, 63, 185
Farmers' Union, 80–1, 104
Federal Aircraft Company, 227
Federal Light and Traction of New
York, 37
Ferguson, Howard, 173
Fielding, W.S., 78–9
"finance capital," 8
Financial Post, 33, 38, 46–7, 52–3,
96–8, 101, 187, 202, 223;
criticism of Liberal government,
225–8. *See also* Chalmers, Floyd
Finkel, Alvin, 14, 241
Finlayson, R.D., 108
First World War, 36, 222; financial
impact of, 5, 121; Thornton,
Henry, role in, 125; veterans of,
193–4

Fisher, W. Shives, 43
Flavelle, Joseph, 92, 123, 126, 130,
132, 164–5, 222, 303n36; business
philosophy of, 133; CPR monop-
oly, opposition to, 124, 133
Flint, Michigan, 157, 163, 195
Fong, William, 223
Forbes, E.R., 205, 235
Ford, Henry, 163, 177
Fordism, 177
Ford Model T, 177
Ford Motors, 158; of Canada, 163,
177, 181, 220, 224, workforce of,
172; Highland Park plant, 177
Forsey, Eugene, 10, 70, 148,
312–3n167
Fort William, Ontario, 205, 207, 224
Fort William Liberal Association,
208
Foster, W.E., 36–7, 40, 266–7n40
Fowler, Frank O., 83, 89
Fraser, Donald, 44, 48
Fraser Companies, 42, 44, 48
Frost, Stanley Brice, 149
Fullerton, C.P., 211, 213

Gardiner, Jimmy, 76–7, 86, 89, 92
Gelech, William, 189, 197–8
General Motors (U.S.), 166–9, 181;
marketing innovations of, 178;
UAW-CIO, and, 189
General Motors of Canada, 92; Bank
of Montreal, account with, 185;
corporate paternalism of, 169;
expansion of, 170–1, 177, 187–8;
formation of, 166–9; Industrial
Relations Department of, 178;
McLaughlin Carriage Company,
origins as, 159–63; McLaughlin

Motor Car Company, formation of, 163; national economy, as exemplar of changes in, 18, 199; Ontario government, relationship to, 190; strikes at, (1928) 159, 179–81, (1937) 157–8, 160, 188–98; women at, 182; workforce, ethnic composition of, 172; working conditions at, 179–82

Germany, 8

Gibb, Sir Alexander (and Gibb Report), 209

Gibson, Alexander "Boss," 30

Girl Guides, 183

Glassford, Larry, 128

Globe (Saint John), 39

Globe (Toronto), 101, 106, 136, 140–1, 145, 184

Globe and Mail (Toronto), 67, 191, 209. *See also* McCullagh, C. George

Godbout, Adélard, 231, 242

Godin, Sévère, 242

Golden Square Mile. *See* Montreal: Square Mile

Goodenough, F.C., 135

Goodyear Tire, 186

Gordon, Sir Charles, 20, 95, 99, 138, 145, 174, 186

Gordon, W.A. (Wes), 223

Gouin, Lomer, 79, 123

government. *See* bourgeoisie; public debt and spending; public enterprise; passim

Graham, Hugh. *See* Atholstan, Lord

Graham, Roger, 123, 128

Grain Growers' Company (Manitoba), 71

Grain Growers' Guide, 75

grain marketing: cooperative. *See* Saskatchewan Co-operative Elevator Company; Saskatchewan Grain Growers' Association

Grand Falls (hydro-electric project), 44

Grand Trunk Railway, 5, 87, 115–16, 122–3, 129, 161–2, 212

Grand Trunk Pacific Railway, 5, 74, 87, 117, 121–2

Grant, George, 249

Graustein, A.R., 44, 48–9

Great Depression (of the 1930s), 5, 57–60, 102–4; impact of, 92, 116, 128–9, 143, 207, 241, 244, in automobile industry, 159, 182–3, 193, 198, 331n159, in U.S., 240. *See also* Dunning, Charles; Oshawa; pulp and paper industry; railways; Robinson, Howard

Great Eastern Railway, 125

Great Lakes, 117

Great-West Life Assurance, 84

Green, Howard, 217

Group of Seven, 184

Gundy, J.H., 96–7, 99, 173, 186, 215

Halifax, Nova Scotia, 13, 204

Halifax Herald. See Dennis, William

Hall, Alex, 192

Hanna, D.B., 126

Hanson, R.B., 42–3, 46, 50, 53, 59, 129, 134, 222. *See also* Robinson, Howard

Harbours Board Bill, 209–10

Harbours Commissions, 209

Harbord Collegiate, 117–8

Harris, Forbes & Company, 35

Havelock, Eric, 193–4
Haydon, Andrew, 38, 40
Heaps, A.A., 181
Hepburn, Mitchell, 208; anti-CIO coalition government, attempt to form, 196–7; CIO, opposition to, 157, 160, 189–97, 199, 219, 334n185; strike (1937), role in, 190
Heron, Craig, 10
Herridge, W.D., 137
Highfield, J.B., 197, 199
Hilferding, Rudolf, 8
Hobbs, John, 118
Hogarth, Don, 223
Hogg, T.H., 201
Holt, Herbert, 25, 51, 95–6, 130; economic outlook and interests of, 3–5, 7, 20, 35, 124, 186, 242–3; National Government, support for, 138, 145; railway question and, 125, 127; shooting of, 99, 294n151
Holmes Foundry: sit-down strike at, 157; 189
Howe (née Worcester), Alice, 205–7
Howe, C.D., 21–4, 74, 94, 200, 248–9; administrative centralization, advocacy for, 210; big business-state relations, restructuring of, 202, 216–18, 222, 226, 232, 235, 239–40, 243–4, 249; Britain, attitude towards, 208, 349n118; business elite, relationship to, 201–2, 215, 225, 228, 231, 233, 236–8, 240–1, 243–4, 353n156; capitalist ideology of, 203, 218, 230, 232, 234–5, 237–40; CBC, and, 220–1; CCF, opposition to, 229; C.D. Howe & Company,

205–6; CNR, management of, 211–14, 220; continentalism of, 230–1; early life of, 204; Dalhousie University, at, 204–5; decisiveness and management style of, 221, 227–8, 231, 238; "dollar-a-year-men," and, 224–5; engineer, as, 202–3, 218, 235, 240; expertise, attitude towards, 211, 240; gendered ideas and style of, 207–8, 237–8; ideology of, 6–7; labour unions, hostility towards, 203, 207, 231–2, 235–7; Liberal Party, and, 207–8, 238; lobbying, attitude towards, 340n50; managerial ethic of, 203, 206–8, 239; meritocratic style of, 207, 237–8, 240; minister of munitions and supply, as, 222, 224–32; minister of reconstruction, as, 232, 234, 236–7; minister of transport, as, 209–18; national economy and nationalism, vision of, 205, 230–1, 235, 238–9; nonpartisan attitude of, 206, 208; social and cultural life of, 201, 206, 237–8; TCA, formation of, 216–17. See also Beatty, Edward; King, W.L.M.
Howe, Stanley Russell, 230
Hudson, A.B., 83
Hudson Bay Railway, 86, 89, 172
Hudson's Bay Company, 85
Hungerford, S.J., 131–2, 220
Hunter, Horace T., 227
Hyde Park Declaration, 230–1

Ilsley, J.L., 215, 227
Imperial Economic Conference (1932), 94
Imperial Life Assurance Company, 80

Imperial Munitions Board, 165, 222, 225
Intercolonial Railway, 87, 122, 287–8n90
International Nickel Company of Canada (Inco), 159, 185–6
International Paper, 66; Canadian International Paper, parent company of, 48–9, 96–7; Grand Falls, acquisition of, 47–9. *See also* Robinson, Howard; Veniot, Peter
Ireland, 13; Northern, 117
Irving, K.C., 30, 56, 66, 244
Irwin, Roger, 190
Iselin, Ernest, 135

Jackson, Gilbert E., 113
James Richardson & Sons Ltd, 20
J.C. Mackintosh & Company, 34
Johns Hopkins Hospital, 33, 51
Jones, Walter, 107–8
J.P. Morgan & Company, 168

Kaiser, T.E., 172, 193
Kaufman, Louis G., 167
Keller, K.T., 171
Kennedy, John, 76
Keynes, John Maynard, 71. *See also* Keynesianism
Keynesianism, 16, 65, 71, 110
Kilbourn, William, 226, 336n3
Killam, Izaak Walton, 29
King, James H., 38
King, William Lyon Mackenzie, 66, 72, 84, 87, 90, 92, 93, 101–2, 123, 134, 147, 152, 160, 191, 199, 214–15, 219, 222–3; administration of, 129, 134; big business, relationship with, 71, 106, 112,

128, 175, 197, 226, 233, 241; Dunning, Charles, relationship with and view of, 99–100, 105–8; Hepburn, Mitchell, conflict with, 192, 195; Howe, C.D., relationship with and view of, 207–8, 210–11, 236, 238; National Government, opposition to, 135, 138–9, 141–3, 145–6, 307–8n120; railway question, attitude towards, 125–7; Robinson, Howard, attitude towards, 37, 42; *Telegraph-Journal* (Saint John), perception of, 47; western progressives, efforts to court and relationship with, 70, 83, 86–7. *See also* Dunning, Charles; Liberal Party
King-Byng affair, 87
King's County Record (Sussex), 32
Kirkland Lake Gold Mines, 186
Kiwanis Club, 144
Korneski, Kurt, 258n19
Ku Klux Klan, 46, 92–3, 269n65

Labour Party (Britain), example of, 82
Lambert, Norman, 73, 102, 105, 108, 201, 207
Lapointe, Ernest, 83–4, 157, 190, 195, 215, 232
Larabee, J. James, 107
Laurier, Wilfrid, 37, 77
"Laurier boom," 115, 162
Lawson, Ray, 215, 227
Laycock, David, 280n6
Leacock, Stephen, 166
Leadership League, 142, 197, 218–21, 228, 243
League for Social Reconstruction (LSR), 149–50

Lears, Jackson, 11, 84, 237
Leiscestershire, England, 69, 73
Leman, Beaudry, 130
Lend Lease Agreement, 230–31
Lewis, John L., 188, 331n163
liberalism: classical, 71, 81, 102–4, 109–10, 112, 148, 203, 232, 235, 243, antidemocratic association of, 144, 245; during the Second World War, 226
"liberal order," 64, 66, 104
Liberal Party, 72, 145; automobile tariff policy of (federal), 19, 173–7; big business influence within and relationship to, 79, 105, 123, 125–6, 224, 346n89; federal-provincial party relations, 77–9, 83, 86; financing of (federal), 93; King-Hepburn feud, 208; leftward shift within (federal), 110, 229, 232; Quebec, in, 79, 231; SGGA, relationship with (Saskatchewan), 75, 77. See also Canadian National Railways; Canadian Pacific Railway; Dunning, Charles; *Financial Post*; Howe, C.D. King, W.L.M.; protective tariff; Saint John, N.B.
Lichtenstein, Nelson, 195
Lindsay, Sir Charles, 144
Lismer, Arthur, 184
London, England, 97, 129, 141; City of, 135, 151. See also England
London School of Economics, 149
Long Point Company, 185
Lord, J.S., 46
Loree, Leonor Fresnel, 130–3
Loyalists: commemoration of, 61–3
Lucerne-in-Quebec, 105. See also Seigniory Club

Lucerne-in-Quebec Community Association Limited, 95
Luther, Craig & Company, 99
Luther, W.E.J., 99

MacBrien, J.H., 191
Macdonald, Angus L., 201
Macdonnell, J.M., 221
MacDougall, J.H., 208
MacDowell, Laurel Sefton, 194
Macfarlane, John, 232
Mackenzie, Sir William, 5, 87, 115, 128–9
Maclean's, 84, 167
MacMillan, H.R., 226–8, 244
Macpherson, C.B., 75, 245
Macpherson, J.E., 53
Magill, Robert, 205
Maharg, J.A., 78
Mail and Empire (Toronto), 208
Manion, Robert J., 113, 207, 342n70, 344–6n85; Beatty plan, view of, 137; Conservative Party leader, as, 219, 221; minister of railway and canals, as, 129–30, 220; National Government, adoption of, 223; railway unification, position on, 143, 221, 338–9n34, 342–3n75
Manitoba, 71, 76, 80
Mann, Churchill, 184
Mann, Donald, 87, 115, 128–9
Maple Leaf Milling Company, 105
Maritime Board of Trade, 51
Maritime Farmer, 39
Maritime Homestead. See Dennis, William
Maritime Rights. *See* Robinson, Howard
Marquis, Greg, 63 .

Marr, William, 170
Marsh, D'Arcy, 131
Marsh, Leonard, 148–9
Martin, Homer, 188, 192
Martin, W.M., 69, 75, 77, 78
Massachusetts Institute of
    Technology (MIT), 203–4
Massey family, 117
Massey, Vincent, 84, 142
Matheson, W.A., 85
McAvity, G. Clifford, 66
McAvity, George, 37–8
McAvity, J.L., 33
McCarthy, Osler, Hoskin and
    Creelman, 118
McClure, W. Chester S., 108
McConnell, J.W., 15, 20, 113, 186,
    223–4, 297n177, 346n87
McCullagh, C. George, 15, 63,
    67, 199, 215, 219–22, 228–9,
    341–2n69; CIO, opposition
    to, 160, 191, 196–7, 332n176,
    334n186; Dunning, Charles, view
    of, 17; Leadership League, and,
    142, 218–20
McDougald, W.L., 99, 294n150
McDowall, Duncan, 202
McFarlane, Paul, 54–5
McGibbon, J.A., 175
McGibbon, Peter, 129
McGill University, 91, 119, 148–50
McGregor, Gordon M., 163
McIntyre Porcupine Mines Ltd, 186
McIvor, Dan, 207–8
McKay, Ian, 64, 66
McKenna, J.D., 38–9, 56, 287–8n90
McKenzie, J. Vernon, 84
McLaughlin (née Mowbray),
    Adelaide, 164, 179, 182–3

McLaughlin, Christine, 182
McLaughlin, Eleanor (Billie), 164,
    184
McLaughlin, George, 158–9, 167–8,
    323n66; apprenticeship of, 161–2;
    investments of, 186; Oshawa, as
    leader within, 171–2; politics of,
    176, 183, 195, 220
McLaughlin, Isabel, 172, 184
McLaughlin, John James (Jack), 162,
    315–6n12
McLaughlin (née Scott), Mary, 161
McLaughlin, Robert, 158, 167; leg-
    acy of, 169; McLaughlin Carriage
    Company, and, 160–3, 315n10,
    316n16; workers, and, 161–3, 180
McLaughlin, R.S. (Sam), 18–19,
    92, 95, 199–200, 236, 243–4,
    247–8; apprenticeship of, 162;
    automobiles, transition to the
    manufacture of, 158–9, 166–7;
    business type, as, 167; Canadian
    bourgeoisie, integration into, 159,
    185–8; capital accumulation strat-
    egies (and identity) of, 6, 19, 165,
    186–7, 198, 200; Durant, Billy,
    relationship with, 163–4, 166–9;
    early life of, 160–2; GM, sale to,
    167–8, 321n52, influence and
    role within, 168–9, 171, 323n67;
    leisure interests of, 162, 165–6;
    McLaughlin Carriage Company,
    involvement in, 158; meritocratic
    style and beliefs of, 166, 198, 200;
    militia, support for, 172; mining
    interests of, 186–7; National Gov-
    ernment, support for, 160, 196;
    Oshawa, as leader within, 171–2,
    174–6; Parkwood, 164–5, 184–5;

paternalism of, 159, 166, 168, 172,
178–80; protective tariff, defense
of, 173, 175–6; right-wing associations of, 197, 219, 239; Russians,
distrust of, 172; social and cultural
life of, 159, 164–6, 171, 183–5,
201; strike (1937), perception of,
188, 194–5; U.S., connections
to, 162–3, 165, 185–6, 199; U.S.
labour "agitators," perception
of, 180, 195; workers, estrangement from, 19, 158–60, 183, 193,
relationship with, 166, 178–81
McLaughlin Carriage Company.
See General Motors of Canada;
McLaughlin, R.S.
McLean, A. Neil, 49–50
McLean, Angus, 39–40, 43, 47, 57,
270n67; Veniot, Peter, opposition
to, 44–6
McLean, Hugh H., 57
McMaster, Ross, H., 20, 95, 138, 186
McMillan, John F., 137
McNair, J.B., 66
Meighen, Arthur, 14, 40, 57, 87, 176,
223, 229, 295n159; CPR, relation-
ship to, 123, 125, 128, 135, 143–4,
218–19, 221, 228; Conservative
Party, attempt to lead (1942), 63,
197, 228, 243;
St James Street, relationship to,
43. *See also* Beatty, Edward
Meighen, Frank, 95
Meighen, Max, 228
Meredith, Fred, 142
Meredith, Vincent, 125
Messer, Don, 56
Metropolitan Railways, 130
Mewburn, S.C., 20

Michigan, 189
Millard, C.H., 190, 193
Miller, Erastus S., 80
Miller-Barstow, D.H., 118
Mills, C. Wright, 11
Mills, Sean, 150
Miramichi Lumber Company, 44
Mitchell, Walter G., 123
modern corporation, the: interpreta-
tions of, 9; political nature of, 15.
See also Chandler, Alfred
Molson, Herbert, 145, 174
Monarch Life Assurance Company,
85
Moncton *Times*, 41
Monro, C.F., 56
Montebello, Quebec, 93
Montreal, 13, 51, 53–4, 87, 94,
97–9, 102, 105, 108, 113, 115,
123–4, 128, 138, 140–2, 144, 186,
220, 229, 242; bourgeoisie of, 70,
91, 119; businessmen, 148, 218,
attitude towards *Financial Post*,
225–6; relative decline of, 169,
244; Square Mile, 3, 119, 250. *See
also* St James Street
Montreal *Gazette*, 137–9, 145, 229.
See also Bassett, John; White,
Smeaton
Montreal Light, Heat & Power
Consolidated, 242
Montreal *Star*, 67, 123–4, 126, 145,
223
Montreal Stock Exchange, 97, 99,
355n9
Moore, John E., 37
Moorhouse, Hopkins, 73
Moose Jaw, Saskatchewan, 78
Morgan, Arthur Eustace, 149

Morgan, Harry, 185
Morgan, Junius II, 185
Mosher, A.R., 180
Motherwell, W.R., 75–6
Mott, C.S., 186–7
Mount Allison Academy, 32
Mount Royal Club. *See* social
    clubs
Murdoch, James Y., 192, 228; "state
    socialism," fear of, 220
Murphy, Frank, 189
Murray, George, 83
Murray, Gladstone, 221
Murray, Walter Charles, 130

Nash, C.W., 321–2n55
Nassau, Bahamas, 51, 201
Naylor, Tom, 257n17
National Breweries. *See* Dawes,
    Norman
National Club. *See* social clubs.
National Government, 17, 101–2,
    107, 115, 130, 160, 196, 222–4,
    229, 243, 344n81, 344–6n85;
    antidemocratic implications of,
    137, 140; big business support for,
    143, 145, 307n115, 310–1n148;
    British example of, 130, 142;
    campaign for, 135–46; Dunning,
    Charles, association with, 105–6,
    295n159, 297n177, 307n115;
    League for, 144; Liberal opposi-
    tion to, 141–2; public opposi-
    tion to, 146, 152, 224. *See also*
    Beatty, Edward; Bennett, R.B.;
    Canadian Pacific Railway; Holt,
    Herbert; King, W.L.M.; Manion,
    Robert; McLaughlin, R.S.; railway
    question

National Liberal Federation, 102,
    207
National Policy, 161; history of the,
    8; political economy of the, 4, 6,
    8, 50, 68, 115, decline of, 116,
    153, 202, 228, 235, 240–1, 243–4,
    250; CPR role within the, 8, 218.
    See also Prairie West
National Trust Company, 124, 165,
    174
Neatby, Blair, 107
Neill, C.E., 42–3, 268n49
Nelles, H.V., 51
New Brunswick Board of Public
    Utilities Commissioners, 52
New Brunswick Broadcasting Com-
    pany, 56
New Brunswick Electric Power
    Commission, 36
New Brunswick Loyalist Society, 62
New Brunswick Museum, establish-
    ment of, 62–3
New Brunswick Power Company,
    48; founding of, 35; public hear-
    ings on, 37; opposition to, 38;
    Saint John plant, expropriation of,
    55. *See also* Robinson, Howard
New Brunswick Publishing Com-
    pany, 39, 56
New Brunswick Telephone Com-
    pany, 33–4, 42–3, 52–7, 59,
    275n113. *See also* Robinson,
    Howard
New Deal (U.S.): example of, 60–1,
    147; opposition to, 149
New Despotism, The (Hewart), 104
New England, 32
Newfoundland, 13, 152
Newman, Peter C., 9, 56, 228

newspapers: nonpartisan business control over, 15, 40–2, 44, 49, 67; political parties and politicians, relationship to, 37–8, 85–6
Newsprint Institute of Canada, 97
New York, 97, 103, 186; capital from, 48. *See also* General Motors; International Paper
New York Times, 35, 97, 245
Niosi, Jorge, 292n135
Noble, David, 202–3, 238
Noranda Mines, 192, 220
Norman, Montagu, 141

O'Brien, J. Leonard, 48, 349n113
Ogilvie Milling Company of Canada, 20, 113, 224
O'Leary, Richard, 39
Ontario Equitable Life, 93
Ontario Provincial Police (OPP), 157, 190–2
Osgoode Hall, 118
Our Wonderland of Bureaucracy (Beck), 104
Overton, James, 152
Oshawa, 19, 161–2; business community of, 174; Chamber of Commerce, 157; Civic Improvement League, 183; Curling Club, 171, 184; GM, support for, 176; Golf Club, 183; Great Depression, impact in, 182–3; growth of, 172; Lakeview Park, 178–9; Memorial Park, 193; St Andrews Church, 171; strike (1937), 157, 188–98, historiography of, 190, pickets during, 191, local support for, 192–3, 195, settlement of, 194; Standard Bank in, 316n16; Thirty Club, 183; Welfare Fund, 183;

Women's Hospital Auxiliary, 182; workers in, 157–60, 172, 179, 183
Oshawa Daily Reformer, 173, 180
Ottawa, 87, 89, 94, 102, 110, 175–6, 209
Ottawa Journal, 70

Padlock Act (1937), 150
Papineau, Louis-Joseph, 94–5
Parenteau, Bill, 47
Parkdale Collegiate Institute, 118
Parkwood. *See* McLaughlin, R.S.
"passive revolution," 203, 241
Paterson, A.P., 50, 58
Paterson, Donald, 170
Peacock, E.R., 79, 142
Peacock, H.M., 79
Pearson, F.S., 51
Pendergest, James, 181
Pennsylvania Railroad, 125
Phillips, A.C. (Slim), 180–1
Phillips, W.E., 236
Pipeline Debate, 249
Pitfield, Ward C., 29, 145, 263n1, 310n148
Polymer Corporation, 234
Portage la Prairie, Manitoba, 87
Port Arthur, Ontario, 74, 205–6
Powell, R.E., 201, 231
Power, Charles Gavin (Chubby), 209
"power elite." *See* Mills, C. Wright
Prairie West: role within National Policy, 8; colonialism in, 85; farmers' fear of railway monopoly in, 100; politics in, 75, 77
Preston, R.D., 176
Price, William H., 173
Prince Albert, Saskatchewan, 73, 86
Prince Edward Island, 107

Progressive Party, 71, 77–8, 81, 87; criticism of, 172

progressivism, 70–1, 122; businessmen's support of, 60, 85; ideological fracturing of, 81. *See also* Dunning, Charles; Progressive Party

Prosperity League of Canada, 174

protective tariff, 112; automobile industry, and, 159, 163, 164, 169–77, adjustment of, 176–7; big business support of, 79, 122; Conservative Party support of, 90, 128; Liberal Party (federal) position on, 86, 122; Western Canadian view of, 77, 171

Psychology and Industrial Efficiency (Münsterberg), 57

public debt and spending: elite attitudes on and efforts to limit and reverse, 5, 14, 17, 126, 140–1, 160, 183, 197, 213, 309n127, 348n127. *See also* liberalism; National Government; railway question

public enterprise: democratic control of, 131–2; in hydro-electric power, 36–7, 124; New Brunswick election (1925), election issue in, 45–6; popularity of, 47; threat of, 55. *See also* railway question

public opinion: efforts to shape, 64, 113, 116, 126, 148, 214; irrationality of, 140, 148, 308–9n125; opposition to, 114, 132, 134; political constraints created by, 113, 152, 239

pulp and paper industry: Great Depression, impact upon, 96–100; newsprint mills, 49; politics of,

44; rise of, 47–8; structure of, 96. *See also* Canada Power and Paper; International Paper; Robinson, Howard

Purvis, Arthur B., 20, 225

Quebec. *See* Liberal Party; Montreal; Robinson, Howard

Quebec City, 136

Queen's University, 113, 119

railway question, 5, 17, 100–2, 106, 114–16, 121–47, 197, 211–14, 218–19, 221

railways: "democratic management" of, 146; expansion of (1920s), 88, 127; Great Depression, impact upon, 100; relationship to nation-state and role within national economy, 5, 115, 128, 199. *See also* Canadian National Railways; Canadian Pacific Railway

Ralston, J.L., 97, 105–6, 215

Raskob, John J., 168, 178

Rasporich, Anthony, 206

R.D. Robinson Publishers Limited (and R.D. Robinson & Company), 32

Reconstruction Party, 109, 143

Regenstreif, S. Peter, 83

Regher, Ted, 242

Regina, Saskatchewan, 86–7, 92–3

Research Enterprises Limited, 236

responsible government, 64

Richardson, James A., 20, 214–15, 217

Richardson, R.L., 76

Rideau Club. *See* social clubs

Robb, J.A., 83, 90–1, 107, 171, 173, 175

Roberts, David, 167
Robertson, Heather, 180, 190
Robinson, Howard P., 15–16, 70, 130, 147, 222, 243–6; Bracken, John, support for, 60, 63, 349n113; British Empire, attitude towards 36–7; Britishness of, 60–6; business philosophy of, 34; business-government relations, view of, 30; capital accumulation strategy of, 50–1, 63; childhood and early family life of, 31–2; "community-oriented entrepreneur," as, 29–30; CPR, director of, 67; death of, 66; finance capital, proponent of, 38; Fraser Companies, trustee of bondholders of, 48; *Globe* (Saint John), takeover of, 49; government bureaucracy, view of, 65; Grand Falls, attitude towards development of, 44; Great Depression, response to, 58–60; Hanson, R.B., disagreement with, 40–2; health problems of, 33, 51, 66–7; ideology of, 30, 34, 42–3, 50–1, 57–68, 279–80n163; International Paper, director of subsidiary of, 48–9; Irving, K.C., sale of business interests to, 56, 66; Maritime Rights, association with, 31, 50–1, 57, 67; McKenna, J.D., relationship with, 39; New Brunswick Broadcasting Company, interest in, 56; New Brunswick election (1925), role in, 47; New Brunswick Power Company, sale of interest in, 37; New Brunswick Telephone Company, involvement with, 52–6, 67, 274n105; newspapers, reorganization of, 37–43; organized labour, opposition to, 65–6; outside capital, relationship to, 48, 52–6, 271n75; political parties, attitude towards and involvement with, 33–4, 36–7, 40, 47, 50, 60, 67, 229, 270n69; publishing, early career in, 32–3; pulp and paper industry, relationship with, 47–9; Quebec nationalism, perception of, 66; religious beliefs of, 32; St James Street, association with, 52, 66–7; Saint John, departure to, 34; securities business of, 34; social and cultural life of, 51–2, 62–3, 278n145; *Telegraph* (Saint John), attitude towards, 39, 41; *Telegraph-Journal* (Saint John), management of, 45, 47, 67; utilities, early involvement in, 33–5; workers, attitude towards, 56–9. *See also* Beatty, Edward; King, W.L.M.; New Brunswick Publishing Company; Royal Commission on Dominion-Provincial Relations; *Telegraph-Journal* (Saint John)
Robinson (née Stiles), Lavina J., 31–2
Robinson (née Fox), Pearl, 32
Robinson, Robert D., 31–2
Robson, H.A., 93
Rockefeller Foundation, 149
Roebuck, Arthur, 192
Rogers, Norman, 136, 192
Rogers, Robert, 122
Roosevelt, Franklin Delano, 147, 149, 189

Rosenberg, Louis (Watt Hugh Mc-
Collum), 10, 66, 243, 250
Ross, Frank M., 62, 348n104
Ross, Gordon, 105
Rotary Club, 171
Rothesay Collegiate, 52
Rowe, Earl, 196
Rowell-Sirois Commission. *See*
Royal Commission on Dominion-
Provincial Relations
Royal Bank of Canada, 3–4, 20, 29,
52, 66, 91, 96, 98–9, 125, 128,
186. *See also* Holt, Herbert
Royal Canadian Mounted Police
(RCMP), 157, 190–2, 198
Royal Canadian Yacht Club, 184
Royal Commission on Dominion-
Provincial Relations: Robinson,
Howard, appointment to, 51,
272–3n92
Royal Commission to Inquire into
Railways and Transportation in
Canada, 17, 114, 146; formation
of, 130; proceedings of, 131–4;
recommendations of, 135, 211
Royal Trust Company, 185
Royal York Hotel, 135
Rundle, W.E., 173
Russell, T.A., 173

Saint John, New Brunswick:
Conservative Party victories in,
47; deindustrialization of, 36, 47;
Liberal Party in, 37; Loyalist city,
as, 62–3; street railway strike
(1921), 37, 58; Union Club of, 43.
See also Robinson, Howard
Saint John Power Commission:
Musquash dam, 38

Saint John River Power Company, 48
Sarnia, Ontario, 157
Saskatchewan Co-operative Elevator
Company (SCEC), 70, 74, 76–7,
205
Saskatchewan Grain Growers'
Association (SGGA), 70, 73–5,
77, 80
Saturday Night, 197, 240
Saywell, John T., 190
Scotland, 13
Scott, F.R., 148
Scott, Gordon, 227
Scully, Hugh, 226, 348n103
Seager, Allen, 127
Second Industrial Revolution, 169;
southern Ontario, and, 199
Second World War: wartime econ-
omy, 64, 222–32
Seigniory Club, 93–6, 185
Shaughnessy, Thomas (Lord), 14,
118–19, 122; railway plan of
123–4, 126
Shawinigan Falls, Quebec, 98
Shawinigan Water and Power, 20
Shediac, New Brunswick, 130
Sheils, G.K., 225
Sheritt-Gordon Mines, 88, 186
Shipshaw (hydroelectric project),
231
Shore, Marlene, 149
Sifton, Clifford, 80, 126, 173
Sifton, Harry, 94
Simpson, James, 180
Simpson, Wallace, 185
Sinclair, Gordon, 198
Sise, C.F., 34
Sise, C.F. Jr, 20, 55, 186, 201
Sklar, Martin, 187

Slaight, Arthur, 208
Sloan, Alfred P. Jr, 171, 323n66
Smith, Andrew, 258n19
Smith, David, 78
Smith, Julian C., 20
Smiths Falls, Ontario, 143
social clubs: Garrison Club, 136;
    Mount Royal Club, 13, 52, 91,
    105, 119, 124, 159, 174; National
    Club, 289n107; Rideau Club, 13;
    St James's Club, 13, 119; Toronto
    Club, 13; Union Club, 43; York
    Club, 13
Social Credit, 111, 284–5n57
Social Science Research Project, 149
Spain, 59
Square Mile. *See* Montreal
Stadler, John, 98
Stairs, John F., 30
Standard (Saint John), 37
St Andrews, New Brunswick, 66
Steel Company of Canada (Stelco),
    113; strike (1946), 236. *See also*
    McMaster, Ross
Stevens, H.H., 106, 143, 145
Stevenson, John A., 130
Stewart, James McGregor, 312n166
St James's Club. *See* social clubs
St James Street, 3, 93, 99–100, 116,
    125, 128, 130, 138, 145, 159, 174,
    185–6, 210, 221, 223–4; CPR-
    Bank of Montreal group, 13, 52,
    119; political failure and decline
    of, 5, 7, 24, 112, 117, 241, 244,
    250. *See also* automobile industry;
    Meighen, Arthur; Montreal;
    Robinson, Howard
St John Railway Company. *See* New
    Brunswick Power Company

St Laurent, Louis: government of,
    234
St Lawrence Sugar Corporation, 20
Stockton, A.A., 34
Stromquist, Shelton, 70
Struthers, James, 241
Sugiman, Pamela, 182
Sussex, New Brunswick, 32, 39
Symington, H.J., 83, 138, 201, 226,
    228, 234, 242

Taschereau, Louis-Alexandre, 91,
    100, 106–7, 136, 242
taxation, 59, 80, 110–11, 218, 225,
    231
Taylor, A.D., 44
Taylor, E.P., 225, 227, 230, 244
Taylor, Frederick W., 177
Telegraph (and *Evening-Times*)
    (Saint John), 37–8. *See also*
    Robinson, Howard
Telegraph-Journal (Saint John),
    56–7; creation of, 39; editorial
    policies of, 40–2, 44–5, 50. *See*
    also King, W.L.M.
Thomas, J.H., 126
Thompson, E.P., 10, 259n23
Thompson, F.B., 34
Thompson, Hugh, 189, 191
Thompson, John Herd, 77
Thompson, T.A., 143
Thornton, Henry, 101, 130, 214, 218;
    campaign to discredit, 129, 134;
    CNR, as president, 125–7, 129,
    212; Dunning, Charles, view of,
    88; organized labour, and, 127,
    303n44; public enterprise, attitude
    towards, 131–2
Thornton, Lady, 129, 131

Thorold, Ontario, 117
Tilley, L.P.D., 45
Tilley, W.N., 20, 95, 119
Toronto, 6, 8, 14, 53–4, 84, 105, 108, 113, 117–18, 127, 140, 142, 186, 236, 244; business elite of, 122–4; businessmen from, 92, 144, 174, 215, 218, 223, 228; Canadian Club of, 135; King Edward Hotel, 190; mining magnates of, 186, 189; workers from, 176
Toronto Club. *See* social clubs
Toronto Stock Exchange, 355n9
Touche & Company, 212–13
Trades and Labour Congress of Canada (TLC), 180–1
Trans-Canada Air Lines Bill, 217
Trans-Canada Air Lines (TCA), 21, 111, 201, 233–4. *See also* Howe, C.D.
Trans Canada Airway, 214–15
transcontinental railways. *See* Canadian National Railways; Canadian Pacific Railway; railways
Traves, Tom, 170, 173–4
Treasure Island (Stevenson), 32
Truman, Harry, 65
Tweedsmuir, Lord, 197
Tyrone, Ontario, 161

UAW, Local 222 (Oshawa): establishment of, 189. *See also* Committee for Industrial Organization
United Automobile Workers of America (UAW), 188–9. *See also* Committee for Industrial Organization
United Church of Canada, 64

Union Club. *See* Saint John, N.B.
Union government, 36–7, 122; Dunning, Charles, relationship to, 77; National Government campaign (1930s), comparison with, 152
United Farmers of Alberta, 81
United Mine Workers of America (UMW), 188
United States, 13, 139–40, 202; automobile manufacturers, dominance of, 164; capitalist expansion of, 8; Chamber of Commerce, 150; comparison with, 70–1; continental linkages from, 130, 158, 186–7, 230–1; direct investment from, 158, 169–70. *See also* automobile industry; Committee for Industrial Organization; continental integration; General Motors; Great Depression; McLaughlin, R.S.; New Deal
university professors, 64, 148; policing of, 149–50
University of Saskatchewan, 130
University of Toronto, 117–18
Upper Canada College, 117

Vancouver, British Columbia, 146
Veblen, Thorstein, 166
Veniot, Peter J., 36, 38, 44; International Paper, purchase of Grand Falls site from, 43. *See also* McLean, Angus
Victoria, British Columbia, 123
Victoria College, 193
Vining, Charles, 119–21

Waltham, Massachusetts, 204
Ward, Norman, 78

Wardaugh, Robert A., 83, 86
War Industries Control Board, 226
War Requirements Board, 227
War Supply Board, 224
wartime economy. *See* Second World
   War
Waterhouse & Company, 213
Waterloo, Ontario, 93
Weatherbee, Thurston B., 225
Webster, John Clarence, 62, 130, 133
Western Canada, 115; CPR,
   opposition to, 124. *See also*
   Prairie West
Western Canadian Airways. *See*
   Canadian Airways Limited (CAL)
Western Prince (ship), 226–7
"Whisper of Death" campaign, 126
Whitaker, Reginald, 79, 223
White, C.T., 33
White, Richard, 5, 115
White, S.H., 33
White, Smeaton, 15, 91, 138, 146
White, Thomas, 113, 124
White Paper on Employment and
   Income, 232
Who Owns Canada? (Rosenberg),
   10, 243
Williams-Taylor, Frederick, 51
Williamson, A.H., 84
Wilson, Alex, 193
Wilson, Morris W., 20, 91
Windsor, Ontario, 172, 177
Windsor Station, 120
Winnipeg, 13, 75, 85, 89, 122
Winnipeg Free Press, 78, 81, 126

Winnipeg General Strike (1919), 79
Winnipeg Grain Exchange, 74
"Winnipeg Sanhedrin," 83
Winnipeg Tribune. See Richardson,
   R.L.
Women Teachers' Association (Port
   Arthur), 207
Wood, E.R., 92
Wood, Gundy & Company, 84, 97
Wood, Henry Wise, 71, 81
Woodward, W.C., 227
World Economic Conference (1934),
   141
Worcester, Joseph, 204–5
workers: autoworkers, 153, 157–8;
   Britain, from, 183; industrial
   unionism, embrace of, 158,
   181, 188–95; journeymen, 161;
   railway, 100, 143, 146; militancy
   of, 153, 179–81; "pressure from
   the labour world," 234. *See also*
   Howe, C.D.: labour unions;
   McLaughlin, Robert; McLaughlin,
   R.S.; Oshawa; Robinson, Howard;
   Thornton, Henry: organized
   labour; working class
working class: conditions of, 182;
   ethic composition of, 12; militancy
   of, 19, 160, 199; Conservative
   Party, being courted by, 47. *See
   also* workers

Yorkton, Saskatchewan, 69, 73
Young Women's Christian
   Association, 183

THE CANADIAN SOCIAL HISTORY SERIES

Terry Copp,
*The Anatomy of Poverty: The Condition
of the Working Class in Montreal, 1897–
1929*, 1974.
ISBN 0-7710-2252-2

Alison Prentice,
*The School Promoters: Education and
Social Class in Mid-Nineteenth Century
Upper Canada*, 1977.
ISBN 0-8020-8692-6

John Herd Thompson,
*The Harvests of War: The Prairie West,
1914–1918*, 1978.
ISBN 0-7710-8560-5

Joy Parr, Editor,
*Childhood and Family in Canadian
History*, 1982.
ISBN 0-7710-6938-3

**Alison Prentice and Susan Mann
Trofimenkoff, Editors,**
*The Neglected Majority: Essays in
Canadian Women's History, Volume 2,*
1985.
ISBN 0-7710-8583-4

Ruth Roach Pierson,
*'They're Still Women After All': The
Second World War and Canadian
Womanhood*, 1986.
ISBN 0-7710-6958-8

Bryan D. Palmer,
*The Character of Class Struggle: Essays
in Canadian Working Class History,
1850–1985*, 1986.
ISBN 0-7710-6946-4

Alan Metcalfe,
*Canada Learns to Play: The Emergence
of Organized Sport, 1807–1914*, 1987.
ISBN 0-7710-5870-5

Marta Danylewycz,
*Taking the Veil: An Alternative to
Marriage, Motherhood, and Spinsterhood
in Quebec, 1840–1920*, 1987.
ISBN 0-7710-2550-5

Craig Heron,
*Working in Steel: The Early Years in
Canada, 1883–1935*, 1988.
ISBN 978-1-4426-0984-6

**Wendy Mitchinson and Janice Dickin
McGinnis, Editors,**
*Essays in the History of Canadian
Medicine*, 1988.
ISBN 0-7710-6063-7

Joan Sangster,
*Dreams of Equality: Women on the
Canadian Left, 1920–1950*, 1989.
ISBN 0-7710-7946-X

Angus McLaren,
*Our Own Master Race: Eugenics in
Canada, 1885–1945*, 1990.
ISBN 0-7710-5544-7

Bruno Ramirez,
*On the Move: French-Canadian and
Italian Migrants in the North Atlantic
Economy, 1860–1914*, 1991.
ISBN 0-7710-7283-X

Mariana Valverde,
*'The Age of Light, Soap and Water':
Moral Reform in English Canada, 1885–
1925*, 1991.
ISBN 978-0-8020-9595-4

Bettina Bradbury,
*Working Families: Age, Gender, and
Daily Survival in Industrializing
Montreal*, 1993.
ISBN 978-0-8020-8689-1

Andrée Lévesque,
Making and Breaking the Rules: Women in Quebec, 1919–1939, 1994.
ISBN 978-1-4426-1138-2

Cecilia Danysk,
Hired Hands: Labour and the Development of Prairie Agriculture, 1880–1930, 1995.
ISBN 0-7710-2552-1

Kathryn McPherson,
Bedside Matters: The Transformation of Canadian Nursing, 1900–1990, 1996.
ISBN 978-0-8020-8679-2

Edith Burley,
Servants of the Honourable Company: Work, Discipline, and Conflict in the Hudson's Bay Company, 1770–1870, 1997.
ISBN 0-19-541296-6

Mercedes Steedman,
Angels of the Workplace: Women and the Construction of Gender Relations in the Canadian Clothing Industry, 1890–1940, 1997.
ISBN 978-1-4426-0982-2

Angus McLaren and Arlene Tigar McLaren,
The Bedroom and the State: The Changing Practices and Politics of Contraception and Abortion in Canada, 1880–1997, 1997.
ISBN 0-19-541318-0

Kathryn McPherson, Cecilia Morgan, and Nancy M. Forestell, Editors,
Gendered Pasts: Historical Essays in Femininity and Masculinity in Canada, 1999.
ISBN 0-978-0-8020-8690-7

Gillian Creese,
Contracting Masculinity: Gender, Class, and Race in a White-Collar Union, 1944–1994, 1999.
ISBN 0-19-541454-3

Geoffrey Reaume,
Remembrance of Patients Past: Patient Life at the Toronto Hospital for the Insane, 1870–1940, 2000.
ISBN 978-1-4426-1075-0

Miriam Wright,
A Fishery for Modern Times: The State and the Industrialization of the Newfoundland Fishery. 1934–1968, 2001.
ISBN 0-19-541620-1

Judy Fudge and Eric Tucker,
Labour Before the Law: The Regulation of Workers' Collective Action in Canada, 1900–1948, 2001.
ISBN 978-0-8020-3793-0

Mark Moss,
Manliness and Militarism: Educating Young Boys in Ontario for War, 2001.
ISBN 0-19-541594-9

Joan Sangster,
Regulating Girls and Women: Sexuality, Family, and the Law in Ontario 1920–1960, 2001.
ISBN 0-19-541663-5

Reinhold Kramer and Tom Mitchell,
Walk Towards the Gallows: The Tragedy of Hilda Blake, Hanged 1899, 2002.
ISBN 978-0-8020-9542-8

Mark Kristmanson,
Plateaus of Freedom: Nationality, Culture, and State Security in Canada, 1940–1960, 2002.
ISBN 0-19-541866-2 (cloth)
ISBN 0-19-541803-4 (paper)

Robin Jarvis Brownlie,
A Fatherly Eye: Indian Agents, Government Power, and Aboriginal Resistance in Ontario, 1918–1939, 2003.
ISBN 0-19-541891-3 (cloth)
ISBN 0-19-541784-4 (paper)

Steve Hewitt,
Riding to the Rescue: The Transformation of the RCMP in Alberta and Saskatchewan, 1914–1872, 2006.
ISBN 978-0-8020-9021-8 (cloth)
ISBN 978-0-8020-4895-0 (paper)

Robert K. Kristofferson,
Craft Capitalism: Craftworkers and Early Industrialization in Hamilton, Ontario, 1840–1871, 2007.
ISBN 978-0-8020-9127-7 (cloth)
ISBN 978-0-8020-9408-7 (paper)

Andrew Parnaby,
Citizen Docker: Making a New Deal on the Vancouver Waterfront, 1919–1939, 2008.
ISBN 978-0-8020-9056-0 (cloth)
ISBN 978-0-8020-9384-4 (paper)

J.I. Little,
Loyalties in Conflict: A Canadian Borderland in War and Rebellion, 1812–1840, 2008.
ISBN 978-0-8020-9773-6 (cloth)
ISBN 978-0-8020-9525-1 (paper)

Pauline Greenhill,
Make the Night Hideous: Four English Canadian Charivaris, 1881–1940, 2010.
ISBN 978-1-4426-4077-1 (cloth)
ISBN 978-1-4426-1015-6 (paper)

Rhonda L. Hinther and Jim Mochoruk,
New Directions in the History of Ukrainians in Canada, 2010.
ISBN 978-1-4426-4134-1 (cloth)
ISBN 978-1-4426-1062-0 (paper)

Reinhold Kramer and Tom Mitchell,
When the State Trembled: How A.J. Andrews and the Citizens' Committee Broke the Winnipeg General Strike, 2010.
ISBN 978-1-4426-4219-5 (cloth)
ISBN 978-1-4426-1116-0 (paper)

Lara Campbell, Dominique Clément, and Greg Kealey
Debating Dissent: Canada and the 1960s, 2012
ISBN 978-1-4426-4164-8 (cloth)
ISBN 978-1-4426-1078-1 (paper)

Janis Thiessen
Manufacturing Mennonites: Work and Religion in Post-War Manitoba, 2013
ISBN 978-1-4426-4213-3 (cloth)
ISBN 978-1-4426-1113-9 (paper)

Don Nerbas
Dominion of Capital: The Politics of Big Business and the Crisis of the Canadian Bourgeoisie, 1914-1947, 2013
ISBN 978-1-4426-4545-5 (cloth)
ISBN 978-1-4426-1352-2 (paper)